NEUROPSYCHOLOGICAL ASSESSMENT AND THE SCHOOL-AGE CHILD

ISSUES AND PROCEDURES

Edited by

GEORGE W. HYND, ED.D.

Associate Professor of Educational Psychology
Department of Educational Psychology
University of Georgia
Athens, Georgia

JOHN E. OBRZUT, PH.D.

Associate Professor of Psychology
Department of Psychology
University of Northern Colorado
Greeley, Colorado

GRUNE & STRATTON

A Subsidiary of Harcourt Brace Jovanovich, Publishers
New York   London
Paris   San Diego   San Francisco   São Paulo
Sydney   Tokyo   Toronto

Library of Congress Cataloging in Publication Data
Main entry under title:

Neuropsychological assessment and the school-age child.

Includes index.
1. Learning disabilities—Diagnosis. 2. Neuropsychology. 3. Psychological tests for children. I. Hynd,
George W. II. Obrzut, John E. [DNLM: 1. Psychological
tests—In infancy and childhood. 2. Psychophysiology—
In infancy and childhood. 3. Neurophysiology—In infancy and childhood. 4. Psychology, Educational—In
infancy and childhood. WM 145 N494]
RJ496.L4N48   618.92'80475   81-2394
ISBN 0-8089-1381-6   AACR2

Grune & Stratton, Inc.
111 Fifth Avenue
New York, New York 10003

Distributed in the United Kingdom by
Academic Press Inc. (London) Ltd.
24/28 Oval Road, London NW 1

Library of Congress Catalog Number 81-2394
International Standard Book Number 0-8089-1381-6

Printed in the United States of America

Contents

Section III DIAGNOSTIC AND CLINICAL PROCEDURES

Section IV NEUROPSYCHOLOGY IN THE SCHOOLS

Acknowledgments

An edited book such as this represents the combined efforts of many. We are especially grateful to the contributors, who were unanimously receptive to our rationale for this volume and gladly gave of their time to write their chapters. The editorial staff of Grune & Stratton deserves our appreciation for continued encouragement, advice, and assistance in making our initial idea a reality. Jerry Harris, Ruben Lozano, Manfred Meier, and Buff Oldridge contributed greatly in their willingness to provide editorial advice and assistance; they are gratefully acknowledged for this. A special word of thanks goes to Fran Pirozzolo for his continued support, encouragement, stimulation, and, most importantly, his friendship. Finally, Cyndie, April, and Brian Hynd and Ann and Krystopher Obrzut gave us their support, patience, and love, which made our efforts enjoyable.

Preface

Since 1970, truly remarkable advances have been made in our understanding of brain–behavior relationships in children. This quantum increase in our knowledge can be largely attributed to the development of sophisticated research techniques and methodologies. The practical result of this research has been the identification of reliable assessment and evaluation procedures that differentially diagnose neuropsychologically based learning and behavioral deficits in children.

This book developed from our recognition that the provision of appropriate educational services to school-age children must incorporate not only these new insights about neurological organization and behavior but also promising neuropsychological assessment and evaluation procedures. Only through the integration of behavioral, educational, and neuropsychological knowledge will children be given the opportunity to perform to their maximum capabilities. Our discussions with school psychologists, clinical child psychologists, trainers, and researchers of child and developmental neuropsychology made it increasingly obvious that a book was needed that would thoroughly yet critically examine the procedures and issues related to neuropsychological assessment of school-age children. As school psychologists who had contributed to the research in child neuropsychology, we felt compelled to edit a book that would meet this need.

In planning this book, we believed that it should provide more than a thorough overview of neuropsychological assessment procedures. First, despite much interest in neuropsychological data among applied psychologists, there is resistance among educators to consider such data when making decisions about school-age children. Second, there are a number of issues critical to our understanding of brain–behavior relationships in children. These issues must be understood and assimilated into a conceptual framework if the neuropsychological assessment is to provide meaningful and useful information. Finally, the use of neuropsychological assessment procedures with school-age children has important implications both for the remediation of children with processing deficits and for the adoption of training and competency standards that will assure school children are given quality services. With these considerations in mind, we divided the book into four sections.

The contributors to each section are eminently qualified to address their particular chapter topics. All have made important contributions to the research literature; are recognized leaders in the field of neuropsychology, and, most importantly, are sensitive to the needs of the applied psychologist who must work daily with learning- and behavior-disordered children.

The chapters in Section I provide a neuropsychological perspective on school-age children. Chapter 1, by Rourke and Gates, serves as an introduction to the book. The authors review research in the neuropsychology of learning disorders, specifically discussing definitional issues, types of investigations, and subtypes of learning-disabled children. They then discuss neuropsychological implications as they relate to the school psychologist. Gaddes (Chapter 2) addresses basic issues about the validity of neuropsychological theory and practice with school-age children. The author outlines in detail various neuropsychological classifications (of brain function) and discusses neuropsychological principles and their value for education.

The second section of the book provides an overview of critical controversial issues in neuropsychology. In Chapter 3, Reynolds makes a distinction between biological and psychological models of intelligence and presents an integrative overview of neuropsychological perspectives of cognitive processing. Kinsbourne and Hiscock, in Chapter 4, discuss the empirical basis of the relationship between learning disorders and cerebral lateralization. They examine the consequences of deviant laterality and whether or not lateralized function develops. Lastly, Pirozzolo and Campanella (Chapter 5) discuss the neuropsychology of developmental speech, language, and learning disorders in children.

Section III presents the major focus of this volume: the various approaches to neuropsychological assessment in children. Selz has written an introductory chapter (Chapter 6) to this section that includes an overview of the Halstead and Reitan children's batteries, methods of inference, the organization of neuropsychological test batteries for children, and her approach to differential diagnoses of children with learning and behavioral problems. Obrzut (Chapter 7) presents a conceptual framework for information processing and suggests a variety of neuropsychological procedures that can assess hierarchies of levels of learning. In Chapter 8, Golden summarizes Luria's conception of the functional units of the brain and presents his own quantitative battery based on Luria's clinical procedures. In contrast to the three preceding chapters, the focus of Aaron's chapter (Chapter 9) is a model for a deductive approach to the differential diagnosis of learning disorders in children. The basis of his approach is a neuropsychological key that helps to identify the learning disordered (and the etiology of the disorder).The key may assist in devising appropriate remedial strategies. In Chapter 10, Knights and Stoddart present a rationale for using a profile approach and pattern analysis in differential diagnosis. They discuss various methods of profile and pattern analysis and consider specific methodological difficulties associated with each approach.

The last section addresses the implications of using a neuropsychological perspective with school-age children. Chapter 11, by Hartlage and Reynolds, presents a sound rationale for using neuropsychological data in planning individualized instructional strategies. Case studies are included that exemplify the use of neuropsychological data in developing the individualized education program. Lastly, in Chapter 12, Hynd examines the issues associated with the provision of neuropsychological services in the schools. He also presents a training model for assuring the competency of school psychologists.

A glossary of technical terms is provided for readers who encounter unfamiliar terminology in this volume.

It is our hope that this book will sufficiently stimulate the reader to pursue further training and experiences in the neuropsychological assessment of school-age children. Only in this way can we ensure that children experiencing neuropsychologically based difficulties in learning and behavior are afforded the services and opportunities they need and deserve.

GEORGE W. HYND, ED.D.
JOHN E. OBRZUT, PH.D.

Contributors

P. G. AARON, PH.D.
Professor of Educational Psychology
Department of Educational Psychology
Indiana State University
Terre Haute, Indiana

DEBRA J. CAMPANELLA, M.S.
Speech Pathologist
Aphasia Unit, Neurology Service
VA Medical Center
Minneapolis, Minnesota

WILLIAM H. GADDES, PH.D.
Professor Emeritus
Department of Psychology
University of Victoria
Victoria, British Columbia

ROBERT D. GATES, M.A.
Department of Psychology
Izaak Walton Killam Hospital for
    Children
Halifax, Nova Scotia

CHARLES J. GOLDEN, PH.D.
Associate Professor of Medical
    Psychology
Department of Psychiatry
The University of Nebraska Medical
    Center
Omaha, Nebraska

LAWRENCE C. HARTLAGE, PH.D.
Professor of Neurology and Pediatrics
Head, Neuropsychology Section
Departments of Neurology and
    Pediatrics
Medical College of Georgia
Augusta, Georgia

MERRILL HISCOCK, PH.D.
Assistant Professor of Psychology and
    Clinical Instructor in Psychiatry
Division of Psychology
University Hospital
Saskatoon, Saskatchewan

GEORGE W. HYND, ED.D.
Associate Professor of Educational
  Psychology
Department of Educational Psychology
University of Georgia
Athens, Georgia

**MARCEL KINSBOURNE, M.R.C.P.,
  D.M.**
Director, Behavioral Neurology Division
Eunice Kennedy Shriver Center for
  Mental Retardation
Waltham, Massachusetts

ROBERT M. KNIGHTS, PH.D.
Professor of Psychology
Department of Psychology
Carleton University
Ottawa, Ontario

JOHN E. OBRZUT, PH.D.
Associate Professor of Psychology
Department of Psychology
University of Northern Colorado
Greeley, Colorado

FRANCIS J. PIROZZOLO, PH.D.
Neuropsychologist
GRECC
VA Medical Center
Assistant Professor

Department of Neurology, Psychiatry,
  and Psychology
University of Minnesota
Minneapolis, Minnesota

CECIL R. REYNOLDS, PH.D.
Associate Professor of Educational
  Psychology and Measurements
Associate Director, Buros Institute of
  Mental Measurements
The University of Nebraska—Lincoln
Lincoln, Nebraska

BYRON P. ROURKE, PH.D.
Professor of Psychology
Department of Psychology
University of Windsor
Head, Department of Neuropsychology
Windsor Western Hospital Center
Windsor, Ontario

MARION SELZ, PH.D.
Clinical Neuropsychologist
Associates in Human Development
Tucson, Arizona

CLARE STODDART, M.A.
Doctoral Candidate
Department of Psychology
Carleton University
Ottawa, Ontario

NEUROPSYCHOLOGICAL ASSESSMENT AND THE SCHOOL-AGE CHILD

SECTION I

Neuropsychological Perspectives on Education

Byron P. Rourke
Robert D. Gates

1

Neuropsychological Research and School Psychology

This chapter provides an overview of those issues and considerations that have arisen in the neuropsychological investigation of children that are relevant to the aims and concerns of school psychologists. The review focuses on the results of research in the neuropsychology of learning disabilities, because it is these results that have received attention.

Although this chapter is designed to introduce the reader to this area of investigation and, as such, can be read without reference to other literature in the field, there are several recent reviews and books that can be profitably consulted. These include Benton's (1975) and Rourke's (1978a) reviews of neurological and neurobehavioral studies of dyslexia, and two volumes dealing with theoretical approaches in the neuropsychology of learning disorders and treatment methods for learning-disabled and hyperactive children (Knights & Bakker, 1976; 1980). Reviews of the methods and models employed in research on the neuropsychology of learning disabilities can also be informative (Rourke, 1975; 1978b; 1981b), as can those works that outline the relevance of these research findings to neuropsychological assessment and educational intervention (Rourke, 1976a; 1981a).

DEFINITIONAL ISSUES

While problems with the definition of *dyslexia* and *specific reading retardation* have been acknowledged throughout the history of research on perceptual and learning disorders, it is only recently that investigations have addressed issues relating to these problems with sophistication and vigor. The traditional ("medical model") approach to these issues has been to rely on refinements based on clinical observation and analysis. After some time, a generally agreed-upon definition of a disorder is arrived at that specifies necessary and sufficient criteria for identification. Such definitions often contain statements about etiology. Improved definitions come, however, not only from concensus, but from research designed to clarify the validity of nosological labels.

It should be clear that the manner in which *learning disability* or *specific reading retardation* or *dyslexia* is defined has a bearing on all phases of research and treatment. For example, epidemiological studies designed to provide estimates of the incidence of a disorder are extremely dependent on how the disorder is defined. Furthermore, since much of the research concerning the etiology of reading disability is characterized by comparisons between "normal" and "disabled" readers, the composition of a reading-disabled group (in terms of cognitive, physical, and/or other variables) is obviously dependent on the criteria used for selection. The greatest challenge to any definition arises in the clinical situation: success in early identification, assessment, and planning treatment programs depends on how well the disorder is conceptualized and understood.

Most investigators now recognize the heterogeneous nature of reading disorders in children. The discovery of reliable subtypes of reading disability can be expected to contribute to improved definitions for both research and treatment. In fact, it would probably be accurate to characterize the recent history of research in this area as an attempt to specify homogeneous subtypes of disabled readers (e.g., Doehring, Hoshko, & Bryans, 1979; Mattis, French, & Rapin, 1975; Petrauskas & Rourke, 1979).

Rutter and Yule provide evidence for a category of specific reading retardation as distinct from a classification that they refer to as *reading backwardness* (Rutter, 1978; Yule & Rutter, 1976). The separation of these two groups stems from a consideration of operational criteria for measuring reading achievement. Most definitions of dyslexia or reading retardation contain some statement to the effect that the affected child is reading at a level substantially below age, grade, or intellectual expectation. Yule and Rutter's reading backwardness group was composed of children who were reading at a level equal to or less than $2\frac{1}{3}$ years below age expectation. Their specific reading retardation group was composed of children who were reading at a level equal to or less than $2\frac{1}{3}$ years below their *predicted* reading level. Predicted reading level was obtained from a regression equation incorporating chronological age and level of psychometric intelligence (prorated full scale IQ). Operationally, then, these two groups differ with respect to the role of psychometric intelligence in accounting for levels of reading achievement.

While there was considerable overlap in the composition of the two groups (approximately 30 percent), Yule and Rutter found several differences between them. The mean prorated IQ of the backward group was lower than that of the reading-retarded group; none of the reading-retarded subjects exhibited any frank neurological disorder, while approximately 11 percent of the backward readers did; and the incidence of other neurodevelopmental deficits was much lower in the reading-retarded group than in the backward group.

Most important, however, was the striking difference in the academic progress of the two groups that emerged at the end of a 4–5-year follow-up period. The reading-retarded subjects made *less* progress in reading and spelling than did the backward readers, but the reading retarded subjects made *greater* gains in arithmetic than did the backward group. These latter findings carry some important educational implications. For example, it should be clear, based even on very general findings such as these, that quite different modes of educational intervention strategies would be appropriate for these two groups of children, all of whom presented at 9-10 years of age with substandard achievement in reading.

In a similar study, Taylor, Satz, and Friel (1979) investigated the validity of the widely circulated World Federation of Neurology (WFN) definition of *specific developmental dyslexia.** Two groups of disabled readers from the Florida Longitudinal Project (Satz, Taylor, Friel, & Fletcher, 1978) were formed using operational criteria derived from the WFN definition. Disabled readers were defined as those children who were reading at a level at least one standard deviation below the mean for the entire sample. Dyslexic disabled readers were those who obtained a normal IQ on the Peabody Picture Vocabulary Test, demonstrated no obvious sensory or neurological handicaps or emotional disorder, came from families of average or better socioeconomic status, and had been exposed to conventional classroom instruction in reading. Nondyslexic disabled readers were those who failed to meet one or more of the above criteria. These two groups of disabled readers were compared in terms of neuropsychological abilities, the frequency of reversal errors in reading, mathematics achievement, parental reading and spelling achievement, neurological status, and personality development.

No consistent differences were found between the two groups, except for significantly lower ranking for socioeconomic status and Peabody IQs in the nondyslexic group (both artifacts of the selection criteria). Interestingly, the

---

*Specific developmental dyslexia is "a disorder manifested by difficulty in learning to read despite conventional instruction, adequate intelligence, and socio-cultural opportunity. It is dependent upon fundamental cognitive disabilities which are frequently of constitutional origin" (Critchley, 1970, p. 11).

parents of the dyslexic group were found to have reached lower levels of achievement in reading and spelling than did the parents of the nondyslexic children, when socioeconomic status was used as a covariate.

Taylor et al (1979) concluded that the WFN definition of dyslexia has little validity, either conceptually or operationally. Rutter (1978) voiced a similar criticism.

A number of issues relating to the definition of dyslexia need to be emphasized at this point. First, the necessity for a multivariate or multidimensional definition should be obvious. Second, an improved definition of dyslexia (if, in fact, such a disorder exists) and other types of reading disabilities appears to be dependent on continued research on the subtype problem. Finally, the lesson for the researcher should be clear: it can no longer be considered acceptable to select disabled readers solely on the basis of poor achievement in reading and approximately normal psychometric intelligence. Differences in levels of achievement in arithmetic, for example, can be reflective of drastically divergent neuropsychological and cognitive characteristics in children who are classified as reading disabled (Rourke & Finlayson, 1978; Rourke & Strang, 1978). The practitioner should be similarly cautious when attempting to formulate remedial plans for reading-disabled children.

It would seem, therefore, that systematic consideration of the definitional dimensions of reading disability—although obviously important for the reasons already mentioned—has done little to illuminate the extent to which neurological dysfunction may be an etiological factor. It was for this reason that, some time ago, a series of investigations was embarked upon, aimed at determining whether and to what extent disordered brain functioning plays a role in learning disorders (including those usually labeled reading, spelling, arithmetic, and social learning disabilities). This research has been summarized in three recent reviews (Rourke, 1975, 1978b, 1981b), but it will be useful at this juncture to discuss at least the general strategy involved.

NEUROPSYCHOLOGY AND LEARNING DISABILITIES

Stimulated by Doehring's (1968) classic study of reading disability, a series of investigations was begun in an attempt to explore fully a neuropsychological approach to the explanation of learning disabilities. Doehring demonstrated that reading-disabled children exhibit serious deficiencies when tested by a wide variety of methods known to be particularly sensitive to brain dysfunction. The results of his study, then, are consistent with the view that reading-disabled children are deficient in many abilities that are mediated by various systems of the brain.

This being the case, it seemed that a series of investigations couched in a model suggested by inferential methods derived from clinical neuropsychological practice would be fruitful. Thus, we adapted the methods and procedures developed by Reitan (see Chapter 6) for this purpose.

Using a comprehensive battery of sensory-perceptual, motor, psychomotor, linguistic, and concept-formation tests (Rourke, 1976a, 1981a), we collected data on over 4000 learning-disabled children who had been referred to our laboratory for assessment and remedial educational programming. These data, and others that were collected under more specific circumstances (sometimes with the use of quite different tests and procedures), were used to test hypotheses suggested by these methods of inference.

For example, brain impairment can result in deficits on a wide variety of psychological tests. Consequently, children were chosen who were very deficient in one or several school subjects, but who were otherwise "normal" (in terms of full scale IQ, cultural and linguistic opportunity, emotional stability, access to education, and freedom from sensory defects), and their performances were compared to those of children of average achievement to establish norms for the tests in question. Not surprisingly, the learning-disabled children performed relatively poorly on a large number of variables (e.g., Pajurkova, Orr, Rourke, & Finlayson, 1976). The results of these studies, when viewed solely in terms of differences in performance levels, are far from conclusive because they do little more than indicate that learning-disabled children perform poorly on a wide variety of tests. Since this may have been due to a negative attitude of the children with respect to tests in general, or to a number of factors other than brain dysfunction, studies designed to capitalize upon modes of inference other than level of performance needed to be conducted.

One such study, which used the *pathognomonic-sign* approach, is especially interesting in this regard (Sweeney & Rourke, 1978). In this study, groups of disabled spellers were selected on the basis of the levels of phonetic accuracy of their misspellings. This criterion was used because it has been well established that (1) phonetically inaccurate misspelling is tantamount to a sign of neurologically based language disorders (aphasia) in adults with well-documented brain lesions, and (2) there is some evidence that the severity of aphasic disturbance and phonetically inaccurate spelling are positively correlated (Kinsbourne & Warrington, 1964; Newcombe, 1969).

The results of the Sweeney and Rourke investigation strongly suggested that older (grade 8) phonetically inaccurate disabled spellers do, indeed, exhibit many more serious deficiencies in psycholinguistic skills than do phonetically accurate retarded spellers. These differences were found despite the fact that the two groups were equated for level of performance in spelling. Although the same differences were not evident among the younger (grade 4) children used in this study, the results of subsequent investigations in this series (Coderre, Sweeney, & Rourke, Note 1; Sweeney, McCabe, & Rourke, Note 3) demonstrated that phonetically inaccurate disabled spellers at this age level are, in fact, much less adept at a wide variety of psycholinguistic skills than are phonetically accurate misspellers.

The important point to emphasize is that a study designed to demonstrate the utility of the pathognomonic-sign approach yielded evidence that was consistent with the view that at least some disabled spellers are suffering from psycholinguistic deficiencies as a result of disordered brain functioning. Although somewhat more conclusive than the results of level-of-performance studies, it is not appropriate to infer that this type of evidence is sufficient to decide the issue. Fortunately, there are ways of approaching this problem that are suggested by other modes of clinical inference. One such mode is the *pattern* or *configurational* analysis approach.

An example of the application of this strategy is the Rourke and Finlayson (1978) investigation. In this study, learning-disabled children were divided into groups based on their patterns of performance on the three subtests of the Wide Range Achievement Test (WRAT; Jastak & Jastak, 1965). Group 1 was markedly impaired on the Reading (word-recognition), Spelling, and Arithmetic subtests. Group 2 was as deficient in reading and spelling as group 1, but performance on the Arithmetic subtest, although impaired, was significantly superior to that of group 1. The arithmetic performance of group 3 was not significantly different from that of group 2, but scores on the Reading and Spelling subtests were somewhat better than average and, of course, markedly superior to those of groups 1 and 2. Comparisons were made of the performances of these three groups on many linguistic and visual-spatial tasks.

The results of this study were clear-cut. Groups 1 and 2 performed at levels significantly inferior to those of group 3 on measures of linguistic skills, whereas their performances were significantly superior to those of group 3 on measures of visual-spatial skills. Thus, although groups 2 and 3 were equated for level of performance in arithmetic, their patterns of performance on measures of linguistic and visual-spatial abilities were markedly divergent. It seems clear that the patterns of performance used to select the groups in this instance were the features that highlighted these differences.

But what does this tell us about the brain? Certainly, the pattern of abilities and deficits exhibited by group 2 is consistent with the view that abilities ordinarily thought to be subserved primarily by the left cerebral hemisphere were relatively impaired, whereas those ordinarily thought to be subserved primarily by the right cerebral hemisphere were relatively intact; the exact opposite state of affairs appeared to be found for group 3. To examine these possibilities further, another study was carried out (Rourke & Strang, 1978) in which these groups' performances on a variety of motor, psychomotor, and tactile-perceptual tests were compared. The results of this second study reinforced the hypotheses of differential hemispheric integrity outlined above, and highlighted differences between groups 1 and 2.

Hence, adapting a neuropsychological clinical inferential strategy for investigative purposes produced data that supported the view that disordered brain function (in the second study, differential hemispheric integrity) plays an important role in the central processing deficiencies responsible for what is termed learning disabilities.

Much evidence has been accumulated on this issue. The interested reader may find the Rourke and Finlayson (1975) and Rourke, Yanni, MacDonald, and Young (1973) studies particularly noteworthy. The former is another example of applying the pattern-analysis approach, and the latter is an example of applying a particular subset of pattern analysis unique to neurology and neuropsychology, that is, comparison of performances on the two sides of the body. Reviews of these studies and the research strategies involved are also available (Rourke, 1975, 1978b, 1981b).

DEVELOPMENTAL INVESTIGATIONS

Cross-Sectional Studies

Rourke, Dietrich, and Young (1973) compared the performances of learning-disabled children at two age levels (5-8 years and 9-14 years) who had been divided into groups on the basis of discrepancies between their verbal IQ and performance IQ scores on the Wechsler Intelligence Scale for Children (WISC). There were three groups at each age level: a high verbal IQ, low performance IQ group; a verbal IQ equal to performance IQ group; and a low verbal IQ, high performance IQ group. The performances of these groups on a variety of linguistic, visual-spatial, motor, and psychomotor tasks were compared. Of interest within the present context was the fact that the patterns of performance in the three groups at the older age level were in accord with hypotheses derived from the results of research on adults with well-documented brain lesions. For example, the older low verbal IQ, high performance IQ group exhibited a pattern of performance on the majority of these measures that would be expected were they suffering from functional deficiencies in systems thought to be subserved primarily by the left cerebral hemisphere, whereas abilities thought to depend on right hemisphere integrity for their development were intact. Precisely the opposite (with respect to differential hemispheric integrity) was found in the older high verbal IQ, low performance IQ group. The situation, however, was far different when similarly composed groups of 5–8-year old children were compared using these same variables. In the latter case, there was some indication that the patterns of performance on measures of linguistic and visual-spatial abilities were comparable to those exhibited by the older age groups, but little similarity was evident in the results for the motor and psychomotor variables.

It is important to note that differences in patterns of performance between the groups at these two age levels were more apparent than were similarities. This attests to the crucial importance of developmental dimensions in the investigation of brain–behavior relationships in children. Specifically, the attempt to compare the patterns of performance exhibited by older children with models derived from neuropsychological studies of adults may very well be fruitful, but this does not seem to be the case with younger children. Perusal of the studies of brain-damaged children that have been reviewed by Reitan (1974) and Boll (1974) leads to much the same conclusion.

However, it may be that the absence of similarities in patterns of performance between younger and older children is, at least in part, a function of a failure to use the proper dependent measure. Consider, for example, the results of the Sweeney and Rourke (1978) study. The investigators found that hypotheses based upon well-established brain–behavior relationships in adult populations were largely confirmed in the case of older (grade 8) children but not with younger (grade 4) children. At the same time, it must be remembered that subsequent investigations (Coderre et al, Note 1; Sweeney et al, Note 3) that employed more challenging—and, possibly, more appropriate—dependent measures revealed marked differences that were in accord with hypotheses derived from the study of adults with acquired cerebral lesions.

At this point, it is rather difficult to understand what this proves about the brain, but the following preliminary conclusions appear to be warranted. First, it is clear that relatively little is known about the relevant neuropsychological dimensions of the ability structures of younger children, and that a concerted effort needs to be made to fill in the gaps in this knowledge. Second, it is obvious that cross-sectional studies have not yielded—and, indeed, cannot yield—sufficient information to allow for satisfactory generalizations to be made about the neuropsychological dimensions that are relevant for intervention. At most, the cross-sectional studies reported to this point (and others like them) have provided potentially valuable clues that seem relevant to the design of longitudinal studies which are necessary to gain the missing information. Fortunately, longitudinal studies have been used with considerable success to test developmental neuropsychological theories of learning disabilities, especially reading disabilities. We will attempt, in the following section, to demonstrate the relevance for education of such studies.

Longitudinal Studies

A major feature of many longitudinal studies is the determination of the developmental precursors of later reading failure. These findings have obvious implications for the design of screening instruments to be used in early identification programs. Also, longitudinal neuropsychological research has provided valuable information regarding the natural history of both normal and disordered reading. It is possible, using longitudinal research, to determine whether and to what extent the deficits demonstrated by younger retarded readers persist throughout the elementary and secondary school years, or whether the patterns of abilities and deficits characteristic of younger retarded readers change with age. A further factor can also be examined: regardless of changes in the pattern of retarded readers' neuropsychological abilities, it is also possible to determine the extent to which the degree of disability in reading improves, remains the same, or becomes worse.

All of these possible outcomes have clear implications for the design of intervention programs. For example, if it were found that a particular pattern of neuropsychological strengths and weaknesses is associated with poor reading in early school grades and with a very poor prognosis for eventually learning to read, then it should be possible to allocate intervention resources more efficiently — that is, to those children who are less likely to catch up in reading achievement. Alternatively, a particular patten of neuropsychological abilities and deficits in some poor readers may follow a regular course of developmental change resulting in normal reading at a later developmental stage. In this instance, remedial programs for younger and older retarded readers should be able to capitalize on the changing nature of the readers' relative cognitive strengths and weaknesses in order to maximize the effects of the (presumably) minimal forms of intervention required. Finally, and perhaps most importantly, longitudinal neuropsychological studies may shed considerable light on possible differences between the development of reading ability in normal and in reading-disabled children. This would lead to improved understanding of the cerebral basis of one of our most complex abilities.

One longitudinal study designed with most of these aims in mind was carried out by Silver and Hagin (1960, 1964). Besides finding a variety of neurodevelopmental deficits in poor readers, Silver and Hagin found that all the reading-disabled children they studied demonstrated deficits in spatial orientation and temporal organization. These findings provide evidence for the importance of the early development of sensory-perceptual abilities for normal reading. In relatively short-term follow-up studies of poor readers, Silver has found that deficits in these abilities continue to be associated with the presence of reading disability (Silver, 1980). Hagin, Silver, and Kreeger (1976) have developed a screening instrument and an intervention program based on these observations.

In one of the most ambitious studies reported in the neuropsychological literature, Satz and associates followed the entire white, male kindergarten population of one county's school system for 6 years (Satz et al, 1978). The theoretical foundation of this investigation, which has come to be known as the Florida Longitudinal Project, is a *neurodevelopmental lag* theory of reading retardation (Satz & Sparrow, 1970). Briefly, this theory postulates that sensory-motor and perceptual abilities normally in ascendance when a child first is taught to read are less well developed in retarded readers than in normal readers. At later stages of the learning-to-read process, when the child attempts to process more complex linguistic and conceptual features of text, retarded readers will exhibit lags in developing such verbal-conceptual abilities. More specifically, Satz and Sparrow (1970) hypothesized that reading-disabled children experience a generalized lag in neural development such that younger retarded readers would be expected to show a relative deficit in early developing sensory-motor and perceptual skills, whereas older retarded readers would be expected to exhibit relatively age-appropriate levels of these skills, but would be delayed in terms of verbal-conceptual abilities. This lag in neural development was conceptualized in neuropsychological terms as a lag in the maturation of the left cerebral hemisphere. One prediction that can be derived from the theory is that younger retarded readers should eventually catch up to their age peers in sensory-motor and perceptual skills.

Satz et al (1978) found that variables grouped in this sensory-motor-perceptual category consistently were the best predictors of later reading achievement. The three variables that most consistently predicted eventual reading achievement were a test for finger localization, an alphabet recitation test, and a visual recognition-discrimination test. An overall correct classification rate of 72 percent was found for an abbreviated test battery in predicting the group membership of severely retarded, mildly retarded, average, and superior readers. In another study based upon the same data, Fletcher and Satz (1980) demonstrated developmental changes in the predictive and concurrent validity of sensory-motor-perceptual and verbal-conceptual variables. Sensory-motor-perceptual variables were the best predictors of younger childrens' early and later reading achievement, whereas verbal-conceptual variables were the best discriminators between older normal and retarded readers.

At the same time, Fennel and Satz (Note 2) found that, in general, the pattern of neuropsychological deficits manifested by younger retarded readers did not change with age—which is in accord with previous studies in this field (e.g., Reed, 1968; Rourke, 1976b). Trites and Fiedorowicz (1976) also reported similar findings in a follow-up study of somewhat older children. Of

particular importance was the fact that, for reading-disabled children, an increasing discrepancy between their age-expected reading level and their actual reading achievement became apparent as they grew older.

In a 4-year follow-up of a small group of retarded and normal readers (Rourke & Orr, 1977), it was demonstrated that a test of visual-perceptual speed and accuracy, the Underlining Test (Doehring, 1968; Rourke & Petrauskas, 1978) was a better predictor of eventual reading and spelling achievement in retarded readers than were measures of psychometric intelligence, reading, and spelling taken in grades 1 and 2. In fact, age-appropriate performance on some components of this test by subjects initially classified as retarded readers was correlated with significant gains in reading achievement by these subjects. It was also found that the predictive accuracy of the various measures used in the study differed for the normal and retarded reading groups. For example, measures of achievement in reading and spelling were the best predictors of eventual reading achievement for the normal readers but not for retarded readers.

In another study of the same two groups of normal and retarded readers (Rourke, 1976b), the relative merits of the developmental lag model (Satz & Sparrow, 1970) were examined as compared to a deficit model for explaining neuropsychological development in reading-retarded children (Rourke, 1976b, pp. 126–127). In addition to the Underlining Test and measures of academic achievement and psychometric intelligence mentioned in connection with the Rourke and Orr (1977) study, both groups were given an extensive battery of neuropsychological tests, including measures of motor, psychomotor, perceptual, psycholinguistic, problem-solving, and reasoning abilities. This battery was administered at intervals of 2, 3, and 4 years following the original assessment in grades 1 and 2. The findings made at the three follow-up intervals were interpreted in the context of seven paradigms constructed to reflect the developmental outcomes predicted by the developmental lag and deficit positions. Results from the Florida Longitudinal Project (Satz, Friel, & Rudegeair, 1974) also were analyzed in terms of these paradigms.

Support for the developmental lag model was found in many measures of fairly simple, early emerging visual-spatial, visual-motor, and verbal-expressive and verbal-encoding abilities. Support for the deficit model was found for measures of more complex, verbal-conceptual, problem-solving, and psycholinguistic abilities. It should be noted that the set of abilities for which a deficit interpretation was the most appropriate included those that are ordinarily thought to be subserved primarily by the left cerebral hemisphere.

For the most part, the results of this investigation did not support the Satz and Sparrow (1970) hypothesis that retarded readers are experiencing the effects of a generalized neurodevelopmental lag or, for that matter, a specific lag in the maturation of the left cerebral hemisphere. Rather, these results were far more compatible with a deficit or difference (Usprich, 1976) position. This view receives added support when considering the results of other longitudinal studies (e.g., Trites & Fiedorowicz, 1976) that demonstrate that greater differences obtain between normal and retarded readers at the end of longitudinal tracking than at the time of initial examination.

Furthermore, many of the variables that differentiated older retarded and normal readers in the Rourke (1976b) study also contributed to the differentiation of the same children when they were younger. It is also the case that many of the test variables for which the retarded readers appeared to catch up to their normal peers may not have been sensitive (or difficult) enough to differentiate the two groups at older ages. This would lend spurious support to the view that sensory-motor abilities are more important at earlier than at later stages of the learning-to-read process. Fletcher and Satz (1980) have considered this issue in designing their more recent investigations.

In a study with a somewhat different emphasis, Peter and Spreen (1979) demonstrated a relationship between the degree of neurological impairment in learning-disabled children and the eventual personality and behavioral adjustment of these children in late childhood and adolescence. Measures of behavioral abnormalities at the end of the follow-up period could be used to discriminate between neurologically impaired and nonimpaired subjects. The learning-impaired subjects (including neurologically impaired and nonimpaired groups) were less well-adjusted than were nondisabled control subjects at the end of the follow-up period. This study demonstrates the pervasive nature of the nonacademic effects of neurological and learning handicaps.

In summary, it is clear that the longitudinal and cross-sectional studies of normal and disabled readers reviewed in this section address several issues relevant for education. While the usual cautions regarding the selection of subjects and the tests used to chart developmental change apply to the interpretation of these studies, several tentative conclusions appear to be warranted.

The application of neuropsychological models to the study of younger children is complicated by the lack of knowledge of the structure of neuropsychological abilities at earlier stages of development. However, there appears to be considerable evidence to support the view that developmentally based differences do exist between younger and older learning-disabled children. In addition, measures of neuropsychological functioning taken during kindergarten or early school years can be used to predict eventual reading achievement with an acceptable level of accuracy. Of equal importance is the conclusion that the neuropsychological dimensions of learning-disabled children that are relevant for the educational process must be viewed within a developmental context.

Furthermore, for most reading-disabled children, virtually all studies indicate that the persistence of neuropsychological deficits is associated with continued substandard reading achievement throughout the school years. This poor achievement often seems to be associated with a host of other behavioral, social, and emotional anomalies.

Finally, the relevance of neuropsychological models for the study of both normal and disabled readers has been established. It remains to be seen whether continued research in this area can be translated into effective early identification and intervention programs.

ELECTROPHYSIOLOGICAL STUDIES

Few studies of event-related brain potentials (ERBP) have been conducted to date with reading-disabled children. Recent reviews of research in this area have been done by Hughes (1976; 1978) and Connors (1978), in which they discuss research concerned with abnormalities of the electroencephalogram (EEG) in learning-disabled children under conditions where the brain is not challenged — as is the case with ERBP studies.

The ERBPs are brief, time-linked recordings of the brain's electrical activity following the presentation of a stimulus. The stimuli used in ERBP research can either be very simple (e.g., a flash of light or an auditory click) or quite complex (e.g., a word). Analyzing these wave forms can be an exceedingly complex enterprise; however, such studies have potential for providing criterion evidence of neurophysiological differences between normal and retarded readers. Furthermore, by using more complex stimuli (which presumably require higher levels of cognitive processing), it should be possible to challenge directly those areas or systems of the brain that are hypothesized to be dysfunctional in retarded readers.

Connors (1971) was the first to report an association between late components of visual ERBPs and reading achievement. In the same study, he also demonstrated that poor readers, as compared to near-normal readers, demonstrated lower amplitudes of later negative components of the visual ERBP. Shields (1973) has shown that the latencies of several components of visual ERBPs are longer in disabled readers than in normal readers. Preston, Guthrie, and Childs (1974) reported finding a flattening of the visual ERBP in retarded readers similar to that reported by Connors (1971). Connors (1971) also found differences between the visual ERBPs of a group of poor readers with high verbal IQ relative to performance IQ and those of a group with low verbal IQ relative to performance IQ.

A recent study by Bakker, Licht, Kok, and Bauma (1980) involved two groups each of normal and disabled readers that had been formed in terms of whether subjects displayed consistent right- or left-ear advantages on a verbal dichotic listening test. As a basis for this study, the authors cited evidence supporting the views that (1) dichotic ear advantages represent cerebral asymmetry for language, and (2) the reading strategies of normal children who display a right-ear advantage are qualitatively different from those of normal children who display a left-ear advantage. For example, Bakker (1979) demonstrated that children showing a left-ear advantage on a verbal dichotic listening task read very slowly, but accurately—an observation consistent with their presumed right-hemisphere language processing. Children who demonstrate a right-ear advantage on verbal dichotic tasks read rapidly, but at the expense of committing many errors—a strategy consistent with their presumed left-hemisphere language processing. Bakker et al (1980) were able to show that, when reading words, normal readers with a right-ear advantage could be clearly differentiated from normal readers with a left-ear advantage in terms of the patterns of electrical activity in the left and right cerebral hemispheres. This relationship was not found in the two groups of poor readers: that is, the poor readers did not show any hemisphere-specific responses when reading a single word. They also found that the latencies of ERBP components were longer in the reading-disabled group than in the nor-normal group. Finally, they suggested that poor readers experience difficulty principally because of their lack of hemisphere-specific control of either the linguistic or the graphemic aspects of word analysis.

The results of these few studies are important within the present context because they support the view that reading-disabled children are experiencing some form of disordered cerebral functioning. In particular, these findings constitute compelling evidence supporting the validity of attempts to differentiate subtypes of retarded readers in terms of neurobehavioral dimensions.

SUBTYPES OF LEARNING-DISABLED CHILDREN

In the 4-year longitudinal study cited previously (Rourke & Orr, 1977), there were some retarded readers (approximately 25 percent) whose reading skills improved to the point that they approached normal (age-appropriate) levels by the fourth and final year of the study. In addition, measures were determined that were highly predictive of membership within one of the two apparent subtypes of retarded readers (that is (1) those who showed a tendency to "recover" from their reading disability and (2) those who made little or no progress, relative to their age, in reading acquisition). This particular study illustrated that not all retarded readers (at the 7–8-year age level) are alike, both in terms of their eventual level of reading acquisition and their initial patterns of abilities and deficits.

In an initial study of spelling disability (Sweeney & Rourke, 1978), it was found that subtypes of 13- and 14-year-old retarded spellers who had been distinguished by the degree of phonetic accuracy they exhibited in their misspellings were clearly distinguishable from one another with respect to many psycholinguistic abilities. In addition, the performances of the phonetically accurate retarded spellers were more similar to those of the normal spellers than to those of the phonetically inaccurate retarded spellers, despite the fact that the phonetically accurate retarded spellers were as disabled, with respect to level-of-performance in spelling, as were the phonetically inaccurate retarded spellers. At the same time, it was obvious that this distinction was not found for these psycholinguistic measures in the case of 9–10-year-old retarded spellers of the two subtypes. However, subsequent studies in this series (Coderre et al, Note 1; Sweeney et al, Note 3) demonstrated that these younger subtypes of retarded spellers can be distinguished on the basis of logical-grammatical reasoning and somewhat more subtle dimensions of psycholinguistic skills. The results of these studies illustrated two important features of spelling-disabled children: (1) there is more than one subtype of retarded speller, and (2) developmental parameters are important dimensions to be considered in determining subtypes of spelling-disabled children.

Another series of studies suggested that subtype analysis was as important in arithmetic disability as in reading and spelling disabilities. The results of the Rourke and Finlayson (1978) investigation, for example, illustrated that groups of children who did not differ in their level of impaired performance in arithmetic, but who were markedly divergent in their reading and spelling skills, were vastly different with respect to their performances on tests for psycholinguistic and visual-spatial skills. In fact, the differences were so dramatic that it would be accurate to say that these groups had virtually nothing in common. A subsequent study (Rourke & Strang, 1978) produced results that led to much the same conclusions about psychomotor and tactile-perceptual abilities.

Based on these studies we were able to conclude that there are meaningful, distinguishable subtypes of learning-disabled children whose problems in cerebral processing are expressed in their profound difficulties in reaching age-appropriate levels of reading, spelling, and/or arithmetic proficiency. At the same time, it became clear that we needed to adopt a different strategy for defining subtypes than we had heretofore employed. In our studies of subtypes of spelling and arithmetic disability, for example, we had determined in an a priori fashion which subgroups we would investigate. That is, we had divided subjects into subgroups of phonetically accurate and phonetically inaccurate retarded spellers, and we had determined that we would investigate subtypes of children who were equated for level-of-performance (deficient) in arithmetic, but who differed widely in their reading and spelling proficiency. What we wanted to do next was use a statistical classification procedure that would determine subtype membership in an empirical fashion, rather than in terms of our clinical intuitions and/or theoretical proclivities with respect to this issue.

It was for this reason that we were attracted by the method of Q factor analysis that was first applied in this field by Doehring (Doehring & Hoshko, 1977). The Q techniue seemed to be particularly applicable to the problem at hand because it emphasizes the pattern of performances exhibited by each subject as the basis for subtype classification and, as has been demonstrated repeatedly, it appears to be the pattern of abilities and deficits exhibited by learning-disabled children that is of particular significance for both theoretical and clinical neuropsychological purposes (Rourke, 1978a, 1978b, 1981a).

Our first attempt to define subtypes of learning-disabled children using the Q technique (Petrauskas & Rourke, 1979) entailed investigating reading-retarded children between the ages of 7 years and 8 years, 11 months. The total sample contained 160 subjects, of whom 133 were retarded readers and 27 were normal readers. It should be noted that these retarded readers were chosen to coincide rigorously with the working definition of reading disability (and other forms of learning disorders) that we adopted for our research program (Rourke, 1975, 1978b).

We used 20 dependent variables that were divided into 6 categories. These categories were chosen to reflect groups of abilities that have been employed frequently in the neuropsychological investigation of children (Reitan, 1974), and especially in the neuropsychology of learning disorders (Rourke, 1978a).

There are several features of the results of this study that merit special comment. Approximately 50 percent of this sample was classified into three reliable subtypes; approximately 20 percent were classified in one, somewhat less reliable subtype; and 30 percent were not classified. Had we chosen less rigorous criteria for designating subytpes, it is likely that many more of these subjects would have been classified. However, given the young age of these subjects and the exploratory nature of this study, a conservative course seemed the best one to follow. Only five normal readers (i.e., 18 percent) were classified into the three reliable retarded-reading subtypes. One normal reader turned up in the less reliable subtype. The remainder of the normal subjects who were classified (seven subjects) appeared in a subtype which contained only one retarded reader. This latter finding, together with the fact that less than 20 percent of the normal readers were classified along with retarded readers into one of the three reliable retarded-reading subtypes, would seem to attest to the essentially qualitative rather than quantitative differences in patterns of performance between normal and retarded readers. In fact, a perusal of the profiles for each of the retarded-reading subtypes indicates that, unlike the normal-reading subtype, these patterns are characterized by normal, near-normal, or above-normal performance on a number of measures within the context of mildly to severely impaired performances on a number of other measures. In other words, the reliably classified retarded readers presented with particular, widely divergent, patterns of abilities and deficits rather than with (1) an approximately even split between average and above-average performances (as is the case for the normal reading subtype), or (2) fairly evenly depressed performances (as might have been expected of children who could be characterized with precision as falling within the mildly retarded range of psychometric intelligence). Thus, in Yule and Rutter's (1976) terms it would seem that we have omitted their group of backward readers in this study and have succeeded in establishing subclassifications (subtypes) of their specific reading retardation group.

Another study in this series (Fisk & Rourke, 1979) differed in several important ways from the previous investigation. In the Fisk and Rourke study, children were chosen who exhibited across-the-board deficiencies in reading, spelling, and arithmetic: all attained centile scores at or below 30 on these three scales of the WRAT. In addition, the subjects were chosen to provide three successive age groups for comparison purposes. Finally, the dependent measures employed were somewhat different than (although couched within the same general categories as) those used in the Petrauskas and Rourke (1979) study.

The data analysis for this study was essentially the same as that for the Petrauskas and Rourke investigation. The Q technique in this instance resulted in the classification of approximately 80 percent of the sample. One reason for this increase in the percentage of classification was probably the advanced age (and, presumably, a corresponding lessening of intrasubject variability) of this sample; another is that we were investigating a much more restricted type of learning-disabled child.

Of particular interest was the persistence across age of the subtypes. To investigate this dimension, we assessed the correlations between each subtype at each age level and compared the profiles visually for each of those subtypes where high correlations were evident. This analysis yielded three replicated subtypes across the age groups studied. For example, the first replicated subtype was composed of subgroup 1 from the 9–10-year-old sample that correlated highest with subgroup 2 from the 11–12-year-old sample ($r = 0.98$) and with subgroup 5 of the 13–14-year-old sample ($r = 0.87$), indicating that the pattern of mean T scores for these subtypes was very similar. It was also evident that there was a high degree of similarity in the levels of performance between these subtypes (i.e., the mean differences between each of the factors for most of the variables were quite modest). Comparable levels of similarity were evident in the two other replicated subtypes.

There are several features of the results of this study that should be emphasized. (1) It appears that classifying learning-disabled children by means of Q-type factor analysis can be done more reliably at ages 9–14 years than at ages 7–9 years. However, there may be more variability associated with the classification of reading-retarded children (as were used in the Petrauskas and Rourke study) than when children with across-the-board learning deficiencies are employed. A separate study would have to be carried out to assess the relative influence of age and learning-disability categorization on classificatory accuracy. (2) The high degree of correlational and level-of-performance similarity within the subtypes that were replicated across age (together with the fact that there were no instances of significant intercorrelations between subtypes for those subgroups that they include) suggests that three qualitatively distinct patterns of abilities and deficits have been isolated using this procedure. (3) It seems clear that these subtypes tend to persist across age, although a longitudinal study would be necessary to decide this issue.

The results of these two studies suggest that subtypes of learning-disabled children can be isolated by applying the Q technique of factor analysis to neuropsychological data. In addition, it appears that there is good reason to maintain that at least some of these subtypes can be expected to persist across age. This latter point, seen within the context of our discussion of the results of other developmental investigations in this area, suggests that the patterns of neuropsychological abilities and deficits that characterize different subtypes of learning-disabled children are anything but epiphenomena. On the contrary, there is sufficient reliable data at this point to support the view that these neuropsychological patterns are crucial reflections of the central processing styles of such children. As such, they would be expected to have an impact on virtually every aspect of the educational enterprise.

NEUROPSYCHOLOGY AND THE SCHOOL PSYCHOLOGIST

It is clear that sophisticated neuropsychological analyses of central processing deficiencies in children have yielded incontrovertible evidence that brain dysfunction can play a major role in the etiology of such deficiencies. This generalization is not meant to suggest that other factors such as emotional disturbance, inadequate instruction, and sensory deficits cannot lead to impaired learning. Rather, it simply emphasizes the point that, once these other factors are ruled out as primary contributors to deficient academic learning, it can be expected that a thorough, comprehensive neuropsychological assessment of such disabled learners will, with a high degree of probability, yield evidence consistent with the presence of some type of cerebral dysfunction. Crucial to testing this generalization, of course, are the provisos that the children be selected in terms of the rigorous definition outlined above and that the mode of neuropsychological assessment employed be comprehensive.

Since developmental considerations have been shown to be paramount in the research results presented in this chapter, it follows that modes of neuropsychological assessment that have as their aim the formulation of habilitational educational plans for the individual child must be designed with these important dimensions in mind. Attention to adequate and applicable norms, test ceilings and floors, and specific developmental applicability of the neuropsychological measures employed are some of the more obvious considerations in this regard.

The findings with respect to subtypes of learning-disabled children have several implications. These include the necessity of adopting procedures for individual assessment that are compatible with modes of interpretation that can transcend simple level-of-performance analysis (including elementary lag or deficit formulations). Specifically, it is clear that assessment procedures should allow for the evaluation of pathognomonic signs, configurational score analyses, and comparisons of performance on the two sides of the body if clinically applicable interpretations are the goal. Failure to do this may lead to the formulation of educational programs that are limited and inappropriate. But perhaps the most important data to emerge from subtype analysis—at least within the context of this volume—are the findings that these subtypes tend to coincide (1) with the intuitive feelings of teachers regarding the relative strengths and weaknesses of children (Doehring & Hoshko, 1977), and (2) with the functional deficiencies thought to be associated with disturbances in specific brain regions and systems (Fisk & Rourke, 1979; Mattis et al, 1975; Petrauskas & Rourke, 1979). It is this type of converging evidence that bodes well for the emerging partnership between school psychology and neuropsychology. What remains is the delicate work necessary to fashion a more permanent bond between the two disciplines. It is up to each reader to decide whether the information provided in the following chapters is sufficient to suggest that this budding love affair will come to fruition!

REFERENCES

Bakker, D. J. Perceptual asymmetries and reading proficiency. In M. Bortner (Ed.), *Cognitive growth and development: Essays in memory of Herbert G. Birch.* New York: Brunner Mazel, 1979.

Bakker, D. J., Licht, R., Kok, A., & Bauma, A. Cortical responses to word reading by right and left eared normal and learning disturbed children. *Journal of Clinical Neuropsychology,* 1980, *2,* 1–12.

Benton, A. L. Developmental dyslexia: Neurological aspects. In W. J. Fried-
    lander (Ed.), *Advances in neurology* (Vol. 7). New York: Raven, 1975.
Boll, T. J. Behavioral correlates of cerebral damage in children aged 9 through
    14. In R. M. Reitan & L. A. Davison (Eds.), *Clinical neuropsychology:
    Current status and applications.* Washington, D.C.: V. H. Winston & Sons,
    1974.
Conners, C. K. Cortical visual evoked responses in children with learning dis-
    orders. *Psychophysiology*, 1971, *7*, 418–428.
Conners, C. K. Critical review of "Electroencephalographic and neurophysio-
    logical studies in dyslexia." In A. L. Benton & D. Pearl (Eds.), *Dyslexia:
    An appraisal of current knowledge.* New York: Oxford University Press,
    1978.
Critchley, M. *The dyslexic child.* London: Heinemann Medical Books, 1970.
Doehring, D. G. *Patterns of impairment in specific reading disability.* Bloom-
    ington: Indiana University Press, 1968.
Doehring, D. G., & Hoshko, I. M. Classification of reading problems by the
    Q-technique of factor analysis. *Cortex*, 1977, *13*, 281–294.
Doehring, D. G., Hoshko, I. M., & Bryans, B. N. Statistical classification of
    children with reading problems. *Journal of Clinical Neuropsychology*,
    1979, *1*, 4–16.
Fisk, J. L., & Rourke, B. P. Identification of subtypes of learning disabled
    children at three age levels: A neuropsychological, multivariate approach.
    Journal of Clinical Neuropsychology, 1979, *1*, 289–310.
Fletcher, J. M., & Satz, P. Developmental changes in the neuropsychological
    correlates of reading achievement: A six-year longitudinal follow-up.
    Journal of Clinical Neuropsychology, 1980, *2*, 23–37.
Hagin, R., Silver, A. A., & Kreeger, H. *TEACH: Learning tasks for the preven-
    tion of learning disability.* New York: Walker Educational Book Corp,
    1976.
Hughes, J. R. Biochemical and electroencephalographic correlates of learning
    disabilities. In R. M. Knights & D. J. Bakker (Eds.), *Neuropsychology of
    learning disorders: Theoretical approaches.* Baltimore, Md.: University
    Park Press, 1976.
Hughes, J. R. Electroencephalographic and neurophysiological studies in dys-
    lexia. In A. L. Benton & D. Pearl (Eds), *Dyslexia: An appraisal of current
    knowledge.* New York: Oxford University Press, 1978.
Jastak, J. F., & Jastak, S. R. *The Wide Range Achievement Test.* Wilmington,
    Del.: Guidance Associates, 1965.
Kinsbourne, M., & Warrington, E. K. Disorders of spelling. *Journal of Neu-
    rology, Neurosurgery and Psychiatry*, 1964, *27*, 224–228.
Knights, R. M., & Bakker, D. J. (Eds.). *Neuropsychology of learning disor-
    ders: Theoretical approaches.* Baltimore, Md.: University Park Press,
    1976.
Knights, R. M., & Bakker, D. J. *Treatment of hyperactive and learning dis-
    ordered children: Current research.* Baltimore, Md.: University Park Press,
    1980.

Mattis, S., French, J. H., & Rapin, I. Dyslexia in children and young adults: Three independent neuropsychological syndromes. *Developmental Medicine and Child Neurology*, 1975, *17*, 150–163.

Newcombe, F. *Missile wounds to the brain.* London: Oxford University Press, 1969.

Pajurkova, E. M., Orr, R. R., Rourke, B. P., & Finlayson, M. A. J. Children's Word Finding Test: A verbal problem-solving task. *Perceptual and Motor Skills*, 1976, *42*, 851–858.

Peter, B. M., & Spreen, O. Behavior rating and personal adjustment scales of neurologically and learning handicapped children during adolescence and early adulthood: Results of a follow-up study. *Journal of Clinical Neuropsychology*, 1979, *1*, 75–91.

Petrauskas, R. J., & Rourke, B. P. Identification of subtypes of retarded readers: A neuropsychological, multivariate approach. *Journal of Clinical Neuropsychology*, 1979, *1*, 17–37.

Preston, M. S., Guthrie, J. T., & Childs, B. Visual evoked responses (VERs) in normal and disabled readers. *Psychophysiology*, 1974, *11*, 452–457.

Reed, J. C. The ability deficits of good and poor readers. *Journal of Learning Disabilities*, 1968, *2*, 134–139.

Reitan, R. M. Psychological effects of cerebral lesions in children of early school age. In R. M. Reitan & L. A. Davison (Eds.), *Clinical neuropsychology: Current status and applications.* Washington, D.C.: V. H. Winston & Sons, 1974.

Rourke, B. P. Brain-behavior relationships in children with learning disabilities: A research program. *American Psychologist*, 1975, *30*, 911–920.

Rourke, B. P. Issues in the neuropsychological assessment of children with learning disabilities. *Canadian Psychological Review*, 1976, *17*, 89–102. (a)

Rourke, B. P. Reading retardation in children: Developmental lag or deficit? In R. M. Knights & D. J. Bakker (Eds.), *Neuropsychology of learning disorders: Theoretical approaches.* Baltimore, Md.: University Park Press, 1976. (b)

Rourke, B. P. Neuropsychological research in reading retardation: A review. In A. L. Benton & D. Pearl (Eds.), *Dyslexia: An appraisal of current knowledge.* New York: Oxford University Press, 1978. (a)

Rourke, B. P. Reading, spelling, arithmetic disabilities: A neuropsychologic perspective. In H. R. Myklebust (Ed.), *Progress in learning disabilities* (Vol. 4). New York: Grune & Stratton, 1978. (b)

Rourke, B. P. Neuropsychological assessment of children with learning disabilities. In S. B. Filskov & T. J. Boll (Eds.), *Handbook of clinical neuropsychology.* New York: Wiley-Interscience, 1981. (a)

Rourke, B. P. Reading and spelling disabilities: A developmental neuropsychological perspective. In U. Kirk (Ed.), *Neuropsychology of language, reading, and spelling.* New York: Academic Press, 1981. (b)

Rourke, B. P., Dietrich, D. M., & Young, G. C. Significance of WISC verbal-performance discrepancies for younger children with learning disabilities. *Perceptual and Motor Skills*, 1973, *36*, 275–282.

Rourke, B. P., & Finlayson, M. A. J. Neuropsychological significance of variations in patterns of performance on the Trail Making Test for older children with learning disabilities. *Journal of Abnormal Psychology,* 1975, *84,* 412–421.

Rourke, B. P., & Finlayson, M. A. J. Neuropsychological significance of variations in patterns of academic performance: Verbal and visual-spatial abilities. *Journal of Abnormal Child Psychology,* 1978, *6,* 121–133.

Rourke, B. P., & Orr, R. R. Prediction of the reading and spelling performances of normal and retarded readers: A four-year follow-up. *Journal of Abnormal Child Psychology,* 1977, *5,* 9–20.

Rourke, B. P., & Petrauskas, R. J. *Underlining Test* (Rev. ed.). Windsor, Ontario: Author, 1978.

Rourke, B. P., & Strang, J. D. Neuropsychological significance of variations in patterns of academic performance: Motor, psychomotor, and tactile-perceptual abilities. *Journal of Pediatric Psychology,* 1978, *3,* 62–66.

Rourke, B. P., Yanni, D. W., MacDonald, G. W., & Young, G. C. Neuropsychological significance of lateralized deficits on the Grooved Pegboard Test for older children with learning disabilities. *Journal of Consulting and Clinical Psychology,* 1973, *41,* 128–134.

Rutter, M. Prevalence and types of dyslexia. In A. L. Benton & D. Pearl (Eds.), *Dyslexia: An appraisal of current knowledge.* New York: Oxford University Press, 1978.

Satz, P., Friel, J., & Rudegeair, F. Differential changes in the acquisition of developmental skills in children who later became dyslexic: A three-year follow-up. In D. Stein, J. Rosen, & N. Butters (Eds.), *Plasticity and recovery of function in the central nervous system.* New York: Academic Press, 1974.

Satz, P., & Sparrow, S. Specific developmental dyslexia: A theoretical formulation. In D. J. Bakker & P. Satz (Eds.), *Specific reading disability: Advances in theory and method.* Rotterdam: Rotterdam University Press, 1970.

Satz, P., Taylor, H. G., Friel, J., & Fletcher, J. M. Some developmental and predictive precursors of reading disabilities: A six-year follow-up. In A. L. Benton & D. Pearl (Eds.), *Dyslexia: An appraisal of current knowledge.* New York: Oxford University Press, 1978.

Shields, D. T. Brain responses to stimuli in disorders of information processing. *Journal of Learning Disabilities,* 1973, *6,* 501–505.

Silver, A. A. An interdisciplinary model for the prevention of learning disability. In R. M. Knights & D. J. Bakker (Eds.), *Treatment of hyperactive and learning disordered children.* Baltimore: University Park Press, 1980.

Silver, A. A., & Hagin, R. Specific reading disability: Delineation of the syndrome and relationship to cerebral dominance. *Comprehensive Psychiatry,* 1960, *1,* 126–134.

Silver, A. A., & Hagin, R. Specific reading disability: Follow-up studies. *American Journal of Orthopsychiatry,* 1964, *34,* 95–102.

Sweeney, J. E., & Rourke, B. P. Neuropsychological significance of phonetically accurate and phonetically inaccurate spelling errors in younger and older retarded spellers. *Brain and Language,* 1978, *6,* 212–225.

Taylor, H. G., Satz, P., & Friel, J. Developmental dyslexia in relation to other childhood reading disorders: Significance and clinical utility. *Reading Research Quarterly,* 1979, *15,* 84–101.

Trites, R. L., & Fiedorowicz, C. Follow-up study of children with specific (or primary) reading disability. In R. M. Knights & D. J. Bakker (Eds.), *The neuropsychology of learning disorders: Theoretical approaches.* Baltimore, Md.: University Park Press, 1976.

Usprich, C. The study of dyslexia: Two nascent trends and a neuropsychological model. *Bulletin of the Orton Society,* 1976, *25,* 34–48.

Yule, W., & Rutter, M. Epidemiology and social implications of specific reading retardation. In R. M. Knights & D. J. Bakker (Eds.), *The neuropsychology of learning disorders: Theoretical approaches.* Baltimore, Md.: University Park Press, 1976.

REFERENCE NOTES

1. Coderre, D. J., Sweeney, J. E., & Rourke, B. P. *Word analysis, visual memory, spelling recognition, and reading in children with qualitatively distinct spelling errors.* Prepublication manuscript.

2. Fennel, E. B., & Satz, P. *A longitudinal test of the lag theory of developmental dyslexia.* Paper presented at the annual meeting of the International Neuropsychological Society, New York, 1979.

3. Sweeney, J. E., McCabe, A. E., & Rourke, B. P. *Logical-grammatical abilities of retarded spellers.* Prepublication manuscript.

William H. Gaddes

2
An Examination of the Validity of Neuropsychological Knowledge in Educational Diagnosis and Remediation

The 1960s and 1970s have seen an explosion in the development of neuro-psychological theory and clinical practices. Since much of this new knowledge has shown great promise for special education, some educators have embraced it with hopeful enthusiasm; others have resisted its promise and have distrusted its efficacy. Much of this wariness stems from a somewhat disreputable image of the practice of "neurologizing" or "physiologizing" behavior. It is quite true that some of the early attempts to relate behavior to its physiological bases were purely speculative, simplistic, incorrect, and not particularly useful. But in the past few years, the improved knowledge and techniques of neurology, neurosurgery, and neuropsychology and its marriage to special education in some instances, have provided a promising and productive union.

In providing a descriptive definition of the neuropsychological approach to learning disabilities, let me state first what it does not mean: it does not mean that every learning-disabled child is brain damaged, and it does not mean that the cause of every learning problem can be traced to a localized brain lesion. It does mean that (1) neuropsychology has much valuable information about the development and functions of the *normal* brain that can help the

---

I am grateful to Dr. Paul Satz for a critical reading of the first draft of this paper and for a number of helpful suggestions.

school psychologist and the teacher better understand perception, cognition, motor response, language development, and learning; (2) clinical studies of children with brain dysfunctions provide much valuable information about the deficits in learning when a child's learning problems are related to an impaired cerebral state; (3) the degree of brain damage covaries with its etiological significance in relation to a child's learning problem, or stated inversely, a neuropsychological approach may be ignored in the case of an underachieving child with a structurally and functionally normal and healthy brain, since pedagogical skills, including a motivational approach and stressing behavior management, should be all that is needed; (4) the locus of a brain lesion (whether it affects the primary cortical language circuits, the primary perceptual areas, the sensorimotor integrating mechanisms, or the cerebral centers mediating memory) may have greater causal significance than the extent or degree of brain dysfunction for a learning disability, because some cortical areas contribute to a greater or lesser degree of intervention in the various perceptual and cognitive processes; and (5) even in a case of documented localized brain damage or dysfunction, this condition is only one of the many etiological organic and psychosocial forces in a child's learning problem, and must be viewed in a total social context.

Neuropsychology implies the study of brain–behavior relationships, and accepts a causal association between these two variables. Because all behavior is mediated by the brain and central nervous system, any serious understanding of behavior must include a knowledge of its mediating structures, particularly when those structures are functionally impaired.

The investigation of these variables requires a collaborating neurologist or a research team of medical specialists that might include a neurosurgeon, a neurologist, an internist, a radiologist, or other medically trained person, and one or more neuropsychologists. When the investigation is designed to study the relationship of brain function and classroom learning disabilities, then the research team will, of course, include the school psychologist and will seek information from all relevant educational personnel, as well as from the child's parent or parents.

There are several levels of investigation that may be undertaken. One method is pure research where an independent variable is introduced under controlled conditions and the resulting behavior changes are observed. This type of investigation is usually done with animals (e.g., using surgically imposed brain lesions), although human subjects are sometimes used (e.g., when conducting drug and electrostimulation studies). Clinical studies may be done of traumatically brain-damaged human subjects, pre- and post-traumatically, where the independent variable is imposed fortuitously (e.g., by a brain infection, required brain surgery, or any type of accident resulting in brain injury). In these two models of neuropsychological research, two sources of data are obtained, one directly from neurology and the other from behavior. This enables correlation studies to be carried out and specific brain-behavior relationships to be discovered (e.g., left hemisphere motor strip lesion and right manual apraxia).

In the two models above, actual invasion of the brain tissue has taken place, either surgically, physically, or pharmacologically, and the nature of this invasion is usually known to the researcher. In the third type of investigation, a congenitally brain-impaired child is studied and only neuropsychological tests are administered. Using a knowledge of the brain-behavior relationships gained from numerous studies such as those described above, probable brain dysfunctions are hypothesized. This is common diagnostic practice in clinical neurology and neuropsychology, but obviously it is not as conclusive or as directly empirically based as the first two models, since observable data are available from only the child's behavior. The success of this type of clinical research depends on the clinician's knowledge of neuropsychology and his or her predictive skills. In some cases predictions regarding neurological status may be tested if the patient undergoes brain surgery.

A fourth level of brain function predictions has emerged in special education by those learning-disabilities specialists who conclude, on the basis of a few psychological tests, that the child suffers from minimal brain dysfunction or some other neurological diagnosis. Some of these clinicians have had no training in clinical neuropsychology, or at best minimal experience, and their diagnoses, if they include neurological statements, are superficial, frequently misleading, and professionally ill-advised.

POTENTIAL PROFESSIONAL PROBLEMS OF NEUROPSYCHOLOGY IN THE SCHOOLS

Let us examine these four levels of neuropsychological investigation again, to recognize their potential value and possible problems when used in a school setting.

Experimental Neuropsychological Research (ER)

This design implies acquiring knowledge about a child's brain from the neurologist or neurosurgeon who performed brain surgery, or through a standard type of examination such as angiography, a brain scan, or a Wada Amytal Test. While these tests are carried out primarily for medical investigation, they provide some valuable data that the neuropsychologically trained school psychologist can interpret for the child's teacher. For example, the amytal test may tell the neurosurgeon that the child's speech is severely interrupted when the left hemisphere is injected, but not the right. The school psychologist can compare his or her dichotic listening test findings (in this hypothetical situation, they showed a strong right ear effect) with the medical findings, and explain to the child's teacher, with a high level of probability, that the child is most likely left-hemisphere dominant for language. If the child, in this case, is left-handed, a pattern of average reading but impaired spelling is likely related to this condition of cerebral-manual ipsilaterality. I have discussed a number of these types of cases in much more clinical detail elsewhere (1980).

Pure research, while it occurs with animals, is not done with humans except peripherally, with some surgical procedure, and if it does not increase the risk or discomfort of the patient. An example is Penfield's electrostimulation of the human cortex with conscious patients during craniotomy. This technique, which he first used in the 1930s, enabled him to plot specific points in the human cortex directed by the patient's oral description of his or her experience during electrostimulation (Penfield & Roberts, 1959). These experiments added much to our understanding of memory and brain function.

Clinical Neuropsychological Studies (CS)

Reitan (1955a, 1959, 1964) originated a clinical procedure in the mid-1950s in which he predicted the locus of a brain lesion preoperatively, purely on the basis of his neuropsychological test findings. Following the craniotomy, the neurosurgeon reported the actual location and nature of the lesion so that Reitan had immediate feedback on the accuracy of his prediction. This is one of the very few instances in clinical psychology in which the psychologist receives immediate and uncompromising confirmation, refinement, or correction of his or her diagnostic statements. The hard-based monitoring of this type of study no doubt has contributed much to the general respect that clinical neuropsychology enjoys in medical–legal circles.

These studies have great value in that they provide information to improve the validity of the neuropsychological test battery, and tell us a great deal about the brain function and cognitive strategies of a child being studied.

A neurosurgeon may report a craniotomy in which he or she had to suture an area of the left parietotemporal area to stop a spontaneous brain hemorrhage in a 9-year-old right-handed girl. The school psychologist, with this knowledge, can alert the child's teacher to the expected postoperative regression in reading and writing, and suggest how to deal with the right hemianopsia, by seating the child on the right side of the classroom.

Neurological Diagnosis (ND)

The first two methods of neuropsychological investigation discussed have involved neurosurgery and the treatment of serious medical and psychological problems. Obviously these are not frequent types of cases for the special educator, but when they do occur, the school psychologist, if trained in clinical neuropsychology, possesses an unusual opportunity to gain knowledge about the child's learning skills not normally available in a school setting.

ND, which includes empirical data from the teacher, parent, and school psychologist, has only speculative data from the medical specialists and the clinical neuropsychologist. Where ER and CS enjoyed two sources of hard data independently generated and experimentally correlated, ND has only one source of direct data—the social and educational input. The other source, the neurological, has to be hypothesized, and as a result is not neuropsychological research in its pure sense. While it is called "neuropsychological assessment," the clinical psychologist practicing it should remember that this is a secondary type of scientific endeavor compared to ER and CS. As a consequence, any diagnostic statements must be presented with caution, true scientific skepticism, and personal humility.

Where ER and CS include the children with hard signs, and neurological pathology is known conclusively, ND includes the children with hard signs, or only a few soft signs, or no neurological signs at all. Neurological pathology, if it exists, is only inferred indirectly. Nevertheless, these children may be experiencing unusual and frequently unaccountable difficulties in learning. This is the major group of learning-disabled children with whom the schools must try to deal, and any school psychologist who elects to include neurological concepts in his or her analysis of this type of child's learning problems will end up on somewhat tenuous grounds scientifically since only a secondary model of experimental investigation can be used. It is this Achilles' heel in the armament of neuropsychological theory and skills that makes the school psychologist a constant target for Coles's type of logical attack (Coles, 1978), and the only protection against this type of assault is a competent knowledge of clinical neuropsychology and considerable clinical experience. To gain this, school psychologists must be given opportunities to obtain superior clinical training in graduate training schools.

One of the most obvious and easiest cases for the school psychologist to deal with in this category is the congenitally hemiplegic child. If a right-handed child has obvious evidence of weakness in his or her left hand and left leg, and on a battery of neuropsychological and educational tests is shown to be normal in language skills but inferior in spatial-constructional tasks, the school psychologist can suspect a right hemisphere lesion. If a large battery of sensorimotor tasks shows consistent normality with the right hand and inferiority with the left, the psychologist, in consultation with the neurologist, may diagnose the presence of chronic dysfunction in the right hemisphere. If trained in neuropsychology, the school psychologist will know that such a pattern of cerebral impairment means problems with learning arithmetic fundamentals, drawing, understanding maps or diagrams, or any task demanding spatial interpretation (Benton, 1969a). I have previously described cases of left and right hemisphere dysfunction in brief detail (1975) and in considerable clinical depth (1980), and have outlined how the school psychologist may interpret this knowledge for the special teacher.

In cases of highly localized or regional dysfunction, the chances are greater that the child's symptoms will have a predictable and limited pattern, as described above (Hartlage & Hartlage, 1977; Luria, 1966, 1970, 1973; Reitan, 1959, 1966a,b; Reitan & Davison, 1974; Rourke, 1975, 1976b). In cases of diffuse brain damage or dysfunction (e.g., postencephalitis, posttraumatic closed head injury, some cases of epilepsy), the child's presentation of symptoms will likely be heterogeneous and unpredictable. In spite of the heterogeneity of the child's symptoms, the school psychologist can obtain much detailed information on the child's strengths and weaknesses in sensory, motor, cognitive, and academic skills from a well-constructed and comprehensive neuropsychological test battery. From this test data he or she, if trained in neuropsychology, can construct a "conceptual nervous system," to use Hebb's term, to provide a system to the diagnostic reasoning and conceptualizing of what might be happening in the child's brain (Luria, Simernitskaya, & Tubylevich, 1970). However, because this procedure is purely speculative, and is constructed as a mental exercise to facilitate a diagnostic consideration of the child, the school psychologist would do well to avoid any diagnostic statements in reports or consultations about the state of the child's brain, other than to repeat what may have been provided in the medical history (e.g., "At age two he suffered from a high temperature for several days, which was followed by convulsions"). Since the hard data includes only the neuropsychological test results, information about the child's learning strategies, and teacher and parent descriptions of behavior, the school psychologist's report should keep exclusively to all this behavioral data. Similarly, the teacher, in conferences with the child's parents, should restrict all remarks to the behavioral and educational data since that is the teacher's area of professional expertise. If the parent asks direct questions about the causes of the child's learning problems, the school psychologist and the teacher should still keep to their areas of competence and avoid statements about brain function. If the parents push for answers about neurological status, they can be referred to the neurologist for that information.

Similarly, neurologists and other medical personnel, unless they have had training in psychometrics, should avoid making statements about the level of a child's intelligence purely on the basis of a few questions and a casual observation of social behavior in the artificial situation of a clinical examination. If clinical psychologists and medical practitioners, in their respective reports and consultations, will make statements within the realm of their respective professional competence, both groups will avoid problem situations that can lead to misdiagnosis and malpractice.

Neuropsychological Screening (NS) in the Schools

Since 1975, papers have begun to appear in educational journals attacking a neuropsychological approach to learning disabilities. Many of these appear to be written with an intent to discredit the theoretical validity of the approach and its practical use, but so far none of these critiques, to my knowledge, has been written by authors familiar with the neuropsychological research literature.

An example of these papers is by Coles (1978). It has been selected because it is articulate and persuasive, and warns against the practice of educators making neurological diagnostic statements about the learning-disabled children with whom they are concerned. This is a legitimate objection and one for which many educators have not shown adequate respect. However, Coles's criticism is not clearly delineated professionally. He talks about learning-disabilities specialists and learning-disabilities authorities. These people, whom he never identifies, would seem to be school psychologists, and he objects to their invalid diagnostic conclusions about a child's alleged neurological dysfunctions, and so do I. If some school psychologists or teachers with little or no training in clinical neuropsychology are willing to make diagnostic statements about a child's brain, using an incomplete battery of tests, most of which were never intended as discriminators of abnormal brain function, then they are inviting a vigorous and justified attack such as Coles's. But that is where my agreement with Coles ends.

Another of his major objections is his disaffection with what he says are the ten tests most commonly used to diagnose learning problems in children. The first major section of his paper is devoted to a careful examination of these ten tests used by the learing-disabilities specialists and their failure to discriminate learning-disabled children from normals. The ten tests are the Illinois Test of Psycholinguistic Abilities, the Bender Visual-Motor Gestalt Test, the Frostig Developmental Test of Visual Perception, the Wepman Auditory Discrimination Test, the Lincoln-Oseretsky Motor Development Scale, the Graham-Kendall Memory for Designs Test, the Purdue Perceptual-Motor Survey, the Wechsler Intelligence Scale for Children, a neurological evaluation by a neurologist, and an electroencephalogram. It is quite true that not one of these tests will discriminate every case of learning-disabled children from a group of normals in a large sample of children, but it is also true that no single test can do this because learning-disabled children are not a homogeneous group, and the syndrome is not a unitary one. To ask a question based on a false premise is to ask a meaningless question and to encourage false negatives in one's findings.

The early research with brain-damaged subjects fell into the same trap. Numerous studies in the 1950s compared brain-damaged subjects with normals and frequently ended up with ambiguous results. It was not until some of the early researchers in the mid-1950s, such as Reitan and Teuber, began to look at subgroups of brain-damaged subjects that they began to discover reliable differences between brain-lesion cases and normal subjects. They knew that brain-damaged subjects were not a homogeneous group, and until the clinical subgroups were recognized, no clear results could be expected. Significant differences were found, on many neuropsychological functions, between left frontal, right frontal, left temporal, right temporal, left posterior, and right posterior lesion cases. Many current critics make invalid evaluations of the neuropsychological approach to learning disabilities because of their ignorance or failure to recognize the specificity of similar brain-lesion cases and the heterogeneity of learning problems across groups of children. Because the syndrome is a multifaceted one, a battery, in order to be successful, must include a selection of tests that draws on all parts of the human cortex and that taps all of the sensorimotor, cognitive, and language skills included in the various forms of learning disorders. Not only that, but a battery that is sensitive to learning problems at one stage of a child's growth will need to be modified at a later stage because of the normal processes of cerebral maturation and the resulting cognitive changes that emerge with normal growth. For all of these reasons, some of the diagnostic test batteries that have been developed to probe all areas of the human cortex, and, that have been tested in various neuropsychology laboratories since 1950, have proven to be of more use. Because they were originally designed to be sensitive to the presence of brain damage and cerebral dysfunctions (Reitan, 1955b, 1959, 1964), and because they indicated growth changes in normal children (Gaddes & Crockett, 1975; Spreen & Gaddes, 1969), it soon became evident that these tests possessed great promise for better understanding learning-disabled children. For these reasons, some clinical neuropsychologists began to recommend using neuropsychological knowledge for the diagnosis and treatment of these children (Benton, 1962b; Gaddes, 1966, 1968, 1969, 1975; Knights, 1970, 1973; Knights & Bakker, 1976; Knights & Ogilvie, 1967; Reitan, 1966b; Reitan & Boll, 1973; Reitan & Davison, 1974; Reitan & Heineman, 1968;

Rourke, 1975, 1976b, 1978a,b; Rourke & Orr, 1977; Rourke, Young, & Flewelling, 1971; Satz & Friel, 1974; Satz, Friel, & Goebel, 1975; Satz, Friel, & Rudegeair, 1974; Satz, Taylor, Friel, & Fletcher, 1978; Spreen, 1978).

ASSESSMENT BATTERIES

While a review of some of the current educational literature led Coles to believe, quite rightly, that the current diagnostic tests used by many learning disabilities specialists failed to identify learning-disabled children, his neglect of the tests that do could lead the reader, unfamiliar with neuropsychological test batteries, to believe that none existed. No attempt will be made to list all of the tests used in neuropsychological clinical diagnosis and research, but it may be useful for the school psychologist to recognize the presence of (1) established batteries that are used by many for clinical diagnosis and research (e.g., Halstead-Reitan Neuropsychological Test Battery; Spreen-Benton Neurosensory Tests and Aphasia Battery), and (2) special batteries, experimentally developed, for the purpose of investigating particular perceptual, cognitive, or motor responses (e.g., Benton's Right-Left Orientation and Finger Localization Tests). Both types of batteries have their own research advantages; the established comprehensive battery over time will provide a large repository of similar and detailed test findings on a large sample of children, and these data banks may enable the researcher to discover a broad knowledge from large samples of children. The special battery, which is problem-oriented, can provide maximum information about a special problem with a minimum of test redundancy.

The test battery I will examine is of the second type and was developed by Satz and his colleagues (Satz et al, 1978) to discover some predictive precursors of reading and learning disabilities. Acknowledging the earlier longitudinal-predictive studies of de Hirsch, Jansky, and Langford (1966), Jansky and de Hirsch (1972), and Silver and Hagin (1975), Satz designed a study which he hoped would fulfill all of the theoretical and methodological requirements that were missing in the earlier studies. To do this, he and his colleagues studied 442 boys from the beginning of kindergarten to the end of grade 5, using multiple cross-validation groups, a substantial time interval between initial testing and criterion follow-up (i.e., 3 years), and the application of mutivariate analysis techniques.

Satz's theory of *maturational lag* implied in the study, has been explained in several papers (Satz, Rardin, & Ross, 1971; Satz & Sparrow, 1970; Satz & Van Nostrand, 1973). Briefly, it assumes that reading disabilities result from a lag in maturation of the child's brain, and this causes a delay in perceptual and motor skills in younger children who are immature.

In older children, this neuropsychological relationship shows itself in delayed conceptual and linguistic skills, although the ontogenetic pattern maintains its normal sequential order. In agreement with Piaget and other theorists, Satz sees child development as including recognized stages of growth with preceding stages resolving into more complex hierarchies of cognitive and adaptive behavior. The lag mechanism, which is not directly observable at present but can be inferred from the behavioral responses on a large number of validated neuropsychological tests, is accepted as a hypothetical construct. Satz sees developmental reading disabilities as disorders in central processing, but he is careful to make clear that the lag may be only temporary and the concept does not necessarily imply structural damage or permanent loss of function. This means that the younger child may catch up but will take longer than normal to learn academic skills. If the child does not catch up then the possibility of a chronic brain dysfunction seems more likely.

At the outset, 16 tests and situation variables were selected as possible predictor variables, and these tests were administered in the early weeks of kindergarten. At the end of grade 2 (i.e., almost 3 years after initial testing), reading ability was measured by teachers' ratings and standardized achievement tests. Readers were assigned to one of four groups on the basis of their reading achievement: *severely* disabled; *mildly* disabled; *average*; and *superior*. A discriminant function analysis, computed on the classroom reading level of 458 of the original group in order to compare the predictive validity of the tests administered almost 3 years earlier, showed a 89 percent correct hit rate on the severe group, and a 94 percent hit rate on the superior readers. Prediction was not as accurate for the mildly disabled and average readers, but the hit rate for the whole group ($N = 458$) was correct for 78 percent of the cases. The most powerful three tests at the end of grade 2 were finger localization, alphabet recitation, and visual form recognition and discrimination. Since these are tests of sensorimotor response and simple language function, they support Satz's developmental theory. When he increased the testing procedure to include classroom reading level plus IOTA Word Recognition, hit rates were even higher: 91 percent for severe; 66 percent for mild; 68 percent for average; and 97 percent for superior. As before, the prediction was better for the extreme reading groups, the false negatives occurring more in the mild and average groups. Even so, the overall hit rate was correct for 76 percent of the total sample. When the same procedure was applied to a cross-validation sample of 175 boys, the correct hit rate, 3 years after initial testing, for the severe group was 89 percent and for the superior group, 93 percent. The overall correct hit rate for the total sample of 175 boys was 72 percent. Satz concluded that, "This predictive accuracy, based on discriminant functions derived from a different sample and with a test-criterion interval of nearly three years, lends convincing support for the intrinsic validity of the tests" (Satz et al, 1978, p. 331).

When the four groups were examined from grade 2 through 5, it was found that the impaired readers also showed problems in arithmetic, spelling, and handwriting, and that their lag in reading ability frequently reflected a broader type of learning disability. By selecting the five strongest predictors (an abbreviated battery that took only about 30 minutes to administer), Satz calculated the probability of reading disability or competence 6 years after the initial kindergarten testing. The probability of reading disability for the next 6 years for the severe group was 85 percent, and for the mild group 88 percent. This means that the school psychologist, armed with this information, would have a highly probable base on which to advise early remedial attention. The probability of reading competence for the next 6 years for the average group was 67 percent, and for the superior group was 100 percent. With this information, the school psychologist would be fairly well prepared to judge which students did not need remediation. The five best predictors were finger localization, alphabet recitation, visual form recognition and discrimination, Beery Visual-Motor Integration Test, and Peabody Picture Vocabulary Test. There was an initial emphasis on perceptual and sensori-motor functions in kindergarten, and a gradual shift to more sensorimotor integration and language competence by grade 5.

This study by Satz and his colleagues in Florida is one of the finest longitudinal-predictive investigations yet carried out, and any school psychologist would be well advised to read the original text in full. I have indicated only some of the significant findings to counter the negative impression produced by Coles's paper that psychometric selection techniques are useless in discriminating learning-disabled children from normals.

Another successful long-term study worthy of note is that of Spreen (1978). It, too, is a 6-year follow-up study covering the period from kindergarten to the end of grade 5. While somewhat similar to Satz's study, it included more children ($N = 1282$) but fewer predictor tests ($N = 4$). The tests were (1) Peabody Picture Vocabulary Test (Dunn, 1965), (2) Coloured Progressive Matrices (Raven, 1965), (3) Revised Visual Retention Test (Benton, 1963b), and (4) the teacher's five-point rating scale to predict the child's future reading ability. The criterion variables were a number of achievement tests in reading, writing, arithmetic, science, and social studies. Using both univariate and multivariate analyses, Spreen found that

> prediction over a 6 year period was maintained on the basis of two tests, the Peabody Picture Vocabulary Test and the Benton Visual Retention Test (copying form). In addition, the Raven Progressive Matrices Test, higher age (within the year of birth) and right-handedness contributed to better success

in the early grades, and male students were achieving slightly better in the later grades.*

The major predictors combined a measure of verbal development and visual-motor competence, and Spreen reported an accuracy of prediction rate ranging from 63 to 86 percent, with an average of about 75 percent.

Most prediction studies, beginning in kindergarten and extending more than 4 years, are unable to improve on the 70-75 percent accuracy rate, although those using multivariate techniques tend to hold up better. Spreen, in commenting on this phenomenon, concludes,

> It is our impression that any prediction of this type based on kindergarten tests and teacher ratings reaches a ceiling, an optimum, which cannot be surpassed unless we consider the many other sources of variance involved in the academic success of a student. These "imponderables" are: the motivation of the student, the teacher's ability to reach a certain student (or just plain "good teaching"), the value placed on educational achievement in the home of the student and the help available in the home. Socioeconomic factors may be the most easily accessible of these and perhaps should be included in future prediction formulas.*

This view, which includes psychometric selection techniques, the recognition of central nervous system processing, and the inclusion of psychosocial factors in future formulas, differs from that of Coles who denies the first two variables and wants to explain all cases of academic underachievement exclusively in terms of primary social factors and what he refers to as "social class injustice" (Coles, 1978, p. 331). While no serious student of behavior will deny the importance of sociogenic forces in molding human behavior, a search of causes of academic failure that concentrates solely on these is likely to lead to a partial understanding of the learning-disabled child with an impairing cortical lesion. For example, a completely behavioral approach could lead to a misdiagnosis and misunderstanding of the dyslexic child with a loving and supportive family, but a severe left parietotemporal dysfunction.

VALIDITY OF NEUROPSYCHOLOGICAL EVALUATION

This brings us to the next point, the inclusion of neuropsychological knowledge in understanding the behavior of both normal and brain-damaged or cerebrally dysfunctioning children. Let us look first at an example of its

---

*From *Prediction of School Achievement from Kindergarten to Grade Five: Review and Report of a Follow-up Study* by O. Spreen. Victoria, V. C.: Department of Psychology, University of Victoria, Research Monograph No. 33, 1978, pp. 46 and 50. With permission.

use with normal children, or a population of average school-age children. Satz's battery in the study described above, was successful largely because the potential predictors were selected in a systematic way within a neuropsychological framework. By contrast, the battery described by Coles, while it includes a number of useful tests, was not comprehensive (it lacked any academic achievement tests as well as several sensorimotor tests), and it varied in coverage from one school system to another. Some school psychologists are reported to favor as few as only three visual-motor or visual-spatial tests (Hynd, Quackenbush, & Obrzut, 1979), hence their chances of selecting learning-disabled subjects would be restricted to those children representing a small segment of the learning-disabled population.

Satz's battery covers biparietal function (finger localization), which is known, from cases of traumatic damage, to be essential to reading, directional sense, body image, and numerous visual-perceptual processes. Alphabet recitation at age 5 suggests competent auditory perception and phonetic discrimination, which is mediated by healthy temporal lobe function. Visual form recognition draws strongly on bioccipital and right-hemisphere occipitoparietal activity, and the Beery test makes maximal demands on the sensorimotor strips (frontal and parietal) and their integrated interaction with the visual (occipital), auditory (temporal), and brainstem centers. The Peabody Picture Vocabulary Test requires a normal language development, verbal memory (increased left-hemisphere activity), pictorial-spatial recognition (increased right-hemisphere activity), and a healthy interhemispheric interaction. It seems highly likely that the success of the batteries of Satz and Spreen in selecting learning-disabled children stems from their wide cerebral coverage. It is interesting to speculate about what might make up the approximately 10 percent of false negatives in the severely disabled category in the study by Satz et al (1978).

Coles's second major complaint concerned the invalid use of the ten tests that he listed to make conclusions about the neurological status of a child's brain, and as already stated, I agree with him on this. I know of no experienced clinical neuropsychologist asked to make a differential diagnosis about a child's possible brain dysfunction, who would want to be restricted to those ten tests. Comprehensive batteries for this purpose characteristically include many more tests of subtle sensorimotor functions, language competence, short- and long-term memory, and measures of both inductive and deductive reasoning (Kløve, 1963; Lezak, 1976; Petrauskas & Rourke, 1979; Reitan, 1955b, 1959; Reitan & Davison, 1974; Rourke, 1975; Smith, 1975; Swiercinsky, 1978). While Coles was correct in warning against the use of invalid test batteries to make neurological diagnostic statements, unfortunately he carried his conclusion further and denied the existence of any psychological tests for neurological diagnosis. He stated quite emphatically and wrongly, that "These tests, in any case, do not yet exist" (Coles, 1978, p. 335). He must be unaware of the early work of Halstead (1947) begun in the early 1940s, and the pioneer work of Reitan, Halstead's most productive student (Reitan, 1955a,b, 1959, 1964). Hebb, in the late 1930s, began collaborative research studies with Wilder Penfield at the Montreal Neurological Institute, and from his influence grew the excellent and flourishing neuropsychological research program headed by Milner (1954, 1962, 1964, 1967, 1975). Reitan was the first to validate a comprehensive neuropsychological test battery for identifying human brain damage and/or dysfunction (Reitan, 1955b), and he soon became proficient in doing this. In a sample of 50 normal and 50 brain-damaged subjects selected on medically documented evidence, Reitan was able, using only his test battery, and with no other knowledge, to pick 96 percent of the brain damaged patients correctly. From a sample of 112 subjects with localized brain lesions (e.g., left or right frontal, left or right posterior, or diffuse) he could identify the locus or type of lesion exactly in 79 percent of the cases, and very closely in 92 percent (Reitan, 1964). His test battery and his methods have been used since about 1955 in many cases, to provide information to the neurosurgeon prior to a craniotomy. Dozens of other research neuropsychologists have developed new tests and batteries for understanding brain function, but no attempt is made to name all of them (Benson & Geschwind, 1968, 1969; Benton, 1959, 1962a, 1963a,b, 1967, 1969b,c; Goodglass & Kaplan, 1972; Kinsbourne, 1972; Luria, 1970; Russell, Neuringer,& Goldstein, 1970; Satz et al, 1978; Smith, 1975; Spreen & Benton, 1969, revised 1977; Teuber, 1959, 1964, 1975).

To summarize the points raised in Coles's paper, we can conclude that (1) School psychologists are ill-advised to make diagnostic statements about a learning-disabled child's brain unless they have had extended and competent training in clinical neuropsychology; they do better to keep to the behavioral data of the child's sensory, cognitive, and motor strengths; (2) While some test batteries have little success in selecting learning-disabled children from normals, there are some batteries developed by neuropsychologists that have a hit rate of 75-78 percent on all categories, and 90-100 percent on the extreme categories; (3) Batteries of neuropsychological tests have been developed and used successfully since about 1955 for making differential diagnoses of brain damage and/or cerebral dysfunction in children and adults; and (4) University and training school faculties should not mislead teacher trainees and educational diagnosticians by describing the administration of a few psychological tests as neuropsychological screening, and implying that these can reliably detect soft neurological signs. Such testing, if it includes three or four tests, is in fact a type of abbreviated educational screening and should be so recognized.

NEUROPSYCHOLOGICAL CLASSIFICATION OF
BRAIN FUNCTION

To give some clarity to the immense intricacy of the various behavior and learning styles and their differing cerebral functional patterns, it is useful to refer to a clinical classification scheme based on behavioral and neurological signs. The basic idea underlying this classification implies that in any large population some subjects have normal and healthy brains that function optimally, while others have damaged or malfunctioning brains. These latter may result from a genetic defect, or maldevelopment of brain tissue (agenesis), or traumatic brain damage incurred prenatally, during the birth process, or postnatally. Along this continuum from normality to severe brain damage is superimposed a random pattern of greater or lesser dysfunction, of thousands of possible loci of the lesion either cortically or subcortically, and of the lesion's extent ranging from highly localized to regional to cerebrally diffuse. Because the brain is the principal mediating organ of behavior, and because brain structure and function across individuals is reliably similar, a knowledge of habitual brain–behavior relationships, both healthy and impaired, will provide the diagnostician with a more detailed understanding of the behavior of the child being studied and a greater probability of predicting the limits of that behavior.

Most clinics develop their own models of classification based on the subject populations they serve. Since any system of groups and subgroups of cases may be made on an infinite number of criteria, the following model is not proposed as a permanent or final classification. It is useful and basically similar to that used in many other clinics, and it serves as a starting point for discussion. It recognizes five broad categories of subjects:

1. Brain damage, with one or more hard neurological signs
2. Borderline dysfunction (minimal brain dysfunction or MBD) with a number of soft neurological signs
3. Learning disabled with no positive neurological signs
4. Normal
5. Psychiatric, emotionally disturbed, or behavior problem

Brain-Damaged Subjects

Frequently the antineuropsychology critics in the educational literature attempt to discredit the use of neuropsychology by implying that its body of knowledge and professional skills are meant exclusively for severely brain-damaged subjects. This, they will tell you, is the responsibility of the neurologist or neurosurgeon, and ultimately the rehabilitation teacher in some remote hospital school. They are likely to point out that most underachieving students in the public school system are not brain-damaged, which is true, and for that reason a purely behavioral approach to teaching is all that is needed. On the surface, such an argument sounds plausible, but its practice, which is still prevalent in most school systems, is likely to neglect or maltreat at least 2 percent of the children in any large elementary school. In a school of 1000 children, this means that 20 or more students needing highly skilled understanding and treatment will be taught in ignorance of the major segment of their behavioral etiology.

The prevalence of learning disabilities, of course, varies in different settings, but in most countries statistics show an incidence of underachievers of about 15 percent (Gaddes, 1976), and about one half of these appear to have both hard and soft signs of neurological damage or dysfunction (Myklebust & Boshes, 1969). The author's own clinical experience indicates that about a third of the children referred to us have neurological signs, and admittedly we have a select clinical sample. These children have conclusive evidence of cerebral dysfunctions, and they suffer the resulting perceptual, cognitive, and/or motor impairments. In light of this clinical experience, an estimate of 2 percent of brain-damaged children in most elementary schools seems to be, in our opinion, a conservative estimate.

These are the children with one or more hard signs (Table 2-1). They have positive evidence of neurological tissue damage which may have become evident during brain surgery, through radiological studies of the brain, from the presence of penetrating head injury, or from specific behavioral signs (e.g., hemiparesis; epileptic seizures; or sudden changes in speech, perception, or cognition, following a cerebral hemorrhage). The electroencephalogram (EEG), if it indicates highly localized and severe dysrhythmias, may be useful in identifying the locus of brain pathology, and in providing the neuropsychologically trained school psychologist with a better predictive understanding of the child's possible learning strategies. A few autopsy studies of learning-disabled children have been reported in clinical detail (Drake, 1968), and while they cannot help the particular child under study, they do provide invaluable knowledge of specific brain–behavior relationships and their possible causal patterns for use in treating future cases.

In the absence of any clear-cut hard signs, a child with at least two or three minor but specific indications may be accepted as brain-damaged. Such signs may include hyperreflexia on one side, marked asymmetry of sensation in hands or face, asymmetry of manual-motor speed between hands, asymmetry of stereognosis between hands, a grade II or III localized dysrhythmia on the EEG, and a large number of other signs evaluated by the neurologist and the clinical neuropsychologist. A child in this category will almost certainly show one or a number of deficits on a neuropsychological battery (e.g.,

Table 2-1
Neuropsychological Clinical Classifications

Brain Damaged: Hard Signs	MBD: Soft Signs	Learning Disability with No Neurological Signs: Specific Learning Disability	Normal: No Learning Problems	Psychiatric: Emotional Disturbance
Conclusive signs of brain tissue damage or dysfunction Examples: brain tumor, bleeding, penetrating injury, EEG, grade iii[a], hemiplegia (half-paralysis), hemiparesis (half-partial paralysis)	Developmental delay, language retardation, motor clumsiness, perceptual deficits, right-left problems, hyperactivity, poor body image, poor hand-eye coordination, EEG, grade i or ii[a]	Examples: reading or arithmetic deficit Cause may be a genetic deficit, or subtle brain dysfunction not detectable on standardized neurological examination	No conclusive neurological or behavioral signs	Learning disability is secondary to inattention, anxiety, or other correlate of emotional disturbance; it may have an organic cause or may result from a biochemical dysfunction

From *Learning Disabilities and Brain Function* by W. H. Gaddes. New York: Springer-Verlag, 1980. Copyright 1980 by Springer-Verlag. With permission.
[a]EEG = electroencephalogram; grades i, ii, and iii indicate minimal, moderate, and severe pathology, respectively.

language retardation, motor incoordination, visual-perceptual deficits, auditory imperception, astereognosis).

In the past, educators have often misunderstood this category of child because of an ignorance of aphasia and its treatment (Myklebust, 1971), and the behavioral sequelae of specific lobular cortical dysfunctions. Although much has yet to be known about the behavioral effects of brain damage, there is a tested body of knowledge available to school psychologists and special teachers that can help to upgrade the remedial programs of brain-damaged children.

Borderline Dysfunction (MBD)

This group makes up about a third of the underachievers or about 5 percent of the school population in most elementary schools. A member of this group is the child with a number of soft signs but no conclusive indicators of brain damage on a standard neurological examination. Because the soft signs are similar to, but usually less intense than, the behavioral deficits of the brain-damaged child, cerebral dysfunctions have been hypothesized by most neurologists on a logical basis (as described above in neuropsychological diagnosis), and in harmony with a model accepting a unity of nature. In essence this is similar to what, in the profession of neurology and neurosurgery, is known as presumptive diagnosis (Penfield, 1977, p. 46), and it is accepted as a scientifically valid clinical practice, based on a sound knowledge of neuroanatomy, neuropathology, and clinical neurology. The neurologist or neurosurgeon who employs it does so using his or her most competent diagnostic skills, and accepts the procedure as useful though imperfect because of the prodigious functional complexity of the human brain. This realistic recognition of the value of presumptive diagnosis has enabled the profession of neurosurgery to develop to its present level of accomplishment, and educators will have to learn to accept it with its potential strengths and weaknesses if educational diagnosis and remediation are to gain by its value and use and if it is to find wide acceptance among well-trained educational diagnosticians.

This category of MBD, which makes up more than half of the constitutionally learning-disabled children, is difficult to define. Since neurological dysfunctions can only be hypothesized, this group is an attractive target for those who wish to defame a neuropsychological approach to learning disabilities; I have indicated above how the school psychologist and educator, wishing to make legitimate use of neuropsychological knowledge, can guard against such critical attacks.

Not only are neurological signs variable, but it is more difficult to obtain as many discriminating psychometric signs as with the brain-damaged category. In Satz's well-controlled predictive study described above, he was able, after 3 years, to obtain a 91 percent successful hit rate with the severely learning-impaired child (with a large number of neuropsychological signs and a high probability of brain dysfunctions) and only a 66 percent hit rate with the mildly impaired child (with few test signs).

Reitan and Boll (1973) have addressed the problem of the difficulties of identifying and classifying the MBD child by comparing a statistical model of analysis and a clinical evaluation of the same groups of children.

In the first part of their study, they examined 94 children with an average age of about 7 years, 5 months. These children were divided into three clinical groups with a fourth matching control group. Group 1 included 25 brain-damaged children selected because of the presence of hard neurological signs (i.e., hemiparesis, accidental brain trauma, etc.). Two groups of MBD children were selected clinically, group 2 ($N = 25$) because they were referred primarily for chronic academic learning problems and group 3 ($N = 19$) because they were referred primarily for behavior problems in the classroom. Soft neurological signs were present in many, but not all, of the subjects in groups 2 and 3, since the primary selection criteria were behavioral for both groups. The control group children, group 4 ($N = 25$), were selected because of no past or present evidence of neurological damage or dysfunction.

When the average scores of each group on the Wechsler (WISC) subtests, on academic achievement, and on a variety of neuropsychological tests (visual and tactile perception, visual-motor integration, spatial memory, concept formation, spatial reasoning, and motor speed and accuracy) were compared, the brain-damaged group consistently had the poorest scores, while the two MBD groups scored in-between. There was a strong trend for the MBD-academic group to score a little lower than the MBD-behavior group, but the differences in their scores were not statistically significant in most cases (Fig. 2-1).

Because clinical neurologists and neuropsychologists agree that the MBD child has a clinically identifiable syndrome, Reitan and Boll began to question the appropriateness of a statistical model of analysis to reveal behavioral deficits associated with minimal brain dysfunctions. They argued that since a statistical model compares average scores of groups, and since minimal brain dysfunctions may affect different brain areas in different children, averaging group scores tends to cancel and mask individual deficits and strengths. In basic terms, since MBD children are not necessarily a homogeneous group either neurologically or behaviorally, it is invalid to use an evaluative and comparative measurement model implying intergroup homogeneity. Because of the differential effects of subtle brain dysfunctions, a child with specific deficits in a particular functional area (e.g., visual-spatial perception and imagery) may measure in the normal or average range of intelligence.

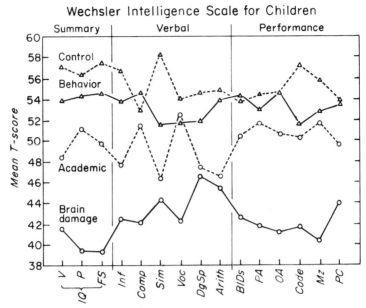

Figure 2-1. Graphic presentation of mean performances on the Wechsler Intelligence Scale for Children for a control group, a brain-damaged group, and minimal brain damage groups with academic deficiencies and school behavior problems. (Redrawn from "Neuropsychological Correlates of Minimal Brain Dysfunction" by R. M. Reitan and T. J. Boll. *Annals of the New York Academy of Sciences,* 1973, *205,* 65–88. With permission.)

To avoid the masking effect of averaging group scores, Reitan and Boll proposed a model of clinical evaluation requiring a sophisticated knowledge and considerable experience of clinical neuropsychology. They studied the scores of each of the 94 children in the total sample, without knowing which of the four groups the scores came from and without knowing the children's history or behavior or learning problems. For each subject they made blind judgements as to whether the test results implied a deficit in each of 16 areas, and the same relative pattern among the four groups emerged. This clinical rating system produced the following average number of deficits for each group: normal, 2.56 deficits; MBD-academic, 7.76; MBD-behavior, 5.53; and brain-damaged, 11.6. All four groups now showed statistical differences. Even the two MBD groups showed a difference (t = 2.59, p < .02) and all the other differences were highly significant (p < .001).

To examine the accuracy of their judgements compared to the actual original groupings, Reitan and Boll assigned three categories of brain function: normal, mildly impaired, and abnormal. They were correct in assigning 64 percent of the control subjects to the normal brain-functioning group, and none to the abnormal group. They misclassified 36 percent of the controls as mildly impaired. Within the brain-damaged group, they classified 96 percent as abnormal, 4 percent as mildly impaired, and none as normal. The two MBD groups were rated very similarly. Not one of these 44 children was judged to have normal brain functions, which is significant since it illustrates that experienced clinicians *can* discriminate differences between MBD children even though these differences fail to show when standard statistical analyses are applied. Reitan and Boll assigned 80 percent of the MBD-academic and 89 percent of the MBD-behavior groups to the mildly impaired classification, only misclassifying 20 percent of the first group and 11 percent of the second by placing them in the abnormal classification.

While these hit rates are high, and can be attained only by thoroughly experienced clinicians, this procedure, like the statistical model, also has inherent methodological weaknesses, which were recognized by Reitan and Boll. Since the original classifications were made in Reitan's laboratory, using the same tests and same selection criteria, it is difficult to run a blind study of this type. And as Reitan has also pointed out, it is difficult to communicate the "artistic" skill in clinical diagnosis. These two authors have realized the weaknesses of both the statistical and the clinical models of diagnosis and conclude that "it is clear that improved methodology is needed in this area" (Reitan & Boll, 1973, p. 80). Regardless of the imperfections of the present methods, it is not true that psychometric and clinical identification of borderline or MBD children is impossible.

Learning-Disabled with No Neurological Signs

This group is particularly interesting because of the complete lack of any clear-cut evidence of physiological correlates. The child in this group usually has normal or above average global intelligence and often possesses superior nonverbal intelligence. He or she is usually free of any obvious perceptual or motor impairments, and in many cases is a good athlete. This is the child with a developmental or congenital learning problem with no known cause. Maybe he or she is an excellent athlete, a gifted graphic artist, and musical performer, but has extreme difficulty in learning to read even at an elementary level (developmental dyslexia). Or by contrast, he or she is an above average student in the language arts, but finds drawing very difficult and numerical calculations almost impossible (developmental acalculia). Probably the most common symptom of the children in this group is a language disability in reading and writing, although usually not in oral language. For some reason or reasons they can talk normally (their receptive and expressive oral language is competent), but they are unable to learn how to decode and encode the graphic representations of oral language (i.e., printing and writing). Such a language disability is psychologically debilitating, not only because these children cannot compete academically on equal terms, but because they are limited in the range with which they can communicate with themselves, develop understanding about themselves and others, and generate well-integrated self images. If children born with language disabilities (e.g., aphasics or those mildly aphasoid) can be taught to improve their receptive and expressive written language skills, a marked improvement in social adjustment commonly results. For anyone, an articulate command of language is one of the most potent and immediate means of controlling one's environment. Anyone who has had the experience of being alone in a foreign country will know the profound feeling of social alienation and personal impotence.

A possible cause of such developmental learning problems is neurological lag, a theory advanced by Satz and colleagues (Satz & Van Nostrand, 1973) and already described briefly. This view postulates a delayed development of the child's central nervous system, particularly the cerebral cortex, the relative functional immaturity of which shows itself in the child's delayed perceptual processes and conceptual abilities. The theory does not necessarily imply a brain lesion, but a cerebral dysfunction stemming from neural immaturity, so that the dyslexic child is viewed as developmentally similar to a younger normal child. Although delayed in the perceptual, cognitive, and motor skills necessary for normal reading, this child may eventually learn them—at a later time than the normal reader. This is an interesting hypothesis and useful for explaining the child who is slow to learn but eventually acquires a normal level of academic achievement. It does not explain, however, the child with a chronic learning disability, who reaches adulthood still plagued with a learning deficit. Presumably this child suffers from a permanent brain lesion or cerebral dysfunction. Rourke (1976a) addressed the question of developmental lag versus cerebral deficit in a number of studies in which normal and retarded readers were examined using a comprehensive neuropsychological battery of tests. Sensory-perceptual tests in all three major perceptual modes, verbal and nonverbal memory tests, tasks of inductive and deductive reasoning, and language and academic achievement tests were used, the results of which led Rourke to conclude that group comparisons indicated that some, if not most, retarded readers suffered from impairing cerebral deficits primarily in the left hemisphere. Since most longitudinal studies (Schonhaut & Satz, 1980) reveal continuing learning disabilities into adulthood, the presence of a chronic brain dysfunction that is interfering with central nervous system processing seems to be justified in many and possibly most of these cases.

In the etiological model under consideration, any such brain lesion would have to be so minimal or subtle as not to show on a standard neurological examination: however, newer neurological techniques and comprehensive batteries of neuropsychological tests are beginning to uncover new evidence strongly suggestive of brain lesions that were previously missed by conventional methods. The computerized tomography (CT) scan has already proven useful in detecting a left posterior lesion in a patient with alexia without agraphia (i.e., Déjerine's syndrome, see Geschwind, 1962, p. 115) where no neurological deficits had been detected on previous neurological examinations (Staller, Buchanan, Singer, Lappin, & Webb, 1978). Also, comprehensive neuropsychological testing has frequently been more sensitive to some types of minimal or subtle brain dysfunctions in some cases of learning disabilities (Gaddes, 1980, Chapter 8; Reitan & Boll, 1973, pp. 81–87).

A third cause of developmental disorders includes abnormal growth of the brain and central nervous system. Such cases of neural agenesis are documented at autopsy, and a few where learning disabilities are involved have been reported (Drake, 1968; Landau, Goldstein, & Kleffner, 1960; Galaburda & Kemper, 1979).

A fourth possible cause of developmental learning problems is a disturbance in cerebral dominance and handedness. Since the 1920s, when Orton related poorly established cerebral dominance with perceptual reversals in reading (Orton, 1925, 1937), this possibility has attracted much research interest. While studies of mixed handedness, eyedness, and footedness may indicate the presence of minimal brain dysfunctions, they are not a reliable predictor of reading disability unless the suspected dysfunction affects the reading circuits of the left hemisphere and certain callosal connections with the right hemisphere. Pathological left-handers are usually left-hemisphere dominant for language (Satz, 1972) and in my experience, this type of ipsilaterality, whether left or right, usually accompanies a reading or more generalized learning disability. In a clinical review of several hundred learning-disabled children whom I have seen since 1960, only one such case of ipsilateral hand-brain conflict has come to my notice free of learning problems. This was a 10-year-old girl, with a verbal IQ of 125, who was a good student. A neurological examination, which included a Wada Amytal Test, was coupled with a comprehensive neuropsychological test battery, which included a dichotic listening test. This knowledge showed the girl to be right-handed and right-hemisphere dominant for language. Three congenital epileptogenic foci were localized in her left temporal lobe, and as a result, her language dominance had shifted to the right side. Her left sensory and motor strips were free of pathology, however, and maintained her handedness on the right side where, presumably, genetic programming had intended it. An analysis of each case, using neuropsychological knowledge, can help the school psychologist to understand in more depth each child's unique learning problem, and to consider the possible remedial approaches that the teacher may use. Although the information from an amytal test is not always available to the school psychologist, a good dichotic tape is and, along with a number of perceptual and motor tests of laterality, may form the basis for a better prediction of the child's cerebral dominance. Also, the manual tests can give added information about the probability of the child's handedness being pathological or genetically determined.

Because current clinical examinations of learning-disabled children in this group usually reveal no clear neurological signs of pathology, the school psychologist must keep in mind that many of them most likely have normal brains and nervous systems, and their academic underachieving is a result of psychological and environmental deficiencies. But because some of them may be affected by some type of subtle and undetected organic determinant (a genetic influence, a neurological immaturity, a distinctive neurological function, or a minimal brain lesion or dysfunction), it falls to the school psychologist to attempt to make this differential diagnosis. A comprehensive test battery will be invaluable because central-processing deficits may emerge with the suspected organic case, while none may emerge with the neurologically normal underachiever. This second group of children can be treated by standard behavior management procedures in which the child's motivation to learn is reinforced (Ross, 1974).

While academic underachievement may be psychogenic or organic in etiology or a mixture of the two, there are physiological causes other than primarily neurological ones, which have been discussed at more length elsewhere (Gaddes, 1978; Ross & Ross, 1976). These other physiological systems are supportive to the healthy function of the human brain which gives us "all our experiences and memories, our imaginations, our dreams" (Eccles, 1973, p. 2). Because of this, a dysfunction in any of the contributory energy systems may produce impaired neural function where no primary neural deficit exists. These supportive systems refer particularly to those forces that affect the chemistry, biology, and genetic variations in the functions of the brain and nervous system, and because their relation to normal brain function is not clear at this time, many learning-impaired children fall in this third category because the physiological substrates cannot be clearly identified and understood.

The first of these possible etiological areas is genetics. Because all behavior is a product of a functional interaction of physiological processes and psychological and social forces, and because the child with a chronic learning disability finds unusual difficulty in academic learning even when the environmental forces are enriched (i.e., remedial teaching), it seems logical to suspect an organic deficit somewhere in the child's system. Familial studies of developmental dyslexia have appeared in the professional literature since the early 1900s, and have indicated a higher incidence of dyslexia among parents, siblings, and relatives of dyslexic subjects than among normal readers (Hallgren, 1950). While Hallgren concluded a dominant mode of inheritance for specific dyslexia, he believed it to be determined by an alternate form of gene on a chromosome other than a sex chromosome (Owen, 1978, pp. 270-272). More recently, other investigators, aware of the heterogeneity of causes of reading and learning problems in children, have looked for subgroups. Owen, Adams, Forrest, Stolz, and Fisher (1971) studied educationally handicapped (EH) and successfully academic (SA) children and their parents. The fathers of the SA children were the best readers, the mothers next, the fathers of the EH children next, and the mothers of the EH children poorest. These findings suggest a genetic and environmental influence on learning deficits. McClearn (1978, pp. 287-297) has hypothesized, for purposes of illustration, that there are three etiological subgroups of developmental dyslexics. The first results from atypical lateralization, the second from interference of audiovisual input, and the third is associated with a reduction in contingent negative variation (a slowly changing negative potential in the brain that may occur between a stimulus and an elected response). If some of these types of reading disabilities are due to single recessive genes, some to dominant genes, some to sex-linked genes, some to polygenic segregation, and some to environmental accidents or different experiences, it becomes obvious, as McClearn has concluded, that unmistakable genetic relationships are impossible to extricate because of the heterogeneity of possible causes. He feels (McClearn, 1978, p. 297) that the behavioral or educational scientist will need to analyze and identify phenotypically distinct entities before the genetic researcher will have much chance of finding specific modes of inheritance. However, in his detailed and scholarly discussion of developmental dyslexia, Benton (1975) concludes that,

Taking all the findings into account, there is impressive evidence for the operation of a hereditary factor in developmental dyslexia. Conceivably this factor is operative in every relatively pure case, i.e., those not ascribable to obvious brain damage, poor educational opportunity, or emotional disturbance (p. 12).

A second possible area of physiological causes lies with the endocrine system. This system of glands secretes hormones directly into the blood stream. Its effects on behavior are those exerted through the central nervous system directly and those involving non-neural structures. Most controlled experiments in biochemistry and endocrinology have been conducted with laboratory animals, chiefly because of ethical reasons. However, the interest in thyroid function and short term memory and the effects of pituitary gland feeding on spelling ability dates back to the 1920s and 1930s (Mateer, 1935). Pancreatic dysfunction may affect the normal secretions of the Islets of

Langerhans, which, in turn, may result in diabetes mellitus (hyperglycemia), or hypoglycemia. This latter condition may be associated with certain types of aphasic symptoms in speech and spelling. School psychologists and special teachers need to be sensitive to possible cases of endocrine pathology. The overweight child with slow mental responses and lack of normal energy is a reasonable candidate for medical referral. A basal metabolism test may reveal a condition of hypothyroidism that can be treated; cases are not uncommon in which an appropriate treatment with thyroxin results in a loss of abnormal weight, an increase in IQ, and an improvement in social adjustment. However, most gland cases are not as clearly understood as the hypothyroid child nor as easily treated, so the school psychologist will need to seek out the best available endocrine diagnosticians for referral purposes. Ongoing medical treatment should be coordinated with educational monitoring so as to evaluate any behavioral and cognitive changes. The whole area of neurochemistry is progressing rapidly and is not yet at a stage that allows more than minimal or segmental explanations of its relation to learning. Eccles (1973) believes "that its period of greatness is yet to come" (p. xiii).

Another possible etiological area is nutrition and its effect on cognition and behavior. Because cell growth depends on adequate nutrition, there is a direct relation between nutrition and the growth and development of the brain and central nervous system. Shneour (1974) has pointed out that because the mature human brain contains about eleven billion neurons, as well as several million glial cells, and because the full complement of neurons is virtually complete at birth, on the average 20,000 neurons per minute must be produced and differentiated throughout the 9 months of normal gestation. Characteristically, the brain has a high and continuous demand for oxygen and nutrients during waking and sleep. Although the adult human brain comprises only 2 percent of the total body weight, it consumes 20 percent of the total oxygen and 20 percent of the total nutrients of the body. The human infant's brain consumes 50 percent of the total oxygen intake. These nourishing resources are carried to the brain by the blood supply whose nutritional richness or deficiency is determined by the child's daily diet.

"Undernutrition during proliferative growth will retard the rate of cell division and result in a permanent reduction in brain cell number" (Winick, Rosso, & Brasel, 1972, p. 199), and since brain growth during gestation is "one of the earliest, most rapid, and most extensive developments of the whole organism" (Shneour, 1974, p. 1) this points up the very real risk of permanent brain damage or maldevelopment occurring during the early stages of development. The pattern of causal relationships in the pregnant mother's diet, the child's diet during early life, and environmental deprivation seems to be the major determinant of the child's physical and mental potential (Von Muralt, 1972). There is growing evidence that native intelligence can be permanently injured by inadequate diet (Shneour, 1974; Winick et al, 1972). It is highly likely that irreversible brain damage results from malnutrition in early life "irrespective of the amounts of protein consumed later" (Altshul [quoted in Johnson, 1967]), but malnutrition later in childhood, following adequate feeding prenatally and during infancy, may have little or no effect (Winick et al, 1972).

Malnutrition does not operate in a social vacuum. Hallahan and Cruickshank (1973) have concluded that

> malnutrition arises from a common group of adverse social conditions, including poverty, ignorance, poor hygiene, overcrowding, parasitic and communicable diseases, superstition, and other factors that collectively and individually limit the availability and/or proper utilization of nutrients by the organism. (p. 17)

No doubt this multicausal pattern, including a large number of social forces that are both difficult to define and to control, has contributed to the difficulties of research in this area. Adams (1968, p. 465) has pointed up the weakness of viewing cultural factors as the major determinant of cognitive development, and viewing nutrition as only one of many minor ones. Instead of asking the question "How does culture affect nutrition, and nutrition in turn affect mental development?" Adams prefers to ask, "How do culture and society affect culture and society when mediated by nutrition and human growth and development?" He sees this whole problem as an adaptive cycle, and in this context the various sociocultural variables involved in problems of nutrition and behavior may be considered as independent, dependent, and intervening variables.

It is estimated that there were 30 million poverty stricken people in the United States in 1967 (Altshul, 1974), and it is plausible to conclude that many of the children in this population may be suffering from subtle forms of brain dysfunctions that could impede their progress in school. These children could reasonably make up a segment of category 3 (learning disabled with no positive neurological signs), since their learning deficits have resulted from complex cultural and physiological variables producing a mild dysgenesis of the brain, too slight to show on a standard neurological examination, but serious enough to interfere with normal thinking.

Interest in nutrition has grown rapidly during the 1970s, and special diets have been recommended for improving concentration, reducing hyperactivity, and resolving many problems of children's behavior. Sometimes these recommendations are based on poor evidence; the school psychologist will want to evaluate their sources and examine their validity.

Other possible sources of learning problems with no detectable neurological deficits include lead poisoning (Ross & Ross, 1976), possible radiation stress from harmful fluorescent lighting (Ott, 1976), drug consumption, smoking, and alcohol use during pregnancy (Ross & Ross, 1976), sensory deficits, and various chronic illnesses.

In summary, it is evident that category 3 may include some children with minimal brain dysfunctions that are undetectable on a standard neurological examination, some children with brain deficits secondary to a large variety of physiological abnormalities, and some children of low socioeconomic status. Because this group may include as many as 5-10 percent of the school population in large urban centers, and because the possible etiologies are so numerous, the school psychologist and special teacher will need to cultivate a multidisciplinary team of consultants to help them understand and treat these children.

Normals

Children free of any health, family, or broad cultural problems, if motivated to learn, should be able to do so by developing their own learning strategies. It is true that some children with known brain damage may fall into this group, but the prevalence of these children is unknown since their brain pathology is not detected unless they seek medical treatment. Two examples come to mind, both children whom I saw in the Neuropsychology Laboratory on medical referral. The first, a bright 8-year-old boy, developed an abscess in his right frontal lobe. Following its surgical excision, he was referred for neuropsychological assessment. His superior pretraumatic verbal IQ still measured in the superior range, and he continued through school and college with excellent marks. He completed an M.A. degree in sociology and is currently employed in a social service center as a counselor.

The second case, a girl with seizures, has been described above. Her left temporal lobe epileptogenic foci were so well localized that they did not interfere with her language. Her brain adapted by shifting language dominance to the right hemisphere, although she remained right-handed. She has been a competent student throughout her school history and her seizures are controlled by anticonvulsive medication.

Sometimes those who try to discredit the neuropsychological approach to learning disabilities have used this type of evidence to establish the "invalidity" of the procedure. But an in-depth clinical study of these types of cases usually shows the brain lesions to be highly localized and outside the cortical areas primarily concerned with mediating language, perception, motor responses, and sensorimotor integration.

Very few children in this category, however, have brain lesions. In fact, almost all of them enjoy normal central nervous system function, a healthy social environment, and a personality free of pathology. They tend to learn in school without special attention. If they happen to be underachieving academically, their treatment, in simple terms, will need an analysis of their motivational pattern and will be by some form of behavior therapy.

Behavior Disorders

Because of space limitations and the enormity of the topic, no attempt will be made to deal with all of the behavior problems of children; only the most common will be mentioned. It is common practice to define behavior as *normal* or *deviant* in terms of agreement with or deviation from the prevailing generally accepted norms of behavior of the group in which the behavior is being rated. Parents and teachers develop certain expectations about child behavior, which usually are somewhat similar to the group norms. The appropriateness of any behavior may be judged in terms of the child's age, the location of its occurrence, its frequency, and its intensity. Since all of these measures involve subjective value judgements, it is obvious that there is no absolute definition of a psychological or behavioral disorder.

Many reports show that hyperactivity is one of the most frequent complaints made by parents about their children (Ross & Ross, 1976, p. 1) and one of the most frequent reasons for clinical referral. One experienced clinical neuropsychologist, Knights, who has directed a research program since 1964 for the study and treatment of learning-disabled children, while recognizing the possibility of neurological deficits in many of these children, lists "problems of hyperactivity" as their most common problem (Knights, 1977). No doubt this is an important behavioral correlate of many children with learning problems, and it should profit the school psychologist and special teacher to examine its relation to neuropsychological knowledge.

Hyperactivity in animals and children may be caused by brain damage, psychosocial frustrations, or a mixture of the two. Lashley (1920) demonstrated many years ago that rats become more active following surgically imposed brain lesions, and clinical interviews with parents of traumatically brain-damaged children (e.g., penetrating head injury or cerebral infection) have frequently revealed increased hyperactivity among these children following their brain injuries. The early general diagnostic impression of brain-injured children, following the influence of Strauss and Lehtinen (1947), implied that hyperactivity always accompanied brain dysfunctions, but we now know this to be false.

Groups of subjects legally convicted of charges involving violent aggressive behavior have been found to demonstrate significantly more signs of brain dysfunctions than a group of nonviolent convicted subjects, as measured by a comprehensive battery of neuropsychological tests. This difference showed both for male adolescents (Spellacy, 1977) and male adults

(Spellacy, 1978). There is a great mass of research and clinical evidence that brain dysfunctions can result in violent, destructive behavior in adults (Mark & Ervin, 1970) and hyperactivity in children (Ross & Ross, 1976).

The hyperactive child with a normally functioning brain, but a deficient or frustrating social environment, whether it be in the home, school, or community, is the more likely referral and the one whom the school psychologist regularly encounters. The assessment of this child requires a search for the nature and location of the source or sources of his or her frustrations and anxieties, and a decision about their management.

Because some children may exhibit both organic and psychological etiological signs, the school psychologist will need to make a differential diagnosis between the two major causal patterns with those children who fall into either one or other of these categories, and will need to decide on the degree of each causal factor with those children in the mixed group. At this point in our knowledge of hyperactive children, a comprehensive battery of neuropsychological tests appears to be the most useful clinical technique for effecting such a differential diagnosis. A competent knowledge of brain structure and function and a familiarity with the current professional literature will enhance the probability of an accurate, or at least useful, diagnosis, which in turn should lead to a more successful program of remediation.

While the primary learning-disabled child may suffer from deficits in perception, language development, intellectual skills, and sensorimotor integration because of cortical or brainstem damage, the hyperactive child may or may not suffer from brain dysfunctions. If he or she does, the learning disability is primary, but if not, impulsivity and distractibility produce a learning problem that is secondary to the hyperactivity. Such a child *can* learn, provided his or her attention can be improved (Douglas, 1976; Meichenbaum, 1976). The reader will remember that in the Reitan and Boll study of MBD children, one of the groups (MBD-behavior) was selected because of classroom behavior problems. It seems quite likely that most of these were hyperactive children, and Reitan and Boll found their test performances close to and sometimes better than those of the normal controls (see Fig. 2-1 through 2-3). No doubt these children's academic achievement in the classroom was not successful because of the interfering effects of their behavior problems, but in the one-to-one relationship with the psychometrician in Reitan's laboratory, they showed that they were capable of normal achievement. This is a common clinical phenomenon. Also, most children find a neuropsychological battery interesting and intriguing and this interest can enhance the child's motivation.

Antisocial behavior among children is a second problem area. Delinquency may have its roots in neural deficits (Spellacy, 1977; Williams, 1969),

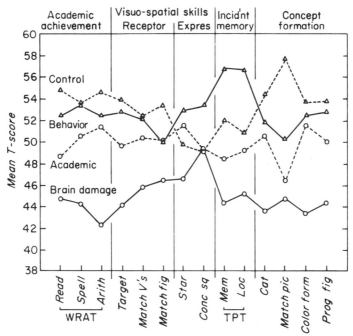

Figure 2-2. Graphic presentation of mean performances on the Wide Range Achievement Test and variables from the Reitan-Indiana Neuropsychological Test Battery for a control group, a brain-damaged group, and minimal brain damage groups with academic deficiencies and school behavior problems. (Redrawn from "Neuropsychological Correlates of Minimal Brain Dysfunction" by R. M. Reitan and T. J. Boll. *Annals of the New York Academy of Sciences,* 1973, *205,* 65–88. With permission.)

psychosocial factors (Glueck & Glueck, 1950; McCord & McCord, 1959; Short & Strodtbeck, 1965), or a mixture of the two. In most textbooks on behavioral disorders in children, which usually present only a behavioral model, organic causes are completely or largely ignored, and social class and community contacts are presented with the implication that the total causal picture has been provided. To avoid misunderstanding the habitual delinquent, a complete neurological and neuropsychological examination should be carried out, either to identify or rule out the possibility of some type of contributing cerebral pathology. Once the school psychologist has done this, he or she is in a position to make a useful differential diagnosis that is not as likely to misdiagnose or mistreat the child.

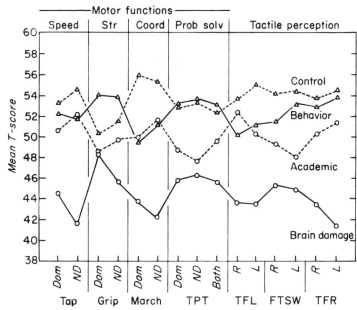

Figure 2-3. Graphic presentation of mean performances for motor and tactile-perceptual tests from the Reitan-Indiana Neuropsychological Test Battery for a control group, a brain-damaged group, and minimal brain damage groups with academic deficiencies and school behavior problems. (Redrawn from "Neuropsychological Correlates of Minimal Brain Dysfunction" by R. M. Reitan and T. J. Boll. *Annals of the New York Academy of Sciences,* 1973, *205,* 65–88. With permission.)

Neurotic withdrawal and psychotic abnormalities among children are primarily a medical or psychiatric responsibility. Remedial teaching programs for these children will usually need to be delayed until the personality problems are resolved or at least improved, since the learning problems in these types of cases are secondary to the children's anxieties and mental preoccupations. Neuropsychological testing is not usually indicated in the case of autistic or psychotic children because of the confounding effects of their apathy or inattention. However, if the tester can attract the child's attention and motivate him or her to cooperate on the tests, the results can be as useful as with the other classes of children for making a differential diagnosis of neurological dysfunction, where that is indicated, or for assembling a detailed profile of the child's sensorimotor and cognitive strengths and weaknesses, which always has value for the special teacher.

NEUROPSYCHOLOGICAL PRINCIPLES AND THEIR VALUE FOR EDUCATION

Cerebral Hemispheric Asymmetry

No neuropsychological phenomenon has attracted as much research attention since about 1955 as the fact that the two cerebral hemispheres have different and unique styles in processing perceptual and cognitive material. With Broca's notable discovery in 1861 that aphasia was correlated with left-hemisphere damage or disease, medical science soon accepted that in right-handed subjects the left hemisphere was dominant for language. The psychological functions of the right hemisphere were not recognized for almost 100 years. Up until about 1955, the right hemisphere was usually labeled nondominant and was frequently considered to be subordinate to the dominant hemisphere. Neuropsychological research in the 1950s (Reitan, 1955a) revealed that left-hemisphere lesion cases had relatively lower verbal IQs (VIQ) than performance IQs (PIQ) on the Wechsler test (VIQ < PIQ), and that right hemisphere lesions showed the reverse pattern (VIQ > PIQ). Since the two halves of the Wechsler test stressed verbal and spatial skills respectively, these abilities became associated with the two halves of the brain, and interest in the brain's asymmetrical functioning increased and expanded at an astounding rate. By 1965, Benton, drawing on the best research in clinical neurology and neuropsychology, made one of the first clear statements on the apparently unique functions of the right hemisphere (Benton, 1965). By 1970, the two hemispheres were described to include language, sequential, and analytical functions for the left hemisphere, and spatial, constructional, and holistic functions for the right.

The evidence for hemispheric asymmetry comes from the study of both abnormal and normal brain functions. Because of the enormity of this research area, I will list only the major sources of this evidence and indicate briefly the value of this knowledge for the school psychologist and the special teacher.

UNILATERAL BRAIN LESIONS

If a child who is left-hemisphere dominant for language suffers traumatic damage to the medial cortical areas of the left hemisphere, he or she will suffer impairment of expressive language (speaking and writing), particularly if the affected area includes the medial cortex extending from the angular gyrus to Broca's area. Receptive language (listening and reading) will be impaired if Wernicke's area in the left temporal lobe, is affected. Thousands of such brain-damaged cases have been reported (Geschwind, 1965; Luria, 1966,

1970, 1973; Milner, 1973; Russell & Espir, 1961). If the right hemisphere is damaged, and the left is spared, then spatial-constructional skills are likely to be impaired, and such a child will have learning problems with arithmetic in the early grades (largely because of its spatial components) and will have difficulty interpreting maps in geography and mechanical diagrams in science, drawing, sewing, and the industrial arts (Gaddes, 1980). This evidence does not mean that verbal processing is exclusively mediated by the left hemisphere, because, as Hughlings Jackson, the eminent nineteenth-century British neurologist pointed out in the mid-1800s, it is not the damaged brain tissue that produces the particular behavioral deficit, but the remaining healthy neural cells (Jackson, 1958). This evidence, however, does show that since unilateral lesions of the left hemisphere produce language deficits in most people (probably at least 94 percent of the adult population) and similar lesions in the right hemisphere do not, the language triangle of the left hemisphere (the cortex within the area bounded by Broca's area, the angular gyrus, and Wernicke's area) is a part of the brain that is essential to normal language mediation. Nevertheless, total brain function must also be present, because the right hemisphere also makes minimal contributions to complete language function (Zaidel, 1973). Interhemispheric functions are mediated by the millions of interconnections in the corpus callosum, and while each hemisphere has its own unique style of processing, healthy input from both hemispheres is needed for normal behavior.

Unfortunately, cerebral laterality has been misunderstood and misrepresented by some popular writers who have described the two hemispheres as functioning differently and separately and by some commercially motivated persons who are promoting books and teaching devices that are alleged to aid learning in either the left or right hemisphere. The implication is that the two hemispheres are functionally independent, which, of course, they are not. This misinformation has been repeated even in a few academic papers, such as the one by Hardyck and Haapanen (1979) in which the reader is told that "the two hemispheres of the human cerebral cortex function very differently and in *an almost noninteractive manner*" (p. 219) (my italics). In the same paper the writers set themselves the task of examining "the belief that our hemispheres function so differently and *so separately*" (p. 219) (my italics). While there is a tremendous body of evidence to support hemispheric asymmetry of function (Kimura, 1973), there is none to support noninteractive function, except in the very rare cases of complete commissurotomy or severe callosal agenesis.

The neuropsychologically trained school psychologist can provide much useful information to the teacher of the child with unilateral penetrating or closed head injury, with one-sided severe cerebral dysrhythmia, and with left or right hemiparesis. These children have frequently been mistreated by the schools because of the ignorance of the cognitive and behavioral sequelae of unilateral brain damage. The teacher who understands the general pattern of hemispherically controlled mental and behavioral skills will have some diagnostic understanding of the unilaterally impaired child, and will be better prepared to decide on an appropriate remedial program.

EXPERIMENTALLY IMPOSED HEMIPARESIS

The same hemiparetic condition may be produced experimentally and temporarily with the Wada Amytal Test. This is a commonly used clinical test in which injections of sodium amytal are made sequentially into the carotid artery on the side of the neck (Wada & Rasmussen, 1960). When the left side is injected, the left hemisphere becomes neurally impaired in a few seconds, and in most subjects aphasia occurs immediately. During the period of the effects of the drug, usually a few minutes, the temporarily aphasic subject may be proficient in pictorial interpretation and completing spatial tasks since the right hemisphere is free of the drug in most cases. When the right carotid artery is injected and the right hemisphere anesthetized, the subject now may be able to speak, follow oral instructions, read and write, but cannot recognize faces, carry out spatial tasks, or interpret pictorial material. Those subjects who are bilateral for language may show both types of cognitive impairment to some extent with injections on either side (Milner, 1973). This clinical procedure is one of the checks on speech laterality prior to brain surgery for the purpose of controlling or terminating intractible epileptic seizures. It also provides immediate and dramatic evidence of the asymmetrical functions of the two cerebral hemispheres. The school psychologist will find this information advantageous, when it is available, for learning more about the child's language dominance and relating it to his or her handedness and other lateral preferences. This information is often crucial in understanding a complex learning problem.

SPLIT BRAIN EXPERIMENTS

As recently as 1951, the two hemispheres were thought to be mirror images of each other, and the real function of the corpus callosum, the large band of interhemispheric fibers, was unknown. The mystery of its function was first revealed by Sperry and colleagues in the 1950s by cutting the corpus callosum and directing perceptual material to one hemisphere or the other. They discovered that the two halves of the brain when completely surgically separated can handle different types of cognitive material, and function quite separately. A skill taught to one hemisphere was completely unknown to the other (Sperry, 1964). No doubt it has been a casual acquaintance with this research that has led to the popular misconception among some educators that the two hemispheres operate uniquely and separately. Since the chances of ever teaching a commissurotomized child are not great, the special educator might reasonably question the educational value of this type of research. It has been extremely valuable in providing knowledge about the asymmetrical functions of the two hemispheres when they cannot communicate (e.g., the left hemisphere understands oral language and can speak, while the right hemisphere usually can understand in a limited way, but cannot speak). It seems certain, however, that each hemisphere does not function this way when normally interconnected, because the energy system is radically changed. Nevertheless, the knowledge of the elemental functions of the separated hemispheres has provided researchers in this area with better grounds for hypothesizing normal brain function. For example, if each hemisphere processes its sensory information in distinctly different ways, as described, then "in the normal intact brain the right and left contributions in any given perceptual experience become fused, making it difficult or impossible to determine which hemisphere is doing what" (Sperry, 1972, p. 131). However, during the 1970s a great interest in research to examine simultaneous stimulation of the two hemispheres in the intact brain occurred, and many of these investigations were inspired by the split brain studies of Sperry and many others.

ELECTROENCEPHALOGRAPHIC EVIDENCE

Attempts to relate patterns of electrical activity in the brain to specific cognitive behaviors have not been decisive. Not only are particular learning strategies believed to draw on all or most parts of the brain, but the various cerebral loci of increased electrical activity appear to change in specific emphasis from moment to moment. In addition to this complex pattern of variability, the EEG picks up electrical changes in a field that may represent not only the focal area of the cortical activity, but background noise from contiguous areas that are electrically induced as well. Put another way, many medical techniques (e.g., surgical and lesion studies) have indicated specific cortical areas that are essential to particular cognitive functions (left hemisphere and language), and while it is believed that most of the bioelectrical activity arises in the cerebral cortices, accurate knowledge is still lacking about the histological structures involved (Hess, 1966). Also, the reliability of inter-rater scores among electroencephalographers is not high because of the subjective aspects of interpreting EEG records.

Because of these confounding contributing variables, much of the early research in this area was confusing, and many educators dismissed the EEG as a useless technique for investigating learning. Nevertheless, there are some indicative findings which have emerged since 1970 and which have shown significant hemispheric differences for different cognitive tasks. In some studies, verbal and spatial skills have been found to correlate with greater electrical activity in the left and right hemispheres, respectively (Galin & Ornstein, 1972). Verbal and nonverbal tasks have shown asymmetrical hemispheric patterns of evoked potential wave forms, and the two patterns have shown greater differences from the left-hemisphere lead (Buchsbaum & Fedio, 1969). Conners (1970) found a flattening of the visual evoked response in the left parietal areas of the six members of a family of dyslexics, although Weber and Omenn (1977) were unable to replicate this with a sample of dyslexic children from 18 other families. The latter researchers account for their failure to match Conners' findings with the possibility that Conners' sample family represented a subgroup of dyslexics not included in their larger sample, or because they used a mastoid reference for the recordings rather than the vertex of the head as Connors had done. These two reference points have been shown to provide differences in recordings (Kooi, 1972). Hemispheric differences have also been found for linguistic tasks of varying difficulty, for the recognition of music (McKee, Humphrey, & McAdam, 1973), and for EEG patterns of subjects classified as field-independent and field-dependent (Oltman, Semple, & Goldstein, 1979). A complete review of this vast literature will not be attempted, but these few examples should provide a reminder of the EEG evidence of hemispheric asymmetry.

CEREBRAL BLOOD FLOW STUDIES

During the 1950s and early 1960s, Ingvar and Risberg and their colleagues in Sweden were developing a fascinating series of studies to investigate the moment-to-moment changes in blood flow at the cortical and subcortical levels during periods of rest and mental activity (Ingvar & Risberg, 1967). These studies have provided normative information regarding total brain, intrahemispheric, and interhemispheric patterns of cerebral blood flow (Gur & Reivich, 1980; Maximilian, Prohovnik, Risberg, & Hakansson, 1978; Risberg, 1980), but in the present discussion we are primarily interested in evidence supporting hemispheric functional asymmetry. "Small but very consistent and statistically significant hemispheric asymmetries were demonstrated for the first time" (Risberg, Halsey, Wills, & Wilson, 1975, p. 523). These investigators found that a verbal analogy test gave increased blood flow in the left hemisphere, while a nonverbal perceptual test gave a right-hemisphere superiority, especially in frontal and parietal regions. Gur and Reivich (1980) also found evidence of small hemispheric blood flow increases for verbal and spatial tasks, although the spatial tasks, while showing a slight increase in right-hemisphere blood volume, did not produce a significant increase in the right relative to the left laterality measure. Risberg (1980) was unable to replicate the findings from his 1975 report, but he accounted for this lack of agreement in terms of the simpler verbal task in the second investigation and its small demand of effort.

This investigative technique has had significant value for neurology, neurosurgery, psychiatry, and neuropsychology, and it offers promise of increasing our understanding of brain function in classroom learning. Already, cerebral blood flow changes have been recorded in conditions of rest, talking, and reading (Ingvar & Schwartz, 1974).

PERCEPTUAL ASYMMETRIES

There is enormous research literature available on this topic, and only a brief reference can be made to the evidence. Visual-perceptual asymmetries in the normal brain can be examined in hemifield tachistoscopic studies, in which a subject is seated before a screen with a fixation point marking its center. While fixating on the central point, the subject reports the nature of visual stimuli flashed to the right or left visual field for periods usually less than 200 msec. It was discovered in the 1950s that verbal material was usually reported more accurately from the right visual field (Heron, 1957). This was thought to result from visual scanning habits acquired through learning to read. However, Kimura (1961b), a neuropsychologist, first proposed that this phenomenon was probably related to the better verbal processing of the left hemisphere in most people, and this hypothesis has led to an immense research literature during the 1960s and 1970s. In subsequent studies, she showed a superiority of recognition of spatial dot designs in the left visual field (right hemisphere) for men under all conditions, and for women under some conditions (Kimura, 1969). The majority of early research studies of hemifield perceptual effects tended to support the right-hemifield superiority for verbal stimuli and the left-hemifield superiority for pictorial and nonverbal stimuli, but occasionally there were ambiguous findings (Bryden & Rainey, 1963; Wyke & Ettlinger, 1961) regarding the perception of nonverbal stimuli. This led investigators in the 1970s to search for other variables in the causal pattern. It is now known that the two hemispheres process both verbal and nonverbal stimuli in varying degrees depending on the familiarity and ease of recognition or complexity of interpretation (Hatta, 1978), and whether the stimuli lend themselves to sequential or holistic analysis. Sex differences also show themselves as early as 5 years of age (Buffery, 1976), and warm-up effects may have an influence on changing performance (Costa, 1980). The perception of verbal stimuli is now believed to involve both hemispheres in terms of their perceived linguistic and spatial- or visual-form recognition qualities. Other variables include ease or difficulty of letter or word recognition (Miller & Butler, 1980), subset size, ease or difficulty of verbalization (Buffery, 1976), and the symbolic, analytic, and phonological associations of the presented words (Segalowitz, Bebout, & Lederman, 1979). It is now believed that the two hemispheres are probably differentially involved in processing visual stimuli in terms of innate facility for particular stimuli (verbal or nonverbal), the experiential background of the subject, and his or her acquired learning strategies.

Kimura's studies of visual perception (1961a) also led her to examine the auditory sense mode. She had already discovered that subjects with left temporal lobectomy, or with lesions in that area, were more impaired in repeating digits than those with right temporal damage. She interpreted this to mean "that the left temporal lobe played a more important part than the right in the perception of spoken material" (Kimura, 1961a, p. 166). This led her to investigate hemispheric processing of auditory stimuli in the normal brain with the dichotic listening technique. Using the Wada Amytal Test to establish the side of language dominance, she found that auditory verbal stimuli were more efficiently processed by the ear contralateral to the language-dominant hemisphere. The effect was independent of handedness and of epileptogenic foci when epileptic subjects were examined. When nonverbal auditory stimuli (hummed melodies, human nonspeech sounds such as laughing, etc.) were presented dichotically, she found a significant left-ear superiority in adults (King & Kimura, 1972) and in children aged 5-8, although boys in this age range tended to identify more nonverbal sounds than girls (Knox & Kimura, 1970).

During the 1970s, research turned to an analysis of task requirements which may have exaggerated or highlighted hemispheric asymmetries. Recent findings suggest that memory functions are more lateralized than perceptual functions (Goodglass & Peck, 1972; Oscar-Berman, Goodglass, & Donnenfeld, 1974) and that by varying the stimulus parameters in dichotic presentations the ear dominance may be varied (Divenyi & Efron, 1979; Efron & Yund, 1974, 1975). For example, not all speech sounds produce a right ear advantage (REA) although most do. Steady state vowel sounds and isolated fricatives show no reliabilility, though voiced consonant vowel syllables (like ba, pa) have been found to produce a reliable REA in boys and girls in kindergarten and grades 2, 4, and 6 (Hynd & Obrzut, 1977). Speech sounds with a temporal structure show a strong tendency to produce a REA in most subjects. Recent research findings have shown that hemispheric asymmetrical function is complex and variable and not dualistically simple as was thought until about 1970.

Hemispheric asymmetries have also been observed in tactile perception. In finger localization tests, children are better at reporting their fingers on their right hands when a verbal report is used, and on their left hands when a nonverbal or spatial type of report is used (Bakker, 1972, p. 83). Tactile nonsense forms are better recognized with the left hand, but recognition of tactile letters is not significantly different between hands (Witelson, 1974), probably because the letters have to be explored spatially during perception prior to being translated into a verbal code. When different forms (letters, digits, lines) are drawn with a stylus simultaneously on both of a subject's up-turned palms (i.e., dichhaptic stimulation) letters show a right hand superiority and lines a left hand advantage. Digits may show no clear hand preferences (Oscar-Berman, Rehbein, Porfert, & Goodglass, 1978).

The Integrative Functions of the Central Nervous System

The neurophysiologists of the nineteenth century first wrote at length about the importance of the integrating functions of the central nervous system. In 1890, William James, who trained first as a physiologist and then as a psychologist, wrote, "The function of the nervous system is to bring each part into harmonious co-operation with every other" (James, 1890, p. 8), and as a psychologist he related man's mental structure to the function of the nervous system. Soon after, Sherrington in England produced his classic book, *The Integrative Action of the Nervous System* (1906), in which, in spite of the current popularity of Pavlov's reflexology, he wrote that a simple reflex "is a convenient, if not a probable, fiction" since "all parts of the nervous system are connected together." By 1944, Herrick reminded us that "integration of bodily activities is a primordial essential; without it no living body can survive."

Following Pavlov's lead, American psychology was dominated until about 1930 by the mechanistic behaviorism of J. B. Watson (1924, 1925) and the connectionism of E. L. Thorndike (1931). These two writers did propose an integration of psychological and physiological processes, but the theoretical neurological base was more segmental and less holistic than the physiologists had proposed before them, or than is currently emerging from neurological and neuropsychological research. However, during this period, there were two holistically oriented psychologists in Europe, Maria Montessori, originally trained in medicine, and Jean Piaget, originally trained in zoology, who proposed psychological theories of behavior with a strong biological base and a broad sociogenic balance. Montessori, at the turn of the twentieth century, pioneered new and successful treatment methods for so-called mentally retarded children, using her knowledge of brain function and sensorimotor development. She stressed early motor activity as an essential precursor to healthy intellectual and personality development (Montessori, 1912). Piaget (1952) since 1920 developed a remarkable model of psychological development in which he proposed that cognitive growth, from early simplicity to mature complexity, parallels brain growth, from elementary synaptic connections to prodigious dendritic intertwining at maturity. He believes all human growth begins in an early stage of sensorimotor activity and awareness, and out of this develops cognitive recognition of concrete perceptual relationships, and finally, in adolescence, the understanding of abstract, conceptual associations is developed. This pattern of ontogeny is a product of the adaptive interaction between the neural functions of the child and the opportunities for expression and the forces of inhibition offered by the immediate environment. Both of these theories described a development of cognition that grew out of the biological and harmonious action of the child's nervous system.

In special education, many practitioners have used this basic type of theoretical orientation to promote a multisensorimotor approach to remediation (e.g., Fernald, 1943; Kephart, 1971). In occupational therapy and psychology, Ayres (1972) has proposed a comprehensive and practical model of diagnosis and treatment of learning-disabled children that stresses improvement of sensorimotor integration as an antecedent condition to competent academic learning.

Luria, the Soviet Union's eminent neuropsychologist, has posited "three principal functional units of the brain" (1973): the brainstem that alerts the cortex to incoming signals, thus providing a necessary mental set; the post-Rolandic cortex that receives, analyzes, and stores information; and the frontal lobes, or pre-Rolandic cortex, that mediates temporal-sequential processes and enables a person to initiate and make plans for the future. Neural and psychological harmonious integration are essential to successful functioning of these three units. Deficit functioning in specific parts of this energy system, as demonstrated by the lesion studies, can result in impaired intellectual functioning of a selective type.

The primary cortical areas are the primary visual cortex (area 17 in the occipital lobes), the primary acoustic cortex (in the Sylvian areas of the temporal lobes), and the somesthetic strips (in the immediate post-Rolandic parts of the parietal lobes). The cortical surfaces contiguous to these highly specialized zones are believed, in the classical model, to be the secondary association areas that contribute meaning to the sensory input. This is believed to result from a cortical integration of thousands of incoming neural impulses that form the neural engram (Lashley, 1950) or cell assembly (Hebb, 1949). This integration is processed by the cortical tissue located on the boundaries of the various association areas. This tissue provides, in a healthy brain, an integration of "visual, auditory, vestibular, cutaneous, and proprioceptive" sensations (Luria, 1973), and forms the neurophysiological substrate of thinking, listening, speaking, reading, and writing. The angular gyrus, in the left parietal lobe in most people, is believed to be such a functional integrating center for the development of language (Geschwind, 1965; Luria, 1966, 1970, 1973).

Due to space limitations, only a brief reference to these important neurological and psychological functions of integration can be made. In the past, integration has not been given enough attention in some teacher training programs. The school psychologist will benefit from a knowledge of experimentally produced conditions of neural dysfunction in which the normal condition of sensorimotor integration is gradually interrupted. An obvious example is delayed auditory feedback, where a bright person becomes unable to speak or read normally because of a deliberate interruption in his or her usual sensorimotor pattern. Delayed visual feedback (Van Bergeijk & David, 1959) can be equally disturbing. Many years ago, Pavlov demonstrated "experimental neurosis" in dogs by conditioning them to respond reliably to an approach and an avoidance stimulation. Once this pattern of expectation was thoroughly established in the dog's nervous system, Pavlov presented an ambiguous stimulus that included both approach and avoidance components. This produced a motivational conflict for the dog because of the psychological condition of disintegration. Similar experiments with monkeys have produced peptic ulcers which were tangible evidence of the neural conflict (Sawrey & Wiesz, 1956).

An obvious behavioral manifestation of neural dysynchrony, or the temporary absence of sensorimotor and neural integration, is epilepsy. The school psychologist not only needs to understand this condition and recommend modes of treatment, but he or she can learn a good deal about cerebral dominance, handedness, and hemispheric asymmetry from epileptic children. Disruptive hyperactivity also may be understood as a condition of sensorimotor disintegration whether its causes are organic or environmental.

In brief summary, sensorimotor integration is essential to normal behavior and learning, and its importance is supported by neurological and neuropsychological studies. This pattern of integration is hierarchical in design—all small units, such as cells, require harmonious intraorganic functioning, and regional groups of cells, such as cortical lobes, require internal consonance free of all conflicts. Because all behavior is mediated by the central nervous system, normal learning implies the system's complete and integrative function, both physically and psychologically.

Sequencing

The neuropsychological processes involved in serial order behavior were not seriously studied until Lashley (1951) drew attention to their importance and complexity. The presence of serial order in all types of behavior is obvious (e.g., walking, talking, reading, writing, thinking). Special educators have frequently included hopping, skipping, trampoline exercises, and clapping rhythmic patterns in their remedial programs, but the educational literature has been almost devoid of research reports to support the validity of including serial order activities. Following Lashley's classic paper, "The Problem of Serial Order in Behavior" (1951), many neuropsychologists began to research this elusive phenomenon, and by the early 1960s many research reports began to appear. Although Lashley believed there must be some type of neural scanning mechanism somewhere in the brain that controlled temporal behavior systematically, he admitted to ignorance about its nature or location. By 1963, Kimble and Pribram concluded that the left hemisphere in monkeys was dominant for the control of sequential behavior, and Efron (1963) concluded the same about right-handed humans and most left-handers. In our laboratory we have found left-hemisphere lesion cases inferior to right-hemisphere lesion cases, and frontal lesion cases worse than posterior lesion cases, in perceiving and remembering serial patterns of single lights on a screen (Gaddes & Tymchuk, 1967). From this evidence, we thought the left frontal part of the human brain was the probable locus of Lashley's scanning mechanism or "ordering system" (Bryden, 1967). Most researchers during the 1960s concluded that the left hemisphere was dominant for sequencing although there were exceptions (Milner, 1962).

One of the first large-scale studies of temporal order perception in school-age children was that of Bakker (1972) in the Netherlands. He investigated visual, auditory, and haptic serial order perception of normal and learning-disabled children in the 7-11-year age range. He concluded that verbal sequential tests discriminate between good and poor readers, and that nonverbal sequential tests do not. Because Bakker's tests were paper and pencil tests with tapping patterns produced at a slow speed, I decided to examine his conclusions by presenting the light patterns (nonverbal) and single letters (verbal) tachistoscopically at very fast speeds (light or letter exposure, 100 msec; interstimulus interval (ISI), 100 msec, Gaddes, 1981), and as a result found that the nonverbal test did discriminate the two groups. Dyslexics, both adult and children, were relatively poorer than normal readers in perceiving sequences of lights at this fast speed. Normal and good readers could report them accurately at both the fast and a slow speed (light exposure, 400 msec and ISI, 1 second); the difference in sequential tempo made no difference to them.

The results of my studies and those of many other researchers have led to the following conclusions: (1) Localized traumatic brain damage usually impairs serial order behaviors more when the damage is in the left hemisphere than in the right. Congenital brain damage anywhere in the brain may affect sequencing behaviors; (2) Sequential perception and sequential memory are discrete abilities. A child may perceive a number of tachistoscopically exposed letters and report them accurately, but in the wrong order (Gaddes, 1978a; Senf, 1969); (3) The speed of cerebral processing and the degree of sequential perceptual accuracy are positively correlated; and (4) The cerebral locus of sequential processing varies with the nature of the immediate task, depending on whether it is verbal or nonverbal, its level of difficulty, the sense mode of the task, and the perceptual strategies of the perceiver. For many tasks, however, the left hemisphere tends to be more involved.

Because of the essential involvement of sequential processing in all academic learning, it is important that more applied research be carried out by educators to examine its value in remediation. The neuropsychological findings are important, but most of them are segmental and only indirectly related to classroom learning.

Cerebral Dominance and Handedness

How the particular parts of the brain tissue control particular parts of the body (e.g., the left motor strip and the right hand) or specific kinds of cognitive material (e.g., left hemisphere and language) is not understood. Because the structural and physiological substrates of cerebral dominance are not understood, it cannot be defined exactly. However, the functional relationships among cortical activities and speech and handedness can be described: (1) cerebral dominance for speech is central, spontaneous, and beyond the conscious control of the subject; (2) lateral preferences (e.g., handedness and footedness) are peripheral, the subject is aware of them and can control or change their sidedness at will; (3) most right-handers and more than half of left-handers are left-hemisphere dominant for language; (4) certain structural asymmetries favoring the left hemisphere suggest a genetic predisposition for language processing (Benson & Geschwind, 1969; Geschwind, 1979; Geschwind & Levitsky, 1968; Wada, Clarke, & Hamm, 1975); and (5) left-handers, although a minority, are more likely to be subject to brain damage or dysfunction (Satz, 1972) and are more variable in their lateral preferences (Zangwill, 1960).

Neuropsychological studies of handedness have uncovered knowledge that can be useful for the school psychologist in classifying children. There is considerable evidence to suggest the following classifications:

Pure right-handers. These children are left-hemisphere dominant for language and strongly right-sided in all their lateral preferences. If free of all neurological dysfunctions and environmental handicaps, these children are normal or superior learners.

Pathological right-handers (Satz, 1972). These children were genetically programmed to be right-hemisphere dominant for language and left-handed, but because of early right-hemisphere brain damage, their left hand is awkward. They have learned to prefer their right hand although they may still be right-hemisphere dominant for language. These children are rare, and likely to be missed as neurologically deviant since they are born into a right-handed world. Their deviance can be detected with careful neurological and neuropsychological analysis.

Mixed right-handers. These children write right-handed, are usually left-hemisphere dominant for language, and show a mixed pattern of eyedness, footedness, and handedness for nonwriting skills. They suffer brain damage or dysfunction in various parts of the cerebral cortex, usually of minimal intensity, and they make up a large number of the learning-disabled population.

Pure left-handers. These children are right-hemisphere dominant for language and consistently left-sided in their lateral preferences. If free of neurological dysfunctions and environmental frustrations, they are normal or superior learners.

Pathological left-handers. These children, for the most part, were intended to be right-handed, but because of spotty bilateral brain lesions, they are left-handed and mixed in their lateral preferences. More than half of them are left-hemisphere dominant for language, some are bilateral, and very few are right-hemisphere dominant. This group, like the group of mixed right-handers, contains many learning-disabled children.

The school psychologist may identify the qualitative nature of a child's cerebral dominance and handedness with careful neuropsychological assessment (Bryden, 1970). Usually this information is basic to understanding the child's learning strategies and for developing a successful remedial prescription.

Reading and Brain Function

Reading problems have been described as the most important learning disorder (Benton, 1975) and in this brief discussion we will look at the four cases, other than primary mental retardation, in which defective brain dysfunction is clearly, or is highly likely to be, the essential etiology. The secondary causes are principally environmental, such as family background and emotional climate, aptitude for and level of language development, personality stability, personal aspirations, and the quality of educational instruction.

The obvious case of organically based reading retardation is traumatic dyslexia, in which the person has suffered measurable reading impairment following traumatic brain injury. The second type, developmental dyslexia, has no clearly established neurological base, but there are strong indications of a genetic deficit in some cases, and/or a number of behavioral correlates, described as soft neurological signs, in many others.

TRAUMATIC DYSLEXIA IN ADULTS

In most of these cases, the brain-injured adult has already demonstrated ability to read pretraumatically and has suffered a sudden reading disability or reduction in reading competence immediately following brain damage.

Large numbers of these cases have been reported because of war injuries (Russell & Espir, 1961), traffic and industrial accidents, strokes (Luria, 1970), and cerebral infections. The causal relationship between sudden left-hemisphere pathology and accompanying dyslexia has been well established, and these cases appear to fall into the following four subgroups (Benson & Geschwind, 1969): (1) Hemialexia manifests itself in an inability to read print or writing in the left visual field with normal reading ability present for verbal stimuli in the right visual field. Vision is normal for nonverbal figures in both full visual fields. This selective reading disability is caused by the cutting of or sudden pathology in the splenium, the posterior part of the corpus callosum, which isolates all verbal input to the right occipital lobe and prevents it from reaching the language analyzer in the left temporal lobe; (2) Alexia without agraphia is frequently referred to as Déjerine's syndrome (Geschwind, 1962), and shows itself in a complete inability to read while still being able to write successfully to dictation and copy. It is caused by a lesion in the splenium and left occipital lobe, damage normally caused by a hemorrhage of the left posterior cerebral artery; (3) In alexia with agraphia the subject suddenly loses the ability to read and write. Widespread damage to the medial parts of the left hemisphere, such as results from hemorrhaging of the left middle cerebral artery, can produce this; and (4) Damage to the left temporal lobe can cause receptive aphasia or an impairment in understanding oral speech. The same aphasic deficit in verbal conceptualizing will impede the understanding of written material.

DEVELOPMENTAL DYSLEXIA IN ADULTS

A developmentally dyslexic adult may appear to be normal in every respect except that he or she has never learned to read, or to read normally. This person may be superior in many other respects. The constitutional cause may be genetic or presumably neurological. Although no neurological deficits are conclusively evident in most of these cases, neuropsychological testing may turn up many soft neurological or mildly deviant behavioral signs. Benton (1975) has discussed these at some length, and has included visuoperceptive deficits, generalized language retardation, poor sequential perception, disturbances in finger recognition, mixed cerebral dominance and handedness, and the presence of abnormal EEG patterns. These subjects usually produce a normal neurological examination, so that, in the past, before the development of comprehensive neuropsychological test batteries, the cause or causes of developmental dyslexia were in most cases totally unknown. With the advent of new neurological test techniques such as the CT scan and the introduction of detailed neuropsychological tests, evidence is increasing to suggest a neurological etiological base.

TRAUMATIC DYSLEXIA IN CHILDREN

A child suffering left-hemisphere brain injury during the preschool period will likely show an impaired ability in learning to read that appears somewhat similar to developmental dyslexia. However, the nature and intensity will depend on the degree of localization, the extent and the locus of lesion, and the age of the child at the time of injury. I have discussed in clinical detail a number of these children elsewhere (Gaddes, 1980, Chapter 8).

DEVELOPMENTAL DYSLEXIA IN CHILDREN

A developmentally dyslexic child usually is one with normal oral language and no obvious physical deficits who has great difficulty in learning to read. His or her neurological examination is typically negative, but on a comprehensive neuropsychological battery of tests the child usually shows a number of neurological soft signs that give the diagnostician useful insight into perceptual, cognitive, and motor strengths and weaknesses. In my experience, I have found such testing invaluable in understanding and treating these children; more abbreviated testing may turn up nothing and hence is a waste of time. Because the prevalence of developmental dyslexia may be only about 3 percent for boys and .5 percent for girls (Benton, 1975), the school psychologist can afford to take 5 or 6 testing hours for diagnostic assessment with these children. Anything less, at this stage of our knowledge, will likely be counterproductive.

More knowledge about subtypes of dyslexics is needed for better definition and diagnostic understanding. Some useful studies have been carried out by neuropsychologists (Doehring, 1968, 1976) using the Q technique of factor analysis (Doehring, Hoshko, & Bryans, 1979) and differential patterns of performance on a comprehensive battery of neuropsychological tests (Mattis, French, & Rapin, 1975; Petrauskas & Rourke, 1979). The increased knowledge of dyslexia gained from these types of studies points up the value and advantages of such assessment procedures for the school psychologist or educational diagnostician. For a fuller discussion, the reader is referred to the excellent book on dyslexia by Benton and Pearl (1978).

DISCUSSION

Because all behavior is motivated both by organically mediating forces and psychological forces, it is necessary that both etiological areas be included in the diagnostic understanding of a child with a neurological dys-

function. A purely behavioral approach to learning disorders is appropriate
only for the child who is free of neurological deficits and whose primary
problem is motivational. While increasing numbers of educators and school
psychologists are accepting the rationale of using neuropsychological knowledge in their problems of diagnosis and remedial prescriptions, it is important that graduate schools give them superior opportunities for sound training
in this discipline. At present many schools are not yet attempting to provide
this type of training except minimally. Unless training programs are strength-
ened, educational assessments and remedial prescriptions relating to neuropsychological problems of learning are likely to be shallow, unknowing, and,
in some cases, inaccurate because of a superficial knowledge of neurological
function and its correlative behavior. No one discipline is adequate to understand and to provide competent treatment for the neurologically impaired
learning-disabled child. Because there are still many gaps in our knowledge,
it is imperative that medicine, psychology, and education collaborate and
pool their knowledge if these children are to have the best chance in the
future.

REFERENCES

Adams, R. N. Cultural aspects of infant malnutrition and mental develop-
ment. In N. S. Scrimshaw & J. E. Gordon (Eds.), *Malnutrition, learning
and behavior.* Cambridge: M.I.T. Press, 1968.
Ayers, A. J. *Sensory integration and learning disorders.* Los Angeles: Western
Psychological Services, 1972.
Bakker, D. J. *Temporal order in disturbed reading.* Rotterdam: Rotterdam
University Press, 1972.
Benson, D. F., & Geschwind, N. Cerebral dominance and its disturbances.
Pediatric Clinics of North America, 1968, 15, 759–769.
Benson, D. F., & Geschwind N. The alexias. In P. J. Vinken & B. W. Bruyn
(Eds.), *Handbook of clinical neurology* (Vol. 4). Amsterdam: North
Holland Publishing, 1969.
Benton, A. L. *Right–left discrimination and finger localization.* New York:
Hoeber-Harper, 1959.
Benton, A. L. The visual retention test as a constructional praxis task. *Con-
finia Neurologica, 1962, 22,* 141–155.(a)
Benton, A. L. Behavioral indices of brain injury in school children. *Child
Development, 1962, 33,* 199–208.(b)
Benton, A. L. Developmental aphasia and brain damage. In S. A. Kirk & W.
Becker (Eds.), *Conference on children with minimal brain impairment.*
Urbana: University of Illinois, 1963.(a)

Benton, A. L. *The revised visual retention test,* (3rd ed.). New York: The Psychological Corporation, 1963. (b)

Benton, A. L. The problem of cerebral dominance. *The Canadian Psychologist,* 1965, *6a,* 332–346.

Benton, A. L. Problems of test construction in the field of aphasia. *Cortex,* 1967, *3,* 42–46.

Benton, A. L. Disorders of spatial orientation. In P. J. Vinken & G. W. Bruyn (Eds.), *Handbook of clinical neurology* (Vol. 3). Amsterdam: North Holland Publishing, 1969.(a)

Benton, A. L. *The three-dimensional praxis test: Manual of instructions.* Victoria, B. C.: Neuropsychology Laboratory, University of Victoria, 1969.(b)

Benton, A. L. *Stereognosis test.* Victoria, B. C.: Department of Psychology, University of Victoria, 1969.(c)

Benton, A. L. Developmental dyslexia: Neurological aspects. In W. J. Friedlander (Ed.), *Advances in neurology.* New York: Raven Press, 1975.

Benton, A. L., & Pearl, D. *Dyslexia: An appraisal of current knowledge.* New York: Oxford University Press, 1978.

Bryden, M. P. A model for the sequential organization of behavior. *Canadian Journal of Psychology,* 1967, *21,* 37–56.

Bryden, M. P. Laterality effects in dichotic listening: Relations with handedness and reading ability in children. *Neuropsychologia,* 1970, *8,* 443–450.

Bryden, M. P., & Rainey, C. A. Left-right differences in tachistoscopic recognition. *Journal of Experimental Psychology,* 1963, *66,* 568–571.

Buchsbaum, M., & Fedio, P. Visual information and evoked responses from the left and right hemispheres. *Electroencephalography and Clinical Neurophysiology,* 1969, *26,* 266–272.

Buffery, A. W. H. Sex differences in the neuropsychological development of verbal and spatial skills. In R. M. Knights & D. J. Bakker (Eds.), *The neuropsychology of learning disorders: Theoretical approaches.* Baltimore: University Park Press, 1976.

Coles, G. S. The learning-disabilities test battery: Empirical and social issues. *Harvard Educational Review,* 1978, *48,* 313–340.

Conners, C. K. Cortical visual evoked responses in children with learning disorders. *Psychophysiology,* 1970, *7,* 418–428.

Costa, L. D. Personal communication, 1980.

de Hirsch, K., Jansky, J. J., & Langford, W. S. *Predicting reading failure.* New York: Harper & Row, 1966.

Divenyi, P. L., & Efron, R. Spectral versus temporal features in dichotic listening. *Brain and Language,* 1979, *7,* 375–386.

Doehring, D. G. *Patterns of impairment in specific reading disability.* Bloomington: Indiana University Press, 1968.

Doehring, D. G. Evaluation of two models of reading disability. In R. M. Knights & D. J. Bakker (Eds.), *The neuropsychology of learning disorders.* Baltimore: University Park Press, 1976.

Doehring, D. G., Hoshko, J. M., & Bryans, B. N. Statistical classification of children with reading problems. *Journal of Clinical Neuropsychology,* *1979,* 1, 5–16.

Douglas, V. I. Perceptual and cognitive factors as determinants of learning disabilities: A review chapter with special emphasis on attentional factors. In R. M. Knights & D. J. Bakker (Eds.), *The neuropsychology of learning disorders.* Baltimore: University Park Press, 1976.

Drake, W. E. Clinical and pathological findings in a child with a developmental learning disability. *Journal of Learning Disabilities,* 1968, 1, 486–502.

Dunn, L. M. *Expanded manual for the Peabody Picture Vocabulary Test.* Circle Pines, Minn.: American Guidance Service, 1965.

Eccles, J. C. *The understanding of the brain.* New York: McGraw-Hill, 1973.

Efron, R. Temporal perception aphasia and déjà vu. *Brain,* 1963, *86,* 403–424.

Efron, R., & Yund, E. W. Dichotic competition of simultaneous tone bursts of different frequency: Dissociation of pitch from lateralization and loudness. *Neuropsychologia,* 1974, *12,* 249–256.

Efron, R., & Yund, E. W. Dichotic competition of simultaneous tone bursts of different frequency: III. The effect of stimulus parameters on suppression and ear dominance functions. *Neuropsychologia,* 1975, *13,* 151–161.

Fernald, G. M. *Remedial techniques in basic school subjects.* New York: McGraw-Hill, 1943.

Gaddes, W. H. The needs of teachers for specialized information on handedness, finger localization and cerebral dominance. In W. M. Cruickshank (Ed.), *The teacher of brain-injured children.* Syracuse, N.Y.: Syracuse University Press, 1966.

Gaddes, W. H. Neuropsychological approach to learning disorders. *Journal of Learning Disabilities,* 1968, 1, 523–534.

Gaddes, W. H. Can educational psychology be neurologized? *Canadian Journal of Behavioral Science,* 1969, 1, 38–49.

Gaddes, W. H. Neurological implications for learning. In W. M. Cruickshank & D. P. Hallahan (Eds.), *Perceptual and learning disabilities in children,* (Vol. 1). Syracuse, N.Y.: Syracuse University Press, 1975.

Gaddes, W. H. Prevalence estimates and the need for definition of learning disabilities. In R. M. Knights & D. J. Bakker (Eds.), *The neuropsychology of learning disorders.* Baltimore: University Park Press, 1976.

Gaddes, W. H. Learning disabilities: The search for causes. In *Bell Canada monograph on learning disabilities.* Montreal: Canadian Association for Children with Learning Disabilities, 1978.

Gaddes, W. H. *Learning disabilities and brain function: A neuropsychological approach.* New York: Springer-Verlag, 1980.

Gaddes, W. H. A review of some research in the area of serial order behavior. In Cruickshank, W. M. & Lerner, J. (Eds.), *The best of ACLD 1981, Vol. 3.* Syracuse, N.Y.: Syracuse University Press, 1981.

Gaddes, W. H., & Crockett, D. J. The Spreen-Benton Aphasia Tests, normative data as a measure of normal language development. *Brain and Language,* 1975, *2,* 257–280.

Gaddes, W. H., & Tymchuk, A. J. *A validation study of the dynamic visual retention test in functional localization of cerebral damage and dysfunction.* Research Monograph No. 38. Victoria, B. C.: University of Victoria, 1967.

Galaburda, A. M., & Kemper, T. L. Cytoarchitectonic abnormalities in developmental dyslexia: A case study. *Annals of Neurology,* 1979, *6,* 94–100.

Galin, D., & Ornstein, R. Lateral specialization of cognitive mode: An EEG study. *Psychophysiology,* 1972, *9,* 412–418.

Geschwind, N. The anatomy of acquired disorders of reading. In J. Money (Ed.), *Reading disability.* Baltimore: Johns Hopkins Press, 1962.

Geschwind, N. Disconnexion syndromes in animals and man. *Brain,* 1965, *88,* 237–294, 585–644.

Geschwind, N. Asymmetries of the brain – New developments. *Bulletin of the Orton Society,* 1979, *29,* 67–73.

Geschwind, N., & Levitsky, W. Human brain: Left–right asymmetries in temporal speech region. *Science,* 1968, *161,* 186–187.

Glueck, S., & Glueck, E. *Unraveling juvenile delinquency.* Cambridge: Harvard, 1950.

Goodglass, H. & Kaplan, E. *The assessment of aphasia and related disorders.* Philadelphia: Lea & Febiger, 1972.

Goodglass, H., & Peck, E. A. Dichotic ear-effects in Korsakoff and normal subjects. *Neuropsychologia,* 1972, *10,* 211–217.

Gur, R. C., & Reivich, M. Cognitive task effects on hemispheric blood flow in humans: Evidence for individual differences in hemispheric activation. *Brain and Language,* 1980, *9,* 78–92.

Hallahan, D. P., & Cruickshank, W. M. *Psychoeducational foundations of learning disabilities.* Englewood Cliffs, N. J.: Prentice-Hall, 1973.

Hallgren, B. Specific dyslexia: A clinical and genetic study. *Acta Psychiatrica et Neurologica,* 1950, *65,* (Suppl.), 1.

Halstead, W. C. *Brain and intelligence.* Chicago: University of Chicago Press, 1947.

Hardyck, C., & Haapanen, R. Educating both halves of the brain: Educational breakthrough or neuromythology? *Journal of School Psychology,* 1979, *17,* 219–230.

Hartlage, L. C., & Hartlage, P. L. Application of neuropsychological principles in the diagnosis of learning disabilities. In L. Tarnopol & M. Tarnopol (Eds.), *Brain function and reading disabilities.* Baltimore: University Park Press, 1977.

Hatta, T. Visual field differences in a mental transformation task. *Neuropsychologia,* 1978, *16,* 637–641.

Hebb, D. O. *Organization of behavior.* New York: Wiley, 1949.

Heron, W. Perception as a function of retinal locus and attention. *American Journal of Psychology,* 1957, *70,* 38–48.

Herrick, C. J. Apparatus of optic and visceral correlation in the brain of amblystoma. *The Journal of Comparative Psychology,* 1944, *37,* 97–105.

Hess, R. *EEG handbook*. Zurich: Sandoz, Sandoz Monographs, 1966.

Hynd, G., & Obrzut, J. E. Effects of grade level and sex on the magnitude of the dichotic ear advantage. *Neuropsychologia*, 1977, *15*, 689–692.

Hynd, G. W., Quackenbush, R., & Obrzut, J. E. *Training school psychologists in neuropsychological assessment: Current practices and trends*. Paper presented at the annual convention of the National Association of School Psychologists, San Diego, California, March, 1979.

Ingvar, D. H., & Risberg, J. Increase of regional cerebral blood flow during mental effort in normals and in patients with focal brain disorders. *Experimental Brain Research*, 1967, *3*, 195–211.

Ingvar, D. H., & Schwartz, M. S. Blood flow patterns induced in the dominant hemisphere by speech and reading. *Brain*, 1974, *97*, 273–288.

Jackson, J. H. *Selected writings of John Hughlings Jackson, Volume II*. London: Staples Press, 1958.

James, W. *The principles of psychology*. New York: Henry Holt & Co., 1890.

Jansky, J., & de Hirsch, K. *Preventing reading failure*. New York: Harper & Row, 1972.

Johnson, W. Protein and poverty, or school lunches are too late. *Child Welfare*, June, 1967.

Kephart, N. C. *The slow learner in the classroom*. Columbus, Oh.: Merrill, 1960 & 1971.

Kimble, D. P., & Pribram, K. H. Hippocampectomy and behavior sequences. *Science*, 1963, *139*, 824–825.

Kimura, D. Some effects of temporal-lobe damage on auditory perception. *Canadian Journal of Psychology*, 1961, *15*, 156–165.(a)

Kimura, D. Cerebral dominance and the perception of verbal stimuli. *Canadian Journal of Psychology*, 1961, *15*, 166–171.(b)

Kimura, D. Spatial localization in left and right visual fields. *Canadian Journal of Psychology*, 1969, *23*, 445–458.

Kimura, D. The asymmetry of the human brain. *Scientific American*, 1973, *228*, 70–78.

King, F. L., & Kimura, D. Left-ear superiority in dichotic perception of vocal nonverbal sounds. *Canadian Journal of Psychology*, 1972, *26*, 111–116.

Kinsbourne, M. *The neuropsychology of learning disabilities*. Victoria B. C.: Seventh Neuropsychology Workshop, University of Victoria, 1972.

Kløve, H. Clinical neuropsychology. *Medical Clinics of North America*, 1963, *11*, 1647–1658.

Knights, R. M. A review of the neuropsychological research program. *Special Education*, Nov., 1970, 9–27.

Knights, R. M. *The effects of cerebral lesions on the psychological test performance of children. Final report*. Ottawa, Ontario: Carleton University, March, 1973.

Knights, R. M. *Comments on the CACLD Definition Paper*. Unpublished paper sent to the Executive Director, Canadian Association of Children with Learning Disabilities, November, 1977.

Knights, R. M., & Bakker, D. J. (Eds.) *The neuropsychology of learning disorders: Theoretical approaches*. Baltimore: University Park Press, 1976.

Knights, R. M., & Ogilvie, R. M. *Comparison of test results from normal and brain damaged children.* London, Ontario: Department of Psychology, University of Western Ontario, Res. Bull. No. 53, July, 1967.

Knox, C., & Kimura, D. Cerebral processing of nonverbal sounds in boys and girls. *Neuropsychologia*, 1970, 8, 227–237.

Kooi, K. A. Letter to the editor. *Psychophysiology*, 1972, 9, 154.

Landau, W. M., Goldstein, R., & Kleffner, F. R. Congenital aphasia: A clinicopathologic study. *Neurology*, 1960, 10, 915–921.

Lashley, K. S. Studies in cerebral function in learning. *Psychobiology*, 1920, 2, 55–136.

Lashley, K. S. In search of the engram. In *Physiological mechanisms in animal behavior.* Society of Experimental Biology Symposium No. 4. Cambridge: Cambridge University Press, 1950.

Lashley, K. S. The problem of serial order in behavior. In L. A. Jeffress (Ed.), *Cerebral mechanisms in behavior. The Hixon symposium.* New York: Wiley and Sons, 1951.

Lezak, M. D. *Neuropsychological assessment.* New York: Oxford University Press, 1976.

Luria, A. R. *Higher cortical functions in man.* New York: Basic Books, 1966.

Luria, A. R. *Traumatic aphasia, its syndromes, psychology and treatment.* The Hague: Mouton, 1970.

Luria, A. R. *The working brain.* Harmondsworth: Penguin Books, 1973.

Luria, A. R., Simernitskaya, E. G., & Tubylevich, B. The structure of psychological processes in relation to cerebral organization. *Neuropsychologia*, 1970, 8, 13–19.

Mark, V. H., & Ervin, F. R. *Violence and the brain.* New York: Harper & Row, 1970.

Mateer, F. *Glands and efficient behavior.* New York: Appleton-Century-Crofts, 1935.

Mattis, S., French, J. H., & Rapin, I. Dyslexia in children and young adults: Three independent neuropsychological syndromes. *Developmental Medicine and Child Neurology*, 1975, 17, 150–163.

Maximilian, V. A., Prohovnik, I., Risberg, J., & Hakansson, K. Regional blood flow changes in the left cerebral hemisphere during word pair learning and recall. *Brain and Language*, 1978, 6, 22–31.

McClearn, G. E. Review of "Dyslexia – Genetic Aspects." In A. L. Benton & D. Pearl (Eds.), *Dyslexia: An appraisal of current knowledge.* New York: Oxford University Press, 1978.

McCord, W., & McCord, J. *Origins of crime: A new evaluation of the Cambridge-Somerville Youth Study.* New York: Columbia University Press, 1959.

McKee, G., Humphrey, B., & McAdam, D. W. Scaled lateralization of alpha activity during linguistic and musical tasks. *Psychophysiology*, 1973, 10, 441–443.

Meichenbaum, D. Toward a cognitive theory of self-control. In G. E. Schwartz & D. Shapiro (Eds.), *Consciousness and self regulation* (Vol. 1). New York: Plenum Press, 1976.

Miller, L. K., & Butler, D. The effect of set size on hemifield asymmetries in letter recognition. *Brain and Language,* 1980, *9,* 307–314.

Milner, B. Intellectual function of the temporal lobes. *Psychological Bulletin,* 1954, *51,* 42–62.

Milner, B. Laterality effects in audition. In V. B. Mountcastle (Ed.), *Interhemispheric relations and cerebral dominance.* Baltimore: Johns Hopkins Press, 1962.

Milner, B. Some effects of frontal lobectomy in man. In J. M. Warren & K. A. Akert (Eds.), *The frontal granular cortex and behavior.* New York: McGraw-Hill, 1964.

Milner, B. Brain mechanisms suggested by studies of temporal lobes. In F. L. Darley (Ed.), *Brain mechanisms underlying speech and language.* New York: Grune & Stratton, 1967.

Milner, B. Hemispheric specialization: Scope and limits. In F. O. Schmitt & F. G. Worden (Eds.), *The neurosciences: Third study program.* Boston: M.I.T. Press, 1973.

Milner, B. Major invited speaker. *Tenth annual neuropsychology workshop,* Victoria, B. C.: University of Victoria, 1975.

Montessori, M. [*The Montessori Method: Scientific pedagogy as applied to child education in the children's houses*] (A. E. George, trans.) New York: F. A. Stokes, 1912.

Myklebust, H. R. Childhood aphasia: An evolving concept, and childhood aphasia: Identification, diagnosis, remediation. In L. E. Travis (Ed.), *Handbook of speech pathology and audiology.* New York: Appleton-Century-Crofts, 1971.

Myklebust, H. R., & Boshes, B. *Final report: Minimal brain damage in children.* Washington, D.C.: Department of Health, Education and Welfare, 1969.

Oltman, P. K., Semple, C., & Goldstein, L. Cognitive style and interhemispheric differentiation in the EEG. *Neuropsychologia,* 1979, *17,* 699–702.

Orton, S. T. "Word-blindness" in school children. *Archives of Neurology and Psychiatry,* 1925, *14,* 581–615.

Orton, S. T. *Reading, writing and speech problems in children.* New York: W. H. Norton, 1937.

Oscar-Berman, M., Goodglass, H., & Donnenfeld, H. Dichotic ear-order effects with nonverbal stimuli. *Cortex,* 1974, *10,* 270–277.

Oscar-Berman, M., Rehbein, L., Porfert, A., & Goodglass, H. Dichhaptic hand-order effects with verbal and nonverbal tactile stimulation. *Brain and Language.* 1978, *6,* 323–333.

Ott, J. N. *Health and light.* New York: Pocket Books, 1976.

Owen, F. W. Dyslexia – Genetic aspects. In A. L. Benton & D. Pearl (Eds.), *Dyslexia: An appraisal of current knowledge.* New York: Oxford University Press, 1978.

Owen, F. W., Adams, P. A., Forrest, T., Stolz, L. M., & Fisher, S. *Learning disorders in children: Sibling studies.* Monographs of the Society for Research in Child Development (Vol. 36). Chicago: University Press, 1971.

Penfield, W. *No man alone.* Toronto: Little, Brown, 1977.

Penfield, W., & Roberts, L. *Speech and brain mechanisms.* Princeton: Princeton University Press, 1959.

Petrauskas, R. J., & Rourke, B. P. Identification of subtypes of retarded readers: A neuropsychological, multivariate approach, *Journal of Clinical Neuropsychology,* 1979, *1,* 17–37.

Piaget, J. *The origins of intelligence in children.* New York: International Universities Press, 1952.

Raven, J. C. *The Coloured Progressive Matrices Test.* London: Lewis, 1965.

Reitan, R. M. Certain differential effects of left and right cerebral lesions in human adults. *Journal of Comparative and Physiological Psychology,* 1955, *48,* 474–477.(a)

Reitan, R. M. Investigation of the validity of Halstead's measures of biological intelligence. *A.M.A. Archives of Neurology and Psychiatry,* 1955, *73,* 28–35.(b)

Reitan, R. M. *The effects of brain lesions on adaptive abilities in human beings.* Indianapolis: Indiana University Medical Center, 1959 (mimeo.).

Reitan, R. M. Psychological deficits resulting from cerebral lesions in man. In J. M. Warren & K. A. Akert (Eds.), *The frontal granular cortex and behavior.* New York: McGraw-Hill, 1964.

Reitan, R. M. Diagnostic inferences of brain lesions based on psychological test results. *The Canadian Psychologist,* 1966, *7a,* (Inst. Suppl.), 368–388.(a)

Reitan, R. M. The needs of teachers for specialized information in the area of neuropsychology. In W. M. Cruickshank (Ed.) *The teacher of brain-injured children.* Syracuse, N.Y.: Syracuse University Press, 1966.(b)

Reitan, R. M., & Boll, T. J. Neuropsychological correlates of minimal brain dysfunction. *Annals of the New York Academy of Sciences,* 1973, *205,* 65–88.

Reitan, R. M., & Davison, L. A. *Clinical neuropsychology: Current status and applications.* Washington: Winston, 1974.

Reitan, R. M., & Heinemann, C. E. Interactions of neurological deficits and emotional disturbances in children with learning disorders: Methods for differential assessment. In J. Hellmuth (Ed.), *Learning disorders* (Vol. 3). Seattle: Special Child Publications, 1968.

Risberg, J. Regional cerebral blood flow measurements by 133 Xe-inhalation: Methodology and applications in neuropsychology and psychiatry. *Brain and Language,* 1980, *9,* 9–34.

Risberg, J., Halsey, J. H., Wills, E. L., & Wilson, E. M. Hemispheric specialization in normal man studied by bilateral measurements of the regional cerebral blood flow: A study with the Xe-inhalation technique. *Brain,* 1975, *98,* 511–524.

Ross, A. O. *Psychological disorders of children: A behavioral approach to theory, research and therapy.* New York: McGraw-Hill, 1974.

Ross, D. M., & Ross, S. A. *Hyperactivity, research, theory, action.* New York: John Wiley & Sons, 1976.

Rourke, B. P. Brain–behavior relationships in children with learning disabilities: A research program. *American Psychologist*, 1975, *30*, 911–920.

Rourke, B. P. Reading retardation in children: Developmental lag or deficit? In R. M. Knights & D. J. Bakker (Eds.), *The neuropsychology of learning disorders*. Baltimore: University Park Press, 1976.(a)

Rourke, B. P. Issues in the neuropsychological assessment of children with learning disabilities. *Canadian Psychological Review*, 1976, *17*, 89–102. (b)

Rourke, B. P. Neuropsychological research in reading retardation: A review. In A. L. Benton & D. Pearl (Eds.), *Dyslexia: An appraisal of current knowledge*. New York: Oxford University Press, 1978.(a)

Rourke, B. P. Reading, spelling and arithmetic disabilities: A neuropsychological perspective. In H. R. Myklebust (Ed.), *Progress in learning disabilities* (Vol. 4). New York: Grune & Stratton, 1978.(b)

Rourke, B. P., & Orr, R. R. Prediction of the reading and spelling performances of normal and retarded readers: A four-year follow-up. *Journal of Abnormal Child Psychology*, 1977, *5*, 9–20.

Rourke, B. P., Young, G. C., & Flewelling, R. W. The relationships between WISC verbal-performance discrepancies and selected verbal auditory-perceptual, visual-perceptual and problem solving abilities in children with learning disabilities. *Journal of Consulting and Clinical Psychology*, 1971, *27*, 475–479.

Russell, E. W., Neuringer, C., & Goldstein, G. *Assessment of brain damage*. New York: Wiley-Interscience, 1970.

Russell, W. R., & Espir, M. L. E. *Traumatic aphasia, a study of aphasia in war wounds of the brain*. London: Oxford University Press, 1961.

Satz, P. Pathological left-handedness: An explanatory model. *Cortex*, 1972, *8*, 121–135.

Satz, P., & Friel, J. Some predictive antecedents of specific disability: A preliminary two year follow-up. *Journal of Learning Disabilities*, 1974, *7*, 437–444.

Satz, P., Friel, J., & Goebel, R. Some predictive antecedents of specific reading disability: A three year follow-up. *Bulletin of the Orton Society*, 1975, *25*, 91–110.

Satz, P., Friel, J., & Rudegeair, F. Some predictive antecedents of specific reading disabilities: A two, three, and four year follow-up. In *The Hyman Blumberg Symposium on Research in Early Childhood Education*. Baltimore: Johns Hopkins Press, 1974.

Satz, P., Rardin, D., & Ross, J. An evaluation of a theory of specific developmental dyslexia. *Child Development*, 1971, *42*, 2009–2021.

Satz, P., & Sparrow, S. S. Specific developmental dyslexia: A theoretical formulation. In D. J. Bakker & P. Satz (Eds.), *Specific Reading Disability: Advances in theory and method*. Rotterdam: Rotterdam University Press, 1970.

Satz, P., Taylor, H. G., Friel, J., & Fletcher, J. M. Some developmental and predictive precursors of reading disabilities: A six year follow-up. In A.

L. Benton & D. Pearl (Eds.), *Dyslexia: An appraisal of current knowledge*. New York: Oxford University Press, 1978.

Satz, P., & Van Nostrand, G. K. Developmental dyslexia: An evaluation of a theory. In P. S. Ross & J. Ross (Eds.), *The disabled learner: Early Detection and intervention*. Rotterdam: Rotterdam University Press, 1973.

Sawrey, W. L., & Wiesz, J. D. An experimental method of producing gastric ulcers. *Journal of Comparative and Physiological Psychology*, 1956, *49*, 269–270.

Schonhaut, S., & Satz, P. Prognosis of the learning disabled child: A review of the follow-up studies. In M. Rutter (Ed.), *Behavioral syndromes of brain dysfunction in childhood*. New York: Guilford Press, in press.

Segalowitz, S. J., Bebout, L. J., & Lederman, S. J. Lateralization for reading musical chords: Disentangling symbolic, analytic and phonological aspects of reading. *Brain and Language*, 1979, *8*, 315–323.

Senf, G. M. Development of immediate memory for bisensory stimuli in normal children and children with learning disorders. *Developmental Psychology Monograph*, 1969, *6*, 1–29.

Sherrington, C. S. *The integrative action of the nervous system*. New York: Scribner, 1906.

Shneour, E. A. *The malnourished mind*. New York: Anchor Press/Doubleday, 1974.

Short, J. F., & Strodtbeck, F. L. *Group process and gang delinquency*. Chicago: University of Chicago Press, 1965.

Silver, A. A., & Hagin, R. A. *Search*. New York: Bellevue Medical Center, 1975.

Smith, A. Neuropsychological testing in neurological disorders. In W. J. Friedlander (Ed.), *Advances in Neurology* (Vol. 7). New York: Raven Press, 1975.

Spellacy, F. J. Neuropsychological differences between violent and nonviolent adolescents. *Journal of Clinical Psychology*, 1977, *33*, 966–969.

Spellacy, F. J. Neuropsychological discrimination between violent and nonviolent men. *Journal of Clinical Psychology*, 1978, *34*, 49–52.

Sperry, R. W. The great cerebral commissure. *Scientific American*, 1964, *210*, 42–53.

Sperry, R. W. Hemispheric specialization of mental faculties in the brain of man. In *Claremont Reading Conference, Thirty-Sixth Yearbook*. Claremont, Ca.: The Claremont Graduate School, 1972.

Spreen, O. *Prediction of school achievement from kindergarten to grade five: Review and report of a follow-up study*. Victoria, B. C.: Department of Psychology, University of Victoria, Research Monograph No. 33, 1978.

Spreen, O., & Benton, A. L. *Neurosensory center comprehensive examination for aphasia*. Victoria, B.C.: Department of Psychology, University of Victoria, 1969, 1977.

Spreen, O., & Gaddes, W. H. Developmental norms for 15 neuropsychological tests ages 6 to 15. *Cortex*, 1969, *5*, 171–191.

Staller, J., Buchanan, D., Singer, M., Lappin, J., & Webb, W. Alexia without agraphia: An experimental case study. *Brain and Language*, 1978, *5*, 378–387.

Strauss, A. A., & Lehtinen, L. E. *Psychopathology and education of the brain-injured child*. New York: Grune & Stratton, 1947.

Swiercinsky, D. *Manual for the adult neuropsychological evaluation*. Springfield, Il.: Charles C Thomas, 1978.

Teuber, H.-L. Some alterations in behavior after cerebral lesions in man. In *Evolution of nervous control*. Washington, D.C.: American Association for the Advancement of Science, 1959.

Teuber, H.-L. The riddle of frontal lobe function in man. In J. M. Warren & K. A. Akert (Eds.), *The frontal granular cortex and behavior*. New York: McGraw-Hill, 1964.

Teuber, H.-L. *Evidence of neural plasticity*. Unpublished speech. Tenth Annual Neuropsychology Workshop, University of Victoria, B.C., Canada, March 1975.

Thorndike, E. L. *Human learning*. New York: The Century Co., 1931.

Van Bergeijk, W. A., & David, E. E. Delayed handwriting. *Perceptual and Motor Skills*, 1959, *9*, 347–357.

Wada, J. A., & Rasmussen, T. Intracarotid injection of sodium amytal for the lateralization of cerebral speech dominance. *Journal of Neurosurgery*, 1960, *17*, 266–282.

Wada, J. A., Clarke, R., & Hamm, A. Cerebral hemispheric asymmetry in humans. *Archives of Neurology*, 1975, *32*, 239–246.

Watson, J. B. *Psychology from the standpoint of a behaviorist*. Philadelphia: J. B. Lippincott, 1924.

Watson, J. B. *Behaviorism*. New York: Norton, 1925.

Weber, B. A., & Omenn, G. S. Auditory and visual evoked responses in children with familial reading disabilities. *Journal of Learning Disabilities*, 1977, *10*, 153–158.

Williams, D. Neural factors related to habitual aggression. *Brain*. 1969, *92*, 503–520.

Winick, M., Rosso, P., & Brasel, J. A. Malnutrition and cellular growth in the brain: Existence of critical periods. In *Ciba Foundation Symposium: Lipids, malnutrition and the developing brain*. Amsterdam: Associated Scientific Publishers, 1972.

Witelson, S. F. Hemispheric specialization for linguistic and non-linguistic tactual perception using a dichotomous stimulation technique. *Cortex*, 1974, *10*, 2–17.

Wyke, M., & Ettlinger, G. Efficiency of recognition in left and right visual fields. *Archives of Neurology*, 1961, *5*, 659–665.

Zaidel, E. *Linguistic competence and related functions in the right cerebral hemisphere of man following commissurotomy and hemispherectomy*. Unpublished doctoral dissertation, California Institute of Technology, 1973.

Zangwill, O. L. *Cerebral dominance and its relation to psychological functions*. London: Oliver & Boyd, 1960.

SECTION II

Issues in
Neuropsychology

Cecil R. Reynolds

3
The Neuropsychological Basis of Intelligence

Cerebral dominance as a mechanism that will lead to an understanding of the neuropsychological basis and processes underlying human mental abilities has dominated the thoughts and research of neuropsychologists throughout the history of the field. Cerebral dominance traditionally refers to the hemisphere responsible for controlling language and most language-mediated functions; for the vast majority of individuals, this is the left hemisphere. Indeed, for some time, the right hemisphere was believed to house few if any important cognitive functions. Cerebral dominance has also been used in some instances to refer to the establishment of handedness. Current thought has presented serious challenges to this traditional approach to the neuropsychology of intelligence. Past concepts of the relationship between handedness and other motoric indices of cerebral dominance are being revolutionized as more contemporary concepts are introduced.

HANDEDNESS, EYEDNESS, AND CEREBRAL DOMINANCE

Handedness and its relationship to cerebral dominance and language functions has been a concern of researchers and theoreticians for some time. Cerebral dominance, as first described informally by Dax in 1836 (Harris, 1980; Joynt & Benton, 1964; Penfield & Roberts, 1959) and later in formal presentations by Broca (1861, 1863; Harris, 1980), meant the hemisphere of the brain responsible for language functions. Handedness itself had been studied extensively since at least the sixteenth century, and theories of how handedness develops abound. In a recent review, Harris (1980) discussed five categories of theories of handedness that have been proffered since the 1400s, a number of which stretch the imagination rather vigorously. The categories of theories reviewed by Harris include structural asymmetry (visceral imbalance, blood flow, weight and density of the cerebral hemispheres, arm length, etc.); positional asymmetry (orientation of infant at time of birth or while in the womb); heredity; cultural conditioning theories (arm used to carry infants, carrying of warshield in left hand to protect heart, etc.); and the ambidextral culture (a movement begun in the late 1800s that proposed humans were "either-handed" and, as such movements seem to do, actually started an educational craze toward training pupils to be ambidextrous). Though it now appears that handedness is a preordained, genetic function for most individuals, deviations from the predetermined state can occur under a variety of conditions. The issue of precisely how and why handedness develops as it does and its subsequent effects on the study of brain–behavior relationships is far from being settled (Annett, 1972; Boklage, 1978; Fuller, 1978; Hardyck & Petrinovich, 1977; Herron, 1980; Morgan & Corballis, 1978).

A number of motor-based programs intended to affect brain-behavior relationships have been developed over the years. Most of these programs assume that the failure to establish hand (and thus cerebral) dominance or consistent lateral preference is an underlying cause of learning or intellectual deficits. (Lateral preference in this instance and as used throughout this chapter refers to consistency of hand, eye, and foot dominance.) The first such program to be established apparently was an exercise therapy program by Buzzard (1882) for the treatment of aphasia on the theory that the various exercises employed would cause the right hemisphere to develop a "convolution for speech." Probably the most influential programs of this nature in American education are those of Orton and Doman and Delacato. Though the Doman and Delacato methods have been principally designed from the maxim "ontogeny recapitulates phylogeny," the notion of cerebral dominance remains central to their theory of brain function and intelligence. Other theories of brain–behavior relationships have affected professional practices in a number of fields (see Harris, 1980).

Samuel T. Orton's Theory

Orton's theory and writings (1925, 1931, 1937) have had marked effect on remedial practices in education, many of which remain today. However, few employing Orton-based techniques can even begin to explain his theory. A very active Orton Society is also quite respected and visible today.

Orton based his theory of cerebral dominance and learning (particularly reading) on the structural symmetry of the brain (though it is now widely known that the human brain does not display perfect morphological or structural symmetry), and he assumed that any event recorded in one hemisphere

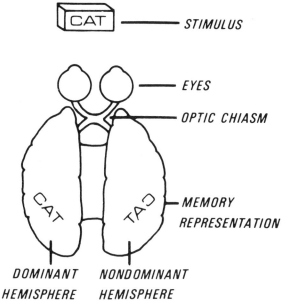

Figure 3-1. Schematic representation of Orton's theory of perception and storage of visual material. (From *The Psychology of Left and Right* by M. C. Corballis and I. L. Beale. Hillsdale, N.J.: Lawrence Erlbaum Associates, 1976. Copyright 1976 by Lawrence Erlbaum Associates. With permission.)

was recorded in its mirror image in the opposite hemisphere. The dominant, or major hemisphere was thought to record perceptual events in their correct spatial orientation. Figure 3-1 provides a schematic representation of the recordings of visual-perceptive events as dictated by Orton's theory. The reversals so often exhibited by dyslexic children were therefore believed to result from competition with the mirror images available in the nondominant, or minor hemisphere. With incomplete, unestablished, or mixed dominance (as determined by lateral preference), the frequency of reversals occurring would be substantially greater due to the intrusion of the minor hemisphere into the process than when a single hemisphere exhibits clear, dominant control over cognitive functions. Orton's (1931) assertions essentially represent a storage or retrieval problem and *not* a problem of initial perception as many believe.

More recently, evidence has proliferated supporting the view that there is no clear relationship between handedness and cerebral dominance (Belmont & Birch, 1963; Benton, 1955, 1959; Hardyck & Petrinovich, 1977; Hardyck,

Petrinovich & Goldman, 1976; Levy & Nagylaki, 1972; Milner, Branch, & Rasmussen, 1964; Naylor, 1980; Penfield & Roberts, 1959; Reynolds, Hartlage, & Haak, 1980). The theoretical basis of Orton's position has also been seriously questioned by Corballis and Beale (1976). As part of their convincing argument, Corballis and Beale put forth that Orton is wrong in his basic assumptions:

> It simply does not follow that the two halves of a symmetrical brain would respond to any given stimulus pattern in mirror-opposite ways. This would only happen in general if the pattern were itself symmetrical with respect to the brain's plane of symmetry. . . . It is not at all clear how perceptual input to the nondominant hemisphere could be veridical, yet leave an engram that is reversed. Neither is it clear why the nondominant hemisphere should be the one to suffer this bizarre malfunction.*

Extensive reviews (Bauer & Wepman, 1955; White, 1969) have indicated that in almost all people the left hemisphere is the dominant hemisphere for symbolic language and speech regardless of the handedness of the subject. Some exceptions have been noted, however. In a review of literature, Witelson (1980) concludes that left-handedness may be associated with a lesser degree of cerebral specialization for speech and language. Dysphasia associated with right-hemisphere lesions in both right- and left-handers has also been reported (e.g., Newcombe & Ratcliff, 1973). Geffen (1978) reports that as many as 6 percent of normal right-handers have other than left-hemisphere specialization for speech.

It is tempting to hypothesize that the lesser degree of lateralization of cognitive processes found with left-handers is responsible for the Orton effect. However, this is contradicted by evidence related to gender differences in the degree of lateral cerebral specialization of cognitive functioning. With regard to lateralization of verbal functions to the left hemisphere and spatial-oriented functions to the right hemisphere, males show consistently greater lateralization of function than females. Females tend to have a less rigid scheme of specialization than do males. If less lateralization of cognitive function is associated with left-handedness and the lack of established dominance, and these two conditions are subsequently related to intellectual or cognitive dysfunctions, why do males (the more highly lateralized sex) outnumber females four to one in classes for learning-disabled children?

Other problems with using handedness or primarily motoric indices as measures of cerebral dominance stem from disagreements about how these

---

*From *The Psychology of Left and Right* by M. C. Corballis and I. L. Beale. Hillsdale, N.J.: Lawrence Erlbaum Associates, 1976, pp. 60–61. Copyright 1976 by Lawrence Erlbaum Associates. With permission.

indices should be measured and from research results which, not surprisingly, can differ dramatically depending upon how handedness is measured. Some researchers approach handedness from a dichotomous perspective; individuals are considered right-handed or nonright-handed. Other researchers define right, left, and no dominance as categories for the study of handedness. More recently, handedness (and hence lateral preference) has come to be considered a continuous variable (Annett, 1972). Subsequently, a variety of efforts have been made to measure lateral preference as a continuous variable, including the use of manual tapping speed (e.g., Peters & Durding, 1978) and self-report inventories questioning hand, eye, and foot preference for a series of activities (e.g., Dean & Kulhavy, 1977).

Measurement of handedness as a continuous variable has not resolved the relationship between dominance and intellectual integrity. Dean (1979), using a self-report measure of lateral preference, recently found that children with higher WISC-R verbal IQs (VIQ) than performance IQs (PIQ) were significantly more bilateral than children with VIQ equal to PIQ and VIQ less than PIQ. The latter children tended to be more right dominant. Orton's theory states that bilaterality underlies cognitive dysfunction in reading disabilities. However, the right-dominant children in Dean's study display the pattern of VIQ–PIQ discrepancies (PIQ greater than VIQ) that are most frequently found with samples of learning-disabled children (Anderson, Kaufman, & Kaufman, 1976; Kaufman, 1979a; Sattler, 1981; Smith, Coleman, Dokecki, & Davis, 1977; Zingale & Smith, 1978), while the bilateral children show the intellectual pattern least often associated with reading deficits. Reynolds, Hartlage, and Haak (1980) attempted to replicate and extend Dean's (1979) findings to determine the relationship between lateral preference and IQ–achievement discrepancies. Instead of relying on self-report studies however, Reynolds et al determined lateral preference (hand, eye, and foot) by summing each child's score on 26 neuropsychological tests that contrasted the two sides of the body. Correlations were then determined between each child's lateral preference score, verbal-performance IQ difference (with and without the sign retained), and the difference between achievement test scores in reading, spelling, and arithmetic and each of the three WISC-R IQs. Of the 12 correlations generated by this method, *none* revealed any significant relationship between lateral preference and the variables described above. Neither was lateral preference significantly related to any of the intellectual or achievement variables when taken in isolation. Although the two studies have contradictory results, both are inconsistent with the Orton hypothesis and other traditional theories of dominance and intellectual function.

Eyedness is an even more complex phenomenon than handedness. Rather than each eye being under the principal control of a single cerebral hemisphere, each hemisphere processes visual information from the contralateral visual hemifield of each eye. In view of the complexity of the eyedness phenomenon, it is not surprising to note the disappointing results of numerous studies that have attempted to relate consistency of eye-hand preference in school-age children to variables such as reading ability (e.g., Balow, 1963; Balow & Balow, 1964; Coleman & Deutsch, 1964; Hillerich, 1964). These results could have been anticipated with the knowledge that 40 percent of the normally functioning $5-8\frac{1}{2}$-year-old population shows mixed eye-hand dominance (Kaufman, 1978), as determined during standardization of the McCarthy Scales of Children's Abilities.

Modifications of Orton's theory have been offered by many researchers since the 1930s. One modification contends that mixed cerebral dominance creates an antagonistic state of affairs, resulting in the right hemisphere fighting for control of language functions to the neglect of its normal involvement in perceptual and spatial functions. The antagonism between the two hemispheres and the subsequent loss of efficiency in perceptual and spatial functions is believed to play a major role in the development of intellectual dysfunctions during childhood. Noble (1968) has offered another, attractive alternative to Orton's proposal, yet he still relies on mirror-image perceptual transfers between hemispheres. Orton's theory and its derivatives continue to rely on the traditional notion of cerebral dominance. It now seems unlikely that measurements based on hands and eyes can bear more than a peripheral relationship to a dynamic understanding of the cognitive aspects of hemispheric functioning. A major fault of eyedness and handedness indices of cerebral dominance concerns attempts to relate dominance of the motor cortex for physical activities to cortical dominance for intellectual functioning and preference for a single mode of cognitive processing. Traditional concepts of dominance must give way to more contemporary notions of hemisphericity in order to better understand the intellectual workings of the brain (Reynolds, 1978, 1980a).

Doman's and Delacato's Theory

The therapeutic system for learning-disabled children known as the Doman and Delacato (D-D) method has been principally described in the writings of Delacato (1959, 1963, 1966). The D-D theory relies on vertical and horizontal development and organization of function within the human brain. The roots of Delacato's theoretical work can be traced directly to Orton's (1928) early writings on dominance. The neuropsychological theory of D-D is based on the biogenetic principle that "ontogeny recapitulates phylogeny" and contends that if one does not follow this sequential continuum of neurological development, problems of mobility and/or communication will develop. The therapeutic methods of D-D are designed to overcome early deficiencies in development so that the optimal level and pattern of neurological organization may be achieved.

Doman and Delacato maintain that there are six major functional attainments of humans: motor skills, speech, writing, reading, understanding, and stereognosis. The attainment of these skills is dependent upon the individual's uninterrupted and successful neuroanatomical progress toward neurological organization.

Neurological organization is that physiologically optimum condition which exists uniquely and most completely in man and is the result of a total uninterrupted ontogenetic neural development. This development recapitulates the phylogenetic neural development of man and begins during the first trimester of gestation and ends at about six and one-half years of age in normal humans. This orderly development progresses *vertically* through the spinal cord and all other areas of the cortex, as it does with all mammals. Man's final and unique developmental progression takes place at the level of the cortex and it is *lateral* (from left to right or from right to left).*

Each higher level of functioning is dependent on successful progression through the earlier levels. It is proffered by the D-D theory that if the highest level of functioning (cerebral dominance) is incomplete or unfunctioning, then a lower level of neurological organization dominates intellectual behavior. The highest level of neurological organization, complete lateral cerebral dominance, is, according to Delacato (1959), what gives humans their great capacity for communication and completely sets them apart from lower animals. Unfortunately for the D-D theory of brain function and intelligence, there is evidence for cerebral dominance in other primates (Dewson, 1977; Gazzaniga, 1971; Johnson & Gazzaniga, 1971a, b; LeMay, 1976; Warren & Nonneman, 1976). In addition, the highest level of neurological organization is deemed to exist only when an individual has achieved consistency of hand, eye, and foot preference. As noted earlier, mixed eye-hand dominance is a common finding in children at least through age 8½ (and likely beyond). Orton and Delacato would have perhaps fared better using a closer review of available literature. Woo and Pearson (1927), after an exhaustive study of 7000 men, concluded that there was "no evidence whatsoever of even a correlation between ocular and manual lateralities. . ." (p. 181). It is not unreasonable to suspect that the lack of completely consistent hand, eye, and foot preference is the rule rather than the exception.

Neurological development is believed to progress upward from the spinal

*From C. H. Delacato, *The Treatment and Prevention of Reading Problems: The Neuropsychological Approach,* 1959, p. 19. Courtesy of Charles C Thomas, Publisher, Springfield, Illinois.

cord through the medulla, the pons, the midbrain (the evolutionarily older portions of the cortex), to the neocortex resulting in lateral hemispheric dominance. While there are any number of cogent theoretical arguments against a theory of neurological organization such as that proposed by D-D (e.g., Bever, 1975; Kinsbourne, 1975), perhaps the more grave damage to the D-D theory is the lack of positive results from studies of the remedial methods D-D derived from their theoretical formulations.

Research support for the effectiveness of the D-D methods has been sparse and fraught with methodological difficulties. Glass and Robbins (1967) reviewed 15 studies cited by Delacato as scientific appraisals of his theory of neurological organization. Five of the studies reviewed failed to control for regression effects, and Glass and Robbins concluded that it was not possible to determine whether gains reported in these studies were due to experimental effects or simple regression effects. In 14 of the 15 studies, no random assignment to groups nor conditions was made although no practical reasons for not doing so existed. Further examinations of D-D's research support indicated that, in all but one study, control and experimental groups met at different times of day, in different classrooms, and with different teachers. Such confounding severely restricts any interpretations of mean group differences. In the study believed to be the best designed of all, the study's author stated that it was his conclusion that all differences found in his study were due to a Hawthorne effect! Glass and Robbins (1967) subsequently offered plausible alternative interpretations of the data presented in the 15 studies, many of which lend themselves to implications directly contrary to the D-D theory. Other studies (e.g., Cornish, 1970; O'Donnell & Eisenson, 1969; Robbins, 1966) continue to find no support for the D-D methods.*

Much of the D-D method is centered around the imposition of patterning exercises on the child, some even during sleep. In this procedure, the child's limbs and head are moved by adults while the child lies limp, not actively participating in the movement. A series of studies with both animals and humans (Held, 1965; Held & Bossom, 1961; Held & Freedman, 1963; Held & Hein, 1963), has demonstrated the ineffectual nature of passive partici-

---

*There are many other objections to the use of the D-D methods that are not pertinent to the discussion here. The reader should note, however, that a fair number of major professional organizations have publicly stated their opposition to the D-D methods, including the American Academy of Cerebral Palsy, American Academy of Physical Medicine and Rehabilitation, American Congress of Rehabilitation Medicine, Canadian Association for Children with Learning Disabilities, Canadian Association for Retarded Children, Canadian Council for the Disabled, National Association for Retarded, American Academy of Pediatrics, American Academy of Neurology, and the American Association on Mental Deficiency. Some writers have gone so far as to condemn the D-D methods as "a brand of charlatanism" (Levine, Brooks, & Shonkoff, 1980).

pation. As an example, in one particular study (Held, 1965), a group of people were fitted with reversible goggles. Half of the group was then allowed to walk around an enclosure with an homogeneous background. The other half of the group was pushed around the same enclosure on a specially designed cart. Those actively participating in moving about the enclosure adapted to the reversible goggles, while the passive-participation group showed *no* adaptation. At least two quite widely held cognitive theories are also in sharp disagreement with D-D (Hunt, 1961).

Traditional dominance-based theories of neurological organization and intelligence find little empirical support. The relationship of dominance to motor functions can only be peripherally related to a preference for intellectual or cognitive processing of information, the forte of intelligent behavior. To cast further doubt upon the functional importance of general dominance by the major hemisphere as indicated by motor indices of dominance, researchers have reported that hemispheric dominance for many cognitive tasks is quite malleable and responds to training and to the principles of reinforcement (e.g., Bever, 1975; Bever & Chiarello, 1974; Bogen, 1969; Johnson & Gazzaniga, 1971a, b).

While traditional concepts of dominance will remain an interesting area of theoretical research, reconceptualization of dominance as related to intellectual functioning is clearly necessary. Several influential theorists have developed neuropsychological models of intellectual functioning with considerably less reliance on traditional notions of cerebral dominance. Luria's theory in particular appears to hold great promise for understanding the neuropsychological basis of intelligence and for developing remedial or compensatory techniques for use with cognitively dysfunctional individuals.

HALSTEAD'S THEORY OF BIOLOGICAL INTELLIGENCE

The early work of Halstead and associates, principally described in Halstead (1947) and Shure and Halstead (1959), has tremendously affected the development of many of the techniques and methods of clinical neuropsychology. Though the Luria-Nebraska Neuropsychological Test Battery is now making headway, the Halstead-Reitan Neuropsychological Test Battery has dominated neuropsychological assessment for more than a quarter of a century.

Halstead's major thesis regarding the relationship between the brain and intelligence was published in 1947. This volume essentially reported the research of Halstead and his colleagues that began in 1935 at the Otho S. S. Sprague Memorial Institute and the Division of Psychiatry of the Department of Medicine at the University of Chicago. Halstead focuses principally on the study of the cortex in relation to intelligence and more specifically on the role of the frontal lobes. (The frontal lobes also play a major role in Luria's conceptualization of intelligence.)

Halstead differentiated between biological intelligence and psychometric intelligence. He considered the latter to be what is measured by intelligence tests and the former to be the true, innate ability of the individual, though he unquestionably realized that the two were not independent of one another. In recognition of this, Halstead, and subsequently Reitan, routinely included a standardized test of intelligence, such as the Henmon-Nelson Tests of Mental Ability or a member of the Wechsler series of intelligence scales, in their neuropsychological test battery. Nevertheless, Halstead's research focused on determining the nature and underlying factors of biological intelligence.

From an original battery of 27 behavioral indicators (i.e., psychological tests), Halstead selected 13 measures for his study of biological intelligence. These 13 tests were selected because they yielded objective scores and because they "seemed likely to reflect some component of biological intelligence" (Halstead, 1947, p. 39). Some of the tests dropped from the larger battery were essentially personality or affective measures (e.g., MMPI, a modified version of the Rorschach); were one-item, dichotomously scored tests (Halstead Closure Test); or were purely sensory measures (e.g., Halstead-Brill Audiometer).

Based on independent factor analyses of the correlation matrix for this set of tests, determined from the responses of a sample of what Halstead considered normal individuals (50 adults fully recovered from a "concussive type" head injury), Halstead extracted four basic factors of biological intelligence, which he labeled *C, A, P,* and *D.** Factor analyses of the data were conducted separately by Karl Holzinger and L. L. Thurstone. Each analysis produced essentially the same results. Halstead defined these four factors as follows.

C, the integrative field factor. Halstead considered this factor to be central to the ability to adapt to new situations and to integrate new information and stimuli that were not a part of one's previous experiences in order to form new symbols and frameworks of orientation when necessary. The *C* fac-

---

*Halstead's use of factor analysis is noteworthy since he was one of the first to pioneer the use of factor analysis in the field that has now become clinical neuropsychology. Factor analysis is a potentially quite valuable statistical method that has been grossly underestimated and underutilized by researchers in clinical neuropsychology, though some progress is evident in the application of factor analysis to problems in clinical neuropsychology in recent years. Some factor analytic investigations (e.g., Reynolds, 1980b) have failed to support some aspects of neuropsychological research, such as sex differences in the organization of cognitive skills, and it is important to the study of intelligence that such conflicting results be resolved.

tor creates order from the chaos of new stimuli from the external world constantly bombarding one and gives these stimuli an internal referent. The C factor was characterized in Halstead's initial factor analysis by large loadings by the Halstead Category Test, the Henmon-Nelson Tests of Mental Ability, the Speech-Sounds Perception Test, the Halstead Finger Oscillation Test, and the Halstead Time-Sense Test.

A, the abstraction factor. The *A* factor represents the aptitude for abstraction. Abstraction is the ability to draw meaning away from a series of events or to hold ideas away from their concrete referents; it is considered difficult. Abstraction includes the ability to grasp essential similarities in the face of apparent differences and vice versa without the use or reliance upon past experience. It also includes the ability to abstract, or draw away, a principle or set of rules governing a series of seemingly unconnected stimuli. The *A* factor was characterized in Halstead's initial factor analysis by large loadings from the Carl Hollow-Square Performance Test for Intelligence, the Halstead Category Test, the Halstead Tactual Performance Test (memory component), and Halstead Tactual Performance Test (localization component).

P, the power factor. Halstead believed *P* to represent the undistorted power factor of the functioning brain and related it analogously to the reserve power available to an amplifier not already functioning at peak wattage. Halstead's description of the *P* factor relies heavily on flicker-fusion research and indicates that the brain with more available power (*P*) has a higher critical fusion frequency. *P* to Halstead was certainly related to the electrical facilitation of cognition (mentation) in the brain and was controlled principally through the frontal lobes. Halstead also proposed some relationships between affect and its effects on intelligence and the *P* factor. The *P* factor was characterized in Halstead's factor analytic study by large loadings by the Halstead Flicker-Fusion Test, the Halstead Tactual Performance Test (recall component), the Halstead Dynamic Visual Field Test (central form), and the Halstead Dynamic Visual Field Test (central color).

D, the directional factor. The *D* factor was, in Halstead's interpretation, the most difficult of his biological factors of intelligence to legitimize statistically through factor analysis. Nevertheless, Halstead seemed satisfied with its existence and determined that *D* was the "medium of exteriorization of intelligence, either from within or from without the individual" (Halstead, 1947, p. 84). *D* then is a modality factor. Intelligence must be expressed, be it through reading, writing, listening, speaking, composing, or painting and Halstead believed that *D* represented the modality of expression of intelligence and was also, in one sense, an attentional factor. For to utilize a modality, one must be able to focus or direct the energy and power of thought towards that modality. (Some theorists contend that hemispheric specialization for methods of cognitive processing are the result of an attentional bias between the two hemispheres.) Results of the factor analysis showed D to be characterized by large loadings by the Halstead Tactual Performance Test (speed component) and the Halstead Dynamic Visual Field Test (peripheral component). A potentially important secondary loading was apparent by the Halstead Tactual Performance Test (incidental localization component). Halstead believed the various agnosias and apraxias to be strongly related to the D factor. However, in the normally functioning human brain, he believed that D faded into the background of the other three factors (C, A, and P) except when a new medium of expression was encountered.

As should be clear by now, C, A, and P were considered the process factors of intelligence and D the factor through which externalization of these processes occurred. In his subsequent research with brain-injured individuals, Halstead observed these various factors in operation and believed that he had thereby demonstrated the biological validity of these basic factors of intelligence. Once having delineated these factors, Halstead and his associates turned their attention to the localization of intelligence in the brain and to the role of these four factors in various types of psychopathology. It is from this latter work that much of current clinical neuropsychology has grown.

The next step in Halstead's validation of his factors of biological intelligence was the development of the now well-known Halstead Impairment Index. Halstead reasoned that if C, A, P, and D were indeed biological factors of intelligence, then individuals with known neuropathology should suffer impairment in their ability to perform tasks representing these factors. In developing the Impairment Index, Halstead was also quite cognizant of its potential pragmatic applications. He found that most of the tests involved in measuring C, A, P, and D differentiated at some level between individuals with a definite history of head injury and a control group with no history of head injury. He then collapsed the ten best discriminating tests into a battery forming the Impairment Index. Although the various tests were not equivalent in their discriminability, each test was given an equal weighting of .10. An individual scoring within the impaired range on a task was thus assigned a score of .10, while scoring in the normal (nonimpaired) range earned a score of 0. Thus, an impairment index of 1.0 represents almost certain brain damage and an index of 0 represents almost certain neurological integrity. Halstead then set out to investigate the neuroanatomical localization of biological intelligence as indicated by the Impairment Index.

Based on a series of findings with neurosurgical patients for whom the exact site of brain lesion was known, Halstead concluded that the factors of biological intelligence were principally controlled through the frontal lobes. Only a very slight difference occurred between left and right frontal lesions; left-sided lesions caused only slightly greater impairment than did right-sided lesions. Frontal lesions (typically in the form of lobotomy) resulted in an impairment index six times that of normal controls and three times that of nonfrontal lesions. The least amount of impairment occurred with occipital lesions, followed by parietal and temporal lesions, though parietal and temporal lesions were very similar in the degree of impairment produced. Although partial replication of these results was provided by Shure and Halstead (1959), the strong relationship between the frontal lobes and Halstead's Impairment Index has not been validated in subsequent research (Reitan, 1975). However, Halstead retained his interest in the localization of the factors of biological intelligence.

Halstead has summarized his theory as follows:

1. Biological intelligence is a basic function of the brain and is essential for many forms of adaptive behavior of the human organism. While it is represented throughout the cerebral cortex, its representation is not equal throughout. It is distributed in a gradient with its maximal representation occurring in the cortex of the frontal lobes.
2. The nuclear structure of biological intelligence comprises four basic factors which, in a unified fashion, enter into all cognitive activities. While these factors make possible the highest reaches of human intellect, their dysfunction, as produced by brain damage, may yield progressively maladaptive forms of behavior, or "biological neurosis."
3. The frontal lobes, long regarded as silent areas, are the portion of the brain most essential to biological intelligence. They are the organs of civilization – the basis of man's despair and of his hope for the future.*

Shortly following the publication of Halstead's 1947 monograph, Reitan and others recognized the need for a more diverse array of neuropsychological tests in order to make more exact and stringent diagnoses of neuropathology. It is important to remember that although Halstead apparently engaged in diagnosing various neurological disorders on the basis of performance on his battery of tests (Reitan, 1975), he was trained as an experimental, physiological psychologist and was principally interested in developing a broad theory of the biology of behavior and concomitant brain–behavior relationships.

Reitan subsequently turned to highly empirical methods in an almost atheoretical fashion in expanding Halstead's original battery of tests. Reitan never developed a comprehensive theory of the biological basis of intelligence, though his contributions to the applied field of clinical neuropsychological assessment have been many and of great significance. Reitan (1964) did engage in some evaluation of Halstead's theory, however. In evaluating the effects of cerebral lesions of various locations within the cortex, Reitan concluded that the consensus of data indicated that nonfrontal lobe lesions are most frequently associated with specific types of disorders while frontal lobe

---

*Reprinted from *Brain and Intelligence* by W. C. Halstead by permission of the University of Chicago Press. © 1947 by the University of Chicago Press.

lesions result in more general disturbances that are difficult to specify in detail. While Reitan apparently felt that these findings disconfirmed Halstead's notion of the frontal lobes as the principal anatomical site of biological intelligence (Reitan, 1975), this is not necessarily the case. If one conceptualizes intelligence as the coordinating and planning activity of the brain (the "executive" branch), and as directing the processing activities of other areas, then damage to the frontal lobes should produce a more generalized, diverse set of disorders.

Reitan's work (Reitan 1955, 1964a, b, 1966, 1975; Reitan & Davison, 1974; Wheeler & Reitan, 1962) has caused researchers and clinicians to appreciate the complexities of elaborating a theory of brain function and intelligence from deficits in the higher cognitive processes following brain lesions. Considerable research has been done with the Halstead-Reitan Neuropsychological Test Battery (HRNTB) regarding brain–behavior relationships. In reviewing this research as it applies to clinical assessment and the development of a comprehensive theory of the neuropsychological basis of intelligence, one must keep in mind the methodological difficulties inherent in this line of research. Many of the methodological problems discussed early by Shure and Halstead (1959) remain. Additionally, researchers have not been vigilant in their reporting of subject descriptions in research utilizing the HRNTB (Hevern, 1980; Parsons & Prigatano, 1978). The following demographic variables are known to affect the outcome of neuropsychological assessment (Hevern, 1980, Parsons & Prigatano, 1978; Reynolds & Gutkin, 1979): age, educational level, sex, socioeconomic status, race, and urban versus rural residence. Hevern's (1980) recent review indicates that for most of these variables, less than half of the studies in the literature since 1975 give adequate information for replication or for accurate comparisons with other studies. Swiercinsky (1979) has also recently questioned the comprehensiveness of assessment with the HRNTB, indicating that important areas of function such as receptive speech, concentration, and other information-processing modes do not receive any independent evaluation through this technique.

A thorough assessment of Halstead's theory of biological intelligence is not yet available. It appears to have fallen by the wayside at present in favor of number-crunching empiricism. A strong theory of the neuropsychological basis of intelligence is requisite to important advances in the field.

THE LURIA MODEL

Alexsandr R. Luria was a Soviet neuropsychologist who was a major force in the development of the scientific discipline of neuropsychology. While his research spans some four decades, his influence on American neuropsychology was minimal until around the mid-1960s. Luria was a prolific researcher and published extensively throughout his career, which ended with his death in 1977. His later work continued to be published into 1979. Luria's major theoretical contributions to understanding the neuropsychological basis of intelligence are well summarized in his publications of 1961, 1964, 1966, 1969, 1970, and 1973. Like Halstead, Luria believed the frontal lobes of man to play a major role in intelligence. Luria's position with respect to the frontal lobes is well reflected in the title of his 1969 address to the 19th International Congress of Psychology – "Cerebral Organization of Conscious Acts: A Frontal Lobe Function." Much of the following presentation is taken from the above references to Luria's work.

Luria was greatly influenced in his clinical and experimental research in neuropsychology by the well-known Soviet psychologist L. S. Vygotski. Throughout Luria's work, one finds that Luria relied extensively on a clinical research methodology not at all unlike the "methodé clinique" of Piaget in addition to his more formalized experimental research. In developing his clinical research methods, Luria designed a rich battery of neuropsychological tests that he used to obtain an essentially qualitative evaluation of an individual's neurological status and integrity. Indeed, it has been the qualitative (often seen as subjective; Golden, Purisch, & Hammeke, 1979), nature of Luria's neuropsychological examination that has fostered the reluctance to adopt his techniques in American neuropsychology. However, over the past several years (unfortunately after Luria's death), a standardized version of the Luria battery has been developed and made available for experimental and clinical use in the United States (Golden, Purisch, & Hammeke, 1979). A children's version of this battery is also under development and should be available imminently (Golden, 1980). However, the quantification and standardization of Luria's assessment techniques has been criticized as tending to remove much of the richness that was the essence of Luria's methods. A clear understanding of Luria's theory of the functional organization of the brain and an appreciation for the brain as a dynamic organ of consciousness should avert the loss of information through the standardization of Luria's methods. Standardization of such methods has a number of advantages that should add to the richness of information about brain function that is available.

Luria conceptualized the working brain as organized into three major components, which he termed "the blocks of the brain." As illustrated in Figure 3-2, the first block of the brain is composed of the brainstem, including the reticular formation and the midbrain as well as the other shaded structures in Figure 3-2. The second block of the brain is essentially composed of the parietal, occipital, and temporal lobes – the sections of the brain frequently referred to as the association areas of the cortex. The third block of the brain is essentially composed of the remaining area of the cortex anterior

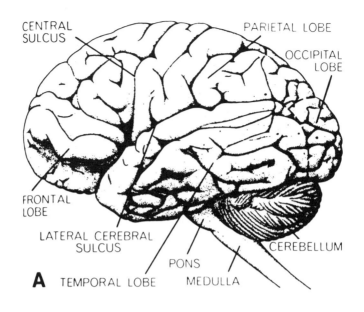

CENTRAL
SULCUS

PARIETAL LOBE

OCCIPITAL
LOBE

FRONTAL
LOBE

LATERAL CEREBRAL
SULCUS

CEREBELLUM

A   TEMPORAL LOBE

PONS

MEDULLA

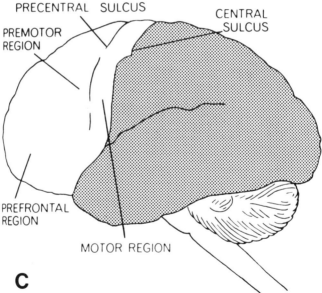

PRECENTRAL SULCUS

CENTRAL
SULCUS

PREMOTOR
REGION

PREFRONTAL
REGION

MOTOR REGION

C

Figure 3-2. Luria's major blocks of the brain. (A) Gross anatomy of the brain, left-hemisphere view. (B) The first block of the brain, the brainstem, and evolutionarily old cortex. (C) The second block of the brain, the association area, composed of the parietal, occipital, and temporal lobes. (D) Shaded

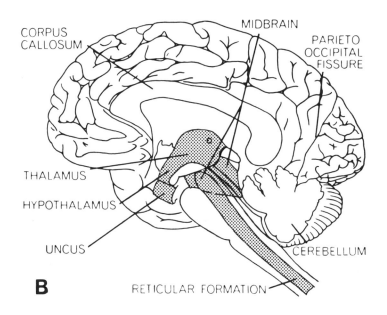

B

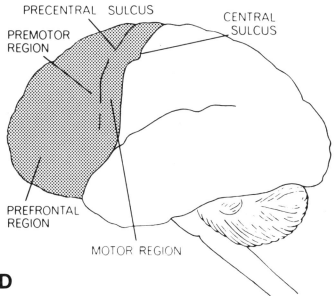

D

area is the third block of the brain, composed of the frontal areas of the brain, anterior to the central sulcus and including the motor strip of the cortex. (From "The Functional Organization of the Brain" by A. R. Luria. *Scientific American,* 1970, **222**, 66-78. Copyright © 1970 by Scientific American, Inc. All rights reserved.)

to the central sulcus, principally the frontal lobes. Before turning to the localization of function within each of the three blocks of the brain, it is important to fully understand the concept of dynamic localization of function in the human brain.

The sensory and motor functions of the brain have highly specific functional localizations. The locations of these functions have been mapped in precise and meticulous detail by neurologists and psychologists over the past decade. Higher-order, complex mental processes require the coordination of many areas of the brain and are not conducive to such rigid or narrow localization of function. While it is well known, for example, that impairment or lesion of the right parietal lobe results in extreme difficulty with the Block Design subtest of the Wechsler series, it is incorrect to consider Block Design performance as being localized to the right parietal lobe. Extensive damage to portions of the frontal or occipital lobes may also produce impaired performance on the Block Design task. Yet, if the parietal lobe remained intact, the *nature* of the difficulty on this task would change as a function of the localization of any neuropathology. Cortical specialization for cognitive tasks is not task- or stimulus-specific; it is much more process-specific, though processing specialization is gross, and any specific type of information processing itself requires coordination of several anatomical sections of the cortex.

The notion of the brain as a dynamic functional system is by no means a new idea. Hughlings Jackson presented a similar premise in the nineteenth century as did Monakow in the twentieth century. The concept of dynamic localization of higher cognitive processes has perhaps been best explained by Luria (1964). According to Luria, the higher mental processes are formed as a function of people's activity in the process of communication with one another and represent "*complex functional systems* based on jointly working zones of the brain cortex."* Once one conceptualizes the brain as an interdependent systemic network, "It becomes completely understandable that a higher (mental) function may suffer as a result of the destruction of *any link which is a part of the structure of a complex functional system* and . . . may be disturbed even when the centres differ greatly in localisation."* Central to this approach is the contention that each link in the system has a particular function in the processing of the problem at hand. Hence, "when one or another link has been lost, the whole functional system will be disturbed in a particular way, and symptoms of disturbance of one or another higher (mental) function will have a *completely different structure, depending on the location of the damage.*"*

By thoroughly analyzing the nature of the difficulty experienced in per-

---

*From "Neuropsychology in the Local Diagnosis of Brain Damage" by A. R. Luria, *Cortex*, 1964, *1*, pp. 11-12. With permission.

forming a task such as reading, writing, or counting, one may determine the localizing significance of the observed disturbance. It was for this purpose that Luria developed his qualitative neuropsychological assessment methods. Keeping the concept of dynamic functional localization in mind, it is appropriate to turn to a functional appraisal of Luria's three blocks of the brain.

Block One

The first block of the brain (Fig. 3-2) is responsible for regulating the energy level and tone of all other portions of the cortex. In serving this regulatory function, the first block provides a stable basis for the conscious organism to organize the various other functions and processes of the brain. The regulatory functions are especially controlled by the reticular formation, the posterior hypothalamic and brainstem portions of which control the waking center of the brain. The reticular formation is responsible for the relative levels of arousal or activation found at any given time in the cortex. The first block of the brain, then, regulates consciousness, and any interruption of impulses from the first block of the brain to the cortex results in complete loss of consciousness. Injuries to the first block can result in coma or a lowering of the level of consciousness in the cortex, giving rise to confused behavior characterized by potentially bizarre associations and great difficulty in stimulus distinction. The subjective experience is not unlike alcohol- or barbiturate-induced intoxication. While involved in all processes of the brain, the first block seems especially important in the maintenance of Halstead's *P* factor.

Block Two

The second block is undoubtedly the most widely and frequently researched area of the brain. It is essentially the area posterior to the central sulcus and is composed principally of the parietal, occipital, and temporal lobes (Fig. 3-2). Most of the cognitive information processing of the brain occurs in the second block. According to Luria's conceptualization, the various areas of block two that are responsible for the analysis and encoding of specific types of stimuli (e.g., auditory in the temporal region, visual or optic in the occipital region, and kinesthetic or tactile in the parietal lobe) are each organized into three hierarchical zones. The *primary zone* of each area is responsible for sorting and recording incoming sensory organization. The *secondary zone* organizes and codes information from the primary zone. The *tertiary zone* is where data are merged from multiple sources of input and collated as the basis for organizing complex behavioral responses.

Damage to the second block of the brain produces the most specific of all behavior changes. For example, damage to the primary zone of the acoustic area of the second block may result in a loss of hearing but is highly unlikely to have any direct effect on the complex, higher mental processes of the brain. As one moves up the hierarchy of processing, however, alterations in behavior become more complex. It is within the second block of the brain that the principal information-processing functions of the brain are carried out. The brain essentially uses two methods of processing information, one a sequential, successive method and the other a method of simultaneous synthesis of information. These two modes of cognitive processing will be explored further when the work of Das is examined.

Block Three

"The third block of the brain, comprising the frontal lobes, is involved in the formation of intentions and programs for behavior" (Luria, 1970, p. 68). The frontal lobes then organize and implement conscious actions on the part of an individual. As Luria points out, the frontal lobes have no responsibility for simple sensory or motor functions. They are, however, intimately involved in every complex, higher-order behavior of humans.

The frontal lobes are also closely tied to the reticular formation and are involved in the activation and regulation of the remainder of the cortex. The frontal lobes serve an important function in regulating and focusing attention in the brain. These are important functions. It is well known that intense anxiety interferes with complex thought and behavior and can produce behavior that appears confused. As a subjective state, anxiety appears to be experienced in the frontal lobes, causing global disruptions of behavior. Violent or highly active victims of psychosis who experience hallucinations are, as a rule, intensely anxious. Treatment of such patients through the psychosurgical process of frontal lobotomy (the severing of nerve fibers between the frontal lobes and the first block of the brain, particularly the thalamus, resulting in considerable bilateral lesions to the frontal lobes) does not effectively stop hallucination or many other psychotic symptoms, but does calm the patient, apparently through reducing the intense anxiety promulgated by the psychotic symptomatology. These patients frequently become listless, however, seeming to lose their "will" to behave. The frontal lobotomy causes the loss of ability to plan, organize, and execute complex behavior functions due to the tremendous loss of communication between the third block and the other blocks of the brain.

The role of the frontal lobes in directing the attentional focus of the association areas is also an extremely important one. The direction of attention is closely related to the method by which information is processed in the brain (simultaneous or successive). Kinsbourne (1978a, b) believes that an attentional bias between hemispheres is one potential basis for hemispheric differences and specialization of processing. Attentional biases in the receipt of sensory information are well documented. These attentional biases are quite likely mediated by the frontal lobes through interaction with the first block of the brain, though the second block is where the principal processing takes place. The view of the frontal lobes as the "executive branch" of intelligence in the human brain is neither new nor unique to Luria's model. It will be recalled that Halstead (1947) considered the frontal lobes to be the central anatomical locus of intelligence. The frontal lobes play an important role in Pribram's (1971) theory of brain function (though this is not surprising since Pribram spent six months in Luria's laboratory studying patients with frontal lobe damage.) Intelligent behavior, in the Luria model, is the product of the dynamic interplay of the three blocks of the brain with activation, regulation, and planning of conscious acts falling to the frontal lobes.

Simultaneous and Successive Cognitive Processes

Simultaneous and successive cognitive processes are the two principal information-processing strategies of the second block of the brain and therefore are central to any neuropsychological theory of intelligence. These two processes seem to be deployed primarily in the secondary and tertiary zones of block two of Luria's model. Simultaneous and successive processes are neither modality- nor stimulus-specific. Any type of stimulus information can be processed through simultaneous or successive means; however, certain functions are processed much more efficiently through one process than the other. For example, language is processed at peak efficiency through successive methods; i.e., placing the elements of the composition into a linear sequence, each part of which is dependent upon its preceding component. Figure copying and solving visual analogies are examples of problems most efficiently solved through simultaneous-processing strategies.

SIMULTANEOUS PROCESSING

As described by Das, Kirby, and Jarman, 1979, "Simultaneous integration refers to the synthesis of separate elements into groups, these groups often taking on spatial overtones. The essential nature of this sort of processing is that any portion of the result is at once surveyable without dependence upon its position in the whole" (p. 49). The creation of a mental image is one excellent example of a simultaneous integration of stimuli.

In their research on simultaneous processing, Das and colleagues use a form of Raven's Matrices, a figure-copying test, and the Graham-Kendall Memory-for-Designs Test as their principal measures (anchor tests) for assessing simultaneous processing. Although the Raven is known to have a large g

factor present, it is used because "solution requires the construction of a spatial pattern or scheme. Only after such a scheme has been formed can the option which correctly completes the pattern be chosen."* Although Das has not discussed the fact that any of these tasks may be successfully completed through a successive method of processing, it is important to note this possibility for any single individual, even though each of the above tasks is undoubtedly performed most efficiently through simultaneous processing. It is also important to note that most traditional tests of spatial abilities show high correlations with simultaneous processing (Kirby & Das, 1977).

SUCCESSIVE PROCESSING

Das et al (1979) describe successive information processing as the "processing of information in a serial order. The important distinction between this type of information processing and simultaneous processing is that in successive processing the system is not totally surveyable at any point in time. Rather, a system of cues consecutively activates the components."* Successive information processing then is of a linear, sequential fashion, with information being dealt with in an interdependent serial order. The syntactical structure of language makes it a task most efficiently processed through successive methods.

Tasks used extensively in research on successive processing by Das and his colleagues are generally tests requiring the maintenance of a temporal order of input of information for the generation of an appropriate response. Examples of the most frequently employed tasks include Digit Span tests, sequential visual short-term memory tests, and serial recall tests. While it is obvious that all of these tasks are memory tests, extensive research (Das et al, 1979) indicates that these tests do not simply define a memory factor. These memory tasks all require the maintenance of a temporal order. Performance on other memory tasks not requiring the maintenance of any serial or temporal order correlate no more highly with the successive memory tasks than they correlate with g (the general ability factor believed to underlie the positive intercorrelation occurring between all cognitive measures). The various successive memory tasks correlate considerably more highly with one another than with general reasoning ability. Various competing theories of information processing have developed from the recent avalanche of research on hemispheric specialization, and it is necessary that this research be reconciled with other major neuropsychological models of intelligence wherever possible.

---

*From *Simultaneous and Successive Cognitive Processing* by J. P. Das, J. R. Kirby, and R. F. Jarman. New York: Academic Press, 1979, pp. 50 and 52. Copyright 1979 by Academic Press. With permission.

HEMISPHERIC SPECIALIZATION AND
SIMULTANEOUS AND SUCCESSIVE COGNITIVE
PROCESSES

The current literature on lateral cerebral specialization of cognitive functions is immense and no attempt will be made to review this literature here. The hemispheric specialization literature is quite complex as well and will be discussed in this section in a simplified fashion, dealing with only very general conclusions. As was recently stated at the 1980 meeting of the International Neuropsychological Society, "To say that the field of hemispheric specialization is in a state of disarray and that the results are difficult to interpret is an understatement. The field can best be characterized as chaotic" (Tomlinson-Keasey & Clarkson-Smith, 1980, p. 1). Nevertheless, research conducted mostly since 1965 or so does allow one to draw some conclusions with an adequate degree of confidence.

For the vast majority of individuals, the left cerebral hemisphere appears to be specialized for linguistic, propositional, serial, and analytic tasks and the right hemisphere for more nonverbal, spatial, appositional, synthetic, and holistic tasks (Bever, 1975; Bogen, 1969; Gazzaniga, 1970; Harnad, Doty, Goldstein, Jaynes, & Krauthamer, 1977; Kinsbourne, 1978a; Schwartz, Davidson, & Maer, 1975; Segalowitz & Gruber, 1977). One will find in the literature a large number of studies of hemispheric specialization attempting to provide anatomical localization of performance on specific, yet higher-order complex tasks. Much of the confusion in the literature stems from the apparently conflicting data of many of these studies. However, the dynamic functional localization principle of Luria, and knowledge that any specific task can be performed through any of the brain's processing modes, should give some insight into the conflicting results that appear in the literature. It is most important to remember that cerebral hemispheric asymmetries of function are *process-specific* and not *stimulus-specific*. Shure and Halstead (1959) noted early in this line of research that manipulation of stimuli was at the root of hemispheric differences, a notion that is well supported by current empirical research (e.g., Ornstein, Johnstone, Herron, & Swencionis, 1980). Bever (1975) has emphasized this point and elaborated on two modes of information processing that are of interest here due to their similarity to simultaneous and successive cognitive processes.

According to Bever (1975), cerebral asymmetries of function result from two fundamental lateralized processes: holistic and analytic processing. Lateralization of these two processes occurs, according to Bever, because these two methods of information processing are incompatible and cannot coexist in the same physical space. Analytic processing appears analogous to successive processing and is lateralized, in most individuals, to the left hemisphere. Holistic processing is analogous to simultaneous processing and is typically lateralized to the right hemisphere.

Bever (1975) has put forth four principles of neural organization to account for this localization of function that may be summarized as follows:

Statement 1. The mind is self-organizing. "[The mind] differentiates in mental space the location of analytic modes of processing from holistic modes of processing."* One will typically have two ways of organizing behavior in response to a given stimulus. "[W]e may analyze the stimulus in terms of component parts, or we may respond to the stimulus if it triggers a holistic behavioral 'template' ... a complex stimulus can itself be processed as a primitive whole or be analyzed in terms of its constituent parts and ... those processes are incompatible ... they cannot occur simultaneously in the same place."*

Statement 2. Analytical processing requires more mental activity than holistic processing. According to Bever this is "essentially a necessary truth" since the recognition of an object or other stimulus through its component parts will ultimately include recognition of the whole.

Statement 3. The dynamic mapping of mental processes onto functional brain structures is maximally simple. Essentially, Bever is asserting here that mental activities that are similar in nature tend to be represented in an anatomically parsimonious fashion and that there is enough flexibility in neural organization to allow for maximal localization of similar processes in the same area of the brain. This view is fundamental to the premise that incompatible processes cannot share the same anatomical location.

Statement 4. The left hemisphere is more adaptable at birth. Since analytical processing requires greater mental activity, it will become localized in the more adaptable or flexible hemisphere, the left hemisphere. Since analytical and holistic processing are anatomically and logically incompatible processes, holistic processing must then be lateralized to the right hemisphere. While Bever (1975) carefully explains that he does not intend to posit here that the right hemisphere is more mature at birth and during the first years of

---

*From "Cerebral Asymmetries in Humans are Due to the Differentiation of Two Incompatible Processes: Holistic and Analytic" by T.G. Bever. In D. Aaronson and R. Reiber (Eds.), *Developmental Psycholinguistics and Communication Disorders.* New York: New York Academy of Sciences, 1975, p. 252. With permission.

life, this does seem an attractive hypothesis for explaining the greater plasticity of the left hemisphere early in life. It also has numerous implications for developmental lag hypotheses of the etiology of learning disabilities. While the evidence is not totally unequivocal, there is a considerable body of literature that implicates greater maturity of the right hemisphere at birth and in the early years (Carmen & Nachson, 1973; Crowell, Jones, Kapunai, & Nakagawa, 1973; Geschwind, 1978; Giannitrapani, 1967; Reynolds & Kaufman, 1980; Seth, 1973; Woods, 1980).

Das et al (1979) do not agree that simultaneous and successive processing are represented in the right and left hemispheres, respectively, but rather believe that each mode of processing is prominently represented in each hemisphere. According to Bever's (1975) line of reasoning, this is an impossible state of affairs in the normally functioning human brain. Additionally, the hemispheric-lateralization literature is highly consistent with the notion of a successive-processing left hemisphere and simultaneous-processing right hemisphere relationship. Das et al (1979) have developed their theory exclusively on the basis of group data, yet they attempt to discredit hemispheric lateralization of cognitive processing by calling upon anecdotal individual case data. Hardly anyone would contend that hemispheric specialization for cognitive processing is the same in every single individual. However, this seems to be the requisite state of affairs for Das et al to accept the hypothesis of lateralization of simultaneous and successive processing. This hardly seems necessary. The sheer weight of evidence at present indicates that, for the vast majority of individuals, the lateralization of simultaneous and successive processes occurs as described above.

HEMISPHERICITY AND COGNITIVE PROCESSING

Hemisphericity, briefly defined, is the tendency of an individual to rely primarily upon the problem-solving or information-processing style of one or the other hemisphere in the course of normal daily functions. *It is vital to understand that hemisphericity is conceptualized as a type of dominance for an information-processing style and is independent of traditional notions of cerebral dominance and unrelated to the motorically determined lateral preference of the individual.* It is a form of dominance for a style of mentation that, if the term had not already acquired an established meaning in psychology, could be described accurately as a true cognitive style. Hemisphericity, meaning the cognitive style of the two hemispheres, has also been described as modes of consciousness (Deikman, 1971; Galin, 1974).

The notion of a dominant or preferential mode of information processing is not new. Bogen, DeZure, TenHouten, and Marsh (1972) describe the concept of hemisphericity as defined above and measure relative hemispheric dependence as a ratio of performance on appositional and propositional tasks. Das et al (1979) frequently refer to individuals who display a "habitual mode of information processing." The development of hemisphericity may occur prior to the age of 3 years, but seems well established in most children by 3½–4 years of age. A variety of studies have indicated the presence of hemisphericity in adult subjects. Hemispheric specialization has begun to replace cerebral dominance as a major concept in our understanding of brain-behavior relationships. Hemisphericity (the dominant or preferential information-processing modality of an individual) holds great promise for helping to understand both normal and dysfunctional intelligence. Normally functioning individuals appear to be able to utilize the two modes of information processing separately or in conjunction with one another and possibly shift at will depending upon the type of information to be processed (Gazzaniga, 1974, 1975), though such decisions are more likely to be made at an unconscious level in interaction between the stimuli to be processed and the direction of hemisphericity. At the highest level of function, the two modes of processing operate in a complementary manner, achieving maximal interhemispheric integration of processing or, in Bogen et al's (1972) terminology, "cerebral complementarity." For example, right-hemisphere function (simultaneous processing) is important in contributing to letter and word recognition during reading, a function handled primarily through successive processing, due to its linguistic nature, in the formative stages of learning to read. Highly skilled readers who have mastered the component skills of reading, making it an automatic function, demonstrate extensive use of both processes in reading (Cummins & Das, 1977).

When first learning to read, successive processing (left-hemisphericity) is most important and many children with difficulties in learning to read have problems with successive processing (Cummins & Das, 1977). This is also consistent with the findings of higher performance than verbal IQ in most groups of reading-disabled children discussed earlier. Performance IQ is almost certainly more closely related to the simultaneous processing of information than to successive processing while the converse relationship holds for the verbal IQ.

A variety of methods are available for measuring hemisphericity (Bogen et al, 1972; Reynolds, Kaltsounis, & Torrance, 1979; Reynolds & Kaufman, 1980; Torrance, Reynolds, & Riegel, 1977), though none are very refined at present. Nevertheless, some interesting relationships have been reported between measures of hemisphericity and cognitive outcome measures. In a blind evaluation of written scenarios of the future (using an objective scoring system developed by Torrance for use in the National Future Problem Solving Program), individuals previously classified as having right-hemisphericity versus left-hemisphericity on the basis of performance on "Your Style of Learning and Thinking" (Torrance, Reynolds, & Riegel, 1977) were compared on the eight scoring scales of the future scenarios (Torrance & Reynolds, 1978). The right-hemisphericity group significantly out-performed the left-hemisphericity group on seven of the eight scales. This had been anticipated since future scenario writing is a creative task, and creative functions seem better subserved by simultaneous-processing methods. This is probably related to the nature of simultaneous processing that makes the entire schema constantly surveyable, making the tryout of new innovations more readily surveyed for outcome and more easily and efficiently modified. Differences in hemisphericity also appear to be partially responsible for black-white IQ discrepancies observed on traditional left-hemisphere oriented intelligence tests (Reynolds & Gutkin, 1980; Reynolds, McBride, & Gibson, in press).

Much research evidence seems to suggest that traditional concepts of dominance should give way to concepts that pertain more to the dynamics of hemispheric specialization and cerebral complementarity. This is especially true since lateralization of cortical functions may be predisposed genetically (Kinsbourne, 1975) and, without specific intervention, continues essentially unaltered throughout the normal life span (Borod & Goodglass, 1980; Elias & Kinsbourne, 1974; Woodruff, 1978; Zelinski & Marsh, 1976). Hemisphericity should take its place in the research literature as a potentially powerful explanatory variable with many pragmatic implications. Although the mode of processing underlying hemisphericity is carried out in the second block of the brain, the first block is undoubtedly the decision-making center that directs and coordinates processing and is thus "in charge" of hemisphericity. Hemisphericity can be altered through trauma or training (Bever & Chiarello, 1974; Reynolds & Torrance, 1978), or by intense emotional responses, especially anxiety. When experiencing high levels of anxiety, individuals tend to lapse into a single, preferential mode of processing.

THE ROLE OF g IN NEUROPSYCHOLOGICAL MODELS OF INTELLIGENCE

It has been in vogue during the 1970s, especially as more is learned about the specialized functioning of the two human cerebral hemispheres, to dismiss the notion of g as outmoded, archaic, and/or having little pragmatic or explanatory value. The dismissal of g has been especially prominent in processing (Das et al, 1979) and componential (Sternberg, 1980) models of intelligence. Even one of the foremost authorities and proponents of intelligence testing has seen fit to relegate g to the past (Kaufman, 1979b).

Das et al (1979) devote much time to arguing against even the existence of g. These researchers have made considerable and important progress in documenting the presence of simultaneous and successive cognitive processes across a variety of ages, races, and cultures. They are able to isolate simultaneous and successive cognitive processes as orthogonal factors in each of the above groups and with separate samples of learning-retarded persons. Das et al maintain that isolation of these orthogonal factors indicates the non-viability of g. Das et al downplay the concept of "ability" as well, indicating that processing and not ability is the more correct variable for study. The study of g and the study of processing and even more specific functions of the brain must be undertaken as complementary, not exclusionary, areas of investigation.

Isolation of simultaneous and successive processes as orthogonal factors does not mean that the performance of these processes is independent of some general ability. Orthogonal isolation only indicates that the two factors can be viewed as distinct, totally separable entities. The mathematics that make this possible do not make performance on the two factors uncorrelated. The verbal and performance IQ factors of the WISC-R are easily isolated as orthogonal factors in many diverse populations (Reynolds, 1981), yet most individuals in the "real world" perform at about the same general level on the two sets of tasks. As Mulaik (1972) has pointed out, factors extracted to be orthogonal in one sample will not be orthogonal in another sample.

However, theories that dismiss g have another, more telling flaw. How can these theories account for individual differences in the level or efficiency of information processing? As Das et al (1979) have noted, mentally retarded individuals demonstrate just as much evidence for the presence of simultaneous and successive cognitive processes as do normal and even higher-functioning individuals. What differentiates these individuals is not whether they can perform cognitive processing or whether there is a "defect" in one component of their cognitive processing, but rather the level and efficiency with which they perform processing. This is what differentiates the high-average- from low-average- and superior- from very-superior-functioning individuals.

This certainly is not true for all intellectual disorders, however. There is excellent evidence at present that one cause of learning disorders is difficulty with specific types of information processing or an over-reliance on a single mode of cognitive processing. Yet the differences between normally functioning individuals with intact brains and cognitive-processing systems cannot be swept under the theoretical rug. Essentially, barring trauma or other insult, g controls the level and efficiency of cognitive processing (though almost certainly in interaction with a number of other factors) any individual is able to undertake. A careful review of the literature will find g to have many pragmatic aspects as well. For example, as Travers (1977) and Luborsky, Auerbach, Chandler, Cohen, and Bachrach (1971) point out, in study after study of psychotherapy-outcome research, the general intellectual level (tantamount to g) of the individual turns out to be the best or one of the best predictors of success. The premorbid level of general intellectual functioning is also the best predictor of rehabilitative success of patients with acute brain trauma and a number of neurological diseases (Golden, 1978).

What is the nature of g? Undoubtedly, g is determined by the particular anatomy, physiology, and chemistry of the brain of the individual. Jensen's (1978) recent research has given some revitalization to the study of g in psychology. The study of the relationship between cortical-evoked potentials and intelligence also gives rise to a physiological determination of g. Jensen's research on reaction times and stimulus complexity and the study of evoked potentials (e.g., Evans, 1977) leads one to define g in much the same terms as used by Head (1926) to describe psychological vigilance. According to Head, psychological vigilance refers to the general physiological efficiency of the central nervous system. Although the term psychological vigilance has taken on a variety of other meanings and connotations, Head's original conceptualization seems to accurately describe what is referred to here as g.

Any comprehensive theory of intelligence must not only take into account the method and components of information processing in the brain, but must also account for the ability to use the available information-processing strategies to their fullest potential. Ignoring g and its basic properties can easily lead one into such simplistic statements as Bijou's (1966) claim that there is no mental retardation only retarded behavior. This directly implies that g can be "taught" through behavior-modification techniques. We have yet to see any individual functioning in the mild, moderate, or lower range of g become a doctor, lawyer, or other successful professional even with the most rigorous behavior-modification program. g cannot be dismissed with such simplistic statements.

DISCUSSION: BIOLOGICAL AND PSYCHOLOGICAL INTELLIGENCE

Are there separate, independent mechanisms of biological and psychological intelligence? Does g represent a biological intelligence based in the physiology of the brain while psychological intelligence is represented by the executive, coordinating, and planning functions of the frontal lobes in interaction with Luria's first two blocks of the brain? The former type of intelligence would seem necessarily to be much more genetically based, though certainly dependent to some extent on the nurturance of the environment pre- and postnatally, much as is height. Psychological intelligence would be under much greater environmental control, though undoubtedly some genetic template is present giving guidance to the functional development of the various anatomical structures of the brain.

Biological intelligence, in referring to higher-order thought, represents the general physiological efficiency of the brain. Psychological intelligence is the mechanism, or processes, through which intelligence is manifest. Biological intelligence is the principal determinant of an individual's level of function, and psychological intelligence is the principal determinant of an individual's method of performing intelligent functions. The theories of Halstead, Luria, Das et al, and others referred to in this chapter are all in reality, theories of psychological intelligence. Their further elaboration will continue to enhance greatly our understanding of how the human brain carries out higher-order thinking. Discovering and elaborating the mechanisms of biological intelligence remains in a primitive state and will likely as not fall to the neurophysiologist and behavioral neurochemist for resolution.

The notion of biological and psychological intelligence briefly described here is relatively new and remains to be elaborated elsewhere in the future. New approaches to dominance such as hemisphericity or habitual modes of information processing should lead to a rich investigation of early learning in school and of school-related subjects. The reconceptualization of dominance may open a whole new era of research in the quest for the aptitude-treatment interaction. Is right- or left-hemisphericity related to performance in particular subject areas? Can accurate measures of hemisphericity be used to predict response to particular curriculum methods? A number of logical connections exist that are amenable to direct experimental investigation. It is not unlikely that an overdependence on right-hemisphere processing will be found to be associated with difficulties in early reading acquisition. Other logical hypotheses associated with the model presented here are outlined by Hartlage and Reynolds (Chapter 11).

It should be clear that level of function, as denoted by g, must be included in any comprehensive theory of the human intellect. Psychological intelligence appears to be best described at present by Luria's model of the three blocks of the brain as elaborated upon by Das et al (1979) and modified here to account for the lateralization of processing in the brain. As new, better, comprehensive measures of psychological intelligence are developed (e.g., Kaufman & Kaufman, in press), our understanding of brain function will increase and our theories will need modification. However, it is through the use of new techniques of measurement based on current theories of intelligence that understanding will come most readily. Perhaps through such methods, the neuropsychologist, the developmentalist, and the psychometrician, all with interests in the origins and development of intelligence, will be able to coalesce their now divergent views of intelligence. Certainly, each has a unique, significant view to contribute to our ultimate understanding of how the human brain processes information.

REFERENCES

Anderson, M., Kaufman, A. S., & Kaufman, N. L. Use of the WISC-R with a learning disabled population: Some diagnostic implications. *Psychology in the Schools*, 1976, *13*, 381–386.

Annett, M. The distribution of manual asymmetry. *British Journal of Psychology*, 1972, *63*, 343–358.

Balow, I. H. Lateral dominance characteristics and reading achievement in the first grade. *Journal of Psychology*, 1963, *55*, 323–328.

Balow, I. H., & Balow, B. Lateral dominance and reading achievement in second grade. *American Educational Research Journal*, 1964, *1*, 139–143.

Bauer, R. W., & Wepman, J. M. Lateralization of cerebral function. *Journal of Speech and Hearing Disorders*, 1955, *20*, 171–177.

Belmont, C., & Birch, H. Lateral dominance, lateral awareness, and reading disability. *Child Development*, 1963, *34*, 257–270.

Benton, A. L. Right–left discrimination and finger localization in defective children. *Archives of Neurology and Psychiatry*, 1955, *74*, 583–589.

Benton, A. L. *Right–left discrimination and finger localization development and pathology*. New York: Hoeber Medical Division, Harper & Row, 1959.

Bever, T. G. Cerebral asymmetries in humans are due to the differentiation of two incompatible processes: Holistic and analytic. In D. Aaronson & R. Reiber (Eds.), *Developmental psycholinguistics and communication disorders*. New York: New York Academy of Sciences, 1975.

Bever, T. G., & Chiarello, R. S. Cerebral dominance in musicians and nonmusicians. *Science*, 1974, *186*, 537–539.

Bijou, S. W. A functional analysis of retarded development. In N. R. Ellis (Ed.), *International review of mental retardation* (Vol. 1). New York: Academic Press, 1966.

Bogen, J. E. The other side of the brain: Parts I, II, and III. *Bulletin of the Los Angeles Neurological Society*, 1969, *34*, 73–105, 135–162, 191–203.

Bogen, J. E., DeZure, R., TenHouten, W., & Marsh, J. The other side of the brain IV: The A/P ratio. *Bulletin of the Los Angeles Neurological Society*, 1972, *37*, 49–61.

Boklage, C. E. On cellular mechanisms for heritably transmitting structural information. *The Behavioral and Brain Sciences*, 1978, *2*, 282–286.

Borod, J. C., & Goodglass, H. Lateralization of linguistic and melodic processing with age. *Neuropsychologia*, 1980, *18*, 79–83.

Broca, P. Remarques sur le siége de la faculté du language articulé, suivies d'une observation d'aphémie (perte de la parole). *Bulletins de la Societé Anatomique*, 1861, *6*, 330–357.

Broca, P. Localisation des functions cérébrales. Siége du language articulé. *Bulletins de la Societé d'Anthropologie de Paris*, 1863, *4*, 200–203.

Buzzard, T. *Clinical lectures on diseases of the nervous system.* London: Churchill, 1882.

Carmen, A., & Nachson, I. Ear asymmetry in perception of emotional nonverbal stimuli. *Acta Psychologica*, 1973, *37*, 351–357.

Coleman, R. I., & Deutsch, C. P. Lateral dominance and right–left discrimination: A comparison of normal and retarded readers. *Perceptual and Motor Skills*, 1964, *19*, 43–50.

Corballis, M. C., & Beale, I. L. *The psychology of left and right.* Hillsdale, N.J.: Lawrence Erlbaum Associates, 1976.

Cornish, R. D. Effects of neurological training on psychomotor abilities of kindergarten children. *Journal of Experimental Education*, 1970, *39*, 15–19.

Crowell, D., Jones, J., Kapunai, L., & Nakagawa, J. Unilateral cortical activity in newborn humans. *Science*, 1973, *180*, 205–208.

Cummins, J., & Das, J. P. Cognitive processing and reading difficulties: A framework for research. *Alberta Journal of Educational Research*, 1977, *23*, 245–256.

Das, J. P., Kirby, J. R., & Jarman, R. F. *Simultaneous and successive cognitive processes.* New York: Academic Press, 1979.

Dean, R. S. Cerebral laterality and verbal-performance discrepancies in intelligence. *Journal of School Psychology*, 1979, *17*, 145–150.

Dean, R. S., & Kulhavy, R. W. *Dean-Kulhavy lateral preference schedule.* Tempe, Az.: Arizona State University (Author), 1977.

Deikman, A. J. Bimodal consciousness. *Archives of General Psychiatry*, 1971, *25*, 481–489.

Delacato, C. H. *The treatment and prevention of reading problems: The neuropsychological approach.* Springfield, Il.: Charles C Thomas, 1959.

Delacato, C. H. *The diagnosis and treatment of speech and reading problems.* Springfield, Il.: Charles C Thomas, 1963.

Delacato, C. H. *Neurological organization and reading.* Springfield, Il.: Charles C Thomas, 1966.

Dewson, J. H. Preliminary evidence of hemispheric asymmetry of auditory function in monkeys. In S. Harnad, R. Doty, L. Goldstein, J. Jaynes, & G. Krauthamer (Eds.), *Lateralization in the nervous system.* New York: Academic Press, 1977.

Elias, M. F., & Kinsbourne, M. Age and sex differences in the processing of verbal and nonverbal stimuli. *Journal of Gerontology*, 1974, *29*, 162–171.

Evans, J. R. Evoked potentials and learning disabilities. In L. Tarnopol & M.

Tarnopol (Eds.), *Brain function and reading disabilities.* Baltimore: University Park Press, 1977.

Fuller, J. L. If genes are not right handed, what is? *The Behavioral and Brain Sciences,* 1978, *2,* 295.

Galin, D. Implications for psychiatry of left and right cerebral specialization. *Archives of General Psychiatry,* 1974, *31,* 78–82.

Gazzaniga, M. S. *The bisected brain.* New York: Appleton, 1970.

Gazzaniga, M. S. Changing hemisphere dominance by changing reward probabilities in split-brain monkeys. *Experimental Neurology,* 1971, *33,* 412–419.

Gazzaniga, M. S. Cerebral dominance viewed as a decision system. In S. Dimond & J. Beaumont (Eds.), *Hemisphere functions in the human brain.* London: Halstead Press, 1974.

Gazzaniga, M. S. Recent research on hemispheric lateralization of the human brain: Review of the split-brain. *UCLA Educator,* May 1975, 9–12.

Geffen, G. Human laterality: Cerebral dominance and handedness. *The Behavioral and Brain Sciences,* 1978, *2,* 295–296.

Geschwind, N. Pathological right-handedness. *The Behavioral and Brain Sciences,* 1978, *2,* 296.

Giannitrapani, D. Developing concepts of lateralization of cerebral functions. *Cortex,* 1967, *3,* 353–370.

Glass, G. V., & Robbins, M. P. A critique of experiments on the role of neurological organization in reading performance. *Reading Research Quarterly,* 1967, *3,* 5–52.

Golden, C. J. *Diagnosis and rehabilitation in clinical neuropsychology.* Springfield, Il.: Charles C Thomas, 1978.

Golden, C. J. Personal communication, 1980.

Golden, C. J., Purisch, A. D., & Hammeke, T. A. *The Luria-Nebraska neuropsychological test battery: A manual for clinical and experimental uses.* Lincoln: The University of Nebraska Press, 1979.

Halstead, W. C. *Brain and intelligence.* Chicago: University of Chicago Press, 1947.

Hardyck, C., & Petrinovich, L. F. Left-handedness. *Psychological Bulletin,* 1977, *84,* 385–404.

Hardyck, C., Petrinovich, L. F., & Goldman, R. D. Left-handedness and cognitive deficit. *Cortex,* 1976, *12,* 266–279.

Harnad, S., Doty, R. W., Goldstein, L., Jaynes, J., & Krauthamer, G. (Eds.). *Lateralization in the nervous system.* New York: Academic Press, 1977.

Harris, L. J. Left-handedness: Early theories, facts, and fancies. In J. Herron (Ed.), *Neuropsychology of left-handedness.* New York: Academic Press, 1980.

Head, H. *Aphasia and kindred disorders of speech* (Vol. 1). New York: MacMillan, 1926.

Held, R. Plasticity in sensory-motor systems. *Scientific American,* 1965, *213,* 84–94.

Held, R., & Bossom, J. Neonatal deprivation and adult rearrangement: Complementary techniques for analyzing plastic sensory-motor coordination. *Journal of Comparative and Physiological Psychology,* 1961, *54,* 33-37.

Held, R., & Freedman, J. Plasticity in human sensory-motor control. *Science,* 1963, *142,* 455-462.

Held, R., & Hein, A. Movement-produced stimulation in the development of visually guided behavior. *Journal of Comparative and Physiological Psychology,* 1963, *56,* 872-876.

Herron, J. (Ed.). *Neuropsychology of left-handedness.* New York: Academic Press, 1980.

Hevern, V. W. Recent validity studies of the Halstead-Reitan approach to clinical neuropsychological assessment. A critical review. *Clinical Neuropsychology,* 1980, *2,* 49-61.

Hillerich, R. L. Eye-hand dominance and reading achievement. *American Educational Research Journal,* 1964, *1,* 121-126.

Hunt, J. McV. *Intelligence and experience.* New York: Ronald Press, 1961.

Jensen, A. R. *"g"–Outmoded concept or unconquered frontier?* Invited address to the annual meeting of the American Psychological Association, New York, September, 1978.

Johnson, J. D., & Gazzaniga, M. S. Some effects of non-reinforcement in split-brain monkeys. *Physiology and Behavior,* 1971, *6,* 703-706.(a)

Johnson, J. D., & Gazzaniga, M. S. Reversal behavior in split-brain monkeys. *Physiology and Behavior,* 1971, *6,* 706-709.(b)

Joynt, R. J., & Benton, A. L. The memoir of Marc Dax on aphasia. *Neurology, Minneapolis,* 1964, *14,* 851-854.

Kaufman, A. S. Personal communication, 1978.

Kaufman, A. S. *Intelligent testing with the WISC-R.* New York: Wiley-Interscience, 1979.(a)

Kaufman, A. S. Cerebral specialization and intelligence testing. *Journal of Research and Development in Education,* 1979, *12,* 96-107.(b)

Kaufman, A. S., & Kaufman, N. L. *Kaufman Assessment Battery for Children.* Circle Pines, Mn.: American Guidance Services, in press.

Kinsbourne, M. The ontogeny of cerebral dominance. In A. Aaronson & R. Reiber (Eds.), *Developmental psycholinguistics and communication disorders.* New York: New York Academy of Sciences, 1975.

Kinsbourne, M. Biological determinants of functional bisymmetry and asymmetry. In M. Kinsbourne (Ed.), *Asymmetrical function of the brain.* Cambridge: Cambridge University Press, 1978.(a)

Kinsbourne, M. Evolution of language in relation to lateral action. In M. Kinsbourne (Ed.), *Asymmetrical function of the brain.* Cambridge: Cambridge University Press, 1978.(b)

Kirby, J. R., & Das, J. P. Reading achievement, IQ, and simultaneous-successive processing. *Journal of Educational Psychology,* 1977, *69,* 564-570.

Kirby, J. R., & Das, J. P. Information processing and human abilities. *Journal of Educational Psychology,* 1978, *70,* 58-66.

LeMay, M. Morphological cerebral asymmetries of modern man, fossil man, and nonhuman primate. *Annals of the New York Academy of Sciences,* 1976, *280,* 349–366.

Levine, M. D., Brooks, R., & Shonkoff, J. P. *A pediatric approach to learning disorders.* New York: John Wiley & Sons, 1980.

Levy, J., & Nagylaki, T. A model for the genetics of handedness. *Genetics,* 1972, *72,* 117–128.

Luborsky, L., Auerbach, A. H., Chandler, M., Cohen, J., & Bachrach, H. M. Factors influencing the outcome of psychotherapy: A review of quantitative research. *Psychological Bulletin,* 1971, *75,* 145–185.

Luria, A. R. *The role of speech in the regulation of normal and abnormal behavior.* Oxford: Pergamon Press, 1961.

Luria, A. R. Neuropsychology in the local diagnosis of brain damage. *Cortex,* 1964, *1,* 3–18.

Luria, A. R. *Higher cortical functions in man.* New York: Basic Books, 1966.

Luria, A. R. *Cerebral organization of conscious acts: A frontal lobe function.* Speech to the 19th International Congress of Psychology, London, England, 1969.

Luria, A. R. The functional organization of the brain. *Scientific American,* 1970, *222,* 66–78.

Luria, A. R. *The working brain.* London: Penguin, 1973.

Milner, B., Branch, C., & Rasmussen, T. Observations on cerebral dominance. In A. V. S. de Rueck & M. O'Conner (Eds.), *Ciba Foundation Symposium on disorders of language,* London: Churchill, 1964.

Morgan, M. J., & Corballis, M. C. On the biological basis of human laterality: II. The mechanisms of inheritance. *The Behavioral and Brain Sciences,* 1978, *2,* 270–277.

Mulaik, S. A. *The foundations of factor analysis.* New York: McGraw-Hill, 1972.

Naylor, H. Reading disability and lateral asymmetry: An information processing analysis. *Psychological Bulletin,* 1980, *87,* 531–545.

Newcombe, F., & Ratcliff, G. Handedness, speech lateralization and ability. *Neuropsychologia,* 1973, *11,* 399–407.

Noble, J. Paradoxical interocular transfer of mirror-image discrimination in the optic chiasm sectioned monkey. *Brain Research,* 1968, *10,* 127–151.

O'Donnell, D. A., & Eisenson, J. Delacato training for reading achievement and visual-motor integration. *Journal of Learning Disabilities,* 1969, *2,* 441–447.

Ornstein, R., Johnstone, J., Herron, J., & Swencionis, C. Differential right hemisphere engagement in visuospatial tasks. *Neuropsychologia,* 1980, *18,* 49–64.

Orton, S. T. "Word-blindness" in school children. *Archives of Neurology and Psychiatry,* 1925, *14,* 581.

Orton, S. T. A physiological theory of reading disability and stuttering in children. *New England Journal of Medicine,* 1928, *199,* 1046–1052.

Orton, S. T. Special disability in reading. *Bulletin of the Neurological Institute of New York*, 1931, *1*, 159–162.

Orton, S. T. *Reading, writing, and speech problems in children.* New York: Norton, 1937.

Parsons, O. A., & Prigatano, G. P. Methodological considerations in clinical neuropsychological research. *Journal of Consulting and Clinical Psychology*, 1978, *46*, 608–619.

Penfield, W., & Roberts, L. *Speech and brain mechanisms.* Princeton: Princeton University Press, 1959.

Peters, M., & Durding, B. M. Handedness measured by finger tapping: A continuous variable. *Canadian Journal of Psychology*, 1978, *32*, 257–261.

Pribram, K. H. *Languages of the brain.* Englewood Cliffs: Prentice-Hall, 1971.

Reitan, R. M. Certain differential effects of left and right cerebral lesions in human adults. *Journal of Comparative and Physiological Psychology*, 1955, *48*, 474–477.

Reitan, R. M. Psychological deficits resulting from cerebral lesions in man. In J. M. Warren & K. Akert (Eds.), *The frontal granular cortex and behavior.* New York: McGraw-Hill, 1964.(a)

Reitan, R. M. Relationships between neurological and psychological variables and their implications for reading instruction. In K. A. Robinson (Ed.), *Meeting individual differences in reading.* Chicago: University of Chicago Press, 1964.(b)

Reitan, R. M. A research program on the psychological effects of brain lesions in human beings. In N. R. Ellis (Ed.), *International review of research in mental retardation.* New York: Academic Press, 1966.

Reitan, R. M. Assessment of brain–behavior relationships. In P. McReynolds (Ed.), *Advances in psychological assessment, Vol. III,* San Francisco: Jossey-Bass, 1975.

Reitan, R. M., & Davison, L. A. (Eds.). *Clinical neuropsychology: Current status and applications.* Washington, D.C.: V. H. Winston, 1974.

Reynolds, C. R. *Current conceptualizations of hemisphericity.* Colloquium presented to the Department of Educational Psychology, the University of Texas–Austin, Austin, Tx., April, 1978.

Reynolds, C. R. *The neuropsychology of intelligence and a reconceptualization of dominance.* Invited address to the Utah State University conference on Brain Research and Teaching, Logan, Ut., August, 1980.(a)

Reynolds, C. R. Differential construct validity of a preschool battery for Blacks, Whites, males, and females. *Journal of School Psychology*, 1980, *18*, 112–125.(b)

Reynolds, C. R. The problem of bias in psychological assessment. In C. R. Reynolds & T. B. Gutkin (Eds.), *The handbook of school psychology.* New York: John Wiley & Sons, 1981.

Reynolds, C. R., & Gutkin, T. B. Predicting the premorbid intellectual status of children using demographic data. *Clinical Neuropsychology*, 1979, *1*, 36–38.

Reynolds, C. R., & Gutkin, T. B. *Intellectual performance of Blacks and Whites matched on four demographic variables: A multivariate analysis.* Paper presented to the annual meeting of the American Psychological Association, Montreal, September, 1980.

Reynolds, C. R., Hartlage, L. C., & Haak, R. *Lateral preference as determined by neuropsychological performance and aptitude/achievement discrepancies.* Paper presented to the annual meeting of the American Psychological Association, Montreal, September, 1980.

Reynolds, C. R., Kaltsounis, W., & Torrance, E. P. A children's form of "Your Style of Learning and Thinking": Preliminary norms and technical data. *Gifted Child Quarterly,* 1979, *23,* 757–767.

Reynolds, C. R., & Kaufman, A. S. Lateral eye movement behavior in children. *Perceptual and Motor Skills,* 1980, *50,* 1023–1037.

Reynolds, C. R., McBride, R. D., & Gibson, L. J. Black-White IQ discrepancies may be related to differences in hemisphericity. *Contemporary Educational Psychology,* in press.

Reynolds, C. R., & Torrance, E. P. Perceived changes in styles of learning and thinking (hemisphericity) through direct and indirect training. *Journal of Creative Behavior,* 1978, *12,* 247–252.

Robbins, M. P. A study of the validity of Delacato's theory of neurological organization. *Exceptional Children,* 1966, *32,* 517–523.

Sattler, J. M. *Assessment of children's intelligence and special abilities.* Boston: Allyn and Bacon, 1981, in press.

Schwartz, G. E., Davidson, R. J., & Maer, F. Right hemisphere lateralization for emotion in the human brain: Interactions with cognition. *Science,* 1975, *190,* 286–288.

Segalowitz, S. J., & Gruber, F. A. (Eds.). *Language development and neurological theory.* New York: Academic Press, 1977.

Seth, G. Eye-hand coordination and handedness: A developmental study of visuo-motor behaviour in infancy. *British Journal of Educational Psychology,* 1973, *43,* 35–49.

Shure, G. H., & Halstead, W. C. Cerebral lateralization of individual processes. *Psychological Monographs: General and Applied,* 1959, *72,* No. 12.

Smith, M. D., Coleman, J. M., Dokecki, P. R., & Davis, E. E. Intellectual characteristics of school labeled learning disabled children. *Exceptional Children,* 1977, *43,* 352–357.

Sternberg, R. J. *Factor theories of intelligence are allright almost.* Paper presented to the annual meeting of the American Educational Research Association, Boston, April, 1980.

Swiercinsky, D. P. Factorial pattern description and comparison of functional abilities in neuropsychological assessment. *Perceptual and Motor Skills,* 1979, *48,* 231–241.

Tomlinson-Keasey, C., & Clarkson-Smith, L. *What develops in hemispheric specialization?* Paper presented to the annual meeting of the International Neuropsychological Society, San Francisco, February, 1980.

Torrance, E. P., & Reynolds, C. R. Images of the future of gifted adolescents: Effects of alienation and specialized cerebral functioning. *Gifted Child Quarterly,* 1978, *22,* 40–54.

Torrance, E. P., Reynolds, C. R., & Riegel, T. R. Your style of learning and thinking, Forms A and B: Preliminary norms, abbreviated technical notes, scoring keys, and selected references. *Gifted Child Quarterly,* 1977, *21,* 563–573.

Travers, R. M. W. *Essentials of learning* (4th ed.). New York: MacMillan, 1977.

Warren, J. M., & Nonneman, A. J. The search for cerebral dominance in monkeys. *Annals of the New York Academy of Sciences,* 1976, *280,* 732–744.

Wheeler, L., & Reitan, R. M. The presence and laterality of brain damage predicted from responses to a short aphasia screening test. *Perceptual and Motor Skills,* 1962, *15,* 783–799.

White, M. J. Laterality differences in perception: A review. *Psychological Bulletin,* 1969, *72,* 387–405.

Witelson, S. W. Neuroanatomical asymmetry in left-handers. In J. Herron (Ed.), *Neuropsychology of left-handedness.* New York: Academic Press, 1980.

Woo, T. L., & Pearson, K. Dextrality and sinistrality of hand and eye. *Biometrika,* 1927, *19,* 165–169.

Woodruff, D. S. Brain activity and development. In P. B. Bates (Ed.), *Life-span development and behavior* (Vol. 1). New York: Academic Press, 1978.

Woods, B. T. The restricted effects of right-hemisphere lesions after age one: Wechsler test data. *Neuropsychologia,* 1980, *18,* 65–70.

Zelinski, E. M., & Marsh, G. R. *Age differences in hemispheric processing of verbal and spatial information.* Paper presented to the annual meeting of the American Psychological Association, Washington, September, 1976.

Zingale, S. A., & Smith, M. D. WISC-R patterns for learning disabled children at three SES levels. *Psychology in the Schools,* 1978, *15,* 199–204.

Marcel Kinsbourne
Merrill Hiscock

4

Cerebral Lateralization and Cognitive Development: Conceptual and Methodological Issues

Education's connection with cerebral lateralization predates the current popularity of the topic. During the 1920s and 1930s, Samuel Orton (1937) promulgated a theory relating a number of language disabilities in children to failure of the dominant hemisphere to achieve functional superiority. Orton's formulation, which was to have immense influence on the theory and practice of special education, proposed that an engram, or physiological representation of a stimulus, is established simultaneously in both cerebral hemispheres. Since the two homologous engrams were thought to be oppositely oriented, i.e., to be mirror images of each other, incomplete suppression of the engram in the nondominant hemisphere supposedly resulted in interhemispheric rivalry which, in turn, led to confusion and inconsistent performance. Thus, developmental language disabilities (termed strephosymbolia, or "twisted symbols") were linked to incomplete left-hemispheric or right-

This chapter is modified from "Cerebral Lateralization and Cognitive Development" by M. Kinsbourne and M. Hiscock. In the Seventy-seventh Yearbook of the National Society for the Study of Education, Part II, entitled *Education and the Brain,* edited by J. S. Chall and A. F. Mirsky. Chicago: The University of Chicago Press, 1978. Copyright 1978 by the National Society for the Study of Education. With permission of the Society.

Preparation of this chapter was supported by the Medical Research Council of Canada through individual grants to author Kinsbourne and author Hiscock.

hemispheric dominance. Orton drew a parallel between the language problems in children with incomplete cerebral dominance and the consequences of damage to the "master" hemisphere in adults. The symptoms of children with developmental strephosymbolia mimicked the symptoms of brain-damaged adults with acquired strephosymbolia (though, in the case of the children, the underlying mechanism was physiological dysfunction rather than damage to the structure of the brain).

Orton's (1937) model still influences education, although the passage of time has diminished its visibility within the educational research literature. Extreme views regarding incomplete lateralization and its remediation have been discredited and seem to be gradually diminishing in popularity (Glass & Robbins, 1967). Nevertheless, belief in an intimate link between cerebral lateralization and cognitive performance persists (e.g., Knights & Bakker, 1976). As Critchley (1970, p. 66) phrased it, "Although this over-simple hypothesis [i.e., Orton's] might not find favour in contemporary thinking, the underlying notion of imperfect cerebral dominance is still acceptable today as one factor of importance [in explaining reading disability]."

LEARNING DISABILITY AND LATERALITY: THE EMPIRICAL BASIS

Many investigators have sought to establish a statistical association between learning disability and some observable characteristic thought to be related to cerebral dominance.

Vernon (1957) notes that, "No other symptom associated with dyslexia has attracted more attention than has defective *lateralization*; that is to say, the apparent failure to establish superior skill in one or the other hand, or to show strong preference for using one hand rather than the other in performing skilled tasks" (p. 138). Despite the attention afforded handedness, the findings are inconclusive (T. T. S. Ingram & Reid, 1956; Vernon, 1957, 1971; Zangwill, 1962). Many authors have reported an elevated incidence of left-handedness among dyslexic children. Others have reported a high incidence of "weak lateralization," or ambidexterity. In fact, reported incidence rates for left-handedness or mixed-handedness (ambidexterity) in samples of learning-disabled children occasionally have reached 75 percent, although most investigators report far more modest statistics. Thus, even though the incidence rates vary markedly, there are numerous claims that deviation from firmly established right-handedness is more common among poor readers than among normal readers. There also are numerous findings that conflict with those claims. Since it is not uncommon among university students (Annett, 1970), ambidexterity per se cannot imply cognitive deficit. Especially in the more recent literature, direct comparisons of poor readers and controls frequently fail to reveal any difference in the incidence of left-handedness or strength of handedness (Balow, 1963; Belmont & Birch, 1965; Clark, 1970; De Hirsh, Jansky, & Langford, 1966; Lyle, 1969; Malmquist, 1958; Rutter, Tizard, & Witmore, 1970).

Many authors, including Orton, have emphasized the consistency of handedness, footedness, and eyedness rather than handedness alone. Orton (1937) considered the risk of strephosymbolia to be no greater for strong left-handers than for strong right-handers. The child at risk was the one with mixed dominance.

Left-eyedness is far more common than left-handedness. In terms of eye preference for sighting, about 30 percent of normal children and adults can be classified as consistently left-eyed (Porac & Coren, 1976). Since no more than 10 percent of the population is left-handed (Hardyck & Petrinovich, 1977; Hicks & Kinsbourne, 1976; Vernon, 1971), many people must be left-eyed but right-handed. On the basis of their number alone, we would expect most to be free of learning disabilities. However, this group (as well as left-handers who sight with their right eye) might be at greater risk than the rest of the population.

Extensive research into the relationship between eyedness and learning disabilities has failed to produce a consensus (Porac & Coren, 1976; Vernon, 1971; Zangwill, 1962). As with deviation from right-handedness, several studies report that deviation from right-eyedness is associated with learning disabilities. Still more studies report that inconsistency between eyedness and handedness (crossed dominance, or mixed dominance) is associated with some form of learning problem. Again, however, many other studies, especially relatively recent ones, show no relationship between eyedness or crossed dominance and learning disabilities (e.g., Balow, 1963; Belmont & Birch, 1965; Coleman & Deutch, 1964; Harris, 1957).

In recent years, attention has shifted from handedness and eyedness to perceptual asymmetries. The study of listening asymmetries, in particular, seemed to be a safe, convenient, and relatively direct means of determining the manner in which speech perception is lateralized in normal and abnormal populations of children and adults (Kimura, 1961a,b; 1963). The technique, called dichotic listening, involves the simultaneous presentation of competing sounds to the two ears. A right-ear superiority for speech sounds is thought to reflect left-hemispheric representation of language. Visual asymmetries also can be obtained if stimuli are flashed briefly to the right or left of fixation (Bryden, 1965; Kimura, 1966; White, 1969). In this case, a right visual half-field superiority for linguistic material is thought to reflect left lateralization of language.

Satz (1976) reviewed 19 studies of perceptual tasks – dichotic listening in most cases—in relation to reading disabilities. Their results were as variable and as incoherent as the handedness and eyedness studies. Satz points out that very few of the studies actually show reduced asymmetry in the learning-disabled group. Mostly, both the learning-disabled children and their controls showed a significant right-ear advantage; in other cases, neither group showed a right-ear advantage (see also Hynd, Obrzut, Weed, & Hynd, 1979). In one visual hemifield study the learning-disabled children actually exhibited a greater mean right-sided advantage than controls (Yeni-Komshian, Isenberg, & Goldberg, 1975). It seems that, even with the aid of modern behavioral techniques, the literature still fails to answer the question of whether reading disabilities, or any other learning disabilities, are linked to anomalous lateralization.

Why has a seemingly straightforward problem proven so intractable? As usual, methodological criticisms may be put forth. Handedness has been defined in various ways, some of which are questionable; there are pitfalls to be avoided in measuring eyedness; dichotic listening and tachistoscopic (visual) tasks may vary along several dimensions; different populations of children have been sampled; sample sizes vary markedly across studies. It is interesting to note that relationships between anomalous laterality and poor reading are often found in clinical studies but not in studies of entire populations of normal children (Yule & Rutter, 1976). Also, it could be that one subtype of reading disability features a right-sided advantage and another does not. If so, different studies might diverge because of sampling variability across subtypes. Pirozzolo and Rayner (1979) have reported exactly such findings in visual half-field viewing with respect to visuospatial and linguistic dyslexics, respectively (cf., the language and the sequencing deficits isolated by Kinsbourne & Warrington, 1963).

The methodological problems, however, are only symptoms of more fundamental problems at the conceptual level. Developing a better handedness questionnaire, increasing sample sizes, or measuring reading skill with greater precision are not likely to resolve the question of whether cerebral lateralization and reading ability are related in some manner. We first should sharpen our understanding of the question we hope to answer and the various implications of that question. Does the question make sense? Are the concepts sufficiently clear? Can the concepts be operationalized? What are we assuming when we ask the question?

THREE BASIC ASSUMPTIONS

Underlying the diverse theoretical positions, experimental methodologies, and criteria for selecting subjects, three assumptions are explicit or implicit in nearly all studies of lateralization and learning disability.

First, postulating a relationship between cognitive performance and cerebral lateralization implies that one can specify what is meant by cerebral lateralization. In practice, a variety of operations have been used to define the presence or degree of lateralization. Is handedness equivalent to lateralization? Is a composite index of handedness, eyedness, and footedness a better measure? Does a right-sided advantage in a perceptual task define language lateralization? Does the concept of *degree* of cerebral lateralization have any meaning?

Second, it is commonly taken for granted that the most prevalent pattern of cerebral organization (i.e., left lateralization of language) is optimal, and that deviations from that norm imply some impairment of function. Thus, left-handedness—which until recently was thought to indicate cerebral specialization in mirror image to right-handers' pattern—frequently has been regarded as contributing to cognitive inefficiency (Critchley, 1964; Kinsbourne & Caplan, 1979).

Third, the rationale for almost all studies in this area and for their interpretation rests squarely on the assumption that lateralization develops ontogenetically. Thus, learning-disabled children are expected to be slow to lateralize. Or, to cite a more complex model, clear-cut lateralization has been claimed to be disadvantageous at one level of development and advantageous at a subsequent level (Bakker, 1973).

WHAT IS LATERALIZATION? HOW IS IT MEASURED?

Definitions

Lateralization may be inferred from results of diverse laterality testing, or the term may be used to refer to a specific behavioral characteristic such as degree of hand preference (Satz, 1976). When applied to specific characteristics, the term is often used in connection with dissimilar operational definitions. Thus, a child may be identified as strongly lateralized on the basis of consistent handedness, footedness, and eyedness or on the basis of marked right-ear superiority in dichotic listening. If the two sets of measures are in agreement, then there may be justification for referring to both as measures of lateralization. But what can one say about lateralization when there is strong right-sided hand, foot, and sighting preference, but left-ear superiority in dichotic listening?

The first problem then, is the ambiguity inherent in common usages of the term lateralization. In attempting to answer questions about the relationship between cerebral lateralization and learning disability, it makes a difference whether one defines lateralization as, say, hand preference or whether one regards lateralization as a property of the brain that cannot be fully measured by any one operation. A further distinction can be made between those who regard lateralization in the brain as having topographical implications only, and those who follow Orton in supposing that the more specialized hemisphere, to which a function is *lateralized,* is also *dominant* in that it successfully competes with (suppresses, inhibits) homologous areas in the other hemisphere that also have the potential to act as substrate for the functions in question. Some indirect evidence for the latter proposition, at least with respect to language, was advanced by Kinsbourne (1974). But the simpler topographical issue itself is so problematical that it is impossible to tell whether the hypothesized contralateral inhibition develops according to the same rules as the lateralized skill itself.

Handedness and Cerebral Lateralization

Today the relationship between the preferred hand and the linguistic cerebral hemisphere is well documented. A hundred years worth of case reports linking side of brain damage and incidence of aphasia (disruption of language) indicates that the great majority — more than 98 percent — of right-handers are left-lateralized for language (Zangwill, 1967). A similar conclusion can be drawn from the results of sodium amobarbitol testing. This procedure (the Wada technique) involves injection of a fast-acting barbituate into the arterial system supplying one side of the cerebrum (Wada & Rasmussen, 1960). The drug incapacitates most of one cerebral hemisphere for a few minutes. Left-sided injections, but not right-sided injections, temporarily impair linguistic functioning in more than 95 percent of right-handers (Rasmussen & Milner, 1975; Rossi & Rosadini, 1967). Therefore, virtually all right-handers are left-lateralized for speech. Left-handers, however, are heterogeneous in speech representation. The aphasia data and results of sodium amobarbitol testing suggest that as many as two thirds of left-handers have left-lateralized speech (Annett, 1975; Ettlinger, Jackson, & Zangwill, 1956; Gloning, Gloning, Haub, & Quatember, 1969; Goodglass & Quadfasel, 1954; Hécaen & Piercy, 1956; Hécaen & Sauget, 1971; Humphrey & Zangwill, 1952; Luria, 1970; Penfield & Roberts, 1959; Rasmussen & Milner, 1975; Roberts, 1969; Rossi & Rosadini, 1967; Russell & Espir, 1961), that is, their speech processor is not contralateral to the dominant hand. Most of the remaining left-handers are right-lateralized for speech, but a minority have some capacity for speech in both hemispheres (Rasmussen & Milner, 1975).

What, exactly, does hand preference tell us about brain organization? It is virtually certain that right-handers have their speech represented in the left cerebral hemisphere. If an adult uses the right hand for everyday unimanual activities (e.g., eating with a spoon, throwing a ball, brushing the teeth), there is only a slight chance that that person's speech is represented anywhere but in the left hemisphere. We have argued elsewhere (Kinsbourne & Hiscock, 1977) that this holds for children as well as for adults. However, if the person shows a preference for the left hand, no safe statement about speech lateralization can be made. Left-hemispheric representation of speech is still most likely, but the odds are only slightly greater than even. Thus, there is only a weak statistical association between hand preference and the likelihood of left-hemispheric speech representation. Apart from the possibility of less-compete lateralization in at least some left-handers, there is no convincing evidence that handedness is related to *degree* of lateralization (Conrad, 1949; Goodglass & Quadfasel, 1954; Hécaen & Piercy, 1956; Rasmussen & Milner, 1975; Zangwill, 1960). This is the very assumption that was made by Orton (1937) and that is implicit in many contemporary viewpoints; that the degree of behavioral asymmetry or "sidedness" reflects the degree to which language is lateralized.

Orton (1937) emphasized the significance of eyedness and, to a lesser degree, footedness—as well as handedness—in the assessment of right- or left-sidedness. In the current era of dichotic listening and tachistoscopic procedures, asymmetrical performance on these tasks can be added to the more traditional indices of sidedness. Sidedness might be defined as the degree of asymmetry on a single measure (e.g., degree of handedness), the concordance among different measures (i.e., the number of these procedures yielding a right-sided preference or superiority), or as some combination of degree of asymmetry on individual tasks and degree of intertask concordance.

Assessing Handedness

The measurement of handedness is not a clear-cut matter. Handedness can be conceived of either as hand preference or as a difference between the hands in skill level. Questionnaire measures of hand preference yield bimodal, *J*-shaped frequency distributions with a large number of scores at the extreme right-hand pole and a much smaller concentration of scores near the left-hand pole (Oldfield, 1971). Right-hand minus left-hand differences on performance measures such as strength and speech form unimodal approximately bell-shaped frequency distributions (Annett, 1972; Woo & Pearson, 1927). It appears that a small right-hand superiority in skill is sufficient to produce a strong preference for the use of the right hand. In any event, asymmetric hand use and asymmetric hand skill are not in proportion, although there does not seem to be an association between these two aspects of handedness (Annett, 1970, 1976).

The investigator who chooses to measure hand preference rather than asymmetry of manual skill must decide how best to sample from the population of manual activities and to weight each activity. Is hand preference for writing equal in importance to hand preference for dealing cards? Does one focus attention on preferences that are likely to be environmentally influenced (e.g., writing, eating, using scissors), or does one concentrate on preferences that seem to be independent of cultural and other environment shaping (Teng, Lee, Yang, & Chang, 1976)? Perhaps it is useful to divide subjects into preference groups on the basis of an association analysis (Annett, 1970) so that questionnaire items are weighted according to their correlations with other items.

If the investigator chooses to define handedness in terms of a performance difference between the hands rather than hand preference, some of the problems inherent in the use of handedness questionnaires can be avoided, but there will be other problems to replace them. Provins and Cunliffe (1972) found statistically significant retest reliability for only two of seven measures of motor-skill asymmetry, one of which was the highly practiced skill of cursive writing. Differences between the hands were unreliable for most tasks despite a short test-retest interval, considerable heterogeneity of hand preference among the (adult) subjects, and adequate retest reliability of performance with the preferred hand. Other studies (Annett, Hudson, & Turner, 1974; Shankweiler & Studdert-Kennedy, 1975) have produced statistically significant but rather modest estimates of retest reliability for the difference between the hands in motor skill. Perhaps because the individual measures are not very reliable, correlations among measures of manual asymmetry tend to be low and, in some instances, even insignificant (Shankweiler & Studdert-Kennedy, 1975). Thus, even if a test of manual-performance asymmetry proves to be reliable, one cannot be sure it is measuring a general dimension of sidedness in motor skill. Fleishman (1972), in fact, has identified several independent factors of motor and perceptual-motor ability, and it is not clear which are most relevant to differences in cerebral organization. Differential experience with the two hands in everyday life constitutes another problem. Highly practiced skills may yield the most reliable differences between the hands, but the magnitude and reliability of these differences probably reflect, in part, differential practice. Even novel tasks may be influenced by facilitative or interfering transfer from similar aspects of everyday tasks. The investigator must decide whether his or her definition of handedness is better embodied in a "pure" (i.e., completely novel) test of skill or in a task that is confounded by the effects of differential experience or practice. Within the testing situation, practice, fatigue, order effects, and other task variables may exert strong influences on the magnitude of performance differences between the hands (Briggs & Brogden, 1953; Hicks and Kinsbourne, 1978; Provins, 1967; Steingrueber, 1975).

Footedness

It is no easy matter to specify the degree to which a person is right- or left-handed. An alternative, as mentioned previously, is to assess the consistency of a person's asymmetry across different pairs of receptors and effectors (e.g., hands, feet, eyes). Presumably, inconsistent sidedness, or mixed dominance, suggests incomplete lateralization (Orton, 1937). What are the implications, and the problems, in this approach? Relatively little is known about footedness, except that foot preference tends to be correlated with hand preference (Annett & Turner, 1974; Clark, 1957). Many of the problems inherent in the measurement of handedness would seem to apply to the measurement of footedness as well. The main issue, though, is the significance of footedness. Does an estimate of hand and foot preference provide more information about brain lateralization than do two measures of hand preference? There is no reason to believe that footedness has any special significance.

Eyedness

Greater claims have been made for the importance of eyedness and the association between crossed eye-hand dominance and cognitive deficit. It is not uncommon today to find clinicians who consider mixed dominance of this kind to be a pathognomonic indicator of learning disability. As noted previously, the evidence is unconvincing. There are many normal students who have crossed eye-hand dominance, and there are many learning-disabled children who do not. Equally important is the lack of theoretical or empirical basis for linking eye dominance and cerebral lateralization. In their comprehensive review of the eye-dominance literature, Porac and Coren (1976) state that "There is little neurological and physiological data to support the presence of any relationship between ocular and cerebral dominance" (p. 886). This statement is based primarily on the lack of an exclusive or preferential relationship between the eye and either cerebral hemisphere. At the optic chiasm, located in the pathway from the retina to the lateral geniculate nuclei, half of the fibers from each eye proceed toward the right hemisphere and half proceed toward the left hemisphere. Consequently, a preference for visual input from, say, the right eye does not imply a left-hemispheric advantage in processing that input. The information from the right eye is transmitted directly to both hemispheres.

Despite the absence of reasons to expect a correlation between handedness and eyedness, several investigators have looked for such a relationship. Of the 20 investigations cited by Porac and Coren (1976), 9 reports claimed associations between the two variables and 11 did not. Porac and Coren

(1976) argue that the positive findings may be "slightly artifactual" because most people are right-handed and also use their right eye for sighting. Especially when subjects are dichotomized or trichotomized with regard to lateral preference, there may be an apparent association between handedness and eyedness even if the two tendencies in fact are orthogonal (Collins & Collins, 1971). The apparent association disappears when quantitative ratings of strength of lateral preference are used (Coren & Kaplan, 1973; Porac & Coren, 1975).

Perceptual Asymmetry: Methodological Problems

Beginning in the 1960s, researchers have shown less interest in the traditional measures of handedness and eyedness than in measures of perceptual asymmetry. Presumably, techniques such as dichotic listening and half-field tachistoscopic presentation provide a more direct assessment of cerebral lateralization. If so, why are the results, as summarized previously, so inconsistent? Inconsistent differences between learning-disabled children and control subjects might be attributed to classification problems discussed elsewhere (see Chapter 5), but the average degree of asymmetry also varies considerably among control groups in these various studies (Satz, 1976).

Some of the variability among dichotic listening studies probably can be attributed to unknown and uncontrolled variations in the acoustical characteristics of the stimulus material. Berlin and colleagues (Berlin & Cullen, 1977; Berlin & McNeil, 1976) have demonstrated the importance of stimulus parameters, such as signal-to-noise ratio, intensity level, band width, and synchrony of stimulus onset. The comparability of results from different studies is jeopardized when these variables are disregarded.

Of particular relevance to the question of anomalous lateralization in learning-disabled children is the difficult problem of how to compare the amount of asymmetry across individuals or groups that differ in overall level of performance. In some cases, floor or ceiling effects may influence asymmetry scores in one group to such a degree that between-group comparison becomes invalid (Kinsbourne & Hiscock, 1977; Satz, 1976). Researchers have a choice of working with raw scores for each ear or visual half-field, or transforming the raw data to one of several laterality indices (Halwes, 1969; Harshman & Krashen, 1972; Kuhn, 1973; Marshall, Caplan, & Holmes, 1975; Studdert-Kennedy & Shankweiler, 1970) in an attempt to make asymmetry scores comparable despite disparate performance levels. Alternatively, they may prefer to use frequency or rank-order data (Bryden, 1970; Bryden & Allard, 1978; Richardson, 1976). But different statistical choices may lead to contradictory conclusions (Sparrow & Satz, 1970).

Perceptual Asymmetry: Conceptual Problems

Although methodological problems are troublesome, the difficulty with perceptual tasks as a measure of cerebral lateralization extends beyond the diversity of technical standards or the intractability of scaling problems. The fundamental problem is conceptual. It is the assumption that the magnitude of listening asymmetry or visual-field asymmetry is a direct measure of the degree to which language is lateralized in an individual or a group. This assumption stems from uncritical reliance on a purely structural model of perceptual asymmetries (Kimura, 1961a, b, 1966, 1967). This model rests on two facts: (1) in most people it is the left hemisphere that is specialized for language processing, and (2) there is preferential access of information coming from one side of space to the contralateral hemisphere. Consequently, it is argued that when speech messages of different content are simultaneously presented to the two ears, it is the message that is on the opposite side of space to the "verbal" hemisphere that gains preferential access to that hemisphere and therefore is better decoded. Those signals that come in through the ear on the same side as the hemisphere dominant for language achieve less priority in processing and therefore are less perfectly recognized. An analogous explanation is used in the visual modality. When verbal information is flashed to one side of the central point of fixation, then, if that is the side opposite the hemisphere dominant for language, the information gains direct access to that hemisphere and is efficiently dealt with. But, if it is presented to the visual half-field on the same side as the language-dominant hemisphere, then it is first conducted contralaterally to the hemisphere that is not so specialized and only secondarily transported, across the corpus callosum, to the verbally competent part of the brain. This additional delay, it is argued, causes the message to lose legibility and to be relatively poorly recognized (McKeever & Huling, 1971).

If perceptual asymmetries are the direct result of the manner in which the afferent pathways are "wired," it seems reasonable to suggest that variations among people in degree of asymmetry might be associated with variations in degree of cerebral specialization. That is, the direct input of information to a cerebral hemisphere would be advantageous only to the degree that the hemisphere is more adept than its counterpart in processing the information. However, the model breaks down immediately when applied to dichotic listening. Kimura (1967) argued that binaural competition is necessary to demonstrate an ear advantage, because listening asymmetries depend on the occlusion of the ipsilateral pathway by the contralateral pathway. However, even the partial occlusion suggested by Kimura would not be a sufficient condition to ensure that the ear advantage is a direct index of lateralization.

Individual differences could be attributed to differences in the degree of occlusion or the degree to which the contralateral pathway is superior to the ipsilateral pathway. Only in the case of total occlusion of one pathway by the other could individual differences be attributed to differences in cerebral lateralization. In fact, occlusion does not appear to be a factor at all. Various investigators have elicited a right-ear advantage for linguistic material without reliance on binaural rivalry (Bakker, 1967, 1968, 1969, 1970; Bever, 1971; Haydon & Spellacy, 1974; Morais & Bertelson, 1973; Morais & Darwin, 1974; Provins & Jeeves, 1975; Simon, 1967).

Thus, even from a structural model of listening asymmetry, it does not follow that differences in degree of asymmetry can necessarily be regarded as indicating differences in degree of cerebral lateralization of language. Such differences might merely reflect variation in the degree to which the pathway from one ear to the language hemisphere is superior to the pathway from the other side as a vehicle for information transmission.

More importantly, there are several grounds on which to question the premise that perceptual asymmetries are, in fact, attributable to structural factors of any nature.

STABILITY OVER TIME

Ear difference scores in dichotic listening are less reliable than measures of a fixed, structural property should be (Blumstein, Goodglass, & Tartter, 1975; Pizzamiglio, De Pascalis, & Vignati, 1974). Blumstein et al (1975) reported test-retest reliability coefficients of .21 for vowels, .46 for music, and .74 for consonants. When frequency data (i.e., the number of subjects showing a right- or left-ear advantage) were analyzed, there was a statstically significant association between test 1 and test 2 only in the case of the musical stimuli. On the consonant and vowel tasks, about one third of the adult subjects shifted ear advantage from test 1 to test 2. There is no reason to believe that the retest reliability of children's ear differences should be any better (Bakker, Hoefkins, & Van der Vlugt, 1979; Hiscock & Kinsbourne, 1977). Visual asymmetries appear to be even less reliable than dichotic listening asymmetries (Hines & Satz, 1974). A portion of the unreliability of these measures may be attributed to a statistical limiting factor: the reliability of difference scores decreases as the correlation between their component scores increase (Hines & Satz, 1974). Nevertheless, perceptual asymmetries are remarkably unstable for indices of a fixed brain characteristic. It is particularly difficult to draw inferences about lateralization in people who show a right-sided preference on initial testing and a left-sided preference upon retesting.

INCIDENCE OF NORMAL AND
DEVIANT LATERALITY

Perceptual tests underestimate the population incidence of left-lateralization of language. For instance, in dichotic listening studies, no more than about 80 percent of a sample of normal, right-handed subjects typically show a right-ear advantage, no matter how small (Bryden & Allard, 1978; Blumstein et al, 1975). Blumstein et al (1975) estimated that 15 percent of their right-handed subjects were consistently left-ear dominant for consonants. These estimates stand in contrast to the 95–99 percent incidence of left-lateralization of language reported for right-handers in both the aphasia literature and the sodium amobarbitol literature (Rasmussen & Milner, 1975; Rossi & Rosadini, 1967; Zangwill, 1967). The significance of this mismatch in incidence estimates has been pointed out vividly by Satz (1977), who used Baysean statistics to demonstrate the fallacy inherent in making inferences about an individual's language lateralization on the basis of dichotic listening asymmetries. If 95 percent of the population actually has speech represented in the left hemisphere, nearly all subjects in any sample will have left-hemispheric language regardless of dichotic listening score. Accordingly, Satz's analysis shows that if 70 percent of a sample shows a right-ear advantage, the probability of left-hemispheric language is .97 for subjects with a right-ear advantage and .90 for subjects with a left-ear advantage. If a subject has a left-ear advantage, the likelihood of right-lateralization is only .10. Thus, the investigator who infers anomalous lateralization from a left-ear advantage may be wrong nine times out of ten with a sample of adult right-handers. There is little reason to believe that the precision of classification of dichotic listening is better among children (Bryden & Allard, 1978; Hiscock & Kinsbourne, 1980b; Kinsbourne & Hiscock, 1977).

SUSCEPTIBILITY TO SITUATIONAL AND
EXPERIENTIAL INFLUENCES

Asymmetries of perception can be modified by certain situational and experiential factors (Studdert-Kennedy, 1975). Kinsbourne (1970; 1973) demonstrated that a concurrent verbal task will introduce a rightward bias in visual perception, and subsequent studies (Hellige & Cox, 1976; Hellige, Cox, & Litvac, 1979) have replicated and elaborated the earlier findings. It has been reported that displacing prisms alter listening asymmetry: if the subject's visual field is shifted to the right, the right-ear advantage is enhanced (Goldstein & Lackner, 1974). Ear asymmetry can be altered by varying the apparent location of the sound source (Morais, 1975; Morais &

Bertelson, 1975). Consequently, the right-ear advantage actually may be a "right-side-of-space" advantage. Other studies (Bartholomeus, 1974; Haggard & Parkinson, 1971; Spellacy & Blumstein, 1970) demonstrate that ear asymmetry is modulated by various aspects of the task. Perhaps the most compelling demonstration of contextual influence is the Spellacy and Blumstein (1970) finding that vowel sounds may yield either a right-ear advantage or no asymmetry depending on whether the context in which the sounds were heard was linguistic or nonlinguistic. Other studies (Bever & Chiarello, 1974; Johnson, 1977; Papcun, Krashen, Terbeek, Remington, & Harshman, 1974; Van Lancker & Fromkin, 1977) suggest that dichotic listening asymmetry depends, in part, on the subject's previous experience with a particular kind of stimulus. Thus, musicians differ from nonmusicians in ear advantage for perception of dichotic melodies (Bever & Chiarello, 1974; Johnson, 1977); Morse code operators differ from naive subjects in ear advantage for certain dot-dash patterns (Papcun et al, 1974); and Thai speakers differ from English speakers in ear advantage for intoned Thai words (Van Lancker & Fromkin, 1977).

TASK DIFFICULTY

The degree of asymmetry varies with the difficulty of the task. This has, for instance, been shown by Geffen and Wale (1979) for dichotic listening, and for verbal-manual interference by Hicks, Bradshaw, Kinsbourne, & Feigin (1978). Not only is this variation in degree of asymmetry unaccounted for by a structural model of laterality, but it also poses serious difficulty for attempts to make neurologically revealing between-group comparisons using these techniques. If females show less right-ear advantage than males on a verbal dichotic listening task, is this because they are "less lateralized," or merely because, insofar as they are verbally more skilled, the task is easier for them? If the same task is given cross-sectionally across a range of ages in childhood, its difficulty cannot be constant. This factor might account for Geffen and Wale's (1979) unusual finding in listening tasks that with fast presentation the right-ear advantage actually decreased with increasing age. If one considers that the more difficult task might more thoroughly engage the responsible hemisphere, causing a greater imbalance in activation and therefore in lateral attention than on easier tasks (Kinsbourne, 1970, 1973), one can understand such a result and escape the embarrassment of having to suppose that lateralization actually diminishes with increasing age.

DISTRIBUTION OF PERCEPTUAL
ASYMMETRY SCORES

Another argument against the assumption of isomorphism between a person's perceptual asymmetry and an underlying dimension of cerebral asymmetry arises from an examination of the manner in which perceptual asymmetries are distributed. The argument is reminiscent of the discussion of the distributions of right–left differences in manual measures. The present argument, however, is different insofar as the disparity exists between perceptual measures and more direct evidence about cerebral specialization. Indeed, the basic issue is whether the concept of varying degrees of brain lateralization (in right-handers) has any meaning.

Perceptual asymmetries tend to be small in magnitude, but more direct (clinical) techniques suggest that lateralization of language in right-handers is virtually an all-or-none phenomenon. Right-ear performance in normal populations seldom exceeds left-ear performance by more than a few percentage points (Berlin & McNeil, 1976; Blumstein et al, 1975). In contrast, unilateral injection of sodium amobarbitol into one of the carotid arteries of right-handers brings about either complete cessation of speech or no change in speech, depending on the side of injection. It is a very rare case in which left-sided and right-sided injections each produce partial disruption of speech in a right-handed patient. It is also very unusual for neither injection to disrupt the speech of a right-hander (Rasmussen & Milner, 1975). Similarly, the aphasia data (e.g., Wyke, 1971; Zangwill, 1967) show that in most right-handers damage to right-hemispheric areas homologous to left-hemispheric speech areas produce no measurable deficit in language functions. Probably all normal asymmetries of human performance are distributed along continuums (Annett, 1972; Shankweiler & Studdert-Kennedy, 1975; Woo & Pearson, 1927). Also, the estimates from clinical data may be biased somewhat by sampling problems (Levy, 1974) and by emphasis on expressive rather than receptive language (Kinsbourne, 1974; Searleman, 1977). Nevertheless, despite these qualifications, it is difficult to relate the continuums of auditory and visual asymmetry to the apparently binary distribution of language lateralization reported for right-handers in the clinical literature.

In discussing perceptual asymmetries, we have argued that the size of an ear advantage or a visual half-field advantage should not be used as an index of degree of cerebral lateralization. We have tried to justify caution in drawing inferences about the brain of a child or a group of children on the basis of ear differences or visual half-field differences. We have *not* argued that the existence of perceptual asymmetries in a population is independent of that population's cerebral lateralization. Indeed, there is no doubt that the asymmetrical organization of the brain underlies most perceptual asymmetries.

We believe that cerebral specialization influences perceptual asymmetry in a way that is fundamentally different from that depicted by a structural model. A structural representation of the human (or infrahuman) nervous system fails to consider that the organism is more than a preprogrammed reactive device that responds to environmental stimulation in a largely mechanical fashion. On the contrary, the organism's behavior is characterized by properties such as selectivity, attention, purposive behavior, expectancy, and planning (Hebb, 1972). Full recognition of the flexibility and adaptability of human behavior leads to a model of hemispheric specialization that can account for the inconsistencies of perceptual asymmetry described above.

This model (Kinsbourne, 1970, 1973, 1974, 1975c) is based on the fact that each cerebral hemisphere directs orientation toward the contralateral side of space. Differential activation of the two hemispheres produces an overt or covert shift of attention away from the side of the more highly activated hemisphere. Although the attentional model has been substantiated primarily by data from visual-perceptual tasks (Hellige & Cox, 1976; Hellige et al, 1979; Kinsbourne, 1970, 1973) and observation of oculomotor activity (Galin & Ornstein, 1974; Gur, 1975; Kinsbourne, 1972; Kocel, Galin, Ornstein, & Merrin, 1972; Schwartz, Davidson, & Maer, 1975), it is equally applicable to auditory phenomena (Hiscock & Kinsbourne, 1977, 1980b; Kinsbourne, 1975b; Morais, 1975; Morais & Bertelson, 1975). When linguistic or other structured auditory stimuli impinge on the neonate, subcortical mechanisms activate the left hemisphere to a greater degree than the right (Gardiner & Walter, 1976; Molfese, 1973, 1977; Molfese, Freeman, & Palermo, 1975). Consequently, attention is biased to the right. Similarly, in older children and adults, listening to speech, speaking, or thinking verbally tends to bias attention toward the right side of space (Kinsbourne, 1972). The species seems to be additionally preprogrammed so that other classes of stimuli elicit different distributions of activation (Davis & Wada, 1977; Gardiner & Walter, 1976; Molfese, 1977). The attentional biases may be relatively automatic and inflexible in the neonate, but, as the organism matures and the cerebrum becomes prepotent in controlling behavior, attentional biases become modulated to an increasing degree by cortical influence. Situational factors become important determinants of orientation in space. Cognitive variables such as mental set, expectancy, and previous experience influence the manner in which stimuli are interpreted and processed. Thus, ambiguous dichotic stimuli might be interpreted either as linguistic or nonlinguistic material, and one or the other hemisphere would be activated accordingly (Spellacy & Blumstein, 1970). Also, as the nervous system becomes increasingly mature, it enables more flexible disposition of attention. The older child or adult can more readily overcome innate biases such as that which connects lateral cerebral activation and lateral biasing orientation. This ability to override voluntarily the way in which a system is wired contributes to the lack of perfect correlation between the direction in degree of asymmetry and the presumed lateralization of language in a given individual.

WHAT ARE THE CONSEQUENCES OF DEVIANT LATERALIZATION?

The manner in which higher mental functions are represented in the cerebral cortex can vary among people along two dimensions (Kinsbourne, 1975a). One dimension might be called degree of specialization. A given function may be represented in a well-defined, circumscribed region of cortex, or the same function may be more diffusely represented over a larger proportion of the cortical mass. The other dimension of individual differences might be called topography. A function may be represented in the "usual" cortical location or it may be represented elsewhere in the cortex. For instance, functions that are found on the left side in most people may be represented on the right side in other people.

As discussed earlier, the present repertoire of noninvasive investigative techniques is not adequate to detect reliably even gross anomalies in the topography of language representation (e.g., right-lateralization of language) among normal people, i.e., in the general rather than the brain-damaged population. Right-handers with speech represented in the right hemisphere are a potential source of data concerning the effects of anomalous topography, but they are rare and the means to pick them out from the general population are not available. Similarly, with respect to degree of specialization, the clinical evidence suggests that in right-handers speech representation seldom, if ever, is so diffuse that speech is represented in both hemispheres (Rasmussen & Milner, 1975). Consequently, very little can be learned about the ramifications of "deviant" lateralization by studying the general population of right-handers.

Language Lateralization in Left-Handers

Left-handers are a group with diverse cerebral representation of language. Consequently, the study of left-handers may shed some light on the significance of anomalous topography and, specifically, on the significance of unusually diffuse representation of language. (The label "left-handers" is used to include ambidextrous people, as well as those showing a clear preference for the left hand, since the pattern of speech lateralization in the two groups appears to be similar) (Branch, Milner, & Rasmussen, 1964; Milner, Branch, & Rasmussen, 1964).

As discussed earlier, clinical evidence indicates that most left-handers have left-lateralized language. However, the proportion of left-handers with right-lateralization far exceeds the proportion of deviant right-handers. The best estimate, from aphasia cases (Annett, 1975; Ettlinger et al, 1956; Gloning et al, 1969; Goodglass & Quadfasel, 1954; Hécaen & Piercy, 1956; Hécaen &

Sauget, 1971; Humphrey & Zangwill, 1952; Luria, 1970; Penfield & Roberts, 1959; Roberts, 1969; Russell & Espir, 1961) and from use of the sodium amobarbitol technique (Rasmussen & Milner, 1975; Rossi & Rosadini, 1967), is that one quarter to one third of left-handers have right-hemispheric speech. One of the best sources is Rasmussen and Milner's (1975) report of the results of sodium amobarbitol tests administered to 140 right-handers and 122 non-right-handers. Of the right-handers, none had bilateral speech and only 6 (4 percent) had right-hemispheric speech. In contrast, 18 (15 percent) of the left-handers and ambidextrous patients had right-hemispheric speech and another 18 showed evidence of some speech representation in each hemisphere. Data obtained from patients after unilateral electroconvulsive therapy (ECT) provide further basis for inferring a markedly elevated incidence of right-hemispheric language among left-handers (Fleminger, de Horne, & Nott, 1970; Pratt & Warrington, 1972; Pratt, Warrington, & Halliday, 1971; Warrington & Pratt, 1973). In normal populations, the average magnitude of the right-ear advantage in dichotic listening and the right visual half-field advantage is usually smaller among left- than right-handers (Hicks & Kinsbourne, 1978).

Ideally, neurologically intact left-handers with deviant lateralization of speech would be identified and then compared to other left-handers and to right-handers on a variety of psychological measures. Such comparisons would provide a powerful means of determining the intellectual consequences, if any, of having a topographical arrangement unlike that of the majority. Unfortunately, no proven noninvasive means of distinguishing among subcategories of left-handedness is available, although one possible method has been suggested (Levy & Reid, 1976, 1978). Consequently, we are forced to capitalize on the rather loose statistical relationship between handedness and the probability of right-lateralization of language. It is clear that any representative sample of left-handers will include a substantial proportion of people with deviant language lateralization. If there is some advantage associated with the norm of left-lateralized language, than a judiciously selected test battery should differentiate the sample of left-handers from a sample of right-handers. Specifically, the left-handers *should* show (1) poorer average performance and (2) greater variability.

Intelligence of Left-Handers

In simplest terms, then, the object is to discover whether left-handers, on the average, are less intelligent than right-handers. Indirect evidence suggests that this may be the case. It has been reported that left-handers are over-represented not only among learning-disabled children but also among the mentally retarded (Bakwin, 1950; Burt, 1950; Doll, 1933, Gordon, 1920;

Hicks & Barton, 1975; Wilson, 1931; Zangwill, 1960) and among children with various language disorders (Morley, 1965).

Although some of the data from normal samples support the hypothesis that left-handers are less intelligent than right-handers, those findings are suspect on the basis of sampling problems. For instance, the two studies (Levy, 1969; Miller, 1971) that reported a selective deficiency in nonverbal ability among left-handers involved small, highly selected groups of university students. Subsequent studies (G. G. Briggs, Nebes, & Kinsbourne, 1976; Hardyck, Petrinovich, & Goldman, 1976; Kocel, 1977; 1980; Newcombe & Ratcliff, 1973), using larger samples of the general population of university students, have not found any notable intellectual deficit in left-handers. Perhaps the last word on the subject has been provided by the authors of a United States Government National Health Survey (Roberts & Engle, 1974), who reported psychometric data for more than 6000 right-handed children and more than 750 left-handed children between the ages of 6 and 11 years. Despite the unusually large sample size and the careful sampling technique, the right- and left-handed children were effectively identical in average performance on verbal and nonverbal tests.

How is it that left-handedness is associated with various kinds of pathology and, yet, left-handers in the general population are as intelligent as their right-handed counterparts? The paradox can be resolved by postulating two distinct etiologies for left-handedness.

Etiologies of Left-Handedness

Most people are left-handed as the result of genetic diversity (Annett, 1964, 1973a, 1974; Chamberlain, 1928; Falek, 1955; Hicks & Kinsbourne, 1976a,b; Hudson, 1975; Levy & Nagylaki, 1972) although the phenotypic expression of the genotype is subject to modification by social pressure and other environmental factors (Bakan, Dibb & Reed, 1973; Collins, 1975; Morgan & Corballis, 1978; Teng et al, 1976). In addition, some people who are genotypic dextrals have become left-handed as a result of lateralized brain insult. This is pathological left-handedness (Satz, 1972; 1973; Satz, Baymur, & Van der Vlugt, in press). Early left-sided damage (probably prenatal or perinatal), even if subtle, may be sufficient to shift handedness from right to left. Of course, right-sided damage would cause left-handers to become right-handed, but there are two reasons why a shift in this direction occurs far less frequently. The main reason is that the pool of left-handers is much smaller than the pool of right-handers. Given equal probability of left- and right-sided injury, the number of pathological left-handers will exceed the number of pathological right-handers by a wide margin. Since the baseline population of left-handers is relatively small, the pathological left-handers will constitute a substantial proportion of left-handers relative to the pathological right-handers, whose number will be miniscule among the vast right-handed population. But, the probability of injury to the two hemispheres is not equal. The frequency of pathological left-handedness may be further elevated because of the left-hemisphere's special vulnerability to injury (Kinsbourne, 1975a). Left occipitoanterior presentation of the fetal head during childbirth, which is the most common, places maximal pressure on the left side of the head and thus increases the likelihood of left-sided damage. In addition, the left hemisphere is more vulnerable to vascular insufficiency, perhaps because the left carotid artery supplies the left hemisphere in a relatively indirect fashion.

The distinction between "natural" and pathological left-handedness must be used cautiously. One cannot assume that sporadic, or nonfamilial, left-handers in the general population are brain-damaged. Although Bakan (1971, Bakan et al, 1973) has claimed that left-handedness in general is associated with adverse birth circumstances, others (Hicks, Evans, & Pellegrini, 1978; Hubbard, 1971; M. Schwartz, 1977; Teng et al, 1976) have been unable to substantiate this claim. Moreover, Wechsler IQ scores of sporadic left-handers are not lower than those of right-handers or familial left-handers (G. G. Briggs et al, 1976). The concept of pathological left-handedness should be applied only to populations known to be deviant on grounds other than handedness (Annett, 1970; Annett & Turner, 1974).

A cautionary note is sounded by one study that, though small in scale, was longitudinal. Swanson, Kinsbourne, and Horn (1980) found intellectual status at age 10 to be maintained at age 13 by right-handers but to drop for non-right-handers. If this finding proves to have generality, it will become important to consider the age at which comparison between handedness groups is made in evaluating this literature. However obscure the reasons for this interaction are, they seem more likely to relate to external (social) factors than to constitutional (maturational) factors.

Anomalous Degree of Specialization

Data concerning left-handers are also relevant to the question of anomalous degree of specialization and its consequences, if any. The individual left-hander's brain specialization is likely to be more diffuse than the right-hander's. That the prognosis for recovery from aphasia due to unilateral insult is better for left-handers than for right-handers (Luria, 1970; Subirana, 1958) could be due to greater neuroplasticity rather than more diffuse lateralization. But other characteristics of language disorder do suggest a more diffuse representation of language in left-handers than in right-handers (Hécaen & Piercy, 1956; Hécaen & Sauget, 1971; Marcie, 1972; Roberts,

1969). Also, unilateral sodium amobarbitol injection has revealed bilateral speech representation in about 15 percent of left-handers (Rasmussen & Milner, 1975). With about half of these patients, injections in either carotid artery arrested speech; however, the duration of speech arrest was shorter than in right-handers. With the other half, injections to either side failed to arrest speech but instead caused dysphasic responses. Frequently, in those patients with bilateral speech representation, one hemisphere seems to be responsible for naming and the other for serial recitation.

Differences between the intellectual skills of normal right- and left-handers might have been attributable to differences in either the topography or the degree of cerebral specialization. Since no differences appear to exist, it seems that neither anomalous topography nor anomalous degree of specialization suffices to produce a performance deficit. Any deficit among left-handers is not necessarily a result of the anomalous manner in which the brains of many left-handers are organized. It is more likely that both the anomalous lateralization and the performance deficit are independently the result of insult to the developing brain.

If deviant states of brain organization are consequences rather than causes, the inconsistent association between left-handedness and learning disability becomes easier to understand. The young brain is vulnerable to various kinds of subtle insult. The insult may or may not produce a left-handed child, and it may or may not lead to cognitive defects serious enough to affect the child's school performance. Among cases of learning disability there may be some whose early insult has produced (pathological) left-handedness *and* circumscribed intellectual impairment.

WHEN DOES THE BRAIN BECOME LATERALIZED?

Inherent in the incomplete lateralization hypothesis of learning disability is the assumption that functions that are at first bilaterally represented become lateralized over time. Thus, cognitive deficits are thought to be related to delayed or incompletely established lateralization of function (T. T. S. Ingram & Reid, 1956). Orton (1943) believed that genetic dispositions underlie the putatively incomplete dominance of strephosymbolic children. However, the presumed critical feature of learning-disabled children is that, during maturation, the neural basis of academically relevant mental abilities fails to become asymmetrical at the usual rate or to the usual degree. The importance of the developmental dimension of cerebral lateralization is also stressed by researchers (Bakker, 1973; Bakker & Reitsma, 1973; Sparrow & Satz, 1970) who postulate that the role of each hemisphere in reading differs as a function of the child's stage of reading acquisition.

What if lateralization does not develop over time? What if the neonate is fully lateralized from the moment of birth? In that case, it would make no sense to speak of delayed lateralization, nor to intervene in the hope of somehow accelerating the course of lateralization. If lateralization is not a developmental phenomenon, it is likely that learning-disabled children are either as fully lateralized as their nondisabled classmates or destined never to acquire the usual form of brain organization. Accepting or rejecting the "progressive lateralization hypothesis" changes quite markedly the way in which one conceptualizes the relationship between cerebral lateralization and learning disorders.

There are many arguments for and against the notion of progressive lateralization (Kinsbourne, 1975b; Kinsbourne & Hiscock, 1977). The idea that cerebral lateralization develops during childhood appeals to "common sense." Neurological development (Gardner, 1968) and behavioral development (Thompson, 1968) both adhere to the principles of growth, differentiation, and organization. Since adults' complex language develops from a nonlinguistic neonatal state, it seems reasonable that the lateralized adult cerebrum develops from a functionally symmetrical neonatal cerebrum (it being alleged that bisymmetry is a simpler, or less evolved, pattern of neural organization than asymmetry).

Lenneberg (1967) constructed an argument for early equipotentiality of the cerebral hemispheres that quickly gained widespread popularity. On the basis of his own clinical experience as well as published case reports — primarily those of Basser (1962) — Lenneberg described the typical course of recovery from aphasia in children at various ages. He inferred two major differences between aphasia in children and in adults: (1) unilateral aphasia-producing cerebral insult in early childhood seldom, if ever, leaves permanent impairment, and (2) right-hemispheric damage produces some language disruption in children much more frequently than in adults. Lenneberg concluded that the two hemispheres are equally good substrates for language at the beginning of language acquisition and that language gradually becomes lateralized in the left hemisphere as the child matures. Language is bilaterally represented at first, but the role of the right hemisphere progressively decreases until, at puberty, language is fully lateralized to the left.

There is another way to interpret Lenneberg's observations. The reported mild and transitory nature of childhood aphasia can be attributed simply to the plasticity of the immature brain. The right hemisphere (or alternative areas within the left hemisphere) of the young child may be able to subserve speech quite adequately in the event of injury to the left-hemispheric speech regions. The concept of neural plasticity in the immature organism is a well-established principle of neurobiology (Isaacson, 1968; Stein, Rosen, & Butters, 1974). In contrast, Lenneberg's concept of a gradually shrinking brain base for a given function is a speculation.

Lenneberg's (1967) second observation is that right-hemisphere damage frequently disrupts language in children. This observation supported Lenneberg's belief that both hemispheres of the child are involved in language processing. However, the observation itself may not be accurate. After examining the case studies on which Lenneberg founded his claims, Krashen (1973) concluded that the development of language lateralization is complete by the age of 5 years. Language disturbance after right-hemisphere lesions does not seem to be more frequent in children above 5 years of age than in adults. Only the relatively sparse data for children below the age of 5 (Basser, 1962; Hécaen, 1976) suggest to Krashen an elevated incidence of language disturbance after right-hemisphere insult, and these data can be discounted on several grounds (Kinsbourne & Hiscock, 1977; Woods & Teuber, 1978).

There are two kinds of sampling problems associated with case reports such as those compiled by Basser (1962). (1) There is a probability that the noteworthy cases (viz., aphasia after right-hemispheric damage) will be reported more often than the commonplace cases (viz., aphasia after left-hemisphere damage and absence of aphasia after right-hemisphere damage). Thus, the high incidence of language disturbance after right-hemisphere insult may be an artifact of selective reporting. (2) Children who suffer brain damage may not be representative of the general population of children. Many of the causes of brain damage in children are potentially recurrent. Consequently, the number of children with right-sided aphasias may be inflated by inclusion of children who switched language lateralization from left to right as a result of earlier damage to the left hemisphere.

Then there is the problem of defining the lesion. For Basser's interpretation to be valid, it is necessary that the lesion be restricted to one hemisphere; however, in many cases, and especially trauma cases, it is impossible to be sure that the damage does not extend to the opposite hemisphere. Thus, bilateral damage frequently cannot be ruled out in cases of apparently right-sided aphasia. Another definitional problem involves the behavioral definition of aphasia. In some cases, the criteria for reporting aphasia are so loose, sparse, or ambiguous that emotionally traumatized children, for instance, might be classified as aphasic simply because they refuse to talk to the examining clinician. Woods and Teuber (1978) reported a pertinent series of cases, which were more thoroughly studied than in the previous literature, and found a striking predominance of left-sided cases of aphasia, even in the youngest children. They also pointed out that most reports emphasizing a high incidence of aphasia as a result of disease involving the right hemisphere date from before 1940, in times when antibiotic and immunization programs were limited in use or unavailable. They infer that many such children might have suffered from encephalopathies involving both sides of the brain. Kinsbourne and Hiscock (1977) reported that as diagnostic criteria for childhood aphasia and laterality of lesion are made more stringent, the preponderance of left-sided cases becomes increasingly striking.

Even if there were an elevated incidence of right-sided aphasia among young children, this would establish only that language is represented in the right hemisphere and not that language is bilaterally represented. Complete redundancy of language in the two hemispheres would imply that language would be unaffected by unilateral damage, regardless of side. Alternatively, if both hemispheres are necessary for language, aphasia would be equally likely in the event of insult to the left or right hemisphere. The bilaterality of speech cannot be firmly established unless both hemispheres of the same child can be studied. Even if there is much validity to Lenneberg's (1967) data base, his inference concerning the bilateral basis of language in young children is unjustified.

Subsequent to the publication of Lenneberg's influential book (1967), much evidence pertinent to the equipotentiality hypothesis has been compiled. This evidence shows clearly that the human cerebral hemispheres are specialized at a very early age.

Evidence of Early Cerebral Specialization

Anatomical asymmetries in the adult cerebrum (Geschwind & Levitsky, 1968; Teszner, Tzavaras, & Gruner, 1972; Wada, Clark, & Hamm, 1975; Witelson & Pallie, 1973; Yeni-Komshian & Benson, 1976) are matched by similar asymmetries in the neonatal cerebrum (Wada et al, 1975; Witelson & Pallie, 1973). In particular, the temporal speech region usually is larger on the left side than on the right. Although structural differences do not necessarily imply functional differences, the neuroanatomical findings are suggestive, and they contradict the classical doctrine of structural identity between the two hemispheres, e.g., the view of Pierre Marie (see Dennis & Whitaker, 1977).

When average evoked potentials—stimulus-dependent patterns of electrical activity—are recorded from the infant brain, the amplitude of the response from each hemisphere depends on the nature of the stimulus (Davis & Wada, 1977; Molfese, 1973, 1977; Molfese et al, 1975). In infants, as in older children and adults, left-hemispheric responses to speech stimuli tend to be greater than right-hemispheric responses, but left-hemispheric responses to music and noise tend to be smaller than right-hemispheric responses. In fact, the asymmetries were reported to be greater in infants than in adults (Molfese, 1977). Other researchers (Gardiner & Walter, 1976), using a different technique have also found early electrophysiological asymmetries in response to speech and music.

Infants display asymmetries of posture and head-turning (Gesell, 1938;

Gesell & Ames, 1950; Liederman & Kinsbourne, 1980a; Siqueland & Lipsitt, 1966; Turkewitz, Gordon, & Birch, 1968; Turkewitz, Moreau, Birch, & Crystal, 1967). The tonic neck reflex, which involves the head and all four limbs, is an inherently asymmetrical posture. Infants (including premature infants) exhibit the tonic neck reflex, and the majority orient more often to the right (Gesell, 1938; Gesell & Ames, 1950). In other words, the head is turned to the right and the right hand is extended. This posture suggests an early prepotency of the left brain. Neonates also turn their heads spontaneously to the right much more often than to the left (Siqueland & Lipsitt, 1966; Turkewitz et al, 1968), and they show a rightward bias when stimulated (Liederman & Kinsbourne, 1980a; Turkewitz et al, 1967). In fact, Siqueland and Lipsitt (1966) found it difficult to study the conditioning of right-turning simply because infants tend to turn to the right spontaneously. The right-ward turning is a motor bias rather than a consequence of differential lateral sensitivity (Liederman & Kinsbourne, 1980a, b), and it may be a precursor of the left lateralization of speech (Kinsbourne & Lempert, 1979).

A right-hand preference has been demonstrated in infants only 3 months old (Caplan & Kinsbourne, 1976); the infants retained an object in the right hand significantly longer than in the left. This finding has been reproduced in infants as young as 17 days (Petrie & Peters, 1980). Previous failures to find very early hand preference (Cernacek & Podivinsky, 1971; Gesell & Ames, 1947; Giesecke, 1936; Seth, 1973) can be attributed to inappropriate choice of response measures. Since infants tend to reach with both hands, and since they usually fail to reach across the midline (Provine & Westerman, 1979), reaching tasks are ill-suited for demonstrating early handedness unless special precautions are taken, in which case the right-handedness becomes manifest (Hawn & Harris, 1979). Infants aged 10 months and over show an overall right-hand tapping preference and rate advantage (Ramsay, 1979).

Infants show perceptual asymmetries that are similar to the perceptual asymmetries observed in older children and adults. Infants are able to discriminate among speech sounds (Eimas, Siqueland, & Jusczyk, 1971; Moffit, 1971; Trehub & Rabinovitch, 1972), and there is an ear advantage associated with this. If pairs of sounds are presented in dichotic competition, infants show a right-ear advantage for the detection of transitions from one speech sound to another. Entus (1977) used a measure of recovery from sucking habituation to demonstrate a right-ear advantage for speech and a left-ear advantage for music in infants as young as 50 days. Glanville, Best, and Levenson (1977) reported similar ear asymmetries in a study that used recovery from cardiac habituation as a measure of auditory perception. Segalowitz and Chapman (in press) even showed differential reduction in limb tremors after speech and music in mildly premature infants: speech had a disproportionate effect on movements of the right limbs.

In addition to the various kinds of experimental evidence against the equipotentiality hypothesis, there is some suggestive clinical evidence (Dennis & Kohn, 1975; Dennis & Whitaker, 1977; Kohn & Dennis, 1974). The lateralization of early damage does not seem to affect the child's ultimate Full Scale IQ, verbal IQ, or performance IQ in any reliable manner (Annett, 1973b; Matarazzo, 1972; Reed & Reitan, 1969), but specific linguistic or visuospatial tasks do elicit the expected pattern of deficits (Dennis & Whitaker, 1977). One way to interpret these data is to conclude that crude or global criteria, such as clinically obvious aphasic signs or IQ scores, are not sufficient to show reliable differences between the right and left hemispheres as substrates for language development. However, carefully selected tasks may show specific deficits that differ according to the hemisphere that is damaged.

Absence of Developmental Change in
Degree of Asymmetry

Rejection of equipotentiality does not preclude the possibility that the degree of hemispheric lateralization increases during childhood, and some investigators (Bryden & Allard, 1978; Satz, Bakker, Teunissen, Goebel, & Van der Vlugt, 1975) have suggested that it does increase. Thus, the issue of degree of lateralization and the ambiguities and problems associated with that concept still exist. In addition, the question of ontogenetic change is a very difficult one. Methodologies appropriate for infants may not be appropriate for slightly older children. Even electrophysiological measures change quite markedly from infancy to adulthood (Gardiner & Walter, 1976; Molfese, 1977). The nature and level of skills change so dramatically during development that the same task may be accomplished in fundamentally different ways at different age levels. As discussed previously, it is difficult to compare the magnitude of asymmetries when performance levels are widely disparate. Moreover, the claims that lateralization increases with age are based primarily on dichotic listening data. Consequently, these claims are founded on the questionable assumption that the magnitude of ear asymmetry reflects the magnitude of cerebral lateralization. In the case of developmental studies of ear asymmetry, the validity of that assumption is moot, for most of the data indicate that the asymmetry does not increase with increasing age.

Several investigators have demonstrated a right-ear advantage for linguistic material in preschool children (Bever, 1971; Geffner & Dorman, 1976; Gilbert & Climan, 1974; Hiscock & Kinsbourne, 1977, 1980b; D. Ingram, 1975; Kinsbourne & Hiscock, 1977; Nagafuchi, 1970; Piazza, 1977). Children as young as 2½ years show the right-ear advantage, and there is no reason to doubt that even younger children would show a similar asymmetry if an appropriate means of testing them were devised. The issue in question, then, is whether the magnitude of the right-ear advantage increases from early childhood to the time of puberty. Neither longitudinal (Bakker et al, 1979) nor cross-sectional data, in general, show an increase in the magnitude of listening asymmetry across this age range (Berlin, Hughes, Lowe-Bell, & Berlin, 1973; Geffen, 1978; Goodglass, 1973; Hiscock & Kinsbourne, 1977, 1980b; Hynd & Obrzut, 1977; Kimura, 1963, 1967; Kinsbourne & Hiscock, 1977; Knox & Kimura, 1970; Schulman-Galambos, 1977). A similar conclusion was reached for visual field asymmetry, using a priming paradigm (Carter & Kinsbourne, 1979). A few studies (Bryden, 1970; Bryden & Allard, 1978; Satz et al, 1975) however, do suggest that the size of the right-ear advantage increases with increasing age. The contradictory evidence may reflect differences among studies in subject selection criteria, stimulus material, technical standards, difficulty level, or statistical treatment (Porter & Berlin, 1975; Satz et al, 1975). The question of ontogenetic changes in the ear advantage is not closed, but the best answer at present is that the right-ear advantage does *not* increase with increasing age.

The argument for constant asymmetries of performance across the childhood years is bolstered by evidence from the study of verbal-manual time sharing in children. It has been shown that, in right-handed adults, speech interferes with right-hand activity more than it interferes with left-hand activity (Hicks, 1975; Kinsbourne & Cook, 1971). This asymmetry of interference is attributed to left-lateralization of speech and the predominantly contralateral control of the limbs (Brinkman & Kuypers, 1972; Gazzaniga, 1970). Left-lateralized speech and skilled right-hand movement both require processing within the left hemisphere, and insofar as the amount of "cross-talk" between two motor systems is proportional to the functional proximity of their respective cerebral representations (Kinsbourne & Hicks, 1978a,b), speech should interfere more with right-hand activity than with left-hand activity (which requires processing within the right hemisphere). Of course, the asymmetrical interference would not be expected to occur unless speech is lateralized. Thus, asymmetrical dual-task performance in preschool children (Kinsbourne & McMurray, 1975) is evidence that speech is lateralized in these children. More importantly, we (Hiscock & Kinsbourne, 1978, 1980a) have shown that the magnitude of the asymmetry remains constant between the ages of 3 and 12 years.

Whereas perceptual and performance asymmetries for a number of verbal tasks occur in young children, and their extent does not interact with age, various other developmental courses characterize the laterality of face recognition (Carey, 1979), Braille reading (Rudel, Denckla, & Hirsch, 1977; Rudel, Denckla & Spalten, 1974; Wagner & Harris, 1979), and, for females, recognition of shapes in a dichhaptic situation (Witelson, 1976). In some of these cases, no asymmetry is found in young children. With increasing age, asymmetry may appear, and then level off, but such a pattern need not be construed as indicating progressive lateralization. Rather, it is consistent with the emergence, within a hemisphere, of functional mechanisms that *supplement* the child's ability to do the task and at the same time render performance asymmetrical. In other words, this pattern shows that a certain lateralized neural faculty has matured into effectiveness. Such findings probably do not reflect a laterally shifting neural base for particular functions, but rather changes in the degree to which the respective functions of each hemisphere are drawn upon in performing the task.

A novel derivation of the progressive lateralization hypothesis has been introduced by Waber (1977). She suggested that sex differences in the spectrum of cognitive skills could be referred back to individual differences in rate of somatosexual maturation (within as well as between the sexes). Specifically, early maturers benefit in verbal development and late maturers in spatial development (males being well known to mature on the average later than females). Waber further linked developmental rate to the rate at which asymmetry evolves in laterality tasks that tap verbal and spatial skills. For present purposes we need only consider the second step of her argument, and note that neither Waber nor anyone subsequently has provided the data necessary to support it. Had it been possible to demonstrate a faster-growing and ultimately more extreme asymmetry for one type of task in one sex, this would still be subject to all the ambiguities in interpretation that we have discussed, and it would still fall short of proving the progressive lateralization hypothesis in this context.

The traditional concepts of hemispheric equipotentiality and progressive lateralization have been discredited by a rapidly expanding body of experimental evidence. Despite a few inconsistencies and lacunae in the data, it seems clear that brain function is lateralized from birth, if not earlier, and that language does not become increasingly lateralized as the child matures. Any relation of lateralization to learning disabilities cannot be due to a simple delay in the lateralization process. Rather, any anomalous cerebral organization existing in learning-disabled children would have to be present at a very early age, and would be expected to persist into adulthood. Since very few right-handed adults have anomalous representation of language, the right-handed learning-disabled children whose disabilities result from anomalous lateralization—if such children exist—would be among those few children who will have right-hemispheric speech as adults.

REFERENCES

Annett, M. A model of the inheritance of handedness and cerebral dominance. *Nature*, 1964, *204*, 59–60.

Annett, M. A classification of hand preference by association analysis. *British Journal of Psychology*, 1970, *61*, 303–321.

Annett, M. The distribution of manual asymmetry. *British Journal of Psychology*, 1972, *63*, 343–358.

Annett, M. Handedness in families. *Annuals of Human Genetics*, 1973, *37*, 93–105. (a)

Annett, M. Laterality of childhood hemiplegia and the growth of speech and intelligence. *Cortex*, 1973, *9*, 4–33. (b)

Annett, M. Handedness in the children of two left-handed parents. *British Journal of Psychology*, 1974, *65*, 129–131.

Annett, M. Hand preference and the laterality of cerebral speech. *Cortex*, 1975, *11*, 305–328.

Annett, M. A co-ordination of hand preference and skill replicated. *British Journal of Psychology*, 1976, *67*, 587–592.

Annett, M., Hudson, P. T. W., & Turner, A. The reliability of differences between the hands in motor skill. *Neuropsychologia*, 1974, *12*, 527–531.

Annett, M., & Turner, A. Laterality and the growth of intellectual abilities. *British Journal of Educational Psychology*, 1974, *44*, 37–46.

Bakan, P. Birth order and handedness. *Nature*, 1971, *229*, 195.

Bakan, P., Dibb, G., & Reed, P. Handedness and birth stress. *Neuropsychologia*, 1973, *11*, 363–366.

Bakker, D. J. Left-right differences in auditory perception of verbal and nonverbal material by children. *Quarterly Journal of Experimental Psychology*, 1967, *19*, 334–336.

Bakker, D. J. Ear-asymmetry with monaural stimulation. *Psychonomic Science*, 1968, *12*, 62.

Bakker, D. J. Ear-asymmetry with monaural stimulation: Task influences. *Cortex*, 1969, *5*, 36–42.

Bakker, D. J. Ear-symmetry with monaural stimulation: Relations to lateral dominance and lateral awareness. *Neuropsychologia*, 1970, *8*, 103–114.

Bakker, D. J. Hemispheric specialization and states in the learning-to-read process. *Bulletin of the Orton Society*, 1973, *23*, 15–27.

Bakker, D. J., Hoefkins, M., & Van der Vlugt, H. Hemispheric specialization in children as reflected in the longitudinal development of ear asymmetry. *Cortex*, 1979, *15*, 619–625.

Bakker, D. J., & Reitsma, P. Ear dominance and reading ability. *Cortex*, 1973, *9*, 301–312.

Bakwin, H. Psychiatric aspects of pediatrics: Lateral dominance, right- and left-handedness. *Journal of Pediatrics*, 1950, *36*, 385–391.

Balow, I. H. Lateral dominance characteristics and reading achievement in the first grade. *Journal of Psychology*, 1963, *55*, 323–328.

Bartholomeus, B. Effects of task requirements on ear superiority for sung speech. *Cortex*, 1974, *10*, 215–223.

Basser, L. W. Hemiplegia of early onset and the faculty of speech with special reference to the effects of hemispherectomy. *Brain*, 1962, *85*, 427–460.

Belmont, L., & Birch, H. G. Lateral dominance, lateral awareness and reading disability. *Child Development*, 1965, *36*, 57–72.

Berlin, C. I., & Cullen, J. K. Acoustic problems in dichotic listening tasks. In S. J. Segalowitz & F. A. Gruber (Eds.), *Language development and neurological theory*. New York: Academic Press, 1977.

Berlin, C. I., Hughes, L. F., Lowe-Bell, S. S., & Berlin, H. L. Dichotic right ear advantage in children 5 to 13. *Cortex,* 1973, *9,* 394-402.

Berlin, C. I., & McNeil, M. R. Dichotic listening. In N. J. Lass (Ed.), *Contemporary issues in experimental phonetics.* Springfield, Ill.: Charles C Thomas, 1976.

Bever, T. G. The nature of cerebral dominance in speech behavior of the child and adult. In R. Huxley & E. Ingram (Eds.), *Language acquisition: Models and methods.* London: Academic Press, 1971.

Bever, T. G., & Chiarello, R. J. Cerebral dominance in musicians and nonmusicians. *Science,* 1974, *185,* 537-539.

Blumstein, S., Goodglass, H., & Tartter, V. The reliability of ear advantage in dichotic listening. *Brain and Language,* 1975, *2,* 226-236.

Branch, C., Milner, B., & Rasmussen, T. Intracarotid sodium amytal for the lateralization of cerebral speech dominance: Observations on 123 patients. *Journal of Neurosurgery,* 1964, *21,* 399-405.

Briggs, G. E., & Brogden, W. J. Bilateral aspects of the trigonometric relationship of precision and angle of linear pursuit – movements. *American Journal of Psychology,* 1953, *66,* 472-478.

Briggs, G. G., Nebes, R. D., & Kinsbourne, M. Intellectual differences in relation to personal and family handedness. *Quarterly Journal of Experimental Psychology,* 1976, *28,* 591-601.

Brinkman, J., & Kuypers, H. G. J. M. Split-brain monkeys: Cerebral control of ipsilateral and contralateral arm, hand and finger movements. *Science,* 1972, *176,* 536-539.

Bryden, M. P. Tachistoscopic recognition, handedness, and cerebral dominance. *Neuropsychologia,* 1965, *3,* 1-8.

Bryden, M. P. Laterality effects in dichotic listening: Relations with handedness and reading ability in children. *Neuropsychologia,* 1970, *8,* 443-450.

Bryden, M. P., & Allard, F. Dichotic listening and the development of linguistic processes. In M. Kinsbourne (Ed.), *The asymmetrical function of the brain.* New York: Cambridge University Press, 1978.

Burt, C. *The backward child* (3rd ed.). London: University of London Press, 1950.

Caplan, P. J., & Kinsbourne, M. Baby drops the rattle: Asymmetry of duration of grasp by infants. *Child Development,* 1976, *47,* 532-534.

Carey, S. The development of face recognition: Is there a maturational component? In M. Hiscock (Chair.), *Symposium on hemispheric specialization in the developing brain.* Symposium presented at the meeting of the International Neuropsychological Society, New York, 1979.

Carter, G. L., & Kinsbourne, M. The ontogeny of right lateralization of spatial mental set. *Development Psychology,* 1979, *15,* 241-245.

Cernacek, J., & Podivinsky, R. Ontogenesis of handedness and somatosensory cortical response. *Neuropsychologia,* 1971, *9,* 219-232.

Chamberlain, H. D. The inheritance of left-handedness. *Journal of Heredity,* 1928, *19,* 557-559.

Clark, M. M. *Left-handedness.* London: University of London Press, 1957.

Clark, M. M. *Reading difficulties in schools.* Harmondsworth, England: Penguin, 1970.

Coleman, R. I., & Deutch, C. P. Lateral dominance and left-right discrimination: A comparison of normal and retarded readers. *Perceptual and Motor Skills,* 1964, *19,* 43–50.

Collins, R. A., & Collins, R. I. Independent eye-hand preference in mentally retarded: Evidence of spurious associations in heterogeneous populations. *American Journal of Optometry & Archives of the American Academy of Optometry,* 1971, *48,* 1031–1033.

Collins, R. L. When left-handed mice live in right-handed worlds. *Science,* 1975, *187,* 181–184.

Conrad, K. Über aphasische Sprachstörungen bei hirnverletzten Linkshändern. *Nervenartz,* 1949, *20,* 148–154.

Coren, S., & Kaplan, C. P. Patterns of ocular dominance. *American Journal of Optometry & Archives of the American Academy of Optometry,* 1973, *50,* 283–292.

Critchley, M. *Developmental dyslexia.* London: Heinemann, 1964.

Critchley, M. *The dyslexic child* (2nd ed.). London: Heinemann, 1970.

Davis, A. E., & Wada, J. A. Hemispheric asymmetries in human infants: Spectral analysis of flash and click evoked potentials. *Brain and Language,* 1977, *4,* 23–31.

DeHirsch, J., Jansky, J. J., & Langford, W. S. *Predicting reading failure.* New York: Harper and Row, 1966.

Dennis, M., & Kohn, B. Comprehension of syntax in infantile hemiplegics after cerebral hemidecortication: Left hemisphere superiority. *Brain and Language,* 1975, *2,* 475–486.

Dennis, M., & Whitaker, H. A. Hemisphere equipotentiality and language acquisition. In S. J. Segalowitz & F. A. Gruber (Eds.), *Language development and neurological theory.* New York: Academic Press, 1977.

Doll, E. A. Psychological significance of cerebral birth lesions. *American Journal of Psychology,* 1933, *45,* 444–452.

Eimas, P. D., Siqueland, E. R., & Jusczyk, P. Speech perception in infants. *Science,* 1971, *171,* 303–306.

Entus, A. K. Hemispheric asymmetry in processing of dichotically presented speech and nonspeech stimuli by infants. In S. Segalowitz & F. A. Gruber (Eds.), *Language development and neurological theory.* New York: Academic Press, 1977.

Ettlinger, G., Jackson, C. V., & Zangwill, O. L. Cerebral dominance in sinistrals. *Brain,* 1956, *79,* 569–588.

Falek, A. Handedness: A family study. *American Journal of Human Genetics,* 1955, *11,* 52–62.

Fleishman, E. A. On the relation between abilities, learning, and human performance. *American Psychologist,* 1972, *27,* 1017–1032.

Fleminger, J. J., de Horne, D. J., & Nott, P. Unilateral electroconvulsive therapy and cerebral dominance: Effect of right- and left-sided electrode placement on verbal memory. *Journal of Neurology, Neurosurgery, and Psychiatry,* 1970, *33,* 408–411.

Galin, D., & Ornstein, R. Individual differences in cognitive style – I. Reflective eye movements. *Neuropsychologia*, 1974, *12*, 367–376.

Gardiner, M. F., & Walter, D. O. Evidence of hemispheric specialization from infant EEG. In S. Harnad, R. W. Doty, & L. Goldstein (Eds.), *Lateralization in the nervous system*. New York: Academic Press, 1976.

Gardner, E. *Fundamentals of neurology* (5th ed.). Philadelphia: Saunders, 1968.

Gazzaniga, M. S. *The bisected brain*. New York: Appleton-Century-Crofts, 1970.

Geffen, G. The development of the right ear advantage in dichotic listening with focused attention. *Cortex*, 1978, *14*, 11–17.

Geffen, G., & Wale, J. Development of selective listening and hemispheric asymmetry. *Developmental Psychology*, 1979, *15*, 138–146.

Geffner, D. G., & Dorman, M. F. Hemispheric specialization for speech perception in four-year-old children from low and middle socio-economic classes. *Cortex*, 1976, *12*, 71–73.

Geschwind, N., & Levitsky, W. Human brain: Left-right asymmetries in temporal speech region. *Science*, 1968, *161*, 186–187.

Gesell, A. The tonic neck reflex in the human infant. *Journal of Pediatrics*, 1938, *13*, 455–464.

Gesell, A., & Ames, L. B. The development of handedness. *Journal of General Psychology*, 1947, *70*, 155–175.

Gesell, A., & Ames, L. Tonic-neck reflex and symmetro-tonic behavior. *Journal of Pediatrics*, 1950, *36*, 165–178.

Giesecke, M. The genesis of hand preference. *Monographs of the Society for Research in Child Development*, 1936, *1* (5, Serial No. 5).

Gilbert, J. H. V., & Climan, I. Dichotic studies in two and three year olds: A preliminary report. *Speech Communication Seminar, Stockholm, Vol 2.* Upsala: Almquist & Wiksell, 1974.

Glanville, B. B., Best, C. T., & Levenson, R. A cardiac measure of cerebral asymmetries in infant auditory perception. *Developmental Psychology*, 1977, *13*, 55–59.

Glass, G. V., & Robbins, M. P. A critique of experiments on the role of neurological organization in reading performance. *Reading Research Quarterly*, 1967, *3*, 5–51.

Gloning, I., Gloning, K., Haub, G., & Quatember, R. Comparison of verbal behavior in right handed and non-right handed patients with anatomically verified lesions of one hemisphere. *Cortex*, 1969, *5*, 41–52.

Goldstein, L., & Lackner, J. R. Sideways look at dichotic listening. *Journal of Acoustical Society of America*, 1974, *55*, 510.

Goodglass, H. Developmental comparison of vowels and consonants in dichotic listening. *Journal of Speech and Hearing Research*, 1973, *16*, 744–752.

Goodglass, H. & Quadfasel, F. A. Language laterality in left-handed aphasics. *Brain*, 1954, *77*, 521–548.

Gordon, H. Left-handedness and mirror writing especially among defective children. *Brain,* 1920, *43,* 313-368.

Gur, R. E. Conjugate lateral eye movements as an index of hemispheric activation. *Journal of Personality and Social Psychology,* 1975, *31,* 751-757.

Haggard, M. P., & Parkinson, A. M. Stimulus and task factors as determinants of ear advantages. *Quarterly Journal of Experimental Psychology,* 1971, *23,* 168-177.

Halwes, T. G. Effects of dichotic fusion on the perception of speech. *Supplement to Status Report on Speech Research.* New Haven, Ct.: Haskins Laboratories, 1969.

Hardyck, C., & Petrinovich, L. F. Left-handedness. *Psychological Bulletin,* 1977, *84,* 385-400.

Hardyck, C., Petrinovich, L. F., & Goldman, R. D. Left handedness and cognitive deficit. *Cortex,* 1976, *12,* 266-279.

Harris, A. J. Lateral dominance, directional confusion and reading disability. *Journal of Psychology,* 1957, *44,* 283-294.

Harshman, R., & Krashen, S. *An unbiased procedure for comparing degree of lateralization of dichotically presented stimuli.* Paper presented at the Eighty-third Meeting, Acoustical Society of America, Buffalo, New York, 1972.

Hawn, P. R., & Harris, L. J. *Hand asymmetries in grasp duration and reacting in two and five month old human infants.* Paper presented at the meeting of the International Neuropsychological Society, New York, 1979.

Haydon, S. P., & Spellacy, F. J. Monaural reaction time asymmetries for speech and non-speech sounds. *Cortex,* 1974, *9,* 288-294.

Hebb, D. O. The problem of consciousness. In D. Singh & C. T. Morgan (Eds.), *Current status of physiological psychology: Readings.* Monterey: Brooks/Cole, 1972.

Hécaen, H. Acquired aphasia in children and the ontogenesis of hemispheric functional specialization. *Brain and Language,* 1976, *3,* 114-134.

Hécaen, H., & Piercy, M. Paroxysmal dysphasia and the problem of cerebral dominance. *Journal of Neurology, Neurosurgery and Psychiatry,* 1956, *19,* 194-201.

Hécaen, H. & Sauget, J. Cerebral dominance in left-handed subjects. *Cortex,* 1971, *7,* 19-48.

Hellige, J. B., & Cox, P. J. Effects of concurrent verbal memory on recognition of stimuli from the left and right visual fields. *Journal of Experimental Psychology: Human Perception and Performance,* 1976, *2,* 210-221.

Hellige, J. B., Cox, P. J., & Litvac, L. Information processing in the cerebral hemispheres: Selective hemispheric activation and capacity limitations. *Journal of Experimental Psychology: General,* 1979, *108,* 251-279.

Hicks, R. A., Evans, E. A., & Pelligrini, R. J. Correlation between handedness and birth order: Compilation of five studies. *Perceptual and Motor Skills,* 1978, *46,* 53-54.

Hicks, R. E. Intrahemispheric response competition between vocal and uni-manual performance in normal adult human males. *Journal of Comparative and Physiological Psychology*, 1975, *89*, 50–60.

Hicks, R. E., & Barton, A. K. A note on left-handedness and severity of mental retardation. *Journal of Genetic Psychology*, 1975, *127*, 323–324.

Hicks, R. E., Bradshaw, G. J., Kinsbourne, M., & Feigin, D. S. Vocal-manual trade-offs in hemispheric sharing of human performance control. *Journal of Motor Behavior*, 1978, *10*, 1–6.

Hicks, R. E., & Kinsbourne, M. On the genesis of human handedness: A review. *Journal of Motor Behavior*, 1976, *8*, 257–266. (a)

Hicks, R. E., & Kinsbourne, M. Human handedness: A partial cross-fostering study. *Science*, 1976, *192*, 908–910. (b)

Hicks, R. E., & Kinsbourne, M. Handedness differences: Human handedness. In M. Kinsbourne (Ed.), *The asymmetrical function of the brain*. New York: Cambridge University Press, 1978.

Hines, D., & Satz, P. Cross modal asymmetries in perception related to asymmetry in cerebral function. *Neuropsychologia*, 1974, *12*, 239–247.

Hiscock, M., & Kinsbourne, M. Selective listening asymmetry in preschool children. *Developmental Psychology*, 1977, *13*, 217–224.

Hiscock, M., & Kinsbourne, M. Ontogeny of cerebral dominance: Evidence from time-sharing asymmetry in children. *Developmental Psychology*, 1978, *14*, 321–329.

Hiscock, M., & Kinsbourne, M. Asymmetry of verbal-manual time sharing in children: A follow-up study. *Neuropsychologia*, 1980, *18*, 151–162. (a)

Hiscock, M., & Kinsbourne, M. Asymmetries of selective listening and attention switching in children. *Developmental Psychology*, 1980, *16*, 70–82. (b)

Hubbard, G. I. Handedness not a function of birth order. *Nature*, 1971, *232*, 276–277.

Hudson, P. T. W. The genetics of handedness – A reply to Levy and Naglaki. *Neuropsychologia*, 1975, *13*, 331–339.

Humphrey, M. E., & Zangwill, O. L. Dysphasia in left-handed patients with unilateral brain lesions. *Journal of Neurology, Neurosurgery, Psychiatry*, 1952, *15*, 184–193.

Hynd, G. W., & Obrzut, J. E. Effects of grade level and sex on the magnitude of the dichotic ear advantage. *Neuropsychologia*, 1977, *15*, 689–692.

Hynd, G. W., Obrzut, J. E., Weed, W., & Hynd, C. R. Development of cerebral dominance: Dichotic listening asymmetry in normal and learning-disabled children. *Journal of Experimental Child Psychology*, 1979, *28*, 445–454.

Ingram, D. Cerebral speech lateralization in young children. *Neuropsychologia*, 1975, *13*, 103–105.

Ingram, T. T. S., & Reid, J. F. Developmental aphasia observed in a department of child psychiatry. *Archives of Disabilities in Childhood*, 1956, *31*, 161–172.

Isaacson, R. (Ed.). *The neuropsychology of development*. New York: Wiley, 1968.

Johnson, P. R. Dichotically-stimulated ear differences in musicians and nonmusicians. *Cortex*, 1977, *13*, 385–389.

Kimura, D. Cerebral dominance and the perception of verbal stimuli. *Canadian Journal of Psychology*, 1961, *15*, 166–171.(a)

Kimura, D. Some effects of temporal-lobe damage on auditory perception. *Canadian Journal of Psychology*, 1961, *15*, 156–165.(b)

Kimura, D. Speech lateralization in young children as determined by an auditory test. *Journal of Comparative and Physiological Psychology*, 1963, *56*, 899–902.

Kimura, D. Dual functional asymmetry of the brain in visual perception. *Neuropsychologia*, 1966, *4*, 275–285.

Kimura, D. Functional asymmetry of the brain in dichotic listening. *Cortex*, 1967, *3*, 163–175.

Kinsbourne, M. The cerebral basis of lateral asymmetries in attention. *Acta Psychologica*, 1970, *33*, 193–201.

Kinsbourne, M. Eye and head turning indicates cerebral lateralization. *Science*, 1972, *176*, 539–541.

Kinsbourne, M. The control of attention by interaction between the cerebral hemispheres. In S. Kornblum (Ed.), *Attention and performance IV*. New York: Academic Press, 1973.

Kinsbourne, M. Mechanisms of hemispheric interaction in man. In M. Kinsbourne & W. L. Smith (Eds.), *Hemispheric disconnection and cerebral function*. Springfield: Charles C Thomas, 1974.

Kinsbourne, M. Cerebral dominance, learning, and cognition. In H. R. Myklebust, (Ed.), *Progress in learning disabilities* (Vol. 3). New York: Grune & Stratton, 1975.(a)

Kinsbourne, M. The ontogeny of cerebral dominance. *Annals of the New York Academy of Sciences*, 1975, *263*, 244–250. (b)

Kinsbourne, M. The mechanism of hemispheric control of the lateral gradient of attention. In P. M. A. Rabbitt & S. Dornic (Eds.), *Attention and performance V*. London: Academic Press, 1975. (c)

Kinsbourne, M., & Caplan, P. J. *Children's learning and attention problems*. Boston: Little, Brown, 1979.

Kinsbourne, M., & Cook, J. Generalized and lateralized effects of concurrent verbalization on a unimanual skill. *Quarterly Journal of Experimental Psychology*, 1971, *23*, 341–345.

Kinsbourne, M., & Hicks, R. E. Functional cerebral space: A model for overflow, transfer and interference effects in human performance. In J. Requin (Ed.), *Attention and performance VII*. Hillsdale: Erlbaum, 1978.(a)

Kinsbourne, M., & Hicks, R. E. Mapping cerebral functional space: Competition and collaboration in human performance. In M. Kinsbourne (Ed.), *Asymmetrical function of the brain*. Cambridge: Cambridge University Press, 1978.(b)

Kinsbourne, M., & Hiscock, M. Does cerebral dominance develop? In S. J. Segalowitz & F. A. Gruber (Eds.), *Language development and neurological theory*. New York: Academic Press, 1977.

Kinsbourne, M., & Lempert, H. Does left brain lateralization of speech arise from right-biased orienting to salient percepts? *Human Development,* 1979, *22,* 270-276.

Kinsbourne, M., & McMurray, J. The effect of cerebral dominance on time sharing between speaking and tapping by preschool children. *Child Development,* 1975, *46,* 240-242.

Kinsbourne, M., & Warrington, E. K. Developmental factors in reading and writing backwardness. *British Journal of Psychology,* 1963, *54,* 145-156.

Knights, R. M., & Bakker, D. J. (Eds.), *The neuropsychology of learning disorders.* Baltimore: University Park Press, 1976.

Knox, C., & Kimura, D. Cerebral processing of nonverbal sounds in boys and girls. *Neuropsychologia,* 1970, *8,* 227-237.

Kocel, K. M. Cognitive abilities: Handedness, familial sinistrality and sex. *Annals of the New York Academy of Sciences,* 1977, *299,* 233-243.

Kocel, K. M. Age-related changes in cognitive abilities and hemispheric specialization. In J. Herron (Ed.), *Neurospychology of left-handedness.* New York: Academic Press, 1980.

Kocel, K., Galin, D., Ornstein, R., & Merrin, E. L. Lateral eye movement and cognitive mode. *Psychonomic Science,* 1972, *27,* 223-224.

Kohn, B., & Dennis, M. Selective impairments of visuo-spatial abilities in infantile hemiplegics after right hemidecortication. *Neuropsychologia,* 1974, *12,* 505-512.

Krashen, S. D. Lateralization, language learning, and the critical period: Some new evidence. *Language Learning,* 1973, *23,* 63-74.

Kuhn, G. M. The phi coefficient as an index of ear differences in dichotic listening. *Cortex,* 1973, *9,* 450-456.

Lenneberg, E. H. *Biological foundations of language.* New York: Wiley, 1967.

Levy, J. Possible basis for the evolution of lateral specialization of the human brain. *Nature,* 1969, *224,* 614-615.

Levy, J. Psychobiological implications of bilateral asymmetry. In S. J. Dimond & J. G. Beaumont (Eds.), *Hemisphere function in the human brain.* London: Paul Elek, 1974.

Levy, J., & Nagylaki, T. A model for the genetics of handedness. *Genetics,* 1972, *72,* 117-128.

Levy, J., & Reid, M. Variations in writing posture and cerebral organization. *Science,* 1976, *194,* 337-339.

Levy, J., & Reid M. Variations in cerebral organization as a function of handedness, hand posture in writing, and sex. *Journal of Experimental Psychology: General,* 1978, *107,* 119-144.

Liederman, J., & Kinsbourne, M. Rightward turning biases in neonates reflect a single neural asymmetry in motor programming. *Infant Behavior and Development,* 1980, *3,* 245-251. (a)

Liederman, J., & Kinsbourne, M. The mechanism of neonatal rightward turning bias: A sensory or motor asymmetry? *Infant Behavior and Development,* 1980, *3,* 223-238. (b)

Luria, A. R. *Traumatic aphasia. Its syndromes, psychology and treatment* (trans. by D. Bowden). Paris: Mouton, 1970.

Lyle, J. G. Reading retardation and reversal tendency: A factorial study. Child Development, 1969, *40*, 833–843.

Malmquist, E. *Factors related to reading disabilities in the first grade of elementary school.* Stockholm: Almquist and Wiksell, 1958.

Marcie, P. Writing disorders in 47 left-handed patients with unilateral cerebral lesions. *International Journal of Mental Health,* 1972, *3*, 30–37.

Marshall, J. C., Caplan, D., & Holmes, J. M. The measures of laterality. *Neuropsychologia,* 1975, *13*, 315–321.

Matarazzo, J. D. *Wechsler's measurement and appraisal of adult intelligence* (5th ed.). Baltimore: Williams & Wilkins, 1972.

McKeever, W. F., & Huling, M. D. Lateral dominance in tachistoscopic word recognition performances obtained with simultaneous bilateral input. *Neuropsychologia,* 1971, *9*, 15–20.

Miller, E. Handedness and the pattern of human ability. *British Journal of Psychology,* 1971, *62*, 111–112.

Milner, B., Branch, T., & Rasmussen, T. Observations on cerebral dominance. In A. V. S. De Rends & M. O'Connor (Eds.), *Ciba foundation symposium on disorders of language.* London: Churchill, 1964.

Moffitt, A. R. Consonant cue perception by twenty to twenty-four week old infants. *Child Development,* 1971, *42*, 717–731.

Molfese, D. L. Central asymmetry in infants, children and adults: Auditory evoked responses to speech and music. *Journal of the Acoustical Society of America,* 1973, *53*, 363–373.

Molfese, D. L. Infant cerebral asymmetry. In S. J. Segalowitz & F. A. Gruber (Eds.), *Language development and neurological theory.* New York: Academic Press, 1977.

Molfese, D. L., Freeman, R. B., & Palermo, D. The ontogeny of brain lateralization for speech and nonspeech stimuli. *Brain and Language,* 1975, *2*, 356–368.

Morais, J. The effects of ventriloquism on the right-side advantage for verbal material. *Cognition,* 1975, *3*, 127–139.

Morais, J., & Bertelson, P. Laterality effects in dichotic listening. *Perception,* 1973, *2*, 107–111.

Morais, J., & Bertelson, P. Spatial position versus ear of entry as determinant of the auditory laterality effects: A stereophonic test. *Journal of Experimental Psychology: Human Perception and Performance,* 1975, *1*, 253–262.

Morais, J., & Darwin, C. J. Ear differences for same-different reaction times to monaurally presented speech. *Brain and Language,* 1974, *1*, 383–390.

Morgan, M. J., & Corballis, M. C. On the biological basis of human laterality: II. The mechanisms of inheritance. *Behavior and Brain Sciences,* 1978, *2*, 270–277.

Morley, M. E. *The development and disorders of speech in childhood* (2nd ed.). Baltimore: William & Wilkins, 1965.

Nagafuchi, M. Development of dichotic and monaural hearing abilities in young children. *Acta Otolaryngologica*, 1970, *69*, 409-414.

Newcombe, F., & Ratcliff, G. Handedness, speech lateralization and ability. *Neuropsychologia*, 1973, *11*, 399-407.

Oldfield, R. C. The assessment and analysis of handedness: The Edinburgh Inventory. *Neuropsychologia*, 1971, *9*, 97-112.

Orton, S. T. *Reading, writing and speech problems in children.* New York: Norton, 1937.

Orton, S. T. Visual functions in strephosymbolia. *Arch Ophthalmol*, 1943, *30*, 707-713.

Papcun, G., Krashen, S., Terbeek, D., Remington, R., & Harshman, R. Is the left hemisphere specialized for speech, language and/or something else? *Journal of Acoustical Society of America*, 1974, *55*, 319-327.

Penfield, W., & Roberts, L. *Speech and brain mechanisms.* Princeton: Princeton University Press, 1959.

Petrie, B. F., & Peters, M. Handedness: Left/right differences in intensity of grasp response and duration of rattle holding in infants. *Infant Behavior and Development*, 1980, *3*, 215-221.

Piazza, D. M. Cerebral lateralization in young children as measured by dichotic listening and finger tapping tasks. *Neuropsychologia*, 1977, *15*, 417-425.

Pirozzolo, F. J., & Rayner, K. Cerebral organization and reading disability. *Neuropsychologia*, 1979, *17*, 485-491.

Pizzamiglio, L. De Pascalis, C., & Vignati, A. Stability of dichotic listening test. *Cortex*, 1974, *10*, 203-205.

Porac, C., & Coren, S. Is sighting dominance a part of generalized laterality? *Perceptual and Motor Skills*, 1975, *40*, 763-769.

Porac, C., & Coren, S. The dominant eye. *Psychological Bulletin*, 1976, *83*, 880-897.

Porter, R. J., & Berlin, C. I. On interpreting developmental changes in the dichotic right ear advantage. *Brain and Language*, 1975, *2*, 186-200.

Pratt, R. T. C., & Warrington, E. K. The assessment of cerebral dominance with unilateral E. C. T. *British Journal of Psychiatry*, 1972, *121*, 327-328.

Pratt, R. T. C., Warrington, E. K., & Halliday, A. M. Unilateral E. C. T. as a test for cerebral dominance, with a strategy for treating left-handers. *British Journal of Psychiatry*, 1971, *119*, 78-83.

Provine, R. R., & Westerman, J. A. Crossing the midline: Limits of early eye-hand behavior. *Child Development*, 1979, *50*, 437-441.

Provins, K. A. Motor skills, handedness, and behaviour. *Australian Journal of Psychology*, 1967, *11*, 137-150.

Provins, K. A., & Cunliffe, P. The reliability of some motor performance tests of handedness. *Neuropsychologia*, 1972, *10*, 199-206.

Provins, K. A., & Jeeves, M. A. Hemisphere differences in response time to simple auditory stimuli. *Neuropsychologia*, 1975, *13*, 207-211.

Ramsay, D. S. Manual preference for tapping in infants. *Developmental Psychology*, 1979, *15*, 437-442.

Rasmussen, T., & Milner, B. Clinical and surgical studies of the cerebral speech areas in man. In K. J. Zulch, O. Creutzfeldt, & G. Galbraith (Eds.), *Otfrid Foerster symposium on cerebral localization.* Heidelberg: Springer-Verlag, 1975.

Reed, J. C., & Reitan, R. M. Verbal and performance differences among brain-injured children with lateralized motor deficits. *Perceptual and Motor Skills,* 1969, *29,* 747–752.

Richardson, J. T. E. How to measure laterality. *Neuropsychologia,* 1976, *14,* 135–136.

Roberts, J., & Engle A. *Family background, early development, and intelligence of children 6–11 years.* National Center for Health Statistics. Data from the National Health Survey, Series II, No. 142, DHEW Publication No. (HRA) 75–1624 (Washington, D.C.: U.S. Government Printing Office, 1974).

Roberts, L. Aphasia, apraxia and agnosia in abnormal states of cerebral dominance. In P. J. Vinken & G. W. Bruyn (Eds.), *Handbook of clinical neurology* (Vol. 4). Amsterdam: North-Holland, 1969.

Rossi, G. F., & Rosadini, G. Experimental analysis of cerebral dominance in man. In C. F. Millikan & F. L. Darley (Eds.), *Brain mechanisms underlying speech and language.* New York: Grune & Stratton, 1967.

Rudel, R. G., Denckla, M. B., & Hirsch, S. The development of left-hand superiority for discriminating braille configurations. *Neurology,* 1977, *27,* 160–164.

Rudel, R. G., Denckla, M. B., & Spalten, E. The functional asymmetry of Braille letter learning in normal, sighted children. *Neurology,* 1974, *24,* 733–738.

Russell, W. R., & Espir, M. L. E. *Traumatic aphasia. A study of aphasia in war wounds of the brain.* London: Oxford University Press, 1961.

Rutter, M., Tizard, J., & Whitmore, K. (Eds.). *Education, health and behaviour.* London: Longmans, 1970.

Satz, P. Pathological left-handedness: An explanatory model. *Cortex,* 1972, *8,* 121–135.

Satz, P. Left-handedness and early brain insult. *Neuropsychologia,* 1973, *11,* 115–117.

Satz, P. Cerebral dominance and reading disability: An old problem revisited. In R. M. Knights & D. J. Bakker (Eds.): *The neuropsychology of learning disorders.* Baltimore: University Park Press, 1976.

Satz, P. Laterality tests: An inferential problem. *Cortex,* 1977, *13,* 208–212.

Satz, P., Bakker, D. J., Teunissen, J., Goebel, R., & Van der Vlugt, H. Developmental parameters of the ear asymmetry: A multivariate approach. *Brain and Language,* 1975, *2,* 171–185.

Satz, P., Baymur, L., & Van der Vlugt, H. Pathological left-handedness. Cross-cultural tests of a model. *Neuropsychologia,* in press.

Schulman-Galambos, C. Dichotic listening performance in elementary and college students. *Neuropsychologia,* 1977, *15,* 577–584.

Schwartz, G. E., Davidson, R. J., & Maer, F. Right hemisphere lateralization for emotion in the human brain: Interactions with cognition. *Science,* 1975, *190,* 236–238.

Schwartz, M. Left-handedness and high-risk pregnancy. *Neuropsychologia*, 1977, *15*, 341–344.

Searleman, A. A review of right hemisphere linguistic capabilities. *Psychological Bulletin*, 1977, *84*, 503–528.

Segalowitz, S. J., & Chapman, J. S. Cerebral asymmetry for speech in neonates: A behavioral measure. *Brain and Language*, in press.

Seth, G. Eye-hand co-ordination and "handedness": A developmental study of visuo-motor behavior in infants. *British Journal of Educational Psychology*, 1973, *43*, 35–49.

Shankweiler, D., & Studdert-Kennedy, M. A continuum of lateralization for speech perception? *Brain and Language*, 1975, *2*, 212–225.

Simon, J. R. Ear preference in a simple reaction-time task. *Journal of Experimental Psychology*, 1967, *75*, 49–55.

Siqueland, E. R., & Lipsitt, L. P. Conditioned head turning in human newborns. *Journal of Experimental Child Psychology*, 1966, *4*, 356–357.

Sparrow, S., & Satz, P Dyslexia, laterality and neuropsychological development. In D. J. Bakker & P. Satz (Eds.), *Specific reading disability: Advances in theory and method.* Rotterdam: Rotterdam University Press, 1970.

Spellacy, F., & Blumstein, S. The influence of language set on ear preference in phoneme recognition. *Cortex*, 1970, *6*, 430–439.

Stein, D. G., Rosen, J. J., & Butters, N. *Plasticity and recovery of function in the nervous system.* New York: Academic Press, 1974.

Steingrueber, H. J. Handedness as a function of test complexity. *Perceptual and Motor Skills*, 1975, *40*, 263–266.

Studdert-Kennedy, M. Dichotic studies II: Two questions. *Brain and Language*, 1975, *2*, 123–130.

Studdert-Kennedy, M., & Shankweiler, D. P. Hemispheric specialization for speech perception. *Journal of the Acoustical Society of America*, 1970, *48*, 579–594.

Subirana, A. The prognosis of aphasia in relation to cerebral dominance and handedness. *Brain*, 1958, *81*, 415–425.

Swanson, J. M. Kinsbourne, M., & Horn, J. M. Cognitive deficit and left-handedness: A cautionary note. In J. Herron (Ed.), *The neuropsychology of left-handedness.* New York, Academic Press, 1980.

Teng, E. L., Lee, P. H., Yang, K. S., & Chang, P. C. Handedness in a Chinese population: Biological, social, and pathological factors. *Science*, 1976, *193*, 1148–1150.

Teszner, D., Tzavaras, A., & Gruner, J. L'asymétrie droite-gauche du planum temporale. A propos de l'étude anatomique de 100 cerveaus. *Revue Neurologique*, 1972, *126*, 444–449.

Thompson, W. R. Development and the biophysical bases of personality. In E. F. Borgatta & W. W. Lambert (Eds.), *Handbook of personality theory research.* Skokie, Ill.: Rand McNally, 1968.

Trehub, S. E., & Rabinovitch, M. S. Auditory-linguistic sensitivity in early infancy. *Developmental Psychology*, 1972, *6*, 74–77.

Turkewitz, G., Gordon, B. W., & Birch, M. G. Head turning in the human neonate: Effect of prandial condition and lateral preference. *Journal of Comparative and Physiological Psychology*, 1968, *59*, 189–192.

Turkewitz, G. Moreau, T., Birch, H., & Crystal, D. Relationship between prior head position and lateral differences in responsiveness to somesthetic stimulation in the human neonate. *Journal of Experimental Child Psychology*, 1967, *5*, 548–561.

Van Lancker, D., & Fromkin, V. A. Hemispheric specialization for pitch and "tone." Evidence from Thai. *Journal of Phonetics*, 1977, *1*, 101–109.

Vernon, M. D. *Backwardness in reading*. London: Cambridge University Press, 1957.

Vernon, M. D. *Reading and its difficulties*. London: Cambridge University Press, 1971.

Waber, D. P. Sex differences in mental abilities, hemispheric lateralization, and rate of physical growth at adolescence. *Developmental Psychology*, 1977, *13*, 29–38.

Wada, J., Clark, R., & Hamm, A. Cerebral hemispheric symmetry in humans. *Archives of Neurology*, 1975, *32*, 239–246.

Wada, J., & Rasmussen, T. Intracarotid injection of sodium Amytal for the lateralization of cerebral speech dominance: Experimental and clinical observations. *Journal of Neurosurgery*, 1960, *17*, 266–282.

Wagner, N. M., & Harris, L. J. *Hand asymmetries in braille letter learning in sighted nine- and eleven-year-olds: A cautionary note on sex differences*. Paper presented at the Annual Meeting of the International Neuropsychology Society, New York, 1979.

Warrington, E. K., & Pratt, R. T. C. Language laterality in left-handers assessed by unilateral E. C. T. *Neuropsychologia*, 1973, *11*, 423–428.

White, M. J. Laterality differences in perception: A review. *Psychological Bulletin*, 1969, *72*, 387–405.

Wilson, M. O., & Dolan, L. B. Handedness and ability. *American Journal of Psychology*, 1931, *43*, 261–268.

Witelson, S. F. Sex and the single hemisphere: Right hemisphere specialization for spatial processing. *Science*, 1976, *193*, 425–427.

Witelson, S. F., & Pallie, W. Left hemisphere specialization for language in the newborn: Neuroanatomical evidence of asymmetry. *Brain*, 1973, *96*, 641–646.

Woo, T. L., & Pearson, K. Dextrality and sinistrality of hand and eye. *Biometrika*, 1927, *19*, 165–199.

Woods, B. T., & Teuber, H. L. Changing patterns of childhood aphasia. *Annals of Neurology*, 1978, *3*, 273–280.

Wyke, M. Dysphasia: A review of recent progress. *British Medical Bulletin*, 1971, *27*, 211–217.

Yeni-Komshian, G. H., & Benson, D. A. Anatomical study of cerebral asymmetry in the temporal lobe of humans, chimpanzees and Rhesus monkeys. *Science*, 1976, *192*, 387–389.

Yeni-Komshian, G., Isenberg, D., & Goldberg, H. Cerebral dominance and

reading disability: Left visual deficit in poor readers. *Neuropsychologia,*
1975, *13,* 83–94.

Yule, W., & Rutter, M. Epidemiology and social implications of specific
reading retardation. In R. M. Knights & D. J. Bakker (Eds.), *The neuropsychology of learning disorders.* Baltimore: University Park Press, 1976.

Zangwill, O. L. *Cerebral dominance and its relation to psychological function.*
London: Oliver and Boyd, 1960.

Zangwill, O. L. Dyslexia in relation to cerebral dominance. In J. Money (Ed.),
Reading disability. Baltimore: Johns Hopkins Press, 1962.

Zangwill, O. L. Speech and the minor hemisphere. *Acta Neurol Psychiatrica
Belgica,* 1967, *67,* 1013–1020.

Francis J. Pirozzolo
Debra J. Campanella

5

The Neuropsychology of Developmental Speech Disorders, Language Disorders, and Learning Disabilities

A significant percentage of school-age children have impaired abilities for acquiring the language skills necessary for school success. Some of these children are brain-injured and handicapped by motor, sensory, or cognitive disabilities. A larger proportion have developmental disorders, disabilities that are probably of fundamental neurologic origin, but have eluded present methods of analysis. These children have the so-called soft neurologic signs, including delayed speech or reading, or have deficits that in the adult would be suggestive of central nervous system disease. Since developmental disorders are relatively common, differential diagnosis is both more difficult and more important. School psychologists must rule out other pathological conditions that present similar symptomatology, and provide a correct diagnosis and remediation plan.

Primary or specific speech and language disorders and secondary speech and language disorders affect approximately 8.5 percent of all preschool children (Bliss, Allen, & Walker, 1978). While a considerable number of children do overcome these difficulties and reach a level of communication skill equivalent to that of their age-mates, one follow-up study (Wolpaw, Nation, & Aram, 1977) shows that 70 percent of children who had pre-school language disorders continue to show signs of impairment at age 9, with 60 percent of these children in special classes. It is clear that childhood speech and language problems are some of the greatest challenges facing the clinical neurosciences.

167

The evaluation of children with suspected developmental disorders should include assessments by an interdisciplinary team of specialists. The following examinations should be considered in the routine differential diagnostic evaluation.

A general physical examination by a pediatrician or pediatric neurologist is important. This evaluation should include a thorough medical history (with emphasis on family history and perinatal history), a general physical examination, and a more specific neurologic examination. Appropriate laboratory tests should be carried out in this part of the evaluation. In addition to the usual blood chemistries and urinanalysis, other procedures performed may include electroencephalography or one or more neuroradiological procedures.

Neuropsychological and/or psychological evaluation is another important part of the diagnostic work-up. Neuropsychological evaluation of the school-age child (see Chapter 7) should include a complete mental status examination. Tests of general intelligence, memory, perceptual, motor, perceptual-motor, speech, and language abilities must be part of the neuropsychological battery. Further evaluation of attention, concentration, and emotional adjustment is also important.

Educational assessment by a specialist is an essential part of the evaluation plan. Testing of reading, writing, spelling, and arithmetic achievement, as well as more specific speech and language evaluation, will provide a sound description of the child's educational status and will aid in the development of a remedial plan.

SPEECH DISORDERS

Articulation Disorders

Articulation disorder refers to deviant oral production of speech sounds. Specific types of articulation errors include (1) substitution of one sound for another, (2) omission of a sound, (3) distortion of sounds, and (4) addition of inappropriate sounds. More than one type of error can occur in a child's speech, but generally one error type will be more prevalent than another. The specific type depends on the etiology of the disorder. Distinct error patterns may emerge with specific organic deficits, such as cleft palate, cerebral palsy, hearing loss, and mental retardation.

Most school-age children who misarticulate, however, do not have organic deficits. In fact, many sound substitutions and omissions occur during the normal developmental sequence of speech acquisition. The specific types of errors observed in normal speech development have been described extensively in the literature (e.g., Templin, 1957; Winitz, 1969). Normal children are frequently observed to substitute "easy" sounds for more "difficult" sounds. Most children master correct articulation of all phonemes by 8 years of age.

Articulation errors that are not due to neurological impairment or organic disorders, and are not considered part of the normal developmental sequence, are sometimes referred to as dyslalia. These errors are usually the result of a simple failure to learn phonological rules (Compton, 1970; Van Riper, 1972b; Winitz, 1969). The probable causes of this presumed mislearning have been studied, but no conclusive results have been shown. Studies of auditory discrimination and pitch discrimination suggest that children with disordered articulation have poorer discrimination skills in these areas than normal speakers (Bradley, 1959; Mange, 1960; Sommers, Meyer & Fenton, 1961; Sommers, Meyer, & Furlong, 1969; Weiner, 1967).

Specific characteristics of articulation errors in children with no apparent structural or neurological abnormalities have not been elucidated yet. However, Compton (1970) has identified some of the most commonly occurring deviant phonological rules in 5- and 6-year-old children. Results suggest that there are, indeed, sound substitutions and omissions that not only occur more frequently than others in the speech of the articulation-disordered child, but that there are distinct patterns of errors that are likely to occur.

ASSESSMENT OF ARTICULATION DISORDERS

Traditionally, articulation tests have been designed to identify the number of defective sounds, types of errors made, and overall intelligibility of speech. Most commonly, a picture is presented to elicit spontaneous production of a word containing the phoneme being tested. Sentence level testing is also included in most standardized tests. Responses are recorded for analysis of features of the errors, and performance is generally compared to norms for specific age groups.

Recent work by Lorentz (1976) suggests that identifying faulty phonemes and analyzing the features of these errors may not be sufficient. He has shown that assessment of articulation disorders should involve more than the limited stimulus–response approach of most articulation techniques. Lorentz suggests that many children with articulation deficits are operating under a set of deviant phonological rules and argues that assessment should include characterization of these rules.

F. L. Darley (1979) has provided a concise summary and description of many popular articulation tests. Frequently used diagnostic tests include the Fisher-Logemann Test of Articulation Competence (H. A. Fisher & Logemann, 1971), Goldman-Fristoe Test of Articulation (Goldman & Fristoe, 1972), and the Templin-Darley Test of Articulation (Templin & Darley, 1969). Popular screening tests include the Denver Articulation Screening

Examination (Drumwright, 1971) and the Photo Articulation Test (Pender-gast, Dickey, Selmar, & Soder, 1969).

TREATMENT OF ARTICULATION DISORDERS

Sommers and Kane (1974) have reviewed the most important approaches to articulation therapy. These approaches vary in their emphasis on sensory and perceptual factors, oral production, and subjective analysis. Traditional approaches have focused on a variety of perceptual and behavioral areas: phonetic placement, motokinesis, ear training, sensorimotor skills, and feed-back. Other therapy approaches emphasize nondirective techniques, carry-over through nonsense materials, and use of teaching machines.

Articulation therapy requires more than eliciting a correct sound in a specific context. Carry-over and generalization are essential to effective treatment. These are often achieved by using operant conditioning principles. Most speech clinicians would agree that measurements of carry-over and generalization are the most difficult aspects of articulation therapy.

Voice Disorders

While no adequate definition exists, voice disorders are disturbances of oral production in which the speaker's voice sounds unpleasant or is in-appropriate for listening (Shanks & Dugauy, 1974). Voice disorders can result from either neuromuscular or functional causes. Most voice disorders are described in terms of deviations of pitch, loudness, or quality of vocal production. These characteristics are the acoustic correlates of features of respiration, phonation, and resonance.

Deviant voice quality is often described by a variety of terms, including hypernasal, denasal, breathy, harsh, and hoarse. Hoarseness appears to be the most common voice disorder observed in the school-age child. This disorder is often associated with vocal abuse, sometimes resulting in a nodule or irritation on the edge of the vocal folds. Excessive use of the voice, inap-propriate loudness, and inappropriate pitch are the most common forms of vocal abuse in children. Hypernasality and denasality, although seen less frequently than hoarse voice quality, are not uncommon. Hypernasality suggests an inability of the soft palate to sufficiently prevent excess air from traveling through the nasal passage. It is usually associated with cleft palate, but also can occur after surgical removal of the adenoids, with diseases causing paralysis of the soft palate, and, sometimes, in the absence of any obvious organic deficiency. Denasality is a term used to describe a voice quality resulting from occlusion of the nasal passages. Nasal consonants are usually distorted and voice quality sounds dull. Enlarged adenoids and abnormal growths in the nasal passage are the most common causes of de-nasality in children.

Pitch deviations occurring in children usually fall into one of the following categories: (1) pitch level too high, (2) pitch level too low, (3) monopitch, and (4) pitch breaks. Pitch breaks refer to involuntary abrupt changes in voice pitch, generally of an octave or more. These are particularly common in boys during puberty. Although pitch breaks diminish after pubescence, boys are sometimes found to have assumed an abnormal habitual pitch in order to reduce these abrupt changes in voice. Other common causes of pitch deviations may be hearing loss, emotional conflict, hormonal problems, tension, or laryngeal abnormality (Boone, 1971; G. P. Moore, 1971).

Loudness disorders can range from complete loss of voice (aphonia) to excessively loud voice. These are generally the least common voice disorders in school-age children. Hearing loss is an important consideration when a child is observed to use an inappropriate loudness level. Deviations in loudness also may result from emotional problems, vocal fold paralysis, and certain neurological deficits.

ASSESSMENT OF VOICE DISORDERS

Two major approaches to evaluating voice disorders are (1) investigation of physiological function of the larynx and (2) auditory analysis of characteristics of the vocal output (G. P. Moore, 1971; Perkins, 1971; Shanks & Duguay, 1974). Physiological analysis deals with features of voice production such as airflow, air pressure, physical characteristics of the vocal folds (stiffness, length, elasticity, contour, degree of vocal fold approximation), and neuromuscular changes accompanying phonation. Auditory analysis deals with assessing characteristics of the sound of the voice. This may be done by using instrumentation to determine fundamental frequency and intensity of the voice, or it may be done by perceptual analysis. Use of instrumentation to measure parameters of voice production and laryngeal functioning is becoming increasingly popular. Instrumentation techniques that have been used are electromyography (Gay & Harris, 1971), fiberoptics (Brewer & McCall, 1974), spectrographic study (Colton, 1972), ultrasound (Kelsey, Minifie, & Hixon, 1969) and ultra-high-speed photography (G. P. Moore, 1975).

Most authors agree that evaluation of voice disorders should include laryngoscopic examination by a qualified specialist (Boone, 1971; G. P. Moore, 1957). This is necessary to check for laryngeal disease and the possible need for surgery. Voice disorders resulting from underlying emotional conflict may also require assessment by a psychologist or psychiatrist.

TREATMENT OF VOICE DISORDERS

Treatment of vocal disturbances is largely based on etiological factors. Where certain types of laryngeal pathology exist, surgery is necessary. In most cases, especially in school-age children, voice disorders are a result of vocal abuse. Methods for eliminating and modifying vocal abuse in children have been suggested (Boone, 1971; G. P. Moore, 1957; Wilson, 1972). These generally require monitoring loudness and excessive use of the voice. Treatment techniques for altering other aspects of voice dysfunction are also described by these authors.

Reed (1980), however, points out that there is little experimental evidence to document the effectiveness of most voice therapy procedures. He states that "there are few useful guidelines for predicting the outcome of voice therapy endeavors. Specifications of behavioral, physiologic, and acoustic measures, combined with appropriate research designs, may allow clinicians to demonstrate accountability for their patients with vocal disorders" (p. 168).

Stuttering

Stuttering is a disruption in the fluency of speech. Although no specific definition of this disorder has been universally agreed upon, most authors describe the symptomatology of stuttering in similar ways (Ainsworth, 1971; Bloodstein, 1969; Van Riper, 1972a). Characteristics usually included in the consideration of stuttering are overt speech behaviors and concomitant variables that often appear to be the result of the stutterer's tension and anxiety. Overt speech behaviors typical of stuttering are repetitions and/or prolongations of sounds, syllables, or words that interrupt the fluency and rhythm of speech. Abnormally long pauses or *blocks* are also considered part of the clinical picture of stuttering. Descriptions of repetitions, prolongations, and pauses have largely been based on perceptual identification by the listener.

The literature also reports physiological changes that often accompany stuttering. In contrast to the perceptual identification of overt behaviors, detection and quantification of these physiological processes have been done with a wide assortment of instruments. Studies have shown alterations in electroencephalographic activity (Freestone, 1942; Sayles, 1971; Travis & Malamud, 1937), dilatation of the pupils (Gardner, 1937), decreases in blood sugar levels (W. E. Moore, 1959), and eye movement abnormalities (Kopp, 1963). Most recent research has shown deviations in articulatory dynamics of stuttering (Zimmerman, 1980a,b), differences in laryngeal behavior among the various types of stuttering (Conture, McCall, & Brewer, 1977), and variations in regional cerebral blood flow (Wood, Stump, McKeehan, Sheldon, & Proctor, 1980).

Many authors have suggested that the features of an individual's stuttering are prone to change over time (Bloodstein, 1969; Bluemel, 1932; Froeschels, 1961; Van Riper, 1972a). It is reported that in the initial phases of stuttering in children 2-6 years old, repetitions and prolongations are relatively effort-less; there is little evidence of concern by the stutterer about the dysfluency of speech. As the stuttering advances, the frequency of dysfluencies increases and specific situation and word fears arise. Stuttering seen in late adolescence and adulthood is often in its most advanced stages. It is frequently associated with avoidance of speech situations, fearful anticipation of stuttering, and frequent word substitutions and circumlocutions (Bloodstein, 1969; Van Riper, 1972b). It is in this late stage of stuttering that many of the con-comitant features, such as extraneous muscle activity, tend to arise. These are presumed to be the result of tension and anxiety.

Most researchers of speech pathology agree that dysfluency in young children is part of the normal developmental sequence of speech acquisition (Bloodstein, 1969; Sheehan & Martyn, 1970; Van Riper, 1972a). There appear to be, however, three distinct schools of thought regarding the per-sistence of stuttering behavior. These three theories are usually grouped as follows: psychoanalytic theories (Barbara, 1954; Glauber, 1958; Travis, 1940); organic or "constitutional" theories (Karlin, 1959; Mysak, 1960; West, 1958); and learning theories (Brutten & Shoemaker, 1967, 1971; Shames & Sherrick, 1963). The reader is referred to Ainsworth (1971) for a review of theories of stuttering.

ASSESSMENT OF STUTTERING

There are few standardized diagnostic tools available for assessment of stuttering. Observations of overt behaviors, measurement of physiological parameters, and paper-and-pencil tests assessing attitudes toward stuttering have all been employed as assessment techniques. Overt speech behaviors are generally measured according to the number and type of fluency failures per specified period of time. The locus and distribution of dysfluencies are usually measured in spontaneous speech production and in oral reading. Physiological parameters measured include heart rate, blood pressure, pulse rate, and galvanic skin response (Webster & Brutten, 1974).

Several of the paper-and-pencil tests requiring self-assessment of behaviors and attitudes are the Iowa Scale of Attitude Toward Stuttering (Ammons & Johnson, 1963); the Scale of Communication Attitudes: S-Scale (Erickson, 1969); and the Southern Illinois University Speech Situations Check List (Brutten & Shoemaker, 1971). These require evaluation of emotional reac-tions to specific speaking situations. Use of these particular tests is more common and more clinically appropriate for evaluation of stuttering in the later stages. For young children, description and quantification of the frequency and nature of dysfluencies are more appropriate measures of performance.

TREATMENT OF STUTTERING

The treatment of stuttering is largely dependent on the individual clinician's perspective toward the etiology of stuttering. Those supporting a psychoanalytic view of stuttering may choose to treat the underlying emotional conflict presumed to be the cause of the disorder (Barbara, 1954). Learning theorists treat the behavioral features of stuttering rather than a presumed underlying cause. Of particular interest is the use of operant conditioning principles to reduce overt dysfluent behaviors. Successful manipulation of stuttering by a variety of reinforcement and punishment techniques has been reported (Flanagan, Goldiamond, & Azrin, 1958; Goldiamond, 1965; Gray & England, 1969). Martin (1968) notes, however, that although some operant conditioning procedures may be successful in particular therapy environments, carry-over to other situations may be limited. Other experimental procedures that have been used to reduce overt symptomatology are delayed auditory feedback (Soderberg, 1968) and drug therapy (Kent, 1963). Van Riper (1973) has provided a comprehensive review of therapies used to reduce stuttering. Specific treatment approaches can be found in a variety of available texts (Bloodstein, 1969; Brutten & Shoemaker, 1967; Sheehan, 1970).

Communication Deficits Associated with Cerebral Palsy

Cerebral palsy is a nonprogressive brain disorder that occurs in the perinatal period. Classification of the different kinds of cerebral palsy is usually based on type and localization of lesions and degree of tonicity of neuromotor disability (Perlstein, 1952). The most common classification is based on the type of neuromuscular disability and includes the following categories: spasticity, athetosis, rigidity, flaccidity, tremor, ataxis, or mixed (Denhoff, 1976). The most prevalent types of cerebral palsy are spastic, athetotic, and mixed.

Disorders of voice, fluency, articulation, and language have all been reported in cerebral palsied children (Lencione, 1976). Voice characteristics that may accompany cerebral palsy are breathiness, aspirate voice quality, abnormal pitch, and loudness disorder. Fluency abnormalities such as short bursts of speech, excessively fast rate, or delay in initiation of voicing have also been reported. These difficulties arise from the numerous respiratory, laryngeal, and pharyngeal dysfunctions that result from central nervous system damage.

Studies of articulation disorders have indicated that omissions, substitutions, and distortions are all likely to occur in the speech of the cerebral palsied child (Irwin, 1972; Mysak, 1971a). Language problems sometimes associated with cerebral palsy include retarded language development, grammatical confusions, substantial lag in oral expression as compared to comprehension, and verbal perseveration (Mysak, 1971a). The literature suggests that qualitative and quantitative differences exist according to type of cerebral palsy (e.g., spastic versus athetoid).

Dysarthria is a term frequently used to describe clusters of speech production difficulties. Darley, Aronson, and Brown (1975) refer to dysarthria as "a collective name for a group of related speech disorders that are due to disturbances in muscular control of the speech mechanism resulting from impairment of any of the basic motor processes involved in the execution of speech" (p. 2). Dysarthria includes motor dysfunctions involving respiration, phonation, articulation, resonance, and prosody. These coexisting disturbances frequently occur in the speech of the cerebral palsied individual and vary with the severity and type of neuromuscular disturbance.

Several authors have addressed the issue of assessment and treatment of communication deficits in the cerebral palsied child (Cruickshank, 1976; DiCarlo, 1974; Mysak, 1971b; Westlake & Rutherford, 1961). Most authors agree that other features in addition to speech and language performance must be evaluated for comprehensive planning of the treatment program. Evaluations of motor impairment, intelligence, hearing, personality characteristics, visual disorders, social environment, and educational potentials should also be included in the neuropsychological assessment program, so that the treatment program will meet the individual needs of the cerebral palsied child.

LANGUAGE DISORDERS

The lack of agreement over definitions of language disorders has led to a plethora of operational definitions. A widely accepted definition is the one given by Bloom and Lahey (1978) who refer to language disorder as "a broad term to describe certain behaviors, or the lack of behaviors, in a child that might be expected considering the child's chronological age" (p. 290). This very general concept of language disorder would include failure to acquire language, delay in language acquisition, and use of inappropriate or "deviant" language structures, regardless of etiology. It would also include both comprehension and expression of language. Specific behaviors that are of interest include use of the sound system (phonology), manner in which words are put together to form sentences (syntax), use of vocabulary (semantics), and use of language in context (pragmatics). Phonological and syntactical rule learning by language-disordered children have been the most extensively studied areas, although some attention has been given to deviant phonology.

Leonard (1972) summarized some of the differences between normal children and deviant speakers. Children with language disorders (1) used indefinite pronouns, personal pronouns, main verbs, and secondary verbs less often than their normal peers; (2) used as many later-developing forms of these structures as their peers; (3) used negation, contraction, and auxiliary "be," and adjective transformations less frequently than their peers; and (4) used deviant forms characterized by verb-phrase omissions, noun-phrase omissions, and article omissions more frequently than normals. Recent studies suggest that language-disordered children generally use linguistic systems that are qualitatively similar to normal-speaking children (Johnston & Schery, 1976; Morehead & Ingram, 1973). The differences, however, are that language-disordered children tend to have marked delays in acquisition of many syntactic rules, that they use certain grammatical structures with less frequency than normal children, and that they do not use their language systems as creatively or efficiently as their normal peers.

Developmental Aphasia

Developmental aphasia refers to the child's inability to develop, or difficulty in developing, a normal understanding and use of language due to injury to the language centers of the central nervous system prenatally, perinatally, or postnatally during the first year of life (Gaddes, 1980). However, the plasticity of the child's brain may enable him or her to either overcome the number and severity of language impairments or to adapt to the neuropathological condition by changing the hemisphere dominant for language.

Children who have adequate sensory capacity and intelligence but who fail to acquire oral speech have been studied for about 150 years. For example, Myklebust (1971) quotes Binet and Simon, who in 1908 identified four basic operations in language development: understanding, speaking, reading, and writing (Binet & Simon, 1908). Binet and Simon noted that each of these specific operations may be suppressed separately by cerebral damage. Since then, a number of investigators have been refining the terminology and classification system. This work has led to the recognition that children who show a marked delay in the development of speech may be mentally normal, have normal hearing, and show no evidence of obvious disease.

Some common symptoms of developmental aphasia include language retardation, receptive deficits (Wernicke's aphasia), expressive deficits (Broca's aphasia), and central processing deficits (semantic aphasia). As Gaddes (1980) indicates, it is important to differentiate the aphasic from the mentally retarded, hard of hearing, or emotionally disturbed. A deficit in auditory language may be recognized during the preschool years whereas other disabilities may go unnoticed until later school years.

Diagnosis will provide information regarding auditory perception, comprehension, integration, and expression, thus indicating the pattern of deficits and relative strengths the child may have. Although the literature is replete with classification systems that divide aphasia into a number of separate syndromes by clustering various symptoms, a definite consistency is demonstrated across studies. Broca's aphasia refers to nonfluent aphasia output, relatively intact comprehension, some difficulty in repetition, and poor spontaneous speech. There is general agreement that individuals with Broca's aphasia will have pathology involving the posterior-inferior portion of the dominant (usually left) hemisphere (Benson, 1979). Wernicke's aphasia refers to verbal output that is fluent but almost invariably contaminated with paraphasia consisting mostly of semantic substitutions. The major language findings are a disturbance of comprehension and a matching disturbance of repetition. The pathology in most cases of Wernicke's aphasia involves the temporal lobe, particularly the auditory association cortex located in the posterior-superior portion of the first temporal gyrus (Benson, 1979).

Semantic aphasia (Luria, 1973) refers to damage or dysfunction that occurs in the left inferior-parietal or parieto-temporo-occipital areas. This causes difficulty in associating individual words or ideas into a meaningful whole. Difficulty understanding sentences, poor memory, and defective association of abstract concepts and symbolic thinking may also occur.

ASSESSMENT OF LANGUAGE DISORDERS

Most standardized language tests are designed to tap a specific aspect of communicative function. Evaluating receptive and expressive components of syntax, vocabulary, and basic language concepts is generally part of the assessment of the language-disordered child. Techniques such as picture description and sentence completion or imitation are used to elicit specific responses. Performance on these tests is then compared with established norms. Recently, emphasis has been placed on collecting samples of the child's spontaneous speech, usually in conversation with an adult, and analyzing various features of syntax, vocabulary, and length of utterance (Lee, 1974). Numerous tests for assessing receptive and expressive components of language are commercially available. Some widely used receptive language tests are the Peabody Picture Vocabulary Test (Dunn, 1965); the Test for Auditory Comprehension of Language (Carrow, 1973); and the Assessment of Children's Language Comprehension (Foster, Giddan, & Stark, 1973). Expressive language tests include the Carrow Elicited Language Inventory (Carrow, 1974) and the Environmental Language Inventory (McDonald,

1978). Tests assessing both receptive and expressive components are the Northwestern Syntax Screening Test (Lee, 1971); the Porch Index of Communicative Ability in Children (Porch, 1975); and the Illinios Test of Psycholinguistic Abilities (Kirk, McCarthy, & Kirk, 1968). Comprehensive reviews of widely used language tests can be found in Cicciarelli, Broen, and Siegel (1976), Darley (1979), and McConnell, Love, and Clark (1974).

TREATMENT OF LANGUAGE DISORDERS

Language treatment programs vary markedly according to the age of the child, the severity of the disorder, the nature of the language deficit, and learning characteristics of the child. Most often, communicative effectiveness and the child's skills in relation to the normal developmental sequence provide the framework for deciding how treatment should proceed. Bloom and Lahey (1978) suggest that prior to the initiation of specific techniques, the clinician should consider behaviors other than language (such as attentional patterns), amount of structure required, and changes in behavior in different environments.

Schiefelbusch (1978a,b) has provided two assessments of the clinical issues surrounding language intervention. In particular, he has analyzed such important issues as providing ongoing assessment, using visual and gestural prompts, using groups for language training, devising programs for nonverbal children, programming for communication therapy, and using parents as intervention agents. Wiig and Semel (1976) have also discussed procedures for remediation of perceptual- and linguistic-processing deficits, language-production abilities, and cognitive-processing deficits.

Another important issue in language treatment concerns the variety of techniques used to elicit and maintain behaviors. Bloom and Lahey (1978) have given an interesting summary of studies of the effectiveness of modeling, imitation, and feedback in language-intervention strategies. There appears to be no single technique that is consistently more effective than another, although responsiveness to techniques has been shown to depend on the learning style of the individual child. Most recent literature suggest that individual learning styles and environments optimal for learning need further investigation.

LEARNING DISABILITIES

In contradistinction to the rich history of the study of language disorders, learning disabilities were first recognized by teachers as well as researchers less than a century ago. Also, in contrast to childhood language disorders, only one form of learning disability has been studied to any considerable degree. Both scientifically and clinically, the study of learning disabilities has been confined largely to the investigation of developmental reading disorders. This fact, however, does not suggest that learning disability is a homogeneous diagnostic entity (Benton, 1978). Even with respect to the specific reading disability, increasing attention has been given to the assumption that several separate subgroups are subsumed under the general clinical category (Pirozzolo, 1979; Satz & Morris, 1980). While this represents some progress in the relatively primitive knowledge about these developmental disorders, some basic problems still exist. One such problem is the lack of agreement on the definition of developmental dyslexia. One popular definition was conceived by the World Federation of Neurology. It states that developmental dyslexia is "a disorder manifested by difficulty in learning to read despite conventional instruction, adequate intelligence, and sociocultural opportunity. It is dependent upon fundamental cognitive disabilities which are frequently of constitutional origin" (Critchley, 1970, p. 11). Among others, Ross (1976) has recognized the inadequacy of this definition. When the exclusion clauses in the definition are omitted, the definition of learning disability becomes "an inability to learn." In addition to this problem, there is very little agreement over the differences between "delayed reading acquisition" or "backward reading" and true developmental dyslexia (Rutter & Yule, 1975). Numerous other basic problems exist over the definitions, nosology, and incidence of these developmental disorders (Pirozzolo, 1979).

Recently, many clinicians have argued that learning disabilities are not a single homogeneous clinical entity but that several syndromes exist (e.g., Mattis, French, & Rapin, 1975). Denckla (1979) has identified ten common syndromes of learning disability. Her subgroups are based on a clinical inferential classification system (Table 5-1).

Several other investigators have found similar subgroups (Boder, 1973; Denckla & Rudel, 1976; Kinsbourne & Warrington, 1963; Mattis, 1980; Pirozzolo & Rayner, 1979). Other attempts to distinguish subtypes of learning disabilities have been based upon a statistical classification system (e.g., Doehring & Hoshko, 1977; Satz & Morris, 1980). A more basic classification of the syndromes described by Denckla was given by Peters, Romine, and Dyckman (1975), who divided these childhood disturbances into learning disabilities and hyperkinesis (or hyperactivity).

Some children are affected by the so-called pure form of hyperactivity, whereas other children are affected by the so-called pure form of learning disabilities, while still other children are affected by both disorders. It is unclear whether learning disabilities and hyperactivity are related etiologically, although clinical intuition suggests such an association. The literature has been

Table 5-1
Learning Disability Subtypes

- Developmental dyslexia with hyperactivity
- Hyperactivity – pure
- Hyperactivity – with EEG disturbances
- Developmental dyslexia – Global language disorder type
- Developmental dyslexia – Anomic – Repetition disorder
  type
- Developmental dyslexia – Articulation – Graphomotor
  disorder type
- Developmental dyslexia – Phonological – Sequencing
  disorder type
- Developmental Gerstmann syndrome
- Prechtl's Choreiform syndrome
- Miscellaneous learning disability

Modified from Denckla (1979).

for the most part separate for these two disorders. They remain two important developmental problems with obscure etiologies.

Attention Deficit Disorder

The American Psychiatric Association's third edition of the *Diagnostic
and Statistical Manual of Mental Disorders* (DSM-III) (1980) refers to childhood disorders that have previously been called hyperactivity, hyperkinesis,
minimal brain dysfunction, minimal brain damage, minimal cerebral dysfunction, and minor cerebral dysfunction as attention deficit disorders (ADD).
The clinical signs of ADD are a developmentally inappropriate short attention
span, excessive overactivity, and impulsivity. The DSM-III identifies two subtypes of ADD, one with hyperactivity and one without hyperactivity. While
previous preference has been given to hyperactivity in the identification of
this disorder, the DSM-III recognizes that in most cases of ADD, hyperactivity decreases markedly or disappears after pubescence.

Developmental Reading Disorder

The DSM-III separates the specific developmental disorders (e.g., developmental reading disorder, developmental arithmetic disorder, developmental
language disorder–expressive type) from other developmental disorders, and
codes them on a separate axis (Axis II). The DSM-III defines a developmental
reading disorder as a significant impairment in the acquisition of reading skills
that is not due to chronological or mental age or educational opportunity.

Among children between the ages of 8 and 13, a 1-2-year discrepancy between expected reading achievement (based on intellectual ability) and actual reading level is considered necessary before the diagnosis can be made. No recommendation is given for the diagnosis of a developmental reading disorder in children under 8.

Children with developmental reading disorders are described as having faulty oral reading with errors involving omissions, additions, and distortions of words. In addition, the DSM-III indicates that there is often reduced comprehension in reading. Associated clinical signs can include subtle language difficulties (e.g., auditory discrimination), behavioral problems, or soft neurological signs such as finger agnosia. The DSM-III takes no position on the prevalence of the disorder, saying only that it is apparently common.

BIOLOGICAL BASIS FOR DEVELOPMENTAL READING DISORDERS

When Morgan (1896) gave the first clinical description of a patient with a developmental reading disorder, he was impressed with the similarity of the features of his patient to the clinical features presented by Hinshelwood's (1895) brain-damaged alexic patients. By this time it had been well established that lesions responsible for reading disorders involved the angular gyrus of the left hemisphere. J. H. Fisher (1910) reasoned that underdevelopment of the left angular gyrus might be responsible for developmental dyslexia. Geschwind (1974) provided a further analogical explanation, arguing that the angular gyrus was among the last brain regions to reach anatomical maturity, and that it was plausible to suggest that in some children this development may be postponed until even later. While the exact nature of the pathophysiology has not been elucidated, the studies below provide some evidence for this hypothesis.

CYTOARCHITECTONIC STUDIES

The first neuropathological study of a case of developmental reading disorder was reported by Drake (1968). The child died from a vascular malformation in the cerebellum. The autopsy revealed an atypical cortical gyral pattern with microgyria and pachygyria, as well as absence of the typical pattern of six well-differentiated layers of cortex. With specific reference to the angular gyrus, the clinicopathological report showed abnormal gyri in the parietal cortex, with thinning of the splenium of the corpus callosum, and ectopic neurons in the subcortical white matter. A more recent study, by Galaburda and Kemper (1979), of a young dyslexic man who died from a fall, reported the results of a serial section autopsy. Inspection of the brain showed no abnormalities in myelination, ventricular size, or callosal thickness. The left hemisphere was found to be wider than the right at all levels of the coronal serial sections. A large percentage of normal brains in both adults (Geschwind & Levitsky, 1968) and young children (Witelson & Pallie, 1973) show a wider left planum temporale—the region on the superior temporal plane that lies posterior to the auditory projection cortex (Heschl's gyrus) and is roughly equivalent of Wernicke's region. The planum temporale in the dyslexic man was not larger on the left than the right. In addition, malformations (polymicrogyria) were found in the structure of Heschl's gyrus and the left planum temporale. The molecular layers of cortex were not clearly differentiated, and there were numerous areas of cortical dysplasias, with abnormally large neurons present in the parietal, occipital, and temporal lobes.

A cause-and-effect relationship cannot be directly inferred from these two studies. In addition to the limitations of the case report method, other confounding factors exist for both studies. In the Drake report, the child died from a cerebellar vascular malformation. The cerebellar abnormality cannot be ruled out completely as a cause of the reading disorder—especially since there is a small minority of investigators who are convinced of the cerebellum's role in developmental reading disorders (Frank & Levinson, 1973). In the second case, the young man suffered from a seizure disorder, which was controlled by the anticonvulsant phenytoin. It is impossible to state whether the cytoarchitectonic abnormalities caused the seizures or the reading disorder. Despite the limitations of these two studies, when they are combined with the results of the reports described below they provide evidence in favor of the hypothesis that underdevelopment of certain left-hemisphere regions known to be involved in language skills may be responsible for developmental reading disorders.

BRAIN TOPOGRAPHY IN DEVELOPMENTAL
READING DISORDERS

Hier, LeMay, Rosenburger, and Perlo (1978) have shown that a large number of dyslexic children have a larger right than left parieto-occipital region. Using computerized tomography, they provided some evidence for Orton's (1937) "reversal of cerebral dominance" hypothesis.

Duffy, Denkla, Bartels, and Santini (1980), reporting the results of electroencephalographic and evoked potential topographic mapping of electrocortical activity in dyslexic boys, have shown that abnormalities can be found in much of the cortical region involved in speech and reading. In their study, electrical activity differed between dyslexics and normals in four brain regions: the medial frontal lobe (the supplemental motor area); the left lateral frontal lobe (Broca's area), the left midtemporal area (auditory association cortex); and the left posterior quadrant (including Wernicke's areas and the left posterior parietal and occipital regions). These findings were based on group data, which could suggest that inclusion of more than one reading-disorder subtype expanded the number of topographic regions from which abnormal electrical activity was recorded.

DISCUSSION

Symptoms of developmental reading and other learning disorders appear in nearly 1 out of every 6 children in the United States. Although the etiology of these disabilities has not been clearly established, there is great progress being made in the areas of neuropsychology, neurolinguistics, and clinical neurology. The consensus of scholarly opinion strongly suggests that cerebral dysfunctions underlie these disorders. Evidence from neuropsychological investigations employing a wide variety of methodologies points to this etiology. Studies of tachistoscopic visual half-field word recognition (Marcel, Katz, & Smith, 1974; Marcel & Rajan, 1975; Pirozzolo & Rayner, 1979; Witelson, 1977; Yeni-Komshian, Isenberg, & Goldberg, 1975), dichotic listening (Obrzut, Hynd, Obrzut, & Pirozzolo, 1981), dichaptic shape discrimination (Witelson, 1977), reading and spelling errors (Boder, 1973; Obrzut, 1979; Pirozzolo & Hess, 1976), language test performance (Myklebust, 1968), eye movements recorded during reading (Pirozzolo, 1979; Pirozzolo & Rayner, 1979; Zangwill & Blakemore, 1972), saccadic latency (Pirozzolo, 1979), and neuropsychological test performance (Mattis et al, 1975) argue for such an explanation.

With respect to reading disorders, neuropsychological research shows that there are probably several subtypes of these disabilities. Two major forms, an auditory-linguistic type and a visual-spatial type, have been delineated within populations of learning-disabled children by numerous investigators (cf. Pirozzolo, 1979), and evidence suggests several other subtypes as well (cf. Denckla, 1979). Auditory-linguistic dyslexia is characterized by an inability to learn the phonological clues to breaking the speech code and a subsequent inability to learn the relationships between the visual appearance and sound of letters and words (Pirozzolo, Rayner, & Whitaker, 1977). This disturbance is probably the most common cause of developmental reading disorder (Mattis et al, 1975). It occurs more often in boys and probably has a genetic or neuroendocrinologic basis. Visual-spatial dyslexia is a less common, but still major, cause of reading disability. It probably occurs with equal frequency within the sexes. Children with visual-spatial dyslexia appear to have normal language development, but are unable to learn the spatial and visual requirements necessary for reading acquisition.

Neuropsychological assessment is helpful in the differential diagnosis of these disorders, and, equally as important, in suggesting remedial methods. A child may have school difficulties or a disorder that resembles ADD because of any one of a number of medical problems. In certain areas in the United States, for example, lead exposure is a common cause of hyperactivity. Other causes include pinworms, allergies, and subacute carbon monoxide exposure – to name only a few. Thus, a complete evaluation must be carried out before a diagnosis is reached. A treatment plan should be written after the diagnosis has been made, i.e., *treatment follows diagnosis*. Frequently, children exhibiting the aforementioned behavioral difficulties are too rapidly and casually diagnosed as learning disabled (or worse, mentally retarded) and are immersed in a treatment program that is entirely inappropriate.

As with the elderly (Maletta & Pirozzolo, 1980), the concept of the "final common pathway" (Sherrington, 1906) is clinically important in the assessment and treatment of children with symptoms of developmental speech, language, and learning disorders. The immature nervous system has a limited means of expression, and this accounts for the high incidence of disturbances of learning, attention span, and activity levels in seemingly disparate disorders.

REFERENCES

Ainsworth, S. Methods for integrating theories of stuttering. In L. E. Travis (Ed.), *Handbook of speech pathology*. New York: Appleton-Century-Crofts, 1971.

American Psychiatric Association, Committee on Nomenclature and Statistics. *Diagnostic and Statistical Manual of Mental Disorders* (3rd ed.). Washington, D.C.: American Psychiatric Association, 1980.

Ammons, R. B., & Johnson, W. Iowa Scale of Attitude Toward Stuttering. In W. Johnson, F. L. Darley, & D. C. Spriestersbach (Eds.), *Diagnostic methods of speech pathology*. New York: Harper and Row, 1963.

Barbara, D. *Stuttering: A psychodynamic approach to its understanding and treatment*. New York: Julian Press, 1954.

Benson, D. F. Aphasia. In K. M. Heilman & E. Valenstein (Eds.), *Clinical neuropsychology*. New York: Oxford University Press, 1979.

Benton, A. Some conclusions about dyslexia. In A. Benton & D. Pearl (Eds.), *Dyslexia: An appraisal of current knowledge*. New York: Oxford University Press, 1978.

Binet, A., & Simon, T. Language et pensée. *Année Psychologie*, 1908, *14*, 284–339.

Bliss, L. S., Allen, D. V., & Walker, G. Sentence structures of trainable and educable mentally retarded subjects. *Journal of Speech and Hearing Research*, 1978, *21*, 722–731.

Bloodstein, O. *A handbook on stuttering*. Chicago: National Easter Seal Society for Crippled Children and Adults, 1969.

Bloom, L., & Lahey, M. *Language development and language disorders*. New York: John Wiley & Sons, 1978.

Bluemel, C. S. Primary and secondary stammering. *Quarterly Journal of Speech*, 1932, *18*, 187–200.

Boder, E. Developmental dyslexia: A diagnostic approach based on three atypical reading-spelling patterns. *Developmental Medicine and Child Neurology*, 1973, *15*, 663–687.

Boone, D. R. *The voice and voice therapy*. Englewood Cliffs, N.J.: Prentice-Hall, 1971.

Bradley, W. H. Some relationships between pitch discrimination and speech development. *Laryngoscope*, 1959, *49*, 422–437.

Brewer, D., & McCall, G. Visible laryngeal changes during voice therapy: Fiber optic study. *Annals of Otology, Rhinology and Laryngology*, 1974, *83*, 423–427.

Brutten, G. J., & Shoemaker, D. J. *The modification of stuttering*. Englewood Cliffs, N.J.: Prentice-Hall, 1967.

Brutten, G. J., & Shoemaker, D. J. A two-factor theory of stuttering. In L. E. Travis (Ed.), *Handbook of speech pathology*. New York: Appleton-Century-Crofts, 1971.

Carrow, E. *Test for auditory comprehension of language*. Boston: Teaching Resources Corp., 1973.

Carrow, E. *Carrow elicited language inventory*. Boston: Teaching Resources Corp., 1974.

Cicciarelli, A., Broen, P., & Siegel, G. Language assessment procedures. In L. L. Lloyd (Ed.), *Communication assessment and intervention strategies*. Baltimore: University Park Press, 1976.

Colton, R. Spectral characteristics of the model and falsetto registers. *Folia Phoniatrica*, 1972, *24*, 337–344.

Compton, A. J. Generative studies of children's phonological disorders: Clinical ramifications. *Journal of Speech and Hearing Disorders*, 1970, *35*, 315–339.

Conture, E., McCall, G., & Brewer, D. Laryngeal behavior during stuttering. *Journal of Speech and Hearing Research*, 1977, *20*, 661–668.

Critchley, M. *The dyslexic child*. London: Heinemann, 1970.

Cruickshank, W. M. *Cerebral palsy*. Syracuse, N.Y.: Syracuse University Press, 1976.

Darley, F. L. *Evaluation of appraisal techniques in speech and language pathology*. Reading, Mass.: Addison-Wesley Publishing, 1979.

Darley, F. R. Aronson, A. E., & Brown, J. R. *Motor speech disorders*. Philadelphia: W. B. Saunders, 1975.

Denckla, M. B. Childhood learning disabilities. In K. Heilman & E. Valenstein (Eds.), *Clinical neuropsychology*. New York: Oxford University Press, 1979.

Denckla, M. B., & Rudel, R. Names of object-drawings by dyslexic and other learning-disabled children. *Brain and Language*, 1976, *3*, 1–15.

Denhoff, E. Medical aspects. In W. M. Cruickshank (Ed.), *Cerebral palsy.* Syracuse, N.Y.: Syracuse University Press, 1976.

DiCarlo, L. M. Communication therapy for problems associated with cerebral palsy. In S. Dickson (Ed.), *Communication disorders: Remedial principles and practices.* Glenview, Il.: Scott, Foresman, 1974.

Doehring, D., & Hoshko, I. Classification of reading problems by the Q-technique of factor analysis. *Cortex,* 1977, *13,* 291-294.

Drake, W. Clinical and pathological findings in a child with a developmental learning disability. *Journal of Learning Disabilities,* 1968, *1,* 9-25.

Drumwright, A. F. *The Denver Articulation Screening Examination.* Denver: Ladoca Project and Publishing Foundation, 1971.

Duffy, F., Denckla, M. B., Bartels, P., & Santini, G. Dyslexia: Regional differences in brain electrical activity by topographic mapping. *Annals of Neurology,* 1980, *7,* 412-420.

Dunn, L. M. *Peabody Picture Vocabulary Test.* Circle Pines, Minn.: American Guidance Service, 1965.

Erickson, R. L. Assessing communication attitudes among stutterers. *Journal of Speech and Hearing Research,* 1969, *12,* 711-724.

Fisher, H. A., & Logemann, J. A. *The Fisher-Logemann Test of Articulation Competence.* Boston, Mass.: Houghton Mifflin, 1971.

Fisher, J. H. Congenital word-blindness. *Transactions of the Ophthalmological Society of the United Kingdom,* 1910, *30,* 216-225.

Flanagan, B., Goldiamond, I., & Azrin, N. Operant stuttering: The control of stuttering behavior through response-contingent consequences. *Journal of Experimental Analysis of Behavior,* 1958, *1,* 173-177.

Foster, R., Giddan, J. J., & Stark, J. *Assessment of children's language comprehension.* Palo Alto, Ca.: Consulting Psychologists Press, 1973.

Frank, J., & Levinson, H. Dysmetric dyslexia and dyspraxia. *Journal of Child Psychiatry,* 1973, *12,* 690-701.

Freestone, N. W. An electroencephalographic study on the moment of stuttering. *Speech Monographs,* 1942, *9,* 28-60.

Froeschels, E. New viewponts on stuttering. *Folia Phoniatrica,* 1961, *13,* 187-201.

Gaddes, W. H. *Learning disabilities and brain function: A neuropsychological approach.* New York: Springer-Verlag, 1980.

Galaburda, A., & Kemper, T. Cytoarchitectonic abnormalities in developmental dyslexia: A case study. *Annals of Neurology,* 1979, *6,* 94-100.

Gardner, W. H. Study of the pupillary reflex with special reference to stuttering. *Psychological Monographs,* 1937, *49,* 1-31.

Gay, T., & Harris, K. Some recent developments in the use of electromyography in speech research. *Journal of Speech and Hearing Disorders,* 1971, *14,* 241-246.

Geschwind, N. The anatomical basis of hemispheric differentiation. In S. J. Dimond & J. G. Beaumont (Eds.), *Hemisphere function in the human brain.* London: Elek Science, 1974.

Geschwind, N., & Levitsky, W. Human brain: Left–right asymmetries in temporal speech region. *Science,* 1968, *161,* 186–187.

Glauber, I. P. Psychoanalysis of stuttering. In J. Eisenson (Ed.), *Stuttering: A symposium.* New York: Harper & Row, 1958.

Goldiamond, I. Stuttering and fluency as manipulable operant response classes. In L. Krasner & L. P. Ullman (Eds.), *Research in behavior modification: New developments and their clinical applications.* New York: Holt, Rinehart and Winston, 1965.

Goldman, R., & Fristoe, M. *Goldman-Fristoe Test of Articulation.* Circle Pines, Minn.: American Guidance Service, 1972.

Gray, B. B., & England, G. *Stuttering and the conditioning therapies,* Monterey, Ca.: Monterey Institute for Speech and Hearing, 1969.

Hier, D. B., LeMay, M., Rosenberger, P. B., & Perlo, V. P. Developmental dyslexia. *Archives of Neurology,* 1978, *35,* 90–92.

Hinshelwood, J. Word blindness and visual memory. *Lancet,* 1895, *2,* 1564–1570.

Irwin, O. *Communication variables of cerebral palsied and mentally retarded children.* Springfield, Il.: Charles C Thomas, 1972.

Johnston, J. R., & Schery, T. K. The use of grammatical morphemes by children with communication disorders. In D. M. Morehead & A. E. Morehead (Eds.), *Normal and deficient child language.* Baltimore: University Park Press, 1976.

Karlin, I. W. Stuttering: Basically an organic disorder. *Logos,* 1959, *2,* 61–63.

Kelsey, C., Minifie, F., & Hixon, T. Applications of ultrasound in speech research. *Journal of Speech and Hearing Disorders,* 1969, *12,* 564–575.

Kinsbourne, M., & Warrington, E. Developmental factors in reading and writing backwardness. *British Journal of Psychology,* 1963, *54,* 145–156.

Kirk, S. A., McCarthy, J. J., & Kirk, W. D. *The Illinois Test of Psycholinguistic Abilities.* Urbana, Il.: University of Illinois Press, 1968.

Kopp, H. G. Eyemovements in reading as related to speech dysfunction in male stutterers. *Speech Monographs,* 1963, *30,* 248.

Lee, L. L. *Northwestern Syntax Screening Test.* Evanston, Il.: Northwestern University Press, 1971.

Lee, L. L. *Developmental sentence analysis.* Evanston, Il.: Northwestern University Press, 1974.

Lecione, R. M. The development of communication skills. In W. M. Cruickshank (Ed.), *Cerebral palsy.* Syracuse, N.Y.: Syracuse University Press, 1976.

Leonard, L. What is deviant language? *Journal of Speech and Hearing Disorders,* 1972, *37,* 427–447.

Lorentz, J. P. An analysis of some deviant phonological rules of English. In D. M. Morehead & A. E. Morehead (Eds.), *Normal and deficient child language.* Baltimore: University Park Press, 1976.

Luria, A. R. *The working brain.* Harmondsworth, England: Penguin Books, 1973.

Maletta, G. J., & Pirozzolo, F. J. (Eds.). *The aging nervous system.* New York: Praeger, 1980.

Mange, C. V. Relationships between selected auditory perceptual factors and articulation ability. *Journal of Speech and Hearing Research,* 1960, *3,* 67-74.

Marcel, T., Katz, K., & Smith, M. Laterality and reading proficiency. *Neuropsychologia,* 1974, *12,* 131-139.

Marcel, T., & Rajan, P. Lateral specialization for recognition of words and faces in good and poor readers. *Neuropsychologia,* 1975, *13,* 489-497.

Martin, R. The experimental manipulation of stuttering behaviors. In H. N. Sleane and B. D. MacAvlay (Eds.), *Operant procedures in remedial speech and language training.* Boston: Houghton Mifflin, 1968.

Mattis, S. Dyslexia syndromes in children: Towards the development of syndrome-specific treatment programs. In F. J. Pirozzolo & M. C. Wittrock (Eds.), *Neuropsychological and cognitive processes in reading.* New York: Academic Press, 1980.

Mattis, S., French, J., & Rapin, I. Dyslexia in children and young adults: Three independent neuropsychological syndromes. *Developmental Medicine and Child Neurology,* 1975, *17,* 150-163.

McConnell, F., Love, R. J., & Clark, B. S. Language remediation in children. In S. Dickson (Ed.), *Communication disorders – remedial principles and practices.* Glenview, Il.: Scott, Foresman, 1974.

McDonald, J. D. *Environmental language inventory.* Columbus, Oh.: Charles E. Merrill Publishing, 1978.

Moore, G. P. Voice disorders associated with organic abnormalities. In L. E. Travis (Ed.), *Handbook of speech pathology and audiology.* New York: Appleton-Century-Crofts, 1957.

Moore, G. P. *Organic voice disorders.* Englewood Cliffs, N.J.: Prentice-Hall, 1971.

Moore, G. P. Ultra high speech photography in laryngeal research. *Canadian Journal of Otolaryngology,* 1975, *4,* 793-799.

Moore, W. E. A study of blood chemistry of stutterers under two hypnotic conditions. *Speech Monographs,* 1959, *26,* 64-68.

Morehead, D. M., & Ingram, D. The development of base syntax in normal and linguistically deviant children. *Journal of Speech and Hearing Research,* 1973, *16,* 330-352.

Morgan, W. P. A case of congenital word-blindness. *British Medical Journal,* 1896, *2,* 1378.

Myklebust, H. R. (Ed.). *Progress in learning disabilities* (Vol. 1). New York: Grune & Stratton, 1968.

Myklebust, H. R. Childhood aphasia: An evolving concept. In L. E. Travis (Ed.) *Handbook of speech pathology and audiology.* New York: Appleton-Century-Crofts, 1971.

Mysak, E. D. Servo theory and stuttering. *Journal of Speech and Hearing Disorders,* 1960, *25,* 188-195.

Mysak, E. D. Cerebral palsy speech syndromes. In L. E. Travis (Ed.), *Handbook of speech pathology and audiology*. New York: Appleton-Century-Crofts, 1971.(a)

Mysak, E. D. Cerebral palsy speech habilitation. In L. E. Travis (Ed.), *Handbook of speech pathology and audiology*. New York: Appleton-Century-Crofts, 1971.(b)

Obrzut, J. E. Dichotic listening and bisensory memory skills in qualitatively diverse dyslexic readers. *Journal of Learning Disabilities*, 1979, *12*, 304–314.

Obrzut, J. E., Hynd, G. W., Obrzut, A., & Pirozzolo, F. J. Effect of directive attention on dichotic ear asymmetries in normal and learning disabled children. *Developmental Psychology*, 1981, *17*, 118–125.

Orton, S. T. *Reading, writing, and speech problems in children*. New York: Norton, 1937.

Pendergast, K., Dickey, S., Selmar, J. W., & Soder, A. L. *Photo Articulation Test*. Danville, Il.: Interstate Printers and Publishers, 1969.

Perkins, W. H. Vocal function: Assessment and therapy. In L. E. Travis (Ed.), *Handbook of speech pathology and audiology*. New York: Appleton-Century-Crofts, 1971.

Perlstein, M. A. Infantile cerebral palsy: Classification and clinical correlations. *Journal of the American Medical Association*, 1952, *149*, 30–34.

Peters, J. E., Romine, J. F., & Dyckman, R. A. A special neurological examination of children with learning disabilities. *Developmental Medicine and Child Neurology*, 1975, *17*, 63–78.

Pirozzolo, F. J. *The neuropsychology of developmental reading disorders*. New York: Praeger, 1979.

Pirozzolo, F. J., & Hess, D. W. *A neuropsychological analysis of the ITPA: Two profiles of reading disability*. Paper presented to the Annual Convention of the New York State Orton Society, Rochester, New York, 1976.

Pirozzolo, F. J., & Rayner, K. Cerebral organization and reading disability. *Neuropsychologia*, 1979, *17*, 485–491.

Pirozzolo, F. J., Rayner, K., & Whitaker, H. A. *Left hemisphere mechanisms in dyslexia: A neuropsychological case study*. Paper presented at the Fifth Annual Meeting of the International Neuropsychology Society, February, 1977.

Porch, B. E. *Porch Index of Communicative Ability in Children*. Palo Alto, Ca.: Consulting Psychologists Press, 1975.

Reed, C. G. Voice therapy: A need for research. *Journal of Speech and Hearing Disorders*, 1980, *45*, 157–169.

Ross, A. *Psychological aspects of learning disabilities and reading disorders*. New York: McGraw-Hill, 1976.

Rutter, M., & Yule, W. The concept of specific reading retardation. *Journal of Child Psychology and Psychiatry*, 1975, *16*, 161–197.

Satz, P., & Morris, R. Learning disability subtypes: A review. In F. J. Pirozzolo & M. C. Wittrock (Eds.), *Neuropsychological and cognitive processes in reading*. New York: Academic Press, 1980.

Sayles, D. G. Cortical excitability, perseveration, and stuttering. *Journal of Speech and Hearing Research,* 1971, *14,* 463-475.

Schiefelbusch, R. (Ed.). *Bases of language intervention.* Baltimore: University Park Press, 1978.(a)

Schiefelbusch, R. (Ed.). *Language intervention strategies.* Baltimore: University Park press, 1978.(b)

Shames, G. H., & Sherrick, C. E. A discussion of nonfluency and stuttering as learned behavior. *Journal of Speech and Hearing Disorders,* 1963, *28,* 3-18.

Shanks, J. C., & Duguay, M. Voice remediation and the teaching of alaryngeal speech. In S. Dickson (Ed.), *Communication disorders: Remedial principles and practices.* Glenview, Il.: Scott, Foresman, 1974.

Sheehan, J. G. *Stuttering: Research and therapy.* New York: Harper and Row, 1970.

Sheehan, J. G., & Martyn, M. M. Stuttering and its disappearance. *Journal of Speech and Hearing Research,* 1970, *13,* 279-289.

Sherrington, C. S. *Integrative action of the nervous system.* New Haven: Yale University Press, 1906.

Soderberg, G. A. Delayed auditory feedback and stuttering. *Journal of Speech and Hearing Disorders,* 1968, *33,* 260-267.

Sommers, R. K., & Kane, A. R. Nature and remediation of functional articulation disorders. In S. Dickson (Ed.), *Communication disorders: Remedial principles and practices.* Glenview, Il.: Scott, Foresman, 1974.

Sommers, R. K., Meyer, W. J., & Fenton, A. K. Pitch discrimination and articulation. *Journal of Speech and Hearing Research,* 1961, *4,* 56-60.

Sommers, R. K., Meyer, W. J. and Furlong, A. K. Pitch discrimination and speech sound discrimination in articulatory defective and normal speaking children. *Journal of Audiological Research,* 1969, *9,* 45-50.

Templin, M. *Certain language skills in children.* Minneapolis: University of Minnesota Press, 1957.

Templin, M. C., & Darley, F. L. *The Templin-Darley Tests of Articulation* (2nd ed.). Iowa City: University of Iowa, Bureau of Eductional Research and Service, 1969.

Travis, L. The need for stuttering. *Journal of Speech and Hearing Disorders,* 1940, *5,* 193-202.

Travis, L. E., & Malamud, W. Brain potentials from normal subjects, stutterers, and schizophrenic patients. *American Journal of Psychiatry,* 1937, *93,* 929-936.

Van Riper, C. *The nature of stuttering.* Englewood Cliffs, N.J.: Prentice-Hall, 1972.(a)

Van Riper, C. *Speech correction.* Englewood Cliffs, N.J.: Prentice-Hall, 1972.(b)

Van Riper, C. *The treatment of stuttering.* Englewood Cliffs, N.J.: Prentice-Hall, 1973.

Webster, M. L., & Brutten, G. J. The modification of stuttering and associated behaviors. In S. Dickson (Ed.), *Communication disorders: Remedial Principles and practices.* Glenview, Il.: Scott, Foresman, 1974.

Weiner, P. Auditory discriminiation and articulation. *Journal of Speech and Hearing Disorders,* 1967, *32,* 19–29.

West, R. An agnostic's speculations about stuttering. In J. Eisenson (Ed.), *Stuttering: A symposium.* New York: Harper & Row, 1958.

Westlake, H., & Rutherford, D. *Speech therapy for the cerebral palsied.* Chicago: National Society for Crippled Children and Adults, 1961.

Wiig, E. H., & Semel, E. M. *Language disabilities in children and adolescents.* Columbus, Oh.: Merrill Publishing, 1976.

Wilson, K. D. *Voice problems in children.* Baltimore, Md.: Williams & Wilkins, 1972.

Winitz, H. *Articulatory acquisition and behavior.* New York: Appleton-Century-Crofts, 1969.

Witelson, S. F. Developmental dyslexia: Two right hemispheres and none left. *Science,* 1977, *195,* 308–311.

Witelson, S. F. & Pallie, W. Left hemisphere specialization of language in the newborn: Neuroanatomical evidence of asymmetry. *Brain,* 1973, *96,* 641–646.

Wolpaw, T., Nation, J., & Aram, D. Developmental language disorders: A follow-up study. In M. S. Burns & J. R. Andrews (Eds.), *Selected papers in language and phonology* (Vol. I). Evanston, Il.: Institute for Continuing Professional Education, 1977.

Wood, F. Stump, D., McKeehan, A., Sheldon, S., & Proctor, J. Patterns of regional cerebral blood flow during attempted reading aloud by stutterers both on and off haloperidol medication: Evidence for inadequate left frontal activation during stuttering. *Brain and Language,* 1980, *9,* 141–144.

Yeni-Komshian, G. H., Isenberg, P., & Goldberg, H. Cerebral dominance and reading disability: Left visual-field in poor readers. *Neuropsychologia,* 1975, *13,* 83–94.

Zangwill, O. L., & Blakemore, C. Dyslexia: Reversal of eye-movements during reading. *Neuropsychologia,* 1972, *10,* 371–373.

Zimmerman, G. Articulatory behaviors associated with stuttering: A cinefluorographic analysis. *Journal of Speech and Hearing Research,* 1980, *23,* 108–121.(a)

Zimmerman, G. Articulatory dynamics of fluent utterances of stutterers and nonstutterers. *Journal of Speech and Hearing Research,* 1980, *23,* 95–107.(b)

SECTION III

Diagnostic and Clinical Procedures

Marion Selz

6

Halstead-Reitan Neuropsychological Test Batteries for Children

Academic and professional interest in the Halstead Neuropsychological Test Battery for Children and the Reitan-Indiana Neuropsychological Test Battery for Children has increased in recent years for a number of reasons. First, there is a growing acceptance of the idea that brain dysfunction or damage under-lies many cases of learning disability and emotional or behavioral disturbance in children. Second, there is a critical need for assessment tools that sample a broader range of abilities. For example, the recent decision in California in the case of *Larry P.* v. *Riles* (Plotkin, 1980), forbidding the use of standard-ized IQ tests for classifying black children as "educable mentally retarded," underscores the need for ability measures that are relatively uncontaminated by cultural influences. Third, as the technology of special education has improved, it has become increasingly evident that disabled learners suffer from a variety of ability deficits and that maximum progress will be achieved by matching the educational program to the individual child's needs and abilities. This matching process can be greatly facilitated by a comprehensive neuropsychological picture of the child's strengths and weaknesses (Rourke & Strang, 1978).

In response to these newly discovered uses for neuropsychological evalua-tion, increasing numbers of clinical psychologists, school psychologists, and psychology graduate students are seeking information about the administra-tion, interpretation, and applications of neuropsychological tests. Although this is an encouraging and positive sign, a word of caution is needed: clinical neuropsychology is a very complex field. The skills required to evaluate and weigh the varied information in a protocol cannot be obtained overnight. Rourke's assertion that 1 year of intensive training in clinical neuropsychology is a minimal prerequisite for a practitioner is well taken (Rourke, 1976).

EVOLUTION OF THE BATTERIES: ORIGINS AND APPLICATIONS

Seminal Work of Halstead and Reitan

Brain functions can be impaired by a variety of different cerebral insults: trauma, vascular problems, tumors, and disease are common causes of impairment. The lesions caused by these different insults vary in terms of the type of cerebral tissue damaged as well as the amount and severity of damage. For example, there will be functional differences between a head injury patient and a vascular accident patient. For a neuropsychological battery to be maximally useful, it needs to be capable of diagnosing the location and approximate size of a lesion, the probable cause of the lesion, and the severity of impairment incurred. Such a battery should include tests that are sensitive to the general adequacy of brain functions as well as the integrity of specific parts of the brain. A broad range of psychological functions subserved by the brain would need to be assessed.

The neuropsychological battery originated in the 1930s and 1940s with Halstead's search for tests that were sensitive to the psychological effects of brain lesions in adults. His work utilized both experimental measures and naturalistic observation of the behavior of persons with brain injuries. Rather than attempting to create a single test capable of diagnosing brain damage, Halstead developed a number of measures intended to sample a range of brain functions and sensitive to a variety of brain lesions. Since brain damage in its various forms can affect sensory, central processing, or motor functions, the original battery included measures of these three stages of the behavioral cycle and consisted of ten tests.

Reitan, who began his neuropsychological research in Halstead's laboratory, understood the potential contribution a standardized battery approach could make to the neuropsychological diagnosis of brain damage. He went on to modify and expand Halstead's original battery and develop two batteries for children. His research and writing since the mid-1950s has been dedicated to explaining the theoretical underpinnings of this approach and exploring the differential effects of brain lesions (Reitan, 1975).

Reitan developed all three batteries by starting with seven of Halstead's original ten measures (three are no longer commonly used because Reitan's validational research [Reitan, 1955] found that they did not reliably discriminate between brain-damaged and control subjects). Other tests were added or new ones developed in accordance with a conceptual framework that Reitan (1980) recently articulated.

According to this framework, a comprehensive neuropsychological test battery must meet three criteria. First, the battery has to be comprehensive: the full range of abilities subserved by the brain must be measured. Second, the battery must include tests that are sensitive to general or overall brain functions as well as tests capable of detecting deficits in particular parts of the brain. Third, the tests must be technically designed to be amenable to valid neuropsychological inference and interpretation based on application of the four methods of inference, which are explained in the next section.

After comparing the performance of hundreds of brain-damaged patients with non-brain-damaged controls on a number of measures, Reitan selected and refined the most sensitive and valid tests. The batteries currently consist of measures of abstraction and concept formation, visual-spatial and spatial-kinesthetic problem solving, attention and discrimination, memory, language skills, and sensory-perceptual and motor skills.

The Four Methods of Inference

One of Reitan's important contributions concerned interpretation of the batteries. Interpretation of most standardized psychological tests relies upon comparison of an individual's score with the performance of a normative sample. If the score is higher than the normative average, the subject is judged to be better at the ability measured than his or her peer group; if the score is lower, he or she is judged to be worse, i.e., slow, or deficient relative to the norm. Although children are rarely accused of scoring higher than their true abilities, it is frequently argued that some children's scores on psychological tests represent an underestimate of their abilities.

To compensate for this weakness in test interpretation and provide a more complete and accurate picture of the individual, Reitan adapted some neurological diagnostic techniques and elaborated his approach into four methods of inference (Reitan, 1967; Reitan & Davison, 1974; Reitan & Heineman, 1968).

LEVEL OF PERFORMANCE

This approach compares an individual's performance with a normative standard. Level-of-performance measures have been widely used by researchers as well as clinicians for several reasons: the significance of a score is fairly obvious (the child is relatively deficient in the ability to perform some task); level-of-performance measures are easy to analyze by conventional statistics; and the continuous scaled nature of this measure facilitates comparison and interpretation. There are, however, several problems with using such scores as the only data for neuropsychological evaluation.

First, a low score may result from factors other than impaired brain functions. Cultural deprivation, educational disadvantages, test-taking anxiety, emotional problems, and many other circumstances all can prevent a child from achieving cognitive potential on a test. Second, the child's previous ability level is not taken into account when assessing the effects of a potential source of brain damage. For example, a child of formerly superior ability may score in the average range on a number of tests after sustaining a head injury. Finally, it is difficult to distinguish between deficit and delay on the basis of level-of-performance scores alone. Thus, a low score may indicate that a child, as a result of cerebral tissue damage, is unable to grasp a cognitive concept or adequately execute a motor task, but the same low score may reflect some slowness in development in a child who has suffered no structural damage to the brain but is simply somewhat delayed in development. Given enough time, the latter child may be capable of adequate performance. The implications of such a distinction can be critical, particularly for educational programming. A child who is delayed may benefit from extra help, extra support, and extra patience. A child who has suffered significant cerebral damage might not benefit from such straightforward "enrichment;" his or her case may require a different educational approach, designed to compensate for individual deficiencies, and perhaps to modify his or her parents' expectations.

PATTERN OF PERFORMANCE

The particular configuration of scores may be of diagnostic significance. For example, the degree of variability of subscale scores on the Wechsler Intelligence Scale for Children-Revised (WISC-R) may be more significant and meaningful than the summary full scale IQ score. Brain-damaged and learning-disabled children often show a much greater amount of variability on the subscale scores than normal or mentally retarded children (the scores of the latter tend to be more uniformly depressed). Similarly, patterns among the neuropsychological measures are important considerations in an interpretation. A depressed score on a particular test may have a range of behavioral implications, depending on the scores on other measures.

RIGHT–LEFT DIFFERENCES

A number of tests can be analyzed not only in terms of overall level; the relative adequacy of performance on the two sides of the body can also be compared. This measure is very useful, since it is not subject to many of the drawbacks of level of performance. Mood, emotion, and educational disadvantage are unlikely to disrupt performance on one side of the body more than on the other. Since sensory and motor performance is governed principally by the contralateral hemisphere, consistent inadequate performance on one side of the body can provide strong support for impairment of the contralateral hemisphere. Inconsistent performance, in which one side is worse on some tests but the other side is relatively inadequate on other measures, often suggests a mild degree of dysfunction, characteristic of a child whose general cerebral development is uneven.

PATHOGNOMONIC SIGNS

Several tests are designed so that a normal child should make few, if any, errors. On one of the sensory-perceptual tests, for example, the examiner lightly touches one or both of the child's hands and asks him or her to identify which hand has been touched. The inability to perceive a light touch to one hand, either alone or when both hands are touched simultaneously, is highly abnormal. On this test, evidence of repeated failure to perceive stimulation can be construed as a strong indication of impaired brain functions.

The measures of the Aphasia Screening Test are usually considered part of the pathognomonic sign approach. This test, originally designed for adults, consists of simple language, arithmetic, and figure-copying tasks in the ability range of nearly any reasonably normal adult. Any failure on the part of an adult with at least minimal education can be interpreted as evidence of impairment in dealing with language and/or spatial configurations, and, if severe, as evidence of brain damage.

The Aphasia Screening Test is considerably more difficult to interpret for children because of the problem of differentiating between limited acquisition versus loss of previously acquired abilities. With adults, one can assume in most instances that the person formerly had the skill, but as a result of brain damage lost it. With children, several possible reasons for failure exist. The child may at one time have had the skill, but as a result of brain damage lost it. Or the child may not have acquired the skill due to impaired brain functions. Or, the child may simply not have acquired the skill because he or she is a little slow, although he or she is capable of doing so with some help. The first two examples represent brain damage that occurred at different ages; the last could be representative of a slow learner.

Interpretation of the Batteries

Reitan's approach to clinical interpretation of the neuropsychological batteries is based on conjoint use of the above four methods of inference (Reitan, 1975) and blind interpretation (Reitan, 1966). Blind interpretation, as practiced in Reitan's laboratory, begins with referring a patient for neuro-psychological assessment who has a suspected or confirmed neurological disorder. A trained technician, having no knowledge of the neurological findings, conducts the tests. The technician scores the test results, and submits these results or test protocol to a neuropsychologist for interpretation. The neuropsychologist bases his or her interpretation exclusively on the data contained in the protocol; information from other sources is not used in reaching conclusions about the patient's brain functions.

This approach is somewhat unconventional in comparison with traditional clinical psychological procedure and may be viewed with suspicion or alarm by psychologists who feel more comfortable with an approach aimed at gathering as much information as possible before drawing conclusions. Reitan's choice of this approach was based on the belief that as long as psychologists use *all* the information that is available, they will not know whether any measure or group of measures constitute a reliable data base for making diagnoses.

During the validational stages of the battery, neuropsychologists performed blind interpretations to ascertain that the neuropsychological information comprised a valid and comprehensive data base for drawing conclusions about brain lesions. By relying exclusively on the neuropsychological battery, Reitan subjected the battery to a rigorous and repeated test with each patient, and was able to demonstrate that neuropsychologists relying solely on the batteries were able to confirm neurological diagnoses and, in some cases, were able to provide pieces of the puzzle the neurological examination failed to detect.

In clinical application, a blind interpretation of the data ensures that the clinician will continue to test and improve his or her neuropsychological skills. The blind interpretation constitutes the first step in a sequential process that includes collecting medical and educational information, interpreting the relative significance of all the pieces of the puzzle, and making recommendations based on all available information.

Refinement Through Research

In the field of research, Reitan initially demonstrated that the battery was able to differentiate between subjects with and without brain lesions (Reitan, 1955). Subsequent studies investigated the effects of brain lesions in more homogenous groups, comparing patients with different types of lesions affecting different parts of the cerebral hemispheres (Reitan, 1964). The general approach has involved starting with the basic question, Can the neuropsychological battery differentiate between damage and normal brain functions? And, gradually moving on to more-refined distinctions in brain lesions, Can the battery differentiate between acute and chronic lesions? Right and left hemisphere? Tumor and vascular disease?

The early research was conducted with adult patients. At the same time that Reitan and associates were exploring the implications of brain lesions in adults, Reitan was modifying the battery to make it suitable for evaluating children. With the development of the children's batteries, neuropsychologists began to address the following questions:

- Is the neuropsychological approach able to differentiate between brain-damaged and normal children?
- Does cerebral damage to developing abilities (i.e., in children) have effects similar to damage to acquired abilities (i.e., in adults)?
- Are there neuropsychological deficits in children who have negative neurological findings, but whose behavior is in some ways similar to that of children with structural brain damage?

As research progresses, it becomes increasingly clear that there is an empirical basis for the assumption that clinical neuropsychology can provide some very important answers to diagnostic questions about children.

Implications and Applications

The implications and applications of clinical neuropsychology only begin with the research. The clinical practitioner will find that comprehensive, objective information about a child's cerebral functions can make a critical difference in both diagnosis and treatment. The problems of children tend to be multifaceted because neurological, environmental, and emotional factors often interact in complex ways.

As an example of such interaction, brain dysfunction in a child can subtly influence the character of that child's interactions and relationships with other family members. Also, the frustrations a child with brain damage experiences or the coping behaviors he or she has adopted may contribute to an impression that the child is emotionally disturbed.

For remediation efforts to be maximally effective, it is vital to know what the source or sources of the problem are. For example, a child may be hostile and aggressive because of frustration over inability to meet performance expectations in school. The emotional disturbance may be very real, and the child very much in need of therapy. Without benefit of neuropsychological insight, the child may be taken to a psychiatrist or clinical psychologist for counseling or play therapy. If the child's school failure has a basis in neuropsychological deficits, a much more effective treatment approach would address and remediate the child's learning problems. This approach could incorporate counseling oriented toward helping the child gain an understanding of the nature of the problems, the relationship between his or her frustration and acting-out behavior, and better ways of dealing with these problems.

As another example, a family may seek counseling because of intrafamily tensions and communication breakdown centering around one child. Perhaps the parents are seeking help because this child chronically refuses to listen to or comply with their requests. This kind of problem can be due to a malfunction in family dynamics, but it can also have neuropsychological underpinnings. The problem may not be that the parents are overly demanding or the child deliberately contrary. It may be that due to weakness in the left hemisphere, the child is unable to process lengthy instructions from his or her parents and may have attempted to comply with what he or she could recall. After experiencing repeated scoldings for not following directions correctly, the child may have found it easier to ignore orders altogether than to try to comply and get punished for incomplete performance. In this situation, the therapist is likelier to improve family harmony by teaching the parents how to communicate in a manner the child will understand than by treating the family members for psychological dysfunction.

In cases of children with multiple problems, such as brain dysfunction, emotional disturbance, and strained family relations, the brain dysfunction is usually a primary problem. Children can become unhappy because of the consequences of deviant brain functions, but unhappiness does not often cause brain damage (at least, not without intervening variables). Therefore, even though by the time a child comes to the attention of a specialist his or her emotional disturbance may appear to be the most serious problem, it is important to address the original (and probably continuing) source of the problem as well as the sequelae. Otherwise, therapeutic efforts directed at the symptoms are destined to fail to alleviate the problem.

Finally, it is important to understand the implications of identifying brain damage or dysfunction in a child. All too often people shy away from the label of brain damage, feeling that it implies a hopeless prognosis. Diagnosing brain damage in a child is not a final step; *brain-damaged* need not be a stamp to be placed on a child's forehead before being dumped into the bin for defective children. Neuropsychological evaluation is a first step, a means of getting an objective and comprehensive handle on the source of a child's problems. An evaluation provides insight into a child's strengths and weaknesses, so that programming can be designed to meet the child's needs. A protocol gives a skilled interpreter a wealth of information about how the child perceives the world and processes information, so that remedial help can be tailored to the individual child, rather than based on vague notions about problem children in general. The promise of neuropsychology is not another label, but better understanding. This is the goal of the testing process and of those engaged in research designed to improve the fine-tuning of the testing process.

CONTENT OF THE BATTERIES

There are two principal batteries for children. The battery for children in the 9–14-year age range, the Halstead Neuropsychological Test Battery for Children (Reitan & Davison, 1974; Selz, 1977), consists of seven of the original Halstead measures (or slight modifications thereof) and other tests that Reitan adapted or developed to ensure that the battery measured a broad and comprehensive range of brain functions (e.g., the Reitan-Kløve Sensory-Perceptual Examination).

The Reitan-Indiana Neuropsychological Test Battery for Children is suitable for children in the 5–8-year age range. Reitan developed this battery because he found that many normal children under 9 years of age had difficulty with the tests in the older children's battery. The Reitan-Indiana battery consists of downward extensions and simplifications of tests in the older children's battery plus six tests that Reitan designed for children in this age range.

There is, at present, no comparable battery suitable for children younger than 5 years of age.

Halstead Neuropsychological Test Battery for Children

HALSTEAD MEASURES

Category Test. This test consists of 168 slides consecutively presented upon a milk-glass screen. An answer panel, consisting of four levers numbered 1 through 4, is located below the screen. The child is told to inspect each stimulus figure as it is presented and depress the lever corresponding to the number of the correct answer. The child receives immediate feedback about his or her response in the form of a bell, indicating a correct choice, or a buzzer, indicating an incorrect response. Following the bell or buzzer, the next slide appears on the screen.

The test is divided into six groups of slides. Within each of the first five groups, a single principle determines the correct answers for the slides in that group. The sixth group consists of slides that have been presented in the first five groups. On the first item of any of the first five groups, the child can only guess at the principle, but the bell or buzzer provides feedback about the correctness of the hypothesis. In this manner, the test procedure allows the subject to test one possible principle after another until finding one that works consistently. The test begins with easy principles: The first group consists of Roman numerals I through IV — and proceeds to more difficult concepts in later groups. This test is not timed.

The Category Test measures abstract reasoning and concept formation. As a result of the format, it also measures the child's ability to utilize positive and negative feedback in solving complex problems. The score is the number of incorrect choices the child makes.

Tactual Performance Test. The Tactual Performance Test (TPT) utilizes a modification of the Seguin-Goddard formboard. There are a total of six spaces on the board. The board is placed with the cross-shaped space in the upper right-hand corner. The child is blindfolded before the test begins and is not permitted to see the board or blocks at any time. After the child has been blindfolded, the examiner sets up the board and runs the child's hand over the outlines of the board to give him or her an idea of the dimensions. The child is told that the task is to fit the blocks into their proper spaces on the board, using only his or her preferred hand. After this task has been completed, the child is instructed to perform the same task using the non-preferred hand only. Then the child is asked to perform the task a third time using both hands.

The time required to complete the task under each of the three conditions is recorded. The time for each hand provides a comparison of the efficiency of performance on the two sides of the body. In addition, three level-of-performance scores are derived from this test. The total time on all three trials constitutes the *Time* score for the test. After the board and blocks have been stored out of sight, the subject is told to draw a diagram of the board representing the blocks in their proper locations. The *Memory* component of TPT consists of the number of blocks correctly reproduced, and the *Localization* component consists of the number of blocks approximately correctly localized.

TPT measures tactile form discrimination, manual dexterity, tactile-visual integration, and incidental memory, all presented in a problem-solving context.

Seashore Rhythm Test. The Seashore Rhythm Test is a subtest of the Seashore Tests of Musical Talent. The child is instructed to write an *S* for *same* or *D* for *different* to indicate which of 30 pairs of rhythmic tests are the same and which are different. This test appears to measure alertness to nonverbal auditory stimuli, sustained attention, and the ability to perceive and compare different rhythmic sequences. The score is the number of correct responses.

Speech-Sounds Perception Test. The Speech-Sounds Perception Test consists of 60 spoken nonsense words recorded on a tape. The beginning and ending consonant sounds of these words vary, while the "ee" vowel sound remains constant. The child's task is to underline the spoken word, selecting one of three alternative spellings printed for each word. This test measures the child's ability to maintain attention through 60 items, perceive the spoken stimulus sound through hearing, and relate the perception through vision to the correct configuration of letters on the test form. The score is the number of errors.

Finger Oscillation Test (Finger Tapping Test). This test measures motor speed using a specially adapted, mounted manual tapper. The child is told to rest his or her hand on the board of the tapper to ensure that the child moves only his or her finger and not the hand and arm. Beginning with the index finger of the preferred hand, the child is asked to tap the finger as fast as possible for 10 seconds. After completing 5 10-second trials with the preferred hand, the child is asked to perform the same task with the index finger of the nonpreferred hand. Rest intervals are provided as needed to prevent fatigue. The score is the average number of taps in a 10-second period, recorded separately for each hand.

TESTS FROM THE REITAN-KLØVE
SENSORY-PERCEPTUAL EXAMINATION

Tactile, Auditory, and Visual Imperception Test. This procedure attempts to determine how accurately the child can perceive bilateral simultaneous sensory stimulation after it has been determined that the child's perception of unilateral stimulation on each side is essentially intact. Each sensory modality is tested separately.

For the tactile assessment, each hand is first touched separately to determine that the child is able to tell which hand is touched. Following this, unilateral stimulation is interspersed with bilateral simultaneous stimulation. Children with lateralized brain lesions are often able to identify unilateral stimulation correctly, but sometimes fail to respond to simultaneous stimulation of the hand contralateral to the damaged hemisphere. Contralateral face–hand combinations are also used with single or double simultaneous stimulation as part of the procedure.

The test for auditory imperception uses an auditory stimulus produced by the examiner lightly rubbing the fingers together very quickly and sharply. A similar procedure is applied in visual examination, with the examiner executing discrete movements of the fingers while the child focuses on the examiner's nose. The test for perception of bilateral simultaneous stimulation is omitted if the child has a serious lateralized tactile, auditory, or visual loss and is not able to respond correctly to unilateral stimulation on the affected side. For all three tests, the score is the number of errors, recorded separately for each side of the body.

Tactile Finger Recognition Test. This test measures the ability to identify individual fingers on each hand on the basis of touch. Before the examination begins, the examiner works out a system with the child for reporting which finger was touched. Usually the child will report by number, but sometimes children prefer to report in other verbal terms. Although the test is given with the subject's eyes closed, it is sometimes necessary to practice with the child's eyes open to be sure he or she is able to report reliably. When the subject is not able to give a reliable verbal report, he or she is asked to point to the finger touched using his or her other hand. Four trials are given for each finger on each hand, yielding a total of 20 trials per hand. The score is recorded as the number of errors for each hand.

Finger-tip Number Writing Perception Test. This measures the child's ability to report numbers written on the fingertips of each hand without the use of vision. The numbers 3, 4, 5, and 6 are written on the fingertips in a standard sequence, with a total of four trials for each finger on each hand. The score is the number of errors for each hand.

Tactile Form Recognition Test. This test uses flat plastic shapes (cross, square, triangle, and circle) that, when placed in the child's hand, must be matched against a set of stimulus figures that are visually exposed. Scores consist of the number of errors on each hand and the total amount of time required to make the identifications.

OTHER TESTS

Aphasia Screening Test. This test is Reitan's modification of the Halstead-Wepman Aphasia Screening Test (Halstead & Wepman, 1949). The test does not provide a continuous scaled distribution reflecting a range of responses on the individual tests. It is intended to identify certain failures of performance and specific deficits by screening for a variety of language-based deficits, including reading, spelling, articulation, and naming problems, right–left confusion, basic problems with arithmetic, and difficulty copying simple geometric shapes.

Grip Strength Test (Dynamometer). This test measures the child's grip strength. Alternating trials for each hand are given using the Smedley Hand

Dynamometer, with a total of two trials for each hand. The score, in kilo-grams, is the average of the two trials for each hand.

Trail Making Test. The Trail Making Test comprises two parts. Part A consists of 15 circles distributed over a white sheet of paper and numbered from 1 to 15. The child is told to connect the circles with a pencil line as quickly as possible, beginning with the number 1 and proceeding in numerical sequence. Part B consists of 15 circles numbered from 1 to 8 and lettered from A to G. The child is told to connect the circles, alternating between numbers and letters as he or she proceeds in sequence.

Scores are the number of seconds required to finish each part. Errors are reflected in increased time, since when an error is made the child is immedi-ately directed to stop, return to the previous circle, and continue to the next correct circle. The test appears to require immediate recognition of the symbolic significance of numbers and letters, ability to scan the page con-tinuously to identify the next number or letter in sequence, flexibility in integrating the numerical and alphabetical sequence, and completion of these requirements under the pressure of time.

Lateral Dominance Examination. Included in this test are a number of measures that ask the child to perform certain activities in order to get a measure of right–left preference. In the name writing test the child is asked to write his or her name and then asked to write it again with the other hand. The time, in seconds, to complete these tasks is recorded.

Reitan-Indiana Neuropsychological Test Battery
for Children

TESTS ADAPTED FROM OLDER CHILDREN'S BATTERY

Category Test. This test was simplified in several ways. First, colored buttons (red, blue, yellow, and green) replaced the numbers 1 through 4 on the answer panel since young children often have trouble comprehending the symbolic significance of numbers. The test was also shortened to 5 sub-tests with 80 stimulus figures. The format of the test remained the same: the main differences are that the child is required to identify the color (rather than the number) that corresponds with the stimulus figure, and the content of the test is simplified to be within the ability range of younger children.

Tactual Performance Test. This test was changed only by placing the formboard horizontally, rather than vertically on the stand (so that the cross is in the upper left-hand corner). This change was introduced so that small children would not have to reach up as far to place the blocks. The task requirements and measures are the same as in the older children's version.

Finger Oscillation Test (Finger Tapping Test). This test was modified by replacing the manual tapper with an electric version. The electric tapper is better suited for small hands and requires the child's finger to transverse a smaller arc.

Sensory-Perceptual Measures. The imperception measures are adapated from the Reitan-Kløve tests described above. The main difference is that whereas older children report verbally, younger children are asked to indicate their responses by moving their hand or pointing. Similarly, in the Tactile Finger Recognition Test, younger children are asked to indicate which finger was touched by pointing to the finger that was touched, rather than identifying each finger by number. These changes were introduced to ensure that verbal confusion would not be responsible for children's mistakes. The Finger-tip Number Writing Perception Test was replaced by the Finger-tip Symbol Writing Recognition Test, in which the symbols X and O are written on the child's fingertips rather than numbers. The Tactile Form Recognition Test is unchanged.

Aphasia Screening Test. The adult Aphasia Screening Test was simplified to be within the ability range of children who were just beginning to read. The child is asked to identify letters, follow directions pertaining to the right and left hands, name objects, copy simple geometric shapes, solve simple arithmetic problems, and identify parts of the body.

Grip Strength Test (Dynamometer). This test is not changed for use with younger children.

Lateral Dominance Examination. This test is not changed for use with younger children.

TESTS DEVELOPED FOR YOUNGER CHILDREN'S BATTERY

In addition to modifiying and incorporating existing techniques, Reitan developed six new tests for the younger children's battery. The Color Form, Progressive Figures, and Matching Pictures Tests were designed to measure cognitive flexibility and concept formation, the Target and Individual Performance Tests to assess reception and expression of visuospatial relationships, and the Marching Test to measure motor coordination.

Color Form Test. The child is shown a test form depicting a number of geometric shapes in different colors and shapes. He or she is shown where to start, and is told that the task is to draw an imaginary line connecting the shapes, first going to a figure with the same shape, and next going to a figure with the same color, and continuing this progression, alternating between shape and color. This test was designed to be analagous to the Trail Making Test, Part B, utilizing the concepts of color and shape instead of numbers and letters.

Progressive Figures Test. This test is similar to the Color Form Test, but somewhat more difficult. The child is shown a page depicting a number of outlined geometric figures. Within each figure is a small and different figure. The child is told to connect the large figures by finding a large figure that matches the small figure where the child is located. In other words, if the child starts with a large circle that has a small square inside, he or she proceeds to a large square. If the large square has a small triangle inside, the child then proceeds to a large triangle. For both the Color Form and Progressive Figures Tests, the task completion time and errors are recorded.

Matching Pictures Test. This test requires the child to match pictures at the top of the page with pictures at the bottom of the page. This test measures a limited amount of generalization and categorization ability, using concrete stimuli. The test begins with easy items, in which the pictures at the bottom are identical to those at the top. On later pages, the task becomes a little harder. For example, on one page the top row depicts women at five different ages and the bottom row depicts men at five different ages; the child must connect each female with the male of the corresponding age. The score is the total correct out of a possible 19.

Target Test. The child is shown a large stimulus figure on which are printed nine dots arranged in a square. He or she is given an answer sheet with 20 similar 9-dot figures, and is shown how the dots on the answer sheet correspond with the ones in the stimulus figure. The test consists of 20 patterns, which the examiner taps out on the large figure. After each pattern the examiner pauses for 3 seconds and then instructs the child to reproduce the pattern on the answer sheet. The first patterns are quite simple, and the later ones are increasingly complex. This test involves a delayed response and the ability to attend to and copy a visual-spatial configuration. The score is the number correct out of 20.

Individual Performance Test. This test consists of four parts:

1. *Matching V's.* The child is shown a strip of cardboard with a row of V's lined up from narrowest to widest. The task is to line up a group of blocks with V's on them so that the blocks correspond with the V's on the strip of cardboard. The score is the time and the number of errors.
2. *Star.* The child is asked to copy a figure of a six-sided star. He or she is shown how the star is made up of two overlapping triangles and is asked to draw the star in the same way. The score is the time and the accuracy of drawing (accuracy is measured by the number of protruding angles).
3. *Matching Figures.* This task is the same as Matching V's except instead of V's, figures ranging from simple to complex are used. The score is time and number of errors.
4. *Concentric Squares.* This task is the same as Star, except that instead of a star, the figure represents three concentric squares. The child is shown how the figure is constructed of three boxes placed inside of each other. The score is the time and accuracy.

Marching Test. This test has two parts. In the first part, the child is shown an $8\frac{1}{2}'' \times 14''$ page with two columns of circles. Each circle is connected to the next by a line. The child is shown how to "march" up the page, marking each circle with a crayon. The child proceeds up the right-sided column marching with the right hand, and goes up the left-sided column marching with the left hand. After the child has practiced the test, he or she is given five pages of circles to march up: with each subsequent page, the pattern of circles becomes more complex and less a straightforward column. The score is the time and number of errors for each hand.

The second part of the test requires the child to "march" with his or her fingers in synchrony with the examiner. The examiner places his or her own index fingers on the first two circles and instructs the child to follow. The child is to alternately move his or her hands so that the index finger is placed onto the circle the examiner has vacated. The examiner "marches" up the page, alternating hands, at a speed of one move per second. After a specified number of errors have been made, this part of the test is discontinued. The score is the total number of circles completed before the test is finished or discontinued.

VALIDATIONAL RESEARCH

The initial studies of the validational research were designed to establish the utility of the neuropsychological approach and the sensitivity of the individual tests to brain damage. Later studies addressed some of the more ambiguous areas such as the neuropsychological patterns in cases of learning disability or minimal brain dysfunction.

Differentiation of Brain-Damaged and Normal Children

Reed, Reitan, and Kløve (1965) matched 50 brain-damaged children between 10 and 14 years of age with 50 normally functioning controls and compared the performance of each pair on 27 measures from the Wechsler-Bellevue Scale and the neuropsychological battery. The t-ratios were significant beyond the .005 level for 24 measures and significant beyond the .02 level for the remaining 3 comparisons. The authors found that the brain-damaged subjects were most frequently impaired in language functions. Since brain damage in adults tends to markedly impair adaptive and problem-solving abilities rather than language skills, these initial results suggest that brain damage sustained in childhood may have a different effect than brain damage sustained in adulthood. In a replication and extension of this study, Boll (1974) found comparable results, supporting the validity of the Wechsler scales and neuropsychological measures as tests for brain damage in older children.

Boll and Reitan (1970) compared 35 brain-damaged subjects in the 9–14-year range with 35 controls on performance of motor and sensory-perceptual measures from the older children's battery. The results indicated significant differences between the groups on one of the three measures of sensory-perceptual functions (Tactile Finger Localization) and all three measures of motor functions (Finger Tapping Test, Tactual Performance Test, and Grip Strength Test).

Turning to the younger children's battery, Reitan (1974) compared 29 brain-damaged children between 5 and 8 years of age with 29 controls on WISC and neuropsychological measures. He found significant differences between the groups on all but 1 of 41 measures (the nonsignificant comparison involved grip strength using the dominant hand). Consistent with Reed et al (1965), the measures of verbal functions frequently showed the largest group differences. In an earlier study utilizing the same groups of subjects, Reitan (1971) found that motor and sensory-perceptual measures alone were able to classify subjects according to group membership with 70–80 percent accuracy.

These studies demonstrate that groups of brain-damaged children consistently achieve lower scores than age-matched controls on the neuropsychological and Wechsler measures. Significant group differences, however, do not automatically translate into clinical applications. For example, the fact that three motor tasks differentiated normal from brain-damaged children (Boll & Reitan, 1970) does not suggest that these measures would comprise an adequate brain-damage test. For an accurate and comprehensive diagnosis of a child's problems, the full battery and utilization of the four methods of inference are necessary.

Damage to Developing as Opposed to Acquired Abilities

The possibility raised by Reed et al (1965) that brain damage may have different effects in adults than in children has been explored in several other studies. In 1965, Fitzhugh and Fitzhugh compared 30 pairs of subjects between 15 and 29 years of age on 22 measures from the Wechsler scales and from the neuropsychological battery for adults. In one group, all subjects had sustained brain damage before 10 years of age; in the other group, all subjects had sustained brain damage after age 12. The after-12-onset group achieved higher mean scores than the before-10-onset group on all 22 measures. The differences between the groups were significant on several Wechsler performance scales; the Trail Making Test, Part A; and TPT—Memory. These results suggest that greater impairment of abilities occurs with early onset than with late onset of brain damage. The longer a person has a normal brain, the more time there is to acquire information and skills.

Support for these conclusions was provided in 1966 by Reed and Fitzhugh in a study comparing four groups of brain-damaged patients with age-matched controls. The brain-damaged groups consisted of older children with mild brain damage; older children with moderate brain damage; adults with recent, mild brain damage; and adults with long-standing moderate brain damage. Results indicated that the controls performed at a higher level than the brain-damaged groups, and that the mildly impaired groups were superior to the moderately impaired groups. The most important aspect of the findings, however, related to the patterns of deficits within the groups. The two groups of brain-damaged children differed from the controls most strikingly on measures of language and symbolic skills. The differences between the normal and brain-damaged children were smaller on the Tactual Performance, Finger Tapping, and Category Tests. The moderately impaired adults had a somewhat similar pattern, showing their greatest impairment on language-related tests.

The mildly impaired adults had a different pattern. They differed from their control groups primarily on measures of immediate problem-solving ability such as the Category Test, Tactual Performance Test—Time, and Wechsler Block Design.

The results are somewhat difficult to interpret, since in the adult groups severity of cerebral impairment was confounded with age of onset. However, the consistency of findings across several studies suggests that brain damage in young children impairs their ability to acquire knowledge in the normal manner, and thus the skills emphasized in the school years—language and symbolic skills—show some of the greatest deficits. If brain damage occurs in adulthood after a normal childhood and adolescence, language and acquired knowledge are usually spared (with the exception of cases of damage to the language area in the brain) and deficits appear primarily in adaptive and problem-solving ability.

Neuropsychological Results for Children Not Clearly Brain Damaged

Many children suffer from a variety of problems including learning difficulties, behavior problems, hyperactivity, and distractibility. These problems, and combinations thereof, have been attributed variously to minimal brain damage, minimal brain dysfunction, or learning disability. Frequently observers reason that since the behavior of these children in some ways resembles that of children with brain damage, they too must have some degree of brain damage or dysfunction. Studies have shown the value of the neuropsychological analysis in discovering such dysfunctions or damage.

Doehring (1968) compared 39 boys between the ages of 10 and 14 years who were retarded in reading but otherwise normal with a control group of 39 boys with normal reading skills. He found that the normal readers were significantly superior to the retarded readers on 62 out of 103 measures, and that the pattern of deficit included visual and verbal impairment. The retarded readers were superior to the normal readers on several measures using somesthetic input. Two experienced neuropsychologists gave the subjects blind ratings of "no cerebral dysfunction" or "definite cerebral dysfunction." The trend for the judges to rate the normal subjects as having no cerebral impairment and the retarded readers as having definite cerebral impairment was significant. For one judge it was beyond the .05 level and for the other judge beyond the .01 level.

Reitan and Boll (1973) evaluated the neuropsychological correlates of minimal brain dysfunction in children in the 5–8-year age range. Their study included four groups of approximately 25 children each. The categories were the following: normal; brain-damaged; minimally brain dysfunctional children whose primary referral was due to academic problems; and minimally brain dysfunctional children who were described as having mainly behavioral problems in the classroom. The test results were subjected to two types of analysis: an analysis of variance supplemented by t tests, and a blind overall judgement of whether each child appeared to have normal, mildly impaired, or abnormal brain functions. Using statistical methods to analyze the level of performance, the authors found that the normal subjects generally achieved the best scores and the brain-damaged subjects the lowest scores, with the two minimally brain dysfunctional (MBD) groups usually scoring in between. The brain-damaged group consistently performed significantly more poorly than the other three groups, but the differences between the two MBD groups and the control subjects generally failed to reach significance. The blind judgement analysis achieved finer distinctions between the groups. Using only the test protocols, the first author of the study identified 64 percent of the brain-damaged children as having abnormal brain functions, approximately 85 percent (averaging the two groups) of the MBD subjects as having mildly impaired brain functions, and 96 percent of the brain-damaged children as having abnormal brain functions.

Selz (1977) examined the neuropsychological differences between normal, learning-disabled, and brain-damaged children in the 9–14-year age range. There were 25 children in each of the three groups. The disabled learners were children with significant academic deficits but no signs of neurological damage on physical neurological exams. Analysis of variance of 3 summary IQ scores and 10 neuropsychological measures indicated significant differences between the groups beyond the .01 level on 11 out of 13 measures, and a significant difference beyond the .05 level on one measure. The t-test comparisons indicated that the learning-disabled subjects performed in a relatively normal manner on measures with a strong motor component. The performance of the disabled learners resembled that of the brain-damaged subjects on tests with strong cognitive or attentional demands. A discriminant analysis that utilized the 13 measures classified subjects according to group membership with 80 percent accuracy. The 20 percent classification errors tended to be in the direction of classifying subjects as less impaired than their group membership implied, e.g., assigning a learning-disabled subject to the control category (Selz & Reitan, 1979a).

A second component of the Selz (1977) work consisted of blind classifications of the subjects. The blind judgments, performed by Reitan, achieved 81.3 percent accuracy, with errors tending in the direction of classifying subjects as more impaired, e.g., assigning a disabled learner to the brain-damaged category. While these numbers would suggest that the blind judgement represented an insignificant degree of improvement over the discriminant analysis, it must be kept in mind that the latter is a statistical technique that takes advantage of the chance characteristics of a group in assigning the weights that will achieve maximum discrimination. The blind judgments, on the other hand, were based on extensive clinical experience but no knowledge of the group memberships of the subjects being judged, and were thus not subject to bias (Selz, 1977).

The third part of this research (Selz & Reitan, 1979b) consisted of the development and validation of a system of rules for classifying children as normal, learning disabled, or brain damaged. These rules, set forth in Table 6-1, are based on the assumption that learning disability is due in many

Table 6-1
Scaled Scores for Rules System

Test	Score			
	0	1	2	3
Level of performance				
1. Category – errors	≤34	35–55	56–74	75+
2. Tactual Performance Test (TPT) – Time (in min)	<6	6–9.9	10–13.9	14+
3. TPT – Memory	6, 5	4	3	2, 1, 0
4. TPT – Localization	3+	2	1	0
5. Trails A – time (in sec)	≤15	16–25	26–35	36+
6. Trails B – time (in sec)	≤39	40–55	56–70	71+
7. Speech – errors	≤10	11–15	16–20	21+
8. Rhythm – correct	25+	21–24	16–20	≤15
9. Verbal IQ	90+	80–89	70–79	≤69
10. Performance IQ	90+	80–89	70–79	≤69
11. Full Scale IQ	90+	80–89	70–79	≤69
12. Tapping, preferred hand – no. of taps	34+	30–33	26–29	≤25
13. Tapping, nonpreferred hand – no. of taps	30+	27–29	23–26	≤22
Pattern				
14. Pattern IQ[a]	≤.99	1.00–1.40	1.41–1.75	1.76+
Right-left differences				
15. Tapping[b]	.04–.16	.03 to –.15	–.16 to –.25	≤–.26
		.17–.30	.31–.40	.41+

(continued)

Table 6-1 (continued)
Scaled Scores for Rules System

Test	Score			
	0	1	2	3
Right-left differences				
16. Grip[b]	.0-.20	-.01 to -.06	-.07 to -.12	≤-.13
		.21-.26	.27-.32	.33+
17. TPT[b]	.11-.49	.10 to -.05	-.06 to .20	≤-.21
		.50-.65	.66-.80	to .81+
18. Name writing—preferred hand (converted score—see Table 6-2)[b]	10, 8	6, 4	2	0
19. Name writing—difference (converted score—see Table 6-2)[b]	6	4	2	1
20. Tactile Finger Recognition. Right hand errors—left hand errors[b]	0, 1	2	3	4+
21. Finger-tip Number Writing, Right hand errors—left hand errors[b]	0-2	3-4	5-6	7+
Pathognomonic signs				
22. Imperception—errors[c]	0	1	2	3+
23. Tactile Finger Recognition—errors[c]	0-3	4-5	6-8	9+
24. Finger-tip Number Writing—errors[c]	0-7	8-10	11-14	15+
25. Tactile Form Recognition—errors[c]	0	1	2	3+

Aphasia battery	Score for deviant performance
26. Constructional dyspraxia	2
27. Dysnomia	3
28. Spelling dyspraxia	1
29. Dysgraphia	2
30. Dyslexia	2
31. Central dysarthria	2
32. Dyscalculia	2
33. Right–left confusion	1
34. Auditory verbal dysgnosia	3
35. Visual number dysgnosia	3
36. Visual letter dysgnosia	3
37. Body dysgnosia	3

From "Rules for Neuropsychological Diagnosis: Classification of Brain Function in Older Children" by M. Selz and R. M. Reitan. *Journal of Consulting and Clinical Psychology*, 1979, *47*, 258–264.(b) Copyright 1979 by the American Psychological Association. Reprinted by permission.

[a]Pattern: Extreme scatter on the subtest scores on the Wechsler scale is abnormal. The following conversion measures the degree of scatter: (largest subscale score – smallest subscale score) ÷ mean of subscale scores.

[b]Right–left differences: The following tests compare performance of the right and left hands. Ratios for 15–17 are derived from this formula: 1 – (nonpreferred hand ÷ preferred hand). The scores in 18 and 19 are derived from the conversion formulas presented in Table 6-2.

[c]Pathognomonic signs: For these tests, normal performance consists of perfect performance. Allowance was made for the fact that even normal children tend to make more errors than adults.

cases to a degree of brain dysfunction that is deviant from normal brain functions but less severe than that resulting from structural brain damage. The rules consist of a four-point scaled scoring system rating 37 aspects of performance on a scale from 0 (normal to excellent performance) to 3 (distinctly abnormal performance). The rules utilized the four methods of inference: rules 1–13 are based on level of performance considerations, 14 analyzes pattern, 15–21 compare right-left differences, and 22–37 evaluate pathognomonic signs.

The rules are derived from analysis of the protocols of 57 pilot subjects. The four-point conversion was developed to facilitate comparisons of scores from different tests. The Aphasia Screening Test (26–37) is scored in the following manner: normal performance is scored 0 and deviant performance is assigned a score of 1, 2, or 3 based on the significance of impaired performance on a particular task. For example, since problems with spelling are considered less significant than inability to correctly identify letters of the alphabet at this age, spelling dypraxia is scored 1, whereas visual letter dysgnosia is scored 3. Rules 18 and 19 are based on a conversion table developed by Reitan (Table 6-2).

After development, the rules were validated on the 75 children in the study. Each protocol was scored, and the scores were added to form a single sum of scaled scores for each subject. The following group cut-offs were selected to result in the fewest misclassifications: 19 or below, control; 20–35, learning disabled; 36 or above, brain-damaged. With these cut-offs, subjects were assigned to groups with 73.3 percent accuracy. The errors in classification tended in the direction of assigning subjects to less impaired groups: eight disabled learners were misclassified as controls, whereas only one control was mistakenly called a disabled learner.

The rules provide a fairly straightforward and objective means of determining the degree of a child's deficits. Furthermore, the scaled score conversion provides a means of evaluating the relative quality of a child's performance in different areas: one can determine quickly whether a child's 3s are cropping up in the areas of motor performance, reasoning, or language skills. At the end of this chapter are two case studies, a learning-disabled child and a brain-damaged child, that illustrate application. These cases are intended to give the reader practice in using the rules.

While it would be premature to base firm conclusions on the outcome of three studies, these studies do support the beliefs that many cases of learning and behavior problems have a basis in a degree of neuropsychological dysfunction and that neuropsychological testing is a valid tool for discovering the nature of the deficit. The next question is, How can information about a child's neuropsychological strengths and weaknesses aid in remediation?

Table 6-2
Name Writing Test Conversions

Preferred Hand		Nonpreferred Hand		Difference Between Hands	
Time (sec)	Converted Score	Time (sec)	Converted Score	Time (sec)	Converted Score
0–9	10	0–29	7	—[a]	2
10–14	8	30–69	6	0–4	4
15–19	6	60–69	4	5–9	10
20–24	4	70–84	2	10–14	8
25–50	2	≥85	1	15–19	6
≥50	0			20–24	4
				25–44	2
				≥45	1

From "Rules for Neuropsychological Diagnosis: Classification of Brain Function in Older Children" by M. Selz and R. M. Reitan. *Journal of Consulting and Clinical Psychology*, 1979, *47*, 258–264.(b) Copyright 1979 by the American Psychological Association. Reprinted by permission.

Note: If subject cannot write name with either hand, classify as brain damaged. Each subject receives three scores: the lower the score, the poorer the performance.

[a]Preferred hand is slower.

IMPLICATIONS FOR REMEDIATION

For children with moderate-to-severe brain damage, the application of the results of a neuropsychological evaluation are fairly straightforward. The evaluation provides an objective data base about the child's abilities and potential limitations. Many children with brain damage appear quite normal, and it can be very useful when counseling parents or advising teachers to have hard data showing that the child does indeed have cerebral problems. Such a child's failures in school are a sign that the child needs extra help or another approach, and the parents or teachers should not blame the child (or themselves) for lack of effort.

A neuropsychological evaluation can be the first step in the very difficult and sensitive task of helping a family come to terms with the implications of brain damage in a child. The objective information can be vital in clarifying for parents that brain damage does not mean that their child is hopeless and degenerating, but it does mean that some revision of hopes and expectations for the child's vocational future may be required. When explained in a nonemotional and nontechnical manner, the neuropsychological report can serve to put a family's fears and apprehensions on a more reality-based level.

The broadest applications of neuropsychology for children, however, probably lie in the area of learning disabilities. It is this group of frequently labeled and discussed, but rarely understood, children who may benefit the most from neuropsychological understanding of their condition. Since the early 1960s, growing awareness of the existence and needs of this large group of children has been accompanied by the arrival and departure of numerous revolutionary new cure-all teaching methods designed to remediate the deficits of the disabled learner. It is unlikely that a single standard program will "cure" the problem, however, since there is no standard learning-disabled child.

Rourke and colleagues (Rourke, 1978; Rourke & Finlayson, 1978; Rourke & Strang, 1978) found that not all disabled learners will respond equally well to a single remedial approach, since not all have the same cognitive problems. Effective programming must be based on an understanding of a specific child's ability structure, rather than general notions about the needs of a homogenous group of disabled learners. This point was borne out by Petrauskas and Rourke (1979), who attempted to identify subtypes of reading-disabled children using a multivariate classification procedure applied to neuropsychological measures. Their procedure produced three reliable subtypes of retarded readers, each with a different pattern of skill deficits.

The next task facing workers in this field is the empirical determination of which remediation approaches achieve the greatest success in ameliorating specific deficits. Establishing links between neuropsychological deficits and specific educational programs will help bridge the gap between neuropsychological research and educational applications. The next few years should see considerable progress in the establishment of a connection that will benefit neuropsychologists, educators, and most of all, children.

CASE STUDIES

The following cases are examples of a right-handed learning-disabled (R. W. J.) and a right-handed brain-damaged (J. H.) child. Both children were subjects in Selz and Reitan's study (1979a). They were selected as typical members of each group. These cases can be used as an exercise. By referring to the protocols (results of neuropsychological examination and Aphasia Screening Test* and to Tables 6-1 and 6-2, each child's performance can be rated and scored according to the rules. The reader can then check his or her results against those on the worksheet following each protocol. The rules are not intended as a substitute or short-cut for training in neuropsychological assessment. For the newcomer to the field, however, they can provide some information about the relative strengths and weaknesses of a particular child, as well as a greater sense of what constitutes a good or poor score on a particular test. A brief commentary about each child's performance follows the worksheet.

---

*The form used for the Aphasia Screening Test is the one for adults and older children.

Results of Neuropsychological Examination

Patient R.W.J. Age 12⁵ Sex M Education in 5 Handedness R

Wechsler Intelligence Scale for Children _____
Wechsler Adult Intelligence Scale _____
Wechsler-Bellvue Scale (Form 1) ___X___

Information	4	Picture Arrangement	8
Comprehension	9	Picture Completion	13
Digit Span	3	Block Design	10
Arithmetic	0	Object Assembly	14
Similarities	8	Digit Symbol (Coding)	6
Vocabulary	5	Mazes	

VIQ 76   PIQ 115   Full Scale IQ 96

Tests from the Halstead Neuropsychological Test Battery:

Category 52   Seashore Rhythm 26
Speech-Sounds Perception 14
Finger Tapping   R 37   L 31
Tactual Performance   R 5.3   L 3.3   Both 1.7
                        Time 10.4   Memory 6
                        Localization 6

Tests from the Reitan-Kløve Sensory-Perceptual Examination:

Tactile Form Recognition   R 0   L 0
Tactile Finger Recognition   R 2/20   L 1/20
Finger-tip Number Writing   R 1/20   L 0/20
Imperception   hand   R 0   L 0
                     ear   R 0   L 0
                     visual   R 0   L 0

Other Tests:

Grip Strength   R 23.5   L 22.0
Name Writing   R 5   L 12
Trail Making   Part   A 33   B 80
WRAT   R 2.7   S 1.9   A _____

Name___R.W.J.___ Age_12^5__ Date_____ Examiner_____

1. Copy SQUARE
    see p. 225
	18. Repeat TRIANGLE
	    okay

2. Name SQUARE
    okay
	19. Repeat MASSACHUSETTS
	    MASSTACHUSESS

3. Spell SQUARE much urging needed, then S-Q-U-W-A-R	20. Repeat METHODIST EPISCOPAL METHIS EPISIPAL

4. Copy CROSS
    see p. 225
	21. Write SQUARE
	    see p. 225

5. Name CROSS TRIANGLE. Ex? and urged S to think of another name, then okay	22. Read SEVEN SEEM (could not improve)
6. Spell CROSS S-H-I DON'T KNOW. Ex urged S to try, then G-R-A-S-E	22a. Repeat SEVEN okay
7. Copy TRIANGLE see p. 225	23. Repeat/Explain HE SHOUTED THE WARNING. okay

8. Name TRIANGLE
    okay
	24. Write HE SHOUTED THE WARNING
	    see p. 225

9. Spell TRIANGLE T-R-I-T-A-N-I-L	25. Compute 85 -27 = see p. 225, Ex then ? S to compute 75 -39 and 29 -17, see p. 225
10. Name BABY okay	26. Compute 17 X 3 = okay, Ex then ? S to compute 13 X 3, done correctly
11. Write CLOCK mumbled CLOCK to himself as he wrote	27. Name KEY okay

12. Name FORK
    okay
	28. Demonstrate use of KEY
	    okay

13. Read 7 SIX 2
    okay
	29. Draw KEY
	    see p. 225

14. Read M G W okay	30. Read PLACE LEFT HAND TO RIGHT EAR. POLICE LEAF THAN TO __ EAR.
15. Reading I okay	31. Place LEFT HAND TO RIGHT EAR placed left hand to left ear
16. Reading II HE IS A __ ONLY, A __ __ OF DOG SHOW.	32. Place LEFT HAND TO LEFT ELBOW

kock

square

He salled the

woning

$\begin{array}{r} \overset{7}{8}\,{}^{1}5 \\ 2\ 7 \\ \hline 5\ 1 \end{array}$

$\begin{array}{r} \overset{6}{\cancel{7}}\,{}^{1}5 \\ -3\ 9 \\ \hline 2\ 6 \end{array}$

$\begin{array}{r} 2\ 9 \\ -1\ 7 \\ \hline 1\ 2 \end{array}$

5 1

3 9

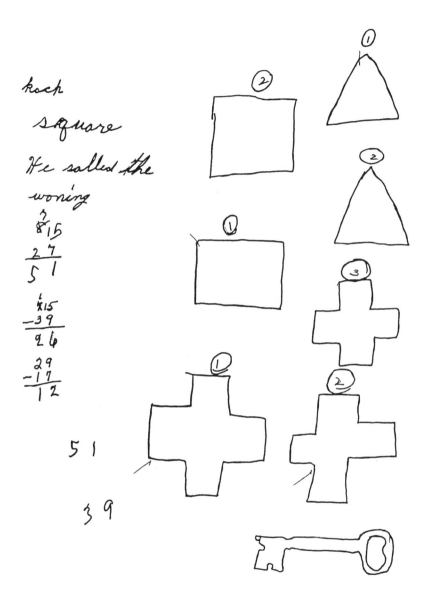

Rules: Worksheet

Name R.W.J.

Rule	Test	Raw	Scaled
1.	Category	52	1
2.	TPT—Time	10.4	2
3.	TPT—Memory	6	0
4.	TPT—Localization	6	0
5.	Trails A—time	33	2
6.	Trails B—time	80	3
7.	Speech—errors	14	1
8.	Rhythm—correct	26	0
9.	Verbal IQ	76	2
10.	Performance IQ	115	0
11.	Full Scale IQ	96	0
12.	Tapping, preferred hand—no. of taps	37	0
13.	Tapping, nonpreferred hand—no. of taps	31	0
14.	Pattern IQ	1.93	3
15.	Tapping	.16	0
16.	Grip	.06	0
17.	TPT	.48	0
18.	Name Writing—preferred (conversion)	10	0
19.	Name Writing—difference (conversion)	10	0
20.	Tactile Finger Recognition, R-L	1	0
21.	Finger-tip Number Writing, R-L	1	0
22.	Imperception—errors	0	0
23.	Tactile Finger Recognition—errors	3	0
24.	Finger-tip Number Writing—errors	1	0
25.	Tactile Form Recognition—errors	0	0
26-37.	Aphasia: dysnomia, spelling dyspraxia, dysgraphia, dyslexia, R-L confusion	9	9

Total   23

Commentary — R. W. J.

SCORING

Rules 1–25 are based on information provided by R. W. J.'s neuropsychological examination and, with the assistance of a calculator, should be fairly simple to derive from Table 6-1. Recall that 18 and 19 also require an intermediate conversion using Table 6-2.

Rules 26–37 are based on the Aphasia Screening Test and require more qualitative judgement. Dysnomia is derived from R. W. J.'s calling a *cross* a *triangle* (5, Aphasia Screening Test, p. 224). Spelling dyspraxia is derived from the definitely dysphonetic spelling of *cross* and *triangle* (6 and 9). Dysgraphia is based primarily on the child's difficulty executing the letter *q* in square. (It is sometimes difficult to make judgements of dysgraphia based on photocopies of original protocols). Dyslexia is derived from the reading problems demonstrated on 16; the sentence should read: "He is a friendly animal, a famous winner of dog shows." Right–left confusion is based on 31: the boy placed his left hand on his left ear, instead of his right ear.

Although the drawings are not good, they are not considered quite poor enough to justify a label of constructional dyspraxia. Similarly, the repetition of *Methodist Episcopal* is not good, but it sounds more like a slur than true confusion of speech sounds, and, therefore, is not labeled central dysarthria.

The sum of the scaled scores is 23 — in the learning-disabled range.

OBSERVATIONS

R. W. J., a right-handed 12½-year-old, was referred for a neuropsychological evaluation because of difficulty in school work. At the time of testing he was in the fifth grade, after having failed 2 years previously. He was having trouble with school work and becoming increasingly nervous. Neurological examination showed no evidence of abnormalities.

Inspection of the scaled scores on the worksheet shows that R. W. J. had no difficulty with lower-level sensory or motor functions. He had definite problems, however, in the Trail Making Test, the Verbal IQ scales, and the aphasia measures. This pattern is quite typical of a learning-disabled child: he is not brain-damaged and in many respects very bright and alert. Tasks with a language component, however, pose very severe difficulties.

His WRAT scores show that R. W. J. has made virtually no progress in school. Particularly for a child with some very good abilities, this situation is extremely frustrating. For children like R. W. J., an intensive remedial program needs to be instituted as early as possible, before frustration builds up to the point that the child gives up altogether.

Results of Neuropsychological Examination

Patient J.H.   Age 10^5 Sex M   Education in 4   Handedness R

Wechsler Intelligence Scale for Children   X
Wechsler Adult Intelligence Scale   _____
Wechsler-Bellvue Scale (Form 1)   _____

Information	9	Picture Arrangement	10
Comprehension	7	Picture Completion	8
Digit Span	6	Block Design	6
Arithmetic	10	Object Assembly	8
Similarities	9	Digit Symbol (Coding)	6
Vocabulary	10	Mazes	6

VIQ 91   PIQ 82   Full Scale IQ 85

Tests from the Halstead Neuropsychological Test Battery:

Category 51   Seashore Rhythm 19
Speech-Sounds Perception 14
Finger Tapping   R 33   L 9
Tactual Performance   R 3.8   L R 1.2   Both 0.8
Time 5.7   Memory 6
Localization 3

Tests from the Reitan-Kløve Sensory-Perceptual Examination:

Tactile Form Recognition   R 0   L 8
Tactile Finger Recognition   R 0/20   L 8/20
Finger-tip Number Writing   R 0/20   L 16/20
Imperception   hand   R 0   L 1
   ear   R 0   L 0
   visual   R 0   L 0

Other Tests:

Grip Strength   R 24.5   L 2.5
Name Writing   R 18   L 72
Trail Making   Part A 27   B 59
WRAT   R 3.7   S 2.5   A 4.9

Aphasia Screening Test

Name ___J.H.___ Age __10^5__ Date _____ Examiner _____

1. Copy SQUARE see p. 231	18. Repeat TRIANGLE okay
2. Name SQUARE okay	19. Repeat MASSACHUSETTS MASSASSCHUSES
3. Spell SQUARE S-T-R-A-E	20. Repeat METHODIST EPISCOPAL MESTHODIS EPISOL
4. Copy CROSS see p. 231	21. Write SQUARE see p. 231
5. Name CROSS okay	22. Read SEVEN okay
6. Spell CROSS C-A- NO, IT'S O- C-O-R-S-T	22a. Repeat SEVEN okay
7. Copy TRIANGLE okay	23. Repeat/Explain HE SHOUTED THE WARNING. okay
8. Name TRIANGLE TRIANGER	24. Write HE SHOUTED THE WARNING okay
9. Spell TRIANGLE T-T-I-A-L-T-O-E	25. Compute 85 - 27 = okay
10. Name BABY okay	26. Compute 17 X 3 = okay
11. Write CLOCK very slow, wrote CLOK but changed to CLOAK	27. Name KEY okay
12. Name FORK okay	28. Demonstrate use of KEY okay
13. Read 7 SIX 2 okay	29. Draw KEY okay
14. Read M G W okay	30. Read PLACE LEFT HAND TO RIGHT EAR. PLEACE LEFT HAND TO RIGHT EAR.
15. Reading I okay	31. Place LEFT HAND TO RIGHT EAR okay
16. Reading II AMINAL (corrected), FRAMOUS SSHOWS, otherwise okay	32. Place LEFT HAND TO LEFT ELBOW tried for a long time to put L hand to L elbow then tried R hand to R elbow

230

1. clobh

square

He shoted the wining

$$\begin{array}{r} 8\,5 \\ -2\,7 \\ \hline 5\,8 \end{array}$$

5 8

Rules: Worksheet

Rule	Test	Raw	Scaled
1.	Category	51	1
2.	TPT—Time	5.7	0
3.	TPT—Memory	6	0
4.	TPT—Localization	3	0
5.	Trails A—time	27	2
6.	Trails B—time	59	2
7.	Speech—errors	14	1
8.	Rhythm—correct	19	2
9.	Verbal IQ	91	0
10.	Performance IQ	82	1
11.	Full Scale IQ	85	1
12.	Tapping, preferred hand—no. of taps	33	1
13.	Tapping, nonpreferred hand—no. of taps	9	3
14.	Pattern IQ	.51	0
15.	Tapping	.73	3
16.	Grip	.90	3
17.	TPT	.68	2
18.	Name Writing—preferred (conversion)	6	1
19.	Name Writing—difference (conversion)	1	3
20.	Tactile Finger Recognition, R-L	8	3
21.	Finger-tip Number Writing, R-L	16	3
22.	Imperception—errors	1	1
23.	Tactile Finger Recognition—errors	8	2
24.	Finger-tip Number Writing—errors	16	3
25.	Tactile Form Recognition—errors	8	3
26-37.	Aphasia: spelling dyspraxia, central dysarthria, R-L confusion	4	4

Total 45

Commentary — J. H.

SCORING

Scoring for rules 1–25 is again straightforward. The aphasic symptoms were derived as follows: spelling dyspraxia is based on the dysphonetic spelling of the words *square, cross,* and *triangle* (3, 6, and 9, Aphasia Screening Test, p. 230). Central dysarthria is based on the pronounciation of *Episcopal* (20), which reflects confusion rather than slurring. Right–left confusion is derived from J. H.'s responses to the directions in 32.

The sum of scaled scores is 45 – in the brain-damaged range.

OBSERVATIONS

At approximately 6 years of age, J. H. was diagnosed as having infantile hemiplegia on the left side with seizures and evidence of right hemiatrophy of the brain. At the time of neuropsychological evaluation he was having problems with spasticity and contractures of the left arm and leg.

The neuropsychological protocol shows that although J. H. had some problems with higher-level conceptual and problem-solving tasks, his major deficits were related to sensory perceptual and motor functions. J. H. has consistent, definite sensory and motor impairment of the left side of his body, severe enough that he was unable to perform the Tactual Performance Test with his left hand. In cases such as this in which a child has strong lateralized sensory and motor impairment, structural brain damage is very probable. In J. H.'s case, the left-sided deficits imply that the damage was primarily to his right cerebral hemisphere.

The IQ and WRAT results are good enough, in light of his deficits, to suggest that J. H. has probably been receiving considerable academic assistance and that he is benefitting from this instruction. The recommendation would be that J. H. continue to receive extra help as well as moral support. Additionally, his parents and teachers should be commended for the very good job they are doing of helping him overcome obstacles and realize his potential.

REFERENCES

Boll, T. J. Behavioral correlates of cerebral damage in children aged 9 through 14. In R. M. Reitan & L. A. Davison (Eds.), *Clinical neuropsychology: Current status and applications.* Washington, D.C.: V. H. Winston and Sons, 1974.

Boll, T. J., & Reitan, R. M. *Motor and sensory-perceptual deficits in brain-damaged children.* Paper presented at Midwestern Psychological Association meeting, 1970.

Doehring, D. G. *Patterns of impairment in specific reading disability: a neuropsychological investigation.* Bloomington: Indiana University Press, 1968.

Fitzhugh, K. B., & Fitzhugh, L. Effects of early and later onset of cerebral dysfunction upon psychological test performance. *Perceptual and Motor Skills,* 1965, *20,* 1099–1100.

Halstead, W. C., & Wepman, J. M. The Halstead-Wepman Aphasia Screening Test. *Journal of Speech and Hearing Disorders,* 1949, *14,* 9–13.

Petrauskas, R. J., & Rourke, B. P. Identification of subtypes of retarded readers: A neuropsychological, multivariate approach. *Journal of Clinical Neuropsychology,* 1979, *1,* 17–37.

Plotkin, R. The view from the courts. *APA Monitor,* 1980, *11,* 12.

Reed, H. B. C., & Fitzhugh, K. B. Patterns of deficits in relation to severity of cerebral dysfunction in children and adults. *Journal of Consulting Psychology,* 1966, *30,* 98–102.

Reed, H. B. C., Reitan, R. M., & Kløve, H. Influence of cerebral lesions on psychological test performance of older children. *Journal of Consulting Psychology,* 1965, *29,* 247–251.

Reitan, R. M. An investigation of the validity of Halstead's measures of biological intelligence. *AMA Archives of Neurological Psychiatry,* 1955, *73,* 28–35.

Reitan, R. M. Psychological deficits resulting from cerebral lesions in man. In J. M. Warren & K. A. Akert (Eds.), *The frontal granular cortex and behavior.* New York: McGraw Hill, 1964.

Reitan, R. M. A research program on the psychological effects of brain lesions in human beings. In N. R. Ellis (Ed.), *International review of research in mental retardation.* New York: Academic Press, 1966.

Reitan, R. M. Psychological assessment of deficits associated with brain lesions in subjects with normal and subnormal intelligence. In J. L. Khanna (Ed.), *Brain damage and mental retardation: A psychological evaluation.* Springfield, Il.: Charles C Thomas, 1967.

Reitan, R. M. Sensorimotor functions in brain-damaged and normal children of early school age. *Perceptual and Motor Skills,* 1971, *33,* 655–664.

Reitan, R. M. Psychological effects of cerebral lesions in children of early school age. In R. M. Reitan & L. A. Davison (Eds.), *Clinical neuropsychology: Current status and applications.* Washington, D.C., V. H. Winston and Sons, 1974.

Reitan, R. M. Human neuropsychology: Assessment of brain–behavior relationships. In P. McReynolds (Ed.), *Advances in psychological assessment* (Vol. III). San Francisco: Josey-Bass, 1975.

Reitan, R. M. *Applications of neuropsychological testing in psychiatric diagnosis.* Unpublished manuscript, 1980.

Reitan, R. M., & Boll, T. J. Neuropsychological correlates of minimal brain dysfunction. *Annals of the New York Academy of Sciences,* 1973, *205,* 65–88.

Reitan, R. M. & Davison, L. A. (Eds.). *Clinical neuropsychology: Current status and applications.* Washington, D.C.: V. H. Winston and Sons, 1974.

Reitan, R. M., & Heineman, C. Interactions of neurological deficits and emotional disturbances in children with learning disorders: methods for their differential assessment. In J. Hellmuth (Ed.), *Learning disorders* (Vol. 3). Seattle, Wash.: Special Child Publication, 1968.

Rourke, B. P. Issues in the neuropsychological assessment of children with learning disabilities. *Canadian Psychological Review,* 1976, *17,* 89-102.

Rourke, B. P. Reading, spelling, arithmetic disabilities: A neuropsychological perspective. In H. R. Myklebust (Ed.), *Progress in learning disabilities* (Vol. IV). New York: Grune & Stratton, 1978.

Rourke, B. P., & Finlayson, M. A. Neuropsychological significance of variations in patterns of academic performance: Verbal and visual-spatial abilities. *Journal of Abnormal Child Psychology,* 1978, *6,* 121-133.

Rourke, B. P., & Strang, J. D. Neuropsychological significance of variation in patterns of academic performance: Motor, psychomotor, and tactile-perceptual abilities. *Journal of Pediatric Psychology,* 1978, *3,* 62-66.

Selz, M. *A neuropsychological model of learning disability: Classification of brain function in 9-14 year old children.* Unpublished doctoral dissertation, University of Washington, 1977.

Selz, M., & Reitan, R. M. Neuropsychological test performance of normal, learning-disabled, and brain-damaged older children. *Journal of Nervous and Mental Disease,* 1979, *167,* 298-302.(a)

Selz, M., & Reitan, R. M. Rules for neuropsychological diagnosis: Classification of brain function in older children. *Journal of Consulting and Clinical Psychology,* 1979, *47,* 258-264.(b).

John E. Obrzut

7
Neuropsychological Procedures with School-Age Children

Traditionally, school psychology has been involved in assessment and intervention techniques borrowed from clinical, counseling, and educational psychology. A variety of techniques and methods including diagnosis and remediation, affective education, curriculum development, teacher consultation, individual and group counseling, behavior management, and parent training have been implemented. As can be seen, the role of a school psychologist is quite varied. This may be the only specialty in psychology that seriously attempts to ameliorate and integrate almost all current practices in psychology, education, and allied fields (Bardon, 1976). As Bardon (1976) has pointed out, the flexibility that characterizes school psychology has probably been the greatest contributor to its receptiveness to growth.

Recently, there has been a growing interest in the area of neuropsychology as it relates to the educational environment (Bogen, 1977; Kaufman, 1979a; Wittrock, 1978). However, this interest in neuropsychology seems to be accompanied by a relatively undeveloped conceptual framework regarding its incorporation into the practice of school psychology. A brief review of some important developments in neuropsychology is an important first step in developing such a framework.

HISTORICAL PERSPECTIVE OF
NEUROPSYCHOLOGICAL ASSESSMENT

A multitude of factors have contributed to the growing interest in clinical neuropsychology in schools. A primary impetus has been the federal legislation (P. L. 94-142) mandating public schools to provide programs for all handicapped children from 3 to 21 years of age. Thus, federal funding is directly related to the number of differentially diagnosed children receiving special instructional services. This means that the need to identify children with handicapping conditions such as dyslexia or developmental aphasia (Federal Register, 1977) has increased the school psychologist's reliance on comprehensive clinical assessment procedures. Since clinical differentiation of learning disorders must encompass some assessment of neuropsychological functioning, school psychologists will be called on to provide an assessment based on brain-behavior relationships. As Gaddes (see Chapter 2) so aptly points out, all behavior is mediated by the brain and central nervous system; thus, any serious understanding of behavior must include a knowledge of its mediating structures, particularly when those structures are functionally impaired.

Neuropsychology developed during the twentieth century because of the inadequate mental status examinations in neurological assessments. Prior to then, the prevailing practice was to ascertain whether a patient's intelligence was intact based on his or her ability to answer a few simple questions. Fritsch and Hitzig (1960) called attention to these superficial methods of examining psychological functions and clarified the need for standardized, objective tools to measure mental, sensory, and motor functions. Thus, the gradual development of formal psychological tests afforded an alternative to the established practice of subjective assessment of mental functions in neurological patients. Initially, such examinations included standardized intelligence tests, projective personality assessment, and, occasionally, specialty tests of mental deterioration designed for use in studies of normal and clinical populations.

The subsequent development of test batteries, including newly developed specialized tests and refinements of earlier techniques, provided diagnostic accuracy and predictive validity. For example, Spreen and Benton (1965) noted that in studies using combined measures, the average of correct predictions was 80 percent, with a maximum of 94 percent. These neuropsychological studies have contributed to neurological diagnoses of (1) traumatic cerebral lesions; (2) acute and chronic cerebral vascular lesions (i.e., strokes); (3) cerebral neoplasms (i.e., tumors); and (4) other progressive neurological disorders, such as Huntington's chorea, Parkinson's disease, multiple sclerosis, and some forms of epilepsy (A. Smith, 1975).

Specifically, neuropsychological studies have contributed objective quantitative and qualitative measures of sensory, motor, language, and mental functions in practical behavioral terms. In addition, neuropsychological tests provide objective measures of mental capabilities during different stages of the underlying disorder, which are essential when considering rehabilitation or special therapy programs. These tests also reveal covert disorders in language, memory, and verbal and nonverbal reasoning that are not revealed in routine psychological evaluations.

Since the school psychologist will be confronted with children who are suffering from learning disorders, some exposure to neuropsychological screening and assessment procedures is needed. The study of neuropsychology can increase our understanding of how the brain affects control of behavior, how the brain is able to compensate when its functions are partially or fully arrested by a brain tumor, and how the brain matures. Answers to these issues are vital to understanding the behavior of school-age children, especially those suspected of having some central nervous system impairment.

According to a recent survey (Hynd, Quackenbush, & Obrzut, 1980), many school psychologists do not have specific training in physiological psychology. However, it is important for school psychologists to understand the structure and function of the brain.

STRUCTURE AND FUNCTIONS OF THE BRAIN

The brain consists of complex neurostructures that grow out of the anterior end of the embryonic neural tube. The posterior portion of the neural tube becomes the spinal cord. The brainstem and spinal cord serve as the pathway for communication between the brain and the rest of the body. Three major anatomical divisions of the brain succeed one another along the brainstem. These are the hindbrain, the midbrain, and the forebrain.

The hindbrain contains the basic life-maintaining centers, that control respiration, blood pressure, and heart beat. The reticular formation is also located here; it mediates important and complex postural reflexes that contribute to the smoothness of muscle activity. The pons and cerebellum also occur in the hindbrain; these structures coordinate postural and kinesthetic information and regulate motor impulses. Dysfunction in this area is commonly reflected in problems with fine motor control and coordination.

The midbrain contains both sensory and motor correlation centers. Midbrain dysfunction is associated with specific movement disabilities, such as tremor, rigidity, and extraneous movements of local muscle groups.

The forebrain consists of two major structures, the thalamus and the hypothalamus. The thalamus is the primary sensory relay center transmitting data to the cerebral cortex. It plays a major role in focusing and shifting attention. Thalamic dysfunction is associated with problems in activation and arousal. The hypothalamus regulates such physiologically based drives as appetite, sex arousal, and thirst. Dysfunction in this part of the system can result in a variety of symptoms, including obesity and changes in drive state and behavior (i.e., fear and rage).

The cerebrum consists of two hemispheres that are almost, but not quite, identical mirror images of each other. The hemispheres are connected by a band of neural fibers, the corpus callosum. Thus, damage to the corpus callosum may result in a lack of interhemispheric communication.

The cerebral cortex is the outer area of gray matter that is composed of nerve cell bodies and their synaptic connections. It is the highest and most complexly organized correlation center of the brain. The patterns of functional localization in the cortex are organized along two spatial planes (1) the lateral plane, which cuts through homologous (corresponding position) areas of both hemispheres; and (2) the longitudinal plane, which runs from the front to the back of the cortex. Thus, the primary sensory and motor centers are homologously positioned within the cortex of each hemisphere in a mirror-image relationship. The centers in each cerebral hemisphere mediate the activities of the contralateral half of the body — with the exception of visual and auditory systems, which are more complex. As shown in Figure 7-1, one half of each visual field is projected onto the contralateral visual cortex, so that destruction of either eye leaves both halves of the visual field intact. The auditory system is organized such that the nerve fibers transmitting auditory stimulation from each ear are projected to the primary auditory centers in the opposite hemisphere. The remaining fibers go to the ipsilateral auditory cortex.

Another kind of organization across the lateral plane differentiates the localization of primary cognitive functions. It has been generally agreed that the distinctiveness of the hemispheres lies not so much in what functions each hemisphere mediates, but in how the information is processed, i.e., what cognitive mode each hemisphere uses (Dimond & Beaumont, 1974; Kinsbourne, 1978; Ornstein, 1977; Segalowitz & Gruber, 1977). In nearly all right-handed individuals, the left hemisphere is thought to process in a sequential analytic linguistic mode, while the right hemisphere processes in a parallel holistic spatial nonlinguistic mode (Witelson, 1977). In general, left-hemisphere dysfunction gives rise to speech and related language disorders, and disorders of symbol formulation. Right-hemisphere dysfunction, on the other hand, leads to difficulties in spatial orientation, perceptual integration of visual and spatial components, and analysis and synthesis of nonverbal conceptual material. Furthermore, the left hemisphere mediates all verbal transformations: receptive and expressive language, reading, writing, verbal ideation, comprehension of verbal symbols traced on the skin, and the musculature of speech. The right hemisphere is responsible for visual-spatial transformations, processing and storage of visual information, tactile and visual recognition of shapes, perception of directional orien-

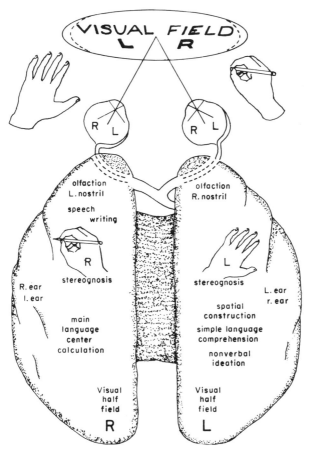

Figure 7-1. Schematic diagram of visual fields, optic tracts, and associated brain areas, showing left and right lateralization in humans. (Redrawn from *Early Experience and Visual Information Processing in Perceptual and Reading Disorders,* 1970, with the permission of the National Academy of Sciences, Washington, D.C.)

tation, copying and drawing geometric and representational designs, and musical ability. Data are organized in the left hemisphere on the basis of conceptual similarity; in the right hemisphere, data are organized on the basis of structural similarity.

The longitudinal organization of the brain refers to the division of hemisphere into four lobes: occipital, parietal, temporal, and frontal (Fig. 7-2). The divisions of the hemispheres are also referred to in terms of anterior and posterior regions. The lobes provide a useful anatomical frame of ref-

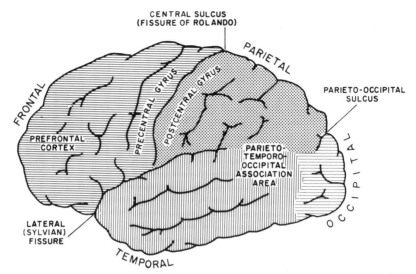

Figure 7-2. The lobes and landmark structures of the cerebral cortex. (Redrawn from *Neuropsychological Assessment* by M. D. Lezak. New York: Oxford University Press, 1976. Copyright by Oxford University Press. With permission.)

erence for functional localization; however, some functionally definable areas overlap two or even three lobes. Theoretically, the left and the right sides may be characterized as the verbal and nonverbal sides, and the posterior and anterior portions as the sensory and motor areas, respectively. However, in reality there is much interweaving of different functional components within the lobes.

The school psychologist should be aware of some behavioral correlates thought to be associated with lesions in the various lobes. The following are common patterns of behavioral impairment associated with damaged anatomical structures. The reader is referred to Lezak (1976) for a more thorough discussion of the following summary.

Occipital Lobe

Lesions of the primary visual cortex result in blind spots in the corresponding parts of the visual fields, although this generally does not alter the comprehension of visual stimuli. Poor visual comprehension, or imperception, is a result of dysfunction in the visual association areas of the occipital lobe. Visual agnosia refers to a variety of disturbances due to dysfunction in visual association areas. In one type of agnosia the affected persons can visually analyze parts but cannot synthesize them into a whole.

They can see letters, words, or parts of symbols, but cannot integrate complete gestalt patterns. Their drawings may be fragmented. In another related difficulty the affected persons cannot recognize an object although they can perceive the visual stimulus. Problems in visual scanning are also included in this category. Left-hemisphere visual agnosia interferes with reading and writing. When just confined to the occipital lobe, the reading problem stems from defects in visual recognition, organization, and scanning, rather than from defective comprehension. Comprehension difficulties usually occur with parietal damage. Writing problems are the result of an inability to recall the visual image of the symbol or the sequence of the symbols, or are a result of faulty scanning. On the other hand, impairment in arithmetic ability results from visual disturbances of symbol perception associated with left occipital cortex lesions. Right occipital dysfunction is more likely to give rise to impaired object perception. Association areas in the parieto-temporo-occipital juncture region are situated in front of the visual association areas and behind the primary sensory strip. These association areas functionally comprehend cortical mediation for all behavior involving vision, touch, body awareness, verbal comprehension, spatial localization, abstract and complex intellectual functions of mathematical reasoning, and logical propositions that have their basis in visuospatial experiences (localization, abstract, and complex intellectual functions of mathematical reasoning and logical propositions that have their basis in visuospatial thinking), such as *inside, bigger,* and/or *instead of.* Therefore, there have been a variety of apraxias and agnosias ascribed to parieto-temporo-occipital dysfunction. Defects from lesions, on either hemisphere, of the posterior association cortex can lead to constructional apraxias of several types. However, there is differential performance depending on the side of the hemisphere damaged. Left-sided dysfunction leads to defects in programming or ordering of movements necessary for constructional activity, whereas right-sided defects lead to visuospatial constructional difficulty. However, puzzle construction in two- to three-dimensional space may be affected by both right- and left-hemisphere dysfunction. Nevertheless, constructional apraxis occurs twice as frequently and with greater severity when the lesion is right-sided.

Defects arising from left-hemisphere lesions on the posterior association cortex primarily result in aphasia and related symbol-processing disabilities. Communication disabilities at this juncture tend to involve impaired or absent recognition and comprehension of symbolic stimuli. Lesions overlapping both the parietal and occipital cortex give rise to reading defects. Writing deficits can occur with lesions limited to either the temporal or parietal lobe, but severity increases when there is damage to the parietal and any one of the other three lobes. Acalculia and agraphia generally occur with other communication disabilities. For example, lesions involving the left parieto-occipital region lead to what is known as Gerstmann's syndrome. This syndrome consists of left-right spatial disorientation, and an inability to identify one's own fingers, i.e., finger agnosia (Benson & Geschwind, 1970; Kinsbourne & Warrington, 1963). Agnosias arising from left-sided lesions just anterior to the visual association area tend to appear as disorientation of personal space. Spatial disorientation of the left hemisphere reflects impaired left-right directional sense and may involve a somatosensory defect as well.

Defects arising from right-hemispheric lesions on the posterior association cortex result in vestibular and occular motor disorders along with constructional apraxia. For example, right-sided acalculia shows up on written calculations as an inability to manipulate numbers in spatial relationships, such as using decimal places, although the subject may be able to compute the arithmetic problem mentally. Difficulty relating and organizing parts of the body to parts of clothing are also the result of defects in this area. Additionally, impaired ability to localize objects in space, such as the hand missing the object when reaching out, commonly occurs with lesions in this area.

Temporal Lobe

Temporal lobe defects affect hearing and related functions such as auditory memory storage and complex perceptual organization. The left temporal lobes mediate the perception of verbal material such as words and numbers and voice recognition. Auditory agnosia (the inability to discriminate and comprehend speech sounds) is associated with lesions in the auditory association cortex commonly known as Wernicke's area. Auditory agnosia, if very pronounced, is one of the most severe communication disorders. However, auditory incomprehension usually does not extend to nonverbal sounds. One of the primary deficits of temporal lobe dysfunction is difficulty with verbal memory. Among the problems resulting are difficulties in recalling words and in remembering long lists, sentences, and complex verbal material.

Right temporal lobe dysfunction leads to problems with nonverbal sound discrimination, recognition, and comprehension. For example, subjects may be unable to appreciate music or rhythmical patterns. Spatial disorientation problems and difficulties in recognizing complex fragmented, or incomplete, visual stimuli will occur. Since the temporal lobes involve recall of memories, bilateral destruction can result in the loss of the ability to learn anything other than new motor skills. However, hemispheric differences persist in unilateral destruction. Loss of the left hippocampus impairs verbal memory in all its modalities; loss of the right hippocampus results in defective recognition and recall of complex, visual, and auditory patterns. The hippocampus resides within the temporal lobes, which are part of the limbic system. This system is subcortical in nature, and its structures mediate both memory and emotional behavior. They direct the focus of attention and thereby determine what is screened out or selected from the perceptual field for registration. Other limbic system structures that have been implicated in memory impairment processes are various portions of the thalamus and the mammillary bodies. Destruction of the mammillary bodies and/or the thalamus can result in what is known as anterograde amnesia, which is impaired ability for new learning, including difficulty in remembering events after the onset of the amnesia, and retrograde amnesia, which is difficulty in remembering events prior to the onset of amnesia.

Information storage is not confined to any cortical area or brain structure. Rather, information involving each modality appears to be stored in the association cortex adjacent to its primary sensory cortex. Thus, retrieval of visual information is impaired by lesions of the visual association cortex of the occipital lobe, and so on. Frontal lobe motor association areas appear to provide the site for programming motor responses.

Frontal Lobe

The frontal lobes are the largest structures of the human brain and are thought to be the seat of highest cognitive functions. Functions believed to be mediated by the frontal lobes are the capacity to form concepts, organize elements in a sequence of adjustments, and solve problems requiring central symbolical or recall processes. The motor strip, or primary motor cortex, and the premotor cortex, or secondary motor association area, are two structures in the frontal lobes. Dysfunction in premotor association areas disrupts the integration of the motor components of complex acts, resulting in discontinuous or uncoordinated movements. For example, in the left hemisphere, the lower portion of the motor association area (Broca's area) mediates the motor organization and patterning of speech. Dysfunction here results in motor pattern apraxia of speech, often called motor aphasia. These disturbances in organizing the muscles of the speech apparatus to form sounds or in patterning groups of sounds into words do not affect comprehension of language. The prefrontal areas, or the anterior portion of the frontal lobes, organize control actions that involve selective perception activities, such as visual scanning. Disturbances of behavior control are one of the basic factors in the pathology of the frontal lobe system. Some typical behavior problems associated with frontal lobe damage are problems of slowed behavior, such as decreased spontaneity, decreased rate at which behavior is emitted, and decrease of initiative. Another behavioral characteristic of frontal lobe dysfunction is difficulty in making mental or behavioral shifts, whether these are shifts in attention, changes in movement, or flexibility in attitude. This is often called perseveration. Another behavior problem is deficient self-awareness, i.e., the inability to perceive performance errors. A final behavior problem associated with damage to the frontal lobe is the inability to use foresight and planning in problem solving.

Intellectual impairment associated with frontal lobe damage may not appear as a loss of specific skills or problem-solving ability, but often results in perseverative behavior that lowers a score on an intelligence test. Some specific cognitive defects that result from frontal lobe dysfunction are difficulties in suppressing response tendencies (impulsive versus reflective cognitive style); defective abstract thinking; inability to use verbal cues to direct, guide, or organize behavior; visual scanning difficulties; impaired registration of incoming stimuli, resulting in decreased short-term memory capacity; and defects of time sense.

Although less marked in frontal lobes, lateralization of cognitive functions does exist. Left-side damage results in decreased verbal fluency and impoverishment of spontaneous speech; right-side involvement results in constructional apraxia in motor rather than perceptual components of a task.

In conclusion, the variations in the size, position, and nature of the lesion and the variations in cortical organization make it impossible to infer with a high degree of certainty the location of a lesion from behavior alone. This is especially valid when dealing with children whose cortical structures are still developing.

RATIONALE FOR A TEST BATTERY

There are several viable approaches to neuropsychological assessment in the schools. One approach is to organize problems into various neurological categories as has been done with adults in the past. Thus, identification of children can be divided into groups such as (1) those suffering from traumatic cerebral lesions, (2) those suffering from acute and chronic cerebral vascular lesions, (3) those that have tumors, and (4) those that have other progressive neurological disorders.

The first category, traumatic cerebral lesions, refers to those neurologic disorders of abrupt onset, such as occur with closed head injuries and accidents (i.e., traumatic- and vascular-type lesions). Although accurate definitions of the nature and extent of focal and diffuse cerebral damage in closed head injuries are important, ancillary diagnostic techniques such as the EEG or radiological studies are of limited value in many cases. Repeated clinical neurological examinations of children in the early post-traumatic stages may indicate complete recovery from initial sensory, motor, and language disabilities. However, psychological testing and neuropsychological follow-up studies often show the later emergence of attenuated mental development, hyperkinesis, seizures, and behavior disorders (Black, Jeffries, Blumer, Wellner, & Walker, 1969; Richardson, 1963).

While the problems in the second category, acute and chronic cerebral vascular lesions such as strokes, infections, and extended high fevers, are not common in school children; those in the third category, tumors, are more prominent. Neuropsychological test data might provide objective definitions of the frequency, range, and types of impairment of higher and lower level cerebral functions associated with different types of intrinsic and extrinsic tumors in various parts of the brain. For example, objective tests of intellectual functions seem to demonstrate consistent and important differences between the effects of left and right frontal tumors (A. Smith, 1966).

The problems of the final category, i.e., other progressive neurological disorders such as Huntington's chorea, are sometimes found in school children. Neuropsychological assessment can evaluate the initial status and subsequent changes in higher and lower level cerebral functions since the mode and rate of development of different symptoms vary. In the initial stages, neurological deficits may be restricted to discernible motor and/or sensory symptoms that do not greatly handicap the student in the activities of daily life. Since aphasic disorders are frequently absent in slowly progressive neurological disease processes, brief psychological assessments may demonstrate that the student has normal speech and verbal comprehension. However, severe memory and other mental defects that are initially masked begin to emerge with time.

Another approach to neuropsychological assessment requires that the school psychologist develop a knowledge of developmental stages of learning acquisition. Neuropsychologically, learning can be viewed as a hierarchy of information processing that involves sensation, perception, memory, symbolization, and conceptualization (Johnson & Myklebust, 1967). A breakdown at any level of this hierarchy could result in school-related learning problems. Sensation is the lowest level of behavior since it refers only to activation of sensory neurostructures. Behavioral concomitants of central nervous system functioning begin with perception, which is the organization and integration of sensory input. Perception in this stage of the hierarchy includes visual, auditory, tactile, and kinesthetic processing. Memory represents the recall of sensations already perceived. Revisualization and reauditorization are the two major types of memory involved in learning. Symbolization refers to the use of symbols to represent units of experience. Symbolic behavior is highly inclusive, encompassing both verbal and nonverbal types of learning and recall. Language, or verbal symbolic behavior, produces or represents a temporal integration of many diverse experiences. Language is crucial to controlling psychological processes. However, non-verbal symbolic behavior plays a crucial role in learning disabilities. Common deficits include the inability to learn to estimate and to recall time, size, distance, volume, shape, height, speed, and other qualitative aspects of experience. Language development includes two major neuropsychological processes: receptive language and expressive language. Conceptualization, the last step in the hierarchy of learning, refers to the ability to abstract and to categorize. It must be kept in mind that a deficit at any one of these levels of information processing interferes with the ability to form concepts, and often is the result of brain dysfunction. Studies of the frontal lobes indicate that this area of the brain carries a unique responsibility for concept formation (Damasio, 1979).

Although different approaches are used in neuropsychological assessment, the goal is to devise a comprehensive battery that assesses functions in the auditory and visual receptive modalities and the spoken, written, graphic, and constructional response modalities. This battery should screen for perceptual and/or organic problems at a relatively efficient rate. Particularly with school-age children, information obtained from the battery alone may reflect the gross outlines of mental impairment patterns with enough clarity to permit the school psychologist to form a diagnostic impression. The selection of tests in the battery should be sensitive enough to assess all areas of the human cortex, i.e., sensory-motor, cognitive, and language skills, that may show dysfunction as various forms of learning disorders. The objective is to devise comprehensive tests of a wide range of higher and lower level cerebral functions. The rationale suggests two basic principles for making such selections: (1) the tests should include standardized and objective measures of a broad range of language, verbal, and nonverbal reasoning and auditory and visual memory functions; and (2) the tests should be selected to permit differentiation of the sensory and motor modalities involved in perception and execution of the task (or lower level functions) (A. Smith, 1975).

An important approach to neuropsychological assessment in the schools is that suggested by Reitan and associates (Reitan, 1967; Reitan & Davidson, 1974; Reitan & Heinemann, 1968). Reitan adapted some diagnostic techniques and elaborated his approach into four methods of inference. Although these methods of inference are elaborated quite articulately by Selz (see Chapter 6), it is important to comment briefly on their usefulness. The purpose of this approach by Selz and Reitan (1979a) was to improve clinical methods of inference by classifying children according to a system of rules. These taxomomic rules include level of performance (i.e., normative data), patterns of performance among various tests (i.e., relationships among various tests), right-left differences (comparison of performance on the two sides of the body), and pathogonomic signs (i.e., performance is either normal or deviant). This statistical model incorporating all four methods of inference would allow the school psychologist to utilize more of the information inherent in the neuropsychological test results than would a system relying on one method alone, and therefore would achieve an improved degree of success in classifying individual subjects into appropriate categories.

In recent years, Golden, Hammeke, and Purisch (1978) have attempted to validate a standardized version of Luria's neuropsychological technique (Christensen, 1975). This work attempts to make Luria's procedures explicit and move his theoretically guided clinical assessment away from the realm of subjective observation. If valid, this approach would allow new attempts to crossvalidate his theory of the brain and functions of behavior. However, the task of validation is arduous and the need for operational definitions and independent crossvalidation is large. Although Golden et al (1978) and Purisch, Golden, and Hammeke (1978) have embarked on the development of the Luria-Nebraska Neuropsychological Test Battery for Children, further validation studies are needed before clinical use or development of the methodology is undertaken (Adams, 1980).

NEUROPSYCHOLOGICAL ASSESSMENT PROCEDURES

Two purposes guide the development of neuropsychological test batteries. The first, accuracy of prediction, is the hallmark of a good diagnostic instrument (Filskov & Goldstein, 1974). The second purpose involves understanding the nature of organic disabilities. Tests in such batteries measure the major intellectual functions across auditory and visual and verbal and nonsymbolic modalities and provide for comparisons between the modalities for each of the major functions (A. Smith, 1975). Thus, for the school psychologist, a useful battery should aid in diagnosis, give baselines, and supply data for planning and treatment.

The intent of the following is not to recommend a specific test battery but rather to suggest an overall organization that makes sense theoretically and yet allows the school psychologist to function in a familiar role. Thus, the ultimate goal is to develop a procedure that school psychologists can use that is sensitive both to the presence of possible brain damage and/or cerebral dysfunctions and to growth changes in normal children (Gaddes & Crockett, 1975; Spreen & Gaddes, 1969). A school-related approach to neuropsychological assessment will then consist of subtests or items from clinically established batteries, as well as special tests or subtests developed on an experimental basis for investigating levels of information processing. Al-

Table 7-1
Neuropsychological Assessment Procedures

Sensory acuity
  Developmental and medical history
  Visual acuity
  Auditory acuity
Tests of lateral dominance
  Lateral motor preferences
    Halstead-Reitan Lateral Dominance Examination
    The Edinburgh Inventory (Oldfield, 1971)
    Miles ABC Test of Ocular Dominance
  Lateral speech preferences
    Auditory channel: dichotic listening technique
    Visual channel: visual half-field technique
Tests of sensory stimulation
  Sensory perception (unilateral and bilateral)
    Tactile perception
    Auditory perception
    Visual perception
  Sensory recognition
    Tactile Finger Recognition Test
    Finger-tip Number Writing Perception Test
    Tactile Form Recognition Test
Tests of perception
  Auditory perception
    Seashore Rhythm Test
    Flowers-Costello Test of Central Auditory Abilities
  Visual perception
    Bender Visual-Motor Gestalt Test
    Benton Visual Retention Test
    Developmental Test of Visual-Motor Integration
    Trail Making Test
    Draw-A-Person Test
  Tactile-kinesthetic perception
    Tactual Performance Test
Speech and language assessment
  Aphasia Screening Test (receptive, expressive, verbal-symbolic)
  Fluency Test (oral)
  Discrimination tests
    Boston Speech Test
    Speech Perception Test
  Sound-Blending Test
  Sentence Memory Test
  Diagnostic achievement tests
    Wide Range Achievement Test (WRAT)

Table 7-1 (continued)

      Boder Diagnostic Reading-Spelling Test
      Formal reading tests
   Intellectual assessment
      Wechsler Intelligence Scale for Children–Revised (WISC-R)
      Peabody Picture Vocabulary Test (PPVT)
      Raven Progressive Matrices
      Category Test

---

though standardized procedures are the heart of reliable assessment, not enough is known at present to endorse any set of neuropsychological procedures with a full-scale standardization. Current batteries, both formal and informal, are not more than early and tentative efforts to deal with the subtle and complex problems of neuropsychological assessment. This is especially true when dealing with school-age children. There are various measures that assess the theoretical hierarchy of information processing noted above. Table 7-1 lists these measures and is an attempt to reflect this hierarchy of learning. It is also an attempt to assess wide-range cerebral coverage of the central nervous system. In addition, Reitan's four methods of inference can be applied to the data generated by these measures. A description of each measure is provided in the following section along with research or clinical evidence to support the measure's usefulness in the assessment process.*

As other authors have indicated, the neuropsychological assessment of the school age-child should be comprehensive, efficient, and practical (Golden, 1976; Rourke, 1976). Furthermore, when considering the neuropsychological assessment of the school-age child, it is imperative that adequate "floors and ceilings" for the tests used with the age group in question be available. Adequate norms for each of the neuropsychological tests have been collected by Spreen and Gaddes (1969), Knights, and Reitan.

---

    *It should be noted that the mode of approach, testing procedures, and conceptualization of brain–behavior relationships described herein has been derived directly from those formulated by Ralph M. Reitan (Reitan, 1966a, b; Reitan & Davison, 1974). Most of the tests from the Halstead Neuropsychological Test Battery for Children and the Reitan-Indiana Neuropsychological Test Battery for Children are included in the present conceptualization. In addition, the contributions of William H. Gaddes (1966, 1968) and Robert M. Knights and Jan A. Norwood (1979) have been influential to the study of the neuropsychological abilities of school-age children as reflected in the present text.

Sensory Acuity

The developmental and medical history is self-explanatory. However, it must be pointed out that a history of abnormal functioning in any of the tested areas could be important. For example, a recent survey showed a history of ear infection (otitis media) that was the significant discriminator between learning-disabled and normal children on a developmental and medical history interview (DeConde, 1980). This author found learning-disabled children reported five times as many ear infections — which may subsequently affect central auditory-processing abilities — as normal children. Two other recent reviews of this problem and its relation to subsequent learning disorders suggest the need for a thorough developmental history (Howie, 1980; Leviton, 1980).

Tests of Lateral Dominance

The Halstead-Reitan Lateral Dominance Examination is designed to determine the child's preferred and nonpreferred hand, eye, and foot. The determination of the preferred side in performance presumably yields information about cerebral dominance or the extent to which the left and right cerebral hemispheres subserve specific and differential functions. In addition, a measure of motor strength of the upper extremities, as well as the child's knowledge of right–left orientation, is obtained. Although the exact structural and physiological substrates of cerebral dominance have not been determined, Smith has suggested that right–left orientation tends to be disrupted by lesions of the left posterior hemisphere (Lezak, 1976). If the school psychologist has difficulty obtaining the Halstead-Reitan Lateral Dominance Examination then the Edinburgh Inventory (Oldfield, 1971) is an acceptable alternative. This inventory affords a simple and brief method of assessing handedness on a quantitative scale for use in neuropsychological and other clinical and experimental work.

Lateral dominance is also conceived of as comparing the level of performance on one side versus the other to evaluate the efficiency or adequacy of performance on the two sides. Such tests as the Finger Tapping Test, the Grip Strength Test, and the Pegboard Test provide information on the comparative efficiency of functions presumably controlled by either the left or right hemisphere.

The Finger Tapping Test was originally called the Finger Oscillation Test (Halstead, 1947). It is a measure of finger-tapping speed using first the index finger of the preferred hand and then the nonpreferred hand. The test is dependent upon motor speed. Lateralized disability may result in marked slowing of the tapping rate of the contralateral hand.

The Pegboard Test (Knights & Norwood, 1979) is a measure of speed and accuracy in eye-hand coordination. This test may also aid in detecting a lateralized disability. It requires the child to place keyhole-shaped metal pegs into rows of matching holes in a board as quickly as possible, first with the preferred, then with the nonpreferred hand. One-sided slowing suggests a lateralized disability on the contralateral hemisphere; bilateral slowing occurs with diffuse or bilateral brain damage. Thus, children with right-hemisphere involvement may be virtually nonfunctional when using their left hands.

The Grip Strength Test measures motor strength of the upper extremities. It is measured by using a children's dynomometer. It too is used as an aid in detecting a lateralized disability.

Although lateral motor and speed preferences are considered to be under the direction of the peripheral nervous system, cerebral dominance for speed is under the control of the central nervous system. While neuropsychological studies of handedness have contributed greatly to knowledge of lateral motor preferences (Belmont & Birch, 1965; Coleman & Deutsch, 1964), recent research with perceptual asymmetries seems to use direct measures of assessing lateralization. Rather than relying on measures of lateral preference (handedness), which may or may not be related to cognitive ability, researchers have used the dichotic listening technique (Hynd & Obrzut, 1977; Satz, 1977; Zurif & Carson, 1970) and the visual half-field technique (Bryden, 1965; Kimura, 1966; Pirozzolo & Rayner, 1977, 1979). Both of these techniques have been employed as means of determining the manner in which speech perception is lateralized in normal and abnormal populations of children and adults. A right-ear advantage (REA) in dichotic listening is thought to reflect the left-hemisphere representation of language while a right visual half-field (R-VHF) superiority for linguistic material is thought to assess the same function. Recent studies comparing a specific population of learning-disabled versus normal children supported the use of the dichotic listening measure as an adequate discriminator between groups (Hynd & Obrzut, 1981; Hynd, Obrzut, Weed, & Hynd, 1979; Obrzut, Hynd, & Obrzut, in press; Obrzut, Hynd, Obrzut, & Leitgeb, 1980). Failure by right-handed individuals to report a high frequency of right-ear stimuli in dichotic listening has been associated with dysfunction of the temporal lobe (Lezak, 1976).

Although the visual half-field technique has not been used as extensively in research with school age children, perhaps findings similar to those found in the auditory channel might be revealed in the visual channel. It is for this reason that these two experimental tasks should be included in a neuropsychological assessment of school-age children.

Tests of Sensory Stimulation

The sensory perception tests discussed here are those used by Knights and Norwood (1979). These tests assess tactile, auditory, and visual perception to determine whether the child is accurately perceiving information in the different modalities. Stimuli are presented unilaterally and bilaterally by touch to both hands and by hand-to-face, by a light finger snap to the ears, and by a hand movement to the eyes. Subjects with lateralized cerebral disability are usually able to identify unilateral stimulation correctly but may fail to respond under circumstances of bilateral simultaneous stimulation on the side contralateral to the damaged hemisphere. Although testing for tactile, auditory, and visual imperception in this manner is adequate, more sophisticated methods for bilateral assessment of the auditory and visual channels, such as the dichotic listening technique and visual half-field technique, respectively, are recommended.

The sensory recognition tests include Finger Recognition (Finger Agnosia), Finger-tip Number Writing Perception, and Tactile Form Recognition. All three of these tests are considered to assess tactile perceptual ability among school-age children. These three techniques present simple recognition or discrimination problems in order to detect defects of touch perception.

Finger Recognition tests the ability of the subject to identify individual fingers on both hands after tactile stimulation. Finger-tip Number Writing requires the subject to report numbers written on the fingertips of each hand without the use of vision. Tactile Form Recognition requires the subject to identify geometric shapes through touch alone. Each hand is tested separately and then both hands are tested simultaneously. Defective performance, regardless of side, implicates a tactile perceptual disability, generally related to the parietal area. When the child displays an error differential between the two hands, a possible contralateral cortical disability is suggested providing that sensory and/or aphasic deficits are ruled out.

Boll, Berent, and Richards (1977) investigated the influence, as assessed by these three tests, of tactile perception on various human abilities such as language acquisition, visuospatial problem solving, concept formation, motor skills, memory, and learning. They found that tactile perceptual performance discriminated children with documented evidence of impaired brain functions (i.e., seizure disorders with EEG abnormalities) from children without evidence or suspicion of neurological impairment. The results suggested that tactile perceptual ability exerts an important effect on the adequacy of a broad range of human abilities and that it may be more important in the general psychological abilities of brain-injured children than normals.

Tests of Perception

The following auditory and visual perceptual tests are the most useful and practical assessment devices that can be used by school psychologists. The Seashore Rhythm Test (Knights & Norwood, 1979) is a subtest of the Seashore Test of Musical Talent (Seashore, Lewis, & Saetveit, 1960) incorporated by Halstead into his test battery and later by Reitan in his neuropsychological assessment program. Two sound patterns presented via a tape recorder require the child to discriminate between like and unlike pairs of sounds. The test requires alertness, sustained attention to the task, and the ability to perceive and compare different rhythmic sequences.

The Flowers-Costello Test of Central Auditory Abilities (Flowers, Costello, & Small, 1970) evaluates the central hearing function or interpretation of speech once the message has been successfully transmitted to the brain by the ear. This test measures all the basic auditory factors such as frequency and intensity as well as all the higher level auditory perceptual functions and/or factors, e.g., selective listening, resistance to distortion, vigilance, storage, and discrimination.

So much of the child's behavior in school is organized around verbal signals that nonverbal auditory functions are often overlooked. However, the recognition, discrimination, and comprehension of nonsymbolic sound patterns are also subject to impairment. Defects of nonverbal auditory perception tend to be associated with brain dysfunction of the right temporal lobe (Bogen & Gordon, 1971; Milner, 1962, 1971).

Tests of visual perception or visuopractic functions combine perceptual-spatial activity with motor response. The Bender Visual-Motor Gestalt Test can be used to demonstrate the tendency of the perceptual system to organize visual stimuli into a gestalt or configurational whole. The complex visuographic copying task requires a high level of integrative behavior that is not necessarily specific to visuopractic functions. Difficulties with the Bender designs are likely to appear in patients with parietal lobe lesions (Garron & Cheifetz, 1965), especially those with dysfunctions of the right parietal lobe (Diller, Ben-Yishar, Gerstman, Goodkin, Gordon, & Weinberg, 1974; Hirschenfang, 1960).

The Benton Visual Retention Test is a widely used visual memory test (Benton, 1974) with three similar forms that permit variations in administration. Administrations A and C are recommended for use with children because of the availability of norms. The Benton Test measures sensitivity to visual inattention, visual memory span, and spatial organization. Practic disabilities have been related to defects in the execution or organization of the drawings, in contrast to perceptual disabilities associated with rotations and consistent design distortions. Patients with right-hemisphere lesions tend to perform more poorly than patients with left-hemisphere lesions; patients with parieto-occipital lesions are more likely to make errors than patients whose lesions are more anterior (Benton, 1974).

The Developmental Test of Visual-Motor Integration (Berry, 1967) is designed primarily for preschool and early primary grade children, although the age range is 2 to 15. It was devised as a measure of the degree to which visual perception and motor behavior are integrated in young children. The copying of geometric forms is well suited for this purpose because there is a close correlation between the visual perception and the motoric expression that is required, and because, unlike letter forms, geometric forms are equally familiar to children of varying backgrounds. Poor performance may indicate dysfunction in the frontal and parietal areas.

The Trail Making Test (Knights & Norwood, 1979) is a test of visual-motor and visual-sequencing skills. The test requires immediate recognition of the symbolic significance of numbers and letters, ability to scan the page continuously to identify the next number or letter in sequence, flexibility in integrating the numerical and alphabetical series, and ability to perform under the time pressure. It also is a test of attention and concentration. Slow performance at any age, on one or both parts, points to likelihood of brain damage, but in itself does not indicate whether the problem is one of motor slowing, incoordination, visual scanning difficulties, poor motivation, or conceptual confusion (Lezak, 1976). Several studies have indicated the usefulness of this test in differentiating brain-injured children from normal children. For example, Reitan (1971) administered a shortened version for use with 35 matched pairs of children with and without cerebral lesions ranging in age from 109 to 179 months. He found that the skills required by either Part A or B of the Trail Making Test are significantly impaired by cerebral damage.

The Draw-A-Person Test is that standard clinical tool used with school-age children as a test of visual-spatial ability. The Goodenough-Harris scoring system (Harris, 1963) is an attempt to measure intellectual maturation in the child. However, focus in the neuropsychological test battery should be on visual-spatial ability. Some characteristics of human figure drawings strongly associated with organic defects are lack of detail, poor integration, noticeable shifting of parts, and inappropriate size or shape of the body parts. In essence, the closer the involvement is to the right occipital lobe, the greater the likelihood that the patient will display some of the more pronounced drawing disabilities associated with right-hemisphere lesions.

The Tactual Performance Test (Tactile Performance Test) is included as a measure of tactile-kinesthetic perception. The Tactual Peformance Test recommended (Knights & Norwood, 1979) is a complex test involving proprioception, visualization of spatial configurations, and tactile memory. The ability to place various blocks in their proper spaces on the board depends on tactile form discrimination, kinesthesis, coordination and movement of the upper extremities, manual dexterity, and visualization of a spatial configuration of the shapes. The test measures a child's problem-solving ability in a novel situation and requires ability to adapt kinesthetic and sensory cues in a problem-solving situation without vision. The three trials include performances from preferred hand, nonpreferred hand, and both hands. The time and difference between the preferred hand and the nonpreferred hand trials may provide a clue to left- or right-hemisphere involvement.

Speech and Language Assessment

Most of the following neuropsychological screening tests are from the Knights and Norwood (1979) test battery.

The Aphasia Screening Test is a test of expressive, receptive, and verbal-symbolic language abilities. The test is designed to sample a large number of language and related behaviors in order to provide a survey of possible aphasic or other deficits. The child is asked to perform relatively simple tasks, each involving a language function. The test includes oral, written, and ideational responses. Left–right discrimination and body orientation tasks are included. The tasks are organized so that various abilities are tested in terms of the particular sensory modalities through which the stimuli are perceived. This organization provides an opportunity for determining whether the limiting deficit is receptive or expressive in nature. This screening measure may signal the presence of an aphasic disorder and may even call attention to its specific characteristics but it does *not* provide the fine discriminations of a complete aphasia test battery.

The Fluency Test is a measure of oral fluency. The child is required to name as many words as possible that begin with a specific consonant sound within 60 seconds.

The Boston Speech Test tests the discrimination of speech sounds and the matching of the sounds to a picture. Discrimination of both vowel and consonant sounds is required. The Speech Perception Test is a measure of the discrimination of speech sounds and of the matching of the sounds to the printed word. The Sound Blending Test involves the blending of sounds into words. Low-level high-familiarity words are used. The Sentence Memory Test is a test of immediate auditory memory for sentences. Twenty-five sentences increasing in difficulty are presented, and the child is asked to repeat each sentence. As on other verbal memory tasks, failure to remember sentences is associated with dysfunction of the left hemisphere. In particular, McFie

(1960) reported that left frontal, temporal, and parietal lobe lesions tend to result in impaired performance on this task.

Several studies have been reported that tend to support the use of many of the tests recommended in this section. One study investigating the neurological competence of children diagnosed with functional articulation disorders found that these children had the greatest difficulty with tasks requiring sensory receptive functions, thereby pointing to the left hemisphere as a possible location of cerebral damage (Frisch & Handler, 1974). In particular, this study proposed that multiple articulation disorders associated with deficits in sensory receptive functions were probably a result of a left-hemisphere dysfunction. Swiercinsky (1979) used factor analysis on 36 neuropsychological test variables and found 8 readily definable factors closely related to subtests measured by the suggested battery in this chapter. For example, factor I reflected a combination of receptive and expressive language skills described as representing dominant (left-) hemisphere functioning. Factor II was defined by tests requiring spatial relationships and object manipulation, functions normally mediated by the nondominant (right) hemisphere. Factor III comprised tests requiring rapid motor coordination. Factor IV involved bilateral tactile acuity. Factor V represented bilateral gross motor speed. Factor VI included right-left grip strength. All of these factors were measured by the neuropsychological assessment battery presented herein.

Diagnostic Achievement Tests

The diagnostic achievement tests include the Wide Range Achievement Test (WRAT) (Jastak & Jastak, 1965), the Boder Diagnostic Reading-Spelling Test (Boder, 1971, 1973), and formal reading tests.

The Wide Range Achievement Test assesses achievement in reading, spelling, and arithmetic from the preschool to the college level. A feature of the WRAT arithmetic test that is particularly valuable for neuropsychological assessment is the variety of mathematical problems it poses. When a child's mathematical performance is defective, the school psychologist can determine by inspection of the worksheet whether the difficulties are due to a spatial dyscalculia, a figure or number alexia, computational deficits, or weakness associated with numerical reasoning.

The Boder Diagnostic Reading-Spelling Test is a screening instrument based on evaluation of the child's ability to perform reading and spelling of phonetic and nonphonetic words, both known (sight) and unknown. The diagnostic test consists of 10 lists of 20 words, each graded from the pre-primer level through grade 12. It assesses an individual's sight vocabulary, nonsight vocabulary, and unknown vocabulary. The spelling test assesses the child's ability to revisualize words in a sight vocabulary and to write good phonetic equivalents of unknown words. On the basis of reading-spelling patterns, each subject is then classified as a normal, nonspecific, or dyslexic (dysphonetic or dyseidetic) reader. Although this procedure is an adequate screening device, recent research (Satz & Morris, 1981) has criticized Boder's system as being too clinical in nature. These authors state that rules for subtype classification need to be more clearly operationalized and validated against external criteria. Nonetheless, the school psychologist may want to distinguish between the dysphonetic reader and the dyseidetic reader. The dysphonetic reader is one who lacks word analysis skills and is inclined to read entirely by recognition of visual gestalts. They often guess from minimal clues and read better in context. They spell "by sight," not "by ear." On the other hand, the dyseidetic reader is considered to be letter blind, misperceiving and reversing visual symbols. They read by phonetic analysis, decoding new words and demonstrating good phonetic misspellings. They spell by ear and demonstrate a weakness in visual recall of whole nonphonetic words (Boder, 1971).

One recent study investigating dichotic listening and bisensory memory skills in readers classified according to the Boder system found that dyseidetic readers were able to attend, store, and retrieve stimuli at two experimental rates of stimulus presentation better than dysphonetic readers (Obrzut, 1979). It was suggested that inability of the dysphonetic group may reflect their difficulty in processing the linguistic (left-hemisphere) and spatial (right-hemisphere) information basic to the reading process. Thus, the school psychologist may find remediation more difficult to implement with certain types of problem readers than with others.

Formal reading tests are necessary for a quantitative estimate of reading and comprehension ability. Since most school psychologists are familiar with the better diagnostic instruments, they will not be reviewed here.

Intellectual Assessment

The intellectual assessment is designed to assess the highest level of cortical functioning that is symbolic and abstract in nature. It is an index of the child's ability to manipulate both verbal and nonverbal symbols and to reason and solve problems. In neuropsychological assessment of school-age children, the most widely used and recommended diagnostic instrument is the Wechsler Intelligence Scale for Children–Revised (WISC-R). Although school psychologists are aware of its utility as a general and specific factor ability test, its sensitivity to the presence of brain dysfunction may not be as apparent.

Intelligence tests were not designed to incorporate neurological theory or research or to correspond to known developmental or neuropsychological constructs. However, the tasks that constitute the IQ test batteries do correspond with issues relevant to subcortical, cortical, and hemispheric specialization functioning. For example, it has been shown that the left hemisphere is specialized for a sequential, analytic, and logical mode of processing information whereas the right hemisphere features a gestalt-like holistic processing mode (Bogen, 1969, 1975; Gazzaniga, 1975). Consequently, performance IQ scores greater than verbal IQ scores may suggest a better developed right hemisphere; whereas, verbal IQ greater than performance IQ may imply more efficient processing dependent on the left hemisphere. Rourke, Young, and Flewelling (1971) found that 9-14-year-old learning-disabled children with verbal greater than performance IQs on the WISC performed better on verbal, language, and auditory perceptual tasks than did youngsters with the reverse discrepancy. In contrast, the performance greater than verbal IQ group was superior on the visual-perceptual tasks. Fedio and Mirsky (1969) found that in a group of temporal lobe epileptics, aged 6-14 years, the direction of the WISC-R verbal-performance discrepancy was predictive of whether the lesion was in the right or left hemisphere. However, there are at least as many studies with children that do not support a direct link-up between Wechsler's verbal and performance scales and the cerebral hemispheres (Binder, 1976; Wener & Templer, 1976).

Although large verbal-performance differences have been frequently associated with possible neurological dysfunction (Black, 1974, 1976; Holroyd & Wright, 1965), Bortner, Hertzig, and Birch (1972) and Kaufman (1976) have found contradictory results. These inconsistencies are probably due to a variety of reasons such as the plasticity of the child's brain or the fact that the two Wechsler scales do not correspond in a one-to-one fashion to the differential specialization of the left and right hemispheres. The lack of definitive studies with children stems from the difficulty in finding children with well-localized brain lesions and in obtaining refined neurological criterion information (Reed, 1976). The WISC-R seems like a perfect dichotomy reflecting left (verbal) and right (performance) hemispheric functioning. But recent research has indicated that hemisphere differences are more related to the mode of processing stimuli than to a left-right dichotomy (Kaufman, 1979b; Segalowitz & Gruber, 1977).

Another approach to the interpretation of the WISC-R is through profile studies. Bannatyne (1971, 1974) has suggested the reorganization of the WISC-R subtests into categorizations based on modes of processing stimuli. His Verbal-Conceptualization Ability-Test consists of Similarities, Vocabulary, and Comprehension; the Spatial Ability Test consists of Picture Completion, Block Design, and Object Assembly; the Sequencing Ability-Test consists of Arithmetic, Digit Span, and Coding; and the Acquired Knowledge-Test consists of Information, Arithmetic, and Vocabulary. Using these groupings, reading-disabled children have been found to show a characteristic WISC-R profile. They score highest on spatial tasks, next highest on verbal conceptualization tasks, and lowest on the sequencing subtest (Rugel, 1974). M. D. Smith, Coleman, Dokecki, and Davis (1977) confirmed this finding and reported that their learning-disabled youngsters performed poorly on the subtest measuring acquired knowledge.

Neuropsychologists have recently suggested that one way to assess the meaning of fluctuations in the WISC-R scales is to analyze children's modes of processing information. Differential processing modes may be viewed from the perspective of right-brain-left-brain functioning (Kaufman, 1979b) or from the related notion of simultaneous versus successive syntheses (Das, Kirby, & Jarman, 1975). According to this framework, a child's verbal scale IQ reflects left-hemisphere processing. However, the performance scale dichotomizes into tasks that seem to require right-brain functioning and tasks that are primarily dependent on a dynamic integration of the cognitive styles of the two hemispheres. The performance scale, because of the different processing demands of the nonverbal task, can be broken down into right-brain processing, which includes Picture Completion and Object Assembly, and integrative functioning, which includes Picture Arrangement, Block Design, Coding, and Mazes (Kaufman, 1979b). The integrated subtests differ from the right-brain tasks in that they require the analytic or sequential processing characteristic of the left hemisphere in addition to the visual, spatial, and nonverbal components that are associated with the right hemisphere. Thus, it is apparent that a variety of Wechsler-like nonverbal tasks demand integrated cerebral function rather than simple right-brain processing.

Finally, Das and colleagues (Das, 1972; Das, Kirby, & Jarman, 1975, 1979; Kirby & Das, 1977; 1978) have suggested a distinction between two modes of processing, successive and simultaneous. Successive processing, a mode featuring serial and temporal handling of information, is presumably disrupted by damage to the frontotemporal area of the cortex; simultaneous processing is believed to be impeded by occipitoparietal damage. According to this model, the type of stimulus is independent of the processing; verbal stimuli are not necessarily associated with successive processing, and visual-spatial stimuli do not automatically demand simultaneous processing. From this neurological model of information processing, the WISC-R performance scale is divided into simultaneous processing (Picture Completion, Block Design, and Object Assembly) and successive processing (Picture Arrangement, Coding, and Mazes). However, these authors have not included the traditional verbal tasks in this schema.

In summary, although the various modes of processing the WISC-R subtests can clearly be related to the cerebral cortex, school psychologists must realize that whatever perspective or model of information processing they subscribe to (i.e., left-hemisphere-right-hemisphere dichotomy, integrative WISC-R tasks, simultaneous or successive processing tasks), this does not imply any specific type of neurological impairment or brain dysfunction. Rather, relative performance on these tasks should give the school psychologist insight into children's mode of processing information and thus into the remedial approach that might be most effective.

The Peabody Picture Vocabulary Test (PPVT) (Dunn, 1965) is an IQ test appropriate for children between the ages of 2½ and 18 years. The test was designed to provide an estimate of an individual's verbal intelligence through measuring his or her hearing vocabulary or receptive knowledge of vocabulary. It is particularly useful for children with known verbal expressive disabilities (i.e., aphasia, apraxia, etc.).

The Raven Progressive Matrices (Raven, 1960) is a nonverbal test of general intellectual ability not dependent on language or academic achievement for success. It requires the subject to conceptualize spatial design and numerical relationships ranging from the very obvious and concrete to the very complex and abstract. The Colored Progressive Matrices (Raven, 1956) provide a simplified alternative form of this test for children aged 5-11. Beside being an objective and quantified measure of nonverbal, visual ideational, or analogous reasoning, the ease of administration and the limited demand on response modalities make this an especially useful test for studying children with severe language, auditory, and physical disabilities. It is therefore particularly useful in evaluating nonverbal reasoning capacities in subjects with aphasia, cerebral palsy, and other severe neurological disorders (A. Smith, 1975). Poor performance on the Raven Progressive Matrices appears to relate consistently to the presence of apraxia and visual field defects. For example, DeRenzi and Faglioni (1965) and Piercy and Smyth (1962) found that Raven Progressive Matrices scores correlate significantly with performance on drawing and constructional tasks.

The Category Test of the Reitan-Indiana Neuropsychological Test Battery for Children is a relatively complex concept-formation test that requires the subject to abstract and apply principles from serially presented visual stimuli. The child must postulate a hypothesis regarding a general principle that applies to each item in a given subtest. The child is able to select one of four possible responses on an answer panel. A bell or buzzer rings to either positively or negatively reinforce the child's response. The test seems to require competence in abstraction ability, especially since the subject is required to postulate in a structured rather than a permissive context. However, this test may be impractical for use by the school psychologist because of its prohibitive expense and the impractical nature of the projection apparatus. The sophisticated equipment is primarily designed for use in a neuropsychological laboratory rather than a school setting.

The Kaufman Assessment Battery for Children (K-ABC) (Kaufman & Kaufman, in press) is an interesting new battery of individually administered tests designed to measure the intellectual (problem-solving) abilities and academic achievement of children ages 3 years, 0 months through 12 years, 11 months. The intellectual tests are divided into those designed to assess simultaneous processing and those designed to assess successive processing. For the purposes of this battery, simultaneous integration refers to the synthesis of separate elements into groups, with these groups often taking on spatial overtones. Successive integration refers to the processing of information in serial order (Das, Kirby, & Jarman, 1979). Characteristic patterns of simultaneous and successive processing have been identified in children who are mentally retarded (Das, 1972), reading disabled (Cummins & Das, 1977), and culturally different (Das, Manos, & Kanungo, 1975). This battery shows promise as a neuropsychological assessment technique that is efficient and practical for use by the school psychologist and yet addresses some of the more important neuropsychological factors that are of concern.

DISCUSSION

The preceding recommended techniques of neuropsychological assessment have been suggested based on the fact that certain neuropsychological disabilities of children with questionable brain disorders persist without obvious neurological signs of impairment. Because of this fact, early assessment of these children should be done to identify deficits that may interfere with normal school learning. Without an adequate profile of adaptive abilities based on an assessment of brain-behavior relationships, children have often been expected to perform adequately in just those areas in which cerebral deficits curtail their abilities (Trupin & Townes, 1976). Neuropsychological assessment provides sufficient information to account for the complexity of possible neurological deficits and how these specific dysfunctions militate against the acquisition of other skills (Reitan, 1974). Thus, it has become increasingly apparent that school-age children with learning disabilities can best be understood from a neuropsychological perspective (Gaddes, 1975; Rourke, 1975). The interest in differentiating learning-disabled from normal children on the basis of neuropsychological assessment procedures stems in large part from the early research of Reitan and his associates, working with brain-injured children (Boll, 1974; Klonoff & Lowe, 1974; Reed, Reitan, & Kløve, 1965; Reitan, 1974).

In terms of research, recent developments have centered on improving the validity of classification rules (Selz & Reitan, 1979b), clarifying the clinical decision-making process (Aaron, 1979), advancing more sophisticated normative approaches to diagnosis (Knights, 1973), examining the utility of various clinical screening instruments (Moore & Burns, 1979), and using neuropsychological assessment procedures to identify clinical subgroups of learning-disabled children (Petraukas & Rourke, 1979; Mattis, French, & Rapin, 1975; Satz & Morris, 1981).

It is crucial to keep in mind that no single test will suffice because of the diverse and subtle effects of brain dysfunction. No single test recommended will discriminate every case in a large sample of learning-disabled children, since the syndrome is not a unitary one, as Fisk and Rourke (1979) point out. With regard to the assessment of children, many researchers are using discriminant function analysis as a useful multivariate approach to neuropsychological research and utilizing many of the tests recommended in this chapter—which are primarily those from the Halstead-Reitan approach (Golden, 1976; Golden, Hammeke, & Purisch, 1978; Obrzut, Hynd, & Obrzut, in press; Selz & Reitan, 1979a; Stuss & Trites, 1977; Swiercinsky, 1976; Tsushima & Towne, 1977). The specific findings of the above-noted studies appear to support the conclusion that neuropsychological deficits or deviations in the absence of medical neurological abnormalities may be relevant in a substantial portion of children with school problems. It is believed that the approach outlined above is oriented towards assessing adequacy of brain–behavior relationships for both differential classification of groups with documented brain damage as well as those school-age children with suspected brain dysfunction.

CASE STUDY

Commentary—C. B.

The following case study is an example of a school-age child (C. B.) diagnosed as having childhood Huntington's chorea. It was selected as a case of a progressive neurological disorder. The neuropsychological evaluation included measures that reflect the theoretical levels of information processing and are amenable to interpretation by the four methods of inference suggested by Selz (see Chapter 6). The school psychologist's task was to evaluate the initial status and subsequent changes in higher- and lower-level cerebral functions as development of the symptoms progressed.

REASON FOR REFERRAL

C. B., an 11-year old fifth grader, was referred by her pediatrician and teachers for a re-evaluation because of apparent lack of progress in school and therapy. The pediatrician expressed concern about the possibility that C. B. was demonstrating symptoms common to Huntington's chorea. Apparently, C. B.'s father has Huntington's chorea and, therefore, she may have acquired the disorder through hereditary transmission.

BEHAVIORAL OBSERVATIONS

C. B. appeared very awkward in balance as she entered the testing room walking with a broad, "drunken" gait. She displayed jerky, irregular motor movements, similar to choreic movements, and appeared slow and lethargic. She further demonstrated difficulty on fine motor tasks, as she seemed clumsy with her hands, which had a slight noticeable tremor. Fine motor control and coordination problems of this nature have been associated with cerebellar dysfunction. C. B. had difficulty maintaining attention in structured problem-solving tasks as well as more informal situations. For example, she fragmented in the middle of a sentence and seemed to lose track of the original thought. C. B. spoke with some dysarthria — she had impaired ability to articulate many sounds and had difficulty with oral motor movements.

C. B. was cooperative throughout testing although her limited attention span interfered with performance.

TEST RESULTS AND INTERPRETATION

The results of the developmental and medical history were nonsignificant other than it is highly probable that Huntington's chorea could have a hereditary basis. C. B. has adequate sensory visual and auditory acuity.

C. B. used her right hand on seven of seven items on the Lateral Dominance Test and preferred her right foot in kicking and stepping. However, she consistently used her left eye on the ABC Ocular Dominance Test, which indicates inconsistent laterality. When asked to show her right hand some confusion was also noted.

On the manual Finger Tapping Test, C. B. tapped $\overline{X} = 26.8$ with the right hand and $\overline{X} = 13.4$ with the left. The norm for her age is $\overline{X} = 38.5$ with the dominant (right) hand and $\overline{X} = 35.4$ with the nondominant (left) hand. Although her right-handed finger tapping was quite slow, it is important to notice that her left-handed finger tapping was severely retarded. This may reflect more involvement of the contralateral (right) hemisphere.

C. B. had a slow response rate on the Tactile Form Recognition test in which a small shape is placed in the subject's hand that must be recognized through the tactile sense alone. Further, she had numerous errors on the Finger-tip Number Writing and the Tactile Finger Recognition Tests. She described pain in the fingertip number writing and seemed very sensitive to touch.

C. B. had considerable difficulty with the Seashore Rhythm Test. This subtest requires the subject to differentiate between 30 pairs of rhythm beats. Deficits related to nonverbal auditory perception tend to be associated with dysfunction of the right temporal lobe. This would appear to require alertness, sustained attention, and ability to perceive and compare rhythmic sequences. C. B. had so few correct answers (7) that the normative data could not be used.

Results of the Bender-Gestalt Test indicated that C. B. scored at a developmental age level similar to that of a 6-year-old. Common errors were angulation, perseveration, and distortion of shapes.

C. B. had an extremely poor performance on the Trail Making Test. This test would appear to require immediate recognition of numerals and letters, ability to scan and continuously sequence, and flexibility in integrating a numerical and alphabetical series. She took 201 seconds (norm, 39–40 seconds) on Part A and 324 seconds on Part B (norm, 91–92 seconds).

C. B. likewise had a very depressed score on the Tactual Performance Test. The subject is blindfolded and asked to place blocks in a formboard with each hand separately, then together. This involves ability to solve problems in spatial relationships, eye-hand coordination, and memory. C. B. performed the task with her dominant hand in 23 minutes, which is quite descrepant with the norm for her age of 3.6 minutes. She took 9.3 minutes with her left hand (norm, 2.4). Her total test time was 32 minutes in comparison to the expected norm of 6.8 minutes. C. B. had severe difficulty with location and memory. She would locate the space with her hand then forget the position of that space within a 1–2 second time interval. When asked to draw the shapes of the blocks from memory, she could not locate any of the forms appropriately.

C. B. demonstrated several errors on the Aphasia Screening Test. She was unable to name certain words of common objects, pronounce multisyllable words, spell certain words, and so on. For example, when shown the graphic figure of a triangle and asked to write the word representing the shape she wrote "sparel." She had difficulty with numerical problems involving mental computations and multiplication. She seemed much more successful when she had a concrete reference for computation. C. B. had 38 correct on the Speech-Sounds Perception (norm, 54.1 correct), which measures ability to process basic speech phonemes. Central and auditory processing deficits are further noted in a report by the school audiologist on the Flowers-Costello Tests of Central Auditory Abilities.

C. B. had a score of 49 on the Category Test, which fell within the low average range or at the thirteenth percentile for her age. This test measures relatively complex concept formation and requires ability in noting similarities or differences. It also measures learning rate in a positive and negative reinforcement situation. In comparison to other subtests, C. B. did quite well on this one.

C. B. demonstrated a dramatic decrease in her intellectual ability in comparison to the initial assessment (Table 7-2).

Table 7-2
The Scores of Patient C. B. on the Wechsler Intelligence Scale
for Children–Revised

Date Tested	Age	Verbal IQ	Perfor- mance IQ	Full Scale IQ
January 23, 1974	6 years, 7 months	92	104	98
September 20, 1976	9 years, 3 months	82	81	80
June 1, 1977	9 years, 11 months	84	75	78
December 19, 1978	11 years, 6 months	66	69	65

These test results reflect C. B.'s performance on tests taken for this case study.

DISCUSSION

In summary, childhood Huntington's chorea is a progressive neurological disease characterized by mental deterioration. In addition, subjects show evidence of cerebellar dysfunction. Motor signs are slow involuntary choreic movements, with rigidity, loss of facial expression, and loss of associated movements. C. B. demonstrated a decline in intellectual capacity as well as evidence of impaired judgment, recent memory, and calculation. She had obvious difficulty with comprehension and remote memory, with some impairment of vocabulary. Her motor movements were similar to individuals with cerebellar dysfunction. All of these signs are indicative of a child with suspected Huntington's chorea. Recommendations are as follows.

1. C. B. should receive medical and neurological follow-up to document Huntington's chorea. These test results suggest that her level of functioning and symptoms are similar to patients with known brain disorders, but more direct measures should be run.
2. C. B. should receive special education services in an educable mentally retarded classroom.
3. Supportive counseling should continue to assist C. B. and her family in adjustment.

REFERENCES

Aaron, P. G. A neuropsychological key approach to diagnosis and remediation of learning disabilities. *Journal of Clinical Psychology*, 1979, *35*, 326–335.

Adams, K. M. In search of Luria's battery: A false start. *Journal of Consulting and Clinical Psychology*, 1980, *48*, 511–516.

Bannatyne, A. *Language, reading, and learning disabilities.* Springfield, Ill.: Charles C Thomas, 1971.

Bannatyne, A. Diagnosis: A note on recategorization of the WISC scaled scores. *Journal of Learning Disabilities,* 1974, *7,* 272-274.

Bardon, J. I. The state of the art (and science) of school psychology. *American Psychologist,* 1976, *31,* 785-791.

Belmont, L., & Birch, H. G. Lateral dominance, lateral awareness, and reading disability. *Child Development,* 1965, *34,* 57-71.

Benson, D. F., & Geschwind, N. Developmental Gerstmann syndrome. *Neurology,* 1970, *20,* 293-298.

Benton, A. L. *The Revised Visual Retention Test.* New York: Psychological Corporation, 1974.

Beery, K. E. *Developmental Test of Visual-Motor Integration.* Chicago: Follett Publishing Company, 1967.

Binder, L. M. Hemispheric specialization. *Journal of Pediatric Psychology,* 1976, *1,* 34-37.

Black, F. W. WISC verbal-performance discrepancies as indicators of neurological dysfunction in pediatric patients. *Journal of Clinical Psychology,* 1974, *30,* 165-167.

Black, F. W. Cognitive, academic, and behavioral findings in children with suspected and documented neurological dysfunction. *Journal of Learning Disabilities,* 1976, *9,* 182-187.

Black, P., Jeffries, J. J., Blumer, D., Wellner, A., & Walker, A. E. The posttraumatic syndrome in children. In A. E. Walker, W. F. Caveness, & M. Critchley (Eds.), *The late effects of head injury.* Springfield, Ill.: Charles C Thomas, 1969.

Boder, E. Developmental dyslexia: A diagnostic screening procedure based on three characteristic patterns of reading and spelling. In B. Bateman (Ed.), *Learning disorders,* (Vol. 4). Washington, D.C.: Special Child Publications, 1971.

Boder, E. Developmental dyslexia: Prevailing diagnostic concepts and a new diagnostic approach. In H. R. Myklebust (Ed.), *Progress in learning disabilities* (Vol. 2). New York: Grune & Stratton, 1973.

Bogen, J. E. The other side of the brain: Parts I, II, and III. *Bulletin of the Los Angeles Neurological Society,* 1969, *34,* 73-105, 135-162, 191-203.

Bogen, J. E. Some educational aspects of hemispheric specialization. *UCLA Educator,* 1975, *17,* 24-32.

Bogen, J. E. *Aspects of neurosociology.* Symposium presented at the annual meeting of the International Neuropsychological Society, Santa Fe, New Mexico, February, 1977.

Bogen, J. E., & Gordon, H. W. Musical tests for functional lateralization with intracarotid amobarbitol. *Nature,* 1971, *230,* 524.

Boll, T. J. Behavioral correlates of cerebral damage in children aged 9 through 14. In R. M. Reitan & L. A. Davison (Eds.), *Clinical neuropsychology: Current status and applications.* Washington, D.C.: V. H. Winston & Sons, 1974.

Boll, T. J., Berent, S., & Richards, H. Tactile-perceptual functioning as a factor in general psychological abilities. *Perceptual and Motor Skills,* 1977, *44,* 535–539.

Bortner, M., Hertzig, M. E., & Birch, H. G. Neurological signs and intelligence in brain-damaged children. *Journal of Special Education,* 1972, *6,* 325–333.

Bryden, M. P. Tachistoscopic recognition, handedness, and cerebral dominance. *Neuropsychologia,* 1965, *3,* 1–8.

Christensen, A. L. *Luria's neuropsychological investigation.* New York: Spectrum, 1975.

Coleman, R. I., & Deutch, C. P. Lateral dominance and left–right discrimination: A comparison of normal and retarded readers. *Perceptual and Motor Skills,* 1964, *19,* 43–50.

Cummins, J., & Das, J. P. Cognitive processing and reading difficulties: A framework for research. *Alberta Journal of Educational Research,* 1977, *23,* 245–256.

Damasio, A. The frontal lobes. In K. M. Heilman & E. Valenstein (Eds.), *Clinical neuropsychology,* New York: Oxford University Press, 1979.

Das, J. P. Patterns of cognitive ability in nonretarded and retarded children. *American Journal of Mental Deficiency,* 1972, *77,* 6–12.

Das, J. P., Kirby, J. R., & Jarman, R. F. Simultaneous and successive syntheses: An alternative model for cognitive abilities. *Psychological Bulletin,* 1975, *82,* 87–103.

Das, J. P., Kirby, J. R., & Jarman, R. F. *Simultaneous and successive cognitive processes.* New York: Academic Press, 1979.

Das, J. P., Manos, J., & Kanungo, R. N. Performance of Canadian native, black and white children on some cognitive and personality tasks. *Alberta Journal of Educational Research,* 1975, *21,* 183–195.

DeConde, C. Personal communication, 1980.

De Renzi, E., & Faglioni, P. The comparative efficiency of intelligence and vigilance tests in detecting hemispheric cerebral damage. *Cortex,* 1965, *1,* 410–433.

Diller, L., Ben-Yishay, Y., Gerstman, L. J., Goodkin, R., Gordon, W., & Weinberg, J. *Studies in cognition and rehabilitation in hemiplegia.* New York: New York University Medical Center Institute of Rehabilitation Medicine, 1974.

Dimond, S. J., & Beaumont, J. G. *Hemisphere function in the human brain.* New York: Wiley & Sons, 1974.

Dunn, L. M. *Expanded manual for the Peabody Picture Vocabulary Test.* Circle Pines, Minn.: American Guidance Service, 1965.

Federal Register. *Education of handicapped children: Implementation of part B of the education of the handicapped act.* Department of Health, Education and Welfare, Vol. 42, No. 163, August, 1977.

Fedio, P., & Mirsky, A. F. Selective intellectual deficits in children with temporal lobe or centrencephalic epilepsy. *Neuropsychologia,* 1969, *7,* 287–300.

Filskov, S. B., & Goldstein, S. G. Diagnostic validity of the Halstead-Reitan Neuropsychology Battery. *Journal of Consulting and Clinical Psychology*, 1974, *42*, 382–388.

Fisk, J. L., & Rourke, B. P. Identification of subtypes of learning disabled children at three age levels: A neuropsychological multivariate approach. *Journal of Clinical Neuropsychology*, 1979, *1*, 289–310.

Flowers, A., Costello, M. R., & Small, V. *Flowers-Costello Tests of Central Auditory Abilities*. Dearborn, Mich.: Perceptual Learning Systems, 1970.

Frisch, G. R., & Handler, L. A neuropsychological investigation of "functional disorders of speech articulation." *Journal of Speech and Hearing Research*, 1974, *17*, 432–445.

Fritsch, G., & Hitzig, E. On the electrical excitability of the cerebrum. In G. von Bonin (Ed.), *Some papers on the cerebral cortex*. Springfield, Ill.: Charles C Thomas, 1960.

Gaddes, W. H. The needs of teachers for specialized information on handedness, finger localization, and cerebral dominance. In W. M. Cruickshank (Ed.), *The teacher of brain-injured children*. Syracuse, N.Y.: Syracuse University Press, 1966.

Gaddes, W. H. A neuropsychological approach to learning disorders. *Journal of Learning Disabilities*, 1968, *1*, 523–534.

Gaddes, W. H. Neurological implications for learning. In W. H. Cruickshank and D. P. Hallahan (Eds.), *Perceptual and learning disabilities in children* (Vol. 1). Syracuse, N.Y.: Syracuse University Press, 1975.

Gaddes, W. H., & Crockett, D. J. The Spreen-Benton Aphasia Tests, normative data as a measure of normal language development. *Brain and Language*, 1975, *2*, 257–280.

Garron, D. C., & Cheifetz, D. I. Comment on "Bender Gestalt discernment of organic pathology." *Psychological Bulletin*, 1965, *63*, 197–200.

Gazzaniga, M. S. Recent research on hemispheric lateralization of the human brain: Review of the split-brain. *UCLA Educator*, 1975, *17*, 9–12.

Golden, C. J. The identification of brain damage by an abbreviated form of the Halstead-Reitan Neuropsychological Battery. *Journal of Clinical Psychology*, 1976, *32*, 821–826.

Golden, C., Hammeke, T., & Purisch, A. Diagnostic validity of a standardized neuropsychological battery derived from Luria's neuropsychological tests. *Journal of Consulting and Clinical Psychology*, 1978, *46*, 1258–1265.

Halstead, W. C. *Brain and intelligence*. Chicago: University of Chicago Press, 1947.

Harris, D. B. Children's drawings as measures of intellectual maturity. New York: Harcourt, Brace, & World, 1963.

Hirschenfang, S. A comparison of Bender-Gestalt reproductions of right and left hemiplegic patients. *Journal of Clinical Psychology*, 1960, *16*, 439.

Holroyd, J., & Wright, F. Neurological implications of WISC Verbal-Performance discrepancies in a psychiatric setting. *Journal of Consulting Psychology,* 1965, *29,* 206-212.

Howie, V. M. Developmental sequelae of chronic otitis media: A review. *Journal of Developmental and Behavioral Pediatrics,* 1980, *1,* 34-38.

Hynd, G. W., & Obrzut, J. E. Effects of grade level and sex on the magnitude of the dichotic ear advantage. *Neuropsychologia,* 1977, *15,* 689-692.

Hynd, G. W., & Obrzut, J. E. Development of reciprocal hemispheric inhibition in normal and learning-disabled children. *Journal of General Psychology,* 1981, *104,* 203-212.

Hynd, G. W., Quackenbush, R., & Obrzut, J. E. Training school psychologists in neuropsychology: Current practices and trends. *Journal of School Psychology,* 1980, *18,* 148-153.

Hynd, G. W., Obrzut, J. E., Weed, W., & Hynd, C. R. Development of cerebral dominance: Dichotic listening asymmetry in normal and learning-disabled children. *Journal of Experimental Child Psychology,* 1979, *28,* 445-454.

Jastak, T. F., & Jastak, S. R. *The Wide Range Achievement Test.* Wilmington, Del.: Guidance Associates, 1965.

Johnson, D. J., & Myklebust, H. R. *Learning disabilities: Educational principles and practices.* New York: Grune & Stratton, 1967.

Kaufman, A. S. A new approach to the interpretation of test scatter on the WISC-R. *Journal of Learning Disabilities,* 1976, *9,* 160-168.

Kaufman, A. S. Cerebral specialization and intelligence testing. *Journal of Research and Development in Education,* 1979, *12,* 96-107. (a)

Kaufman, A. S. *Intelligent testing with the WISC-R.* New York: Wiley-Inter-Science, 1979. (b)

Kaufman, A. S., & Kaufman, N. L. *Kaufman Assessment Battery for Children (K-ABC).* Circle Pines, Minn.: American Guidance Service, in press.

Kimura, D. Dual functional asymmetry of the brain in visual perception. *Neuropsychologia,* 1966, *4,* 275-285.

Kinsbourne, M. (Ed). *Asymmetrical function of the brain.* New York: Cambridge University Press, 1978.

Kinsbourne, M., & Warrington, E. The developmental Gerstmann syndrome. *Archives of Neurology,* 1963, *8,* 490-501.

Kirby, J. R., & Das, J. P. Reading achievement, I.Q., and simultaneous successive processing. *Journal of Educational Psychology,* 1977, *69,* 564-570.

Kirby, J. R., & Das, J. P. Information processing and human abilities. *Journal of Educational Psychology,* 1978, *70,* 58-66.

Klonoff, H., & Lowe, M. Disordered brain function in young children and early adolescents: Neuropsychological and electroencephalographic correlates. In R. M. Reitan & L. A. Davison (Eds.), *Clinical neuropsychology: Current status and applications.* Washington, D.C.: V. H. Winston & Sons, 1974.

Knights, R. M. Problems of criteria in diagnosis: A profile similarity approach. *Annuals of the New York Academy of Sciences,* 1973, *205,* 124-131.

Knights, R. M., & Norwood, J. A. *A neuropsychological test battery for children.* Ottawa, Canada: Psychological Consultants, 1979.

Leviton, A. Otitis media and learning disorders. *Journal of Developmental and Behavioral Pediatrics,* 1980, *1,* 58-63.

Lezak, M. D. *Neuropsychological assessment.* New York: Oxford University Press, 1976.

Mattis, S., French, J. H., & Rapin, I. Dyslexia in children and young adults: Three independent neuropsycholoical syndromes. *Developmental Medicine and Child Neurology,* 1975, *17,* 150-163.

McFie, J. Psychological testing in clinical neurology. *Journal of Nervous and Mental Disease,* 1960, *131,* 383-393.

Milner, B. Laterality effects in audition. In V. B. Mountcastle (Ed.), *Interhemispheric relations and cerebral dominance.* Baltimore: Johns Hopkins University Press, 1962.

Milner, B. Interhemispheric differences in the localization of psychological processes in man. *British Medical Bulletin,* 1971, *27,* 272-277.

Moore, C. L., & Burns, W. J. The performance of neurologically impaired and normal subjects on four screening techniques. *Journal of Clinical Psychology,* 1979, *35,* 420-424.

Obrzut, J. E. Dichotic listening and bisensory memory skills in qualitatively diverse dyslexic readers. *Journal of Learning Disabilities,* 1979, *12,* 304-314.

Obrzut, J. E., Hynd, G. W., & Obrzut, A. Effect of directed attention on cerebral asymmetries in normal and learning-disabled children. *Developmental Psychology,* 1981, *17,* 118-125.

Obrzut, J. E., Hynd, G. W., & Obrzut, A. Neuropsychological assessment of learning disabilities: A discriminant analysis. *Journal of Consulting and Clinical Psychology,* in press.

Obrzut, J. E., Hynd, G. W., Obrzut, A., & Leitgeb, J. L. Time sharing and dichotic listening asymmetry in normal and learning-disabled children. *Brain and Language,* 1980, *11,* 181-194.

Oldfield, R. C. The assessment and analysis of handedness: The Edinburgh Inventory. *Neuropsychologia,* 1971, *9,* 97-113.

Ornstein, R. E. *The psychology of consciousness.* New York: Harcourt, Brace, & Jovanovich, 1977.

Petrauskas, R. J., & Rourke, B. P. Identification of subtypes of retarded readers: a neuropsychological, multivariate approach. *Journal of Clinical Neuropsychology,* 1979, *1,* 17-37.

Piercy, M., & Smyth, V. Right hemisphere dominance for certain non-verbal intellectual skills. *Brain,* 1962, *85,* 775-790.

Pirozzolo, F. J., & Rayner, K. Hemispheric specialization in reading and word recognition. *Brain and Language,* 1977, *4,* 248-261.

Pirozzolo, F. J., & Rayner, K. Cerebral organization and reading disability. *Neuropsychologia,* 1979, *17,* 485-491.

Purisch, A., Golden, C., & Hammeke, T. Discrimination of schizophrenic and brain-injured patients by a standardized version of Luria's neuropsychological tests. *Journal of Consulting and Clinical Psychology,* 1978, *46,* 1266-1273.

Raven, J. C. *Guide to using the Coloured Progressive Matrices.* London: H. K. Lewis, 1956.

Raven, J. C. *Guide to the standard progressive matrices.* London: H. K. Lewis, 1960.

Reed, H. B. C. Pediatric neuropsychology. *Journal of Pediatric Psychology.* 1976, *1,* 5-7.

Reed, H. B. C., Reitan, R. M., & Kløve, H. Influence of cerebral lesions on psychological test performance of older children. *Journal of Consulting Psychology,* 1965, *29,* 247-251.

Reitan, R. M. A research program on the psychological effects of brain lesions in human beings. In N. R. Ellis (Ed.), *International review of research in mental retardation* (Vol. 1). New York: Academic Press, 1966. (a)

Reitan, R. M. The needs of teachers for specialized information in the area of neuropsychology. In W. M. Cruickshank (Ed.), *The teacher of brain-injured children.* Syracuse, N.Y.: Syracuse University Press, 1966. (b)

Reitan, R. M. Psychological assessment of deficits associated with brain lesions in subjects with normal and subnormal intelligence. In J. L. Khanna (Ed.), *Brain damage and mental retardation: A psychological evaluation.* Springfield, Ill.: Charles C Thomas, 1967.

Reitan, R. M. Sensorimotor functions in brain-damaged and normal children of early school age. *Perceptual and Motor Skills,* 1971, *33,* 655-664.

Reitan, R. M. Psychological effects of cerebral lesions in children of early school age. In R. M. Reitan & L. A. Davison (Eds.), *Clinical neuropsychology: Current status and applications.* Washington, D.C.: V. H. Winston and Sons, 1974.

Reitan, R. M., & Davision, L. A. (Eds.), *Clinical Neuropsychology: current status and applications.* Washington, D.C.: V. A. Winston & Sons, 1974.

Reitan, R. M., & Heinemann, C. Interactions of neurological deficits and emotional disturbances in children with learning disorders: Methods for their differential assessment. In J. Hellsmuth (Ed.), *Learning disorders* (Vol. 3). Seattle, Wash.: Special Child Publications, 1968.

Richardson, F. Some effects of severe head injury. *Developmental Medicine and Child Neurology,* 1963, *5,* 471-478.

Rourke, B. P. Brain-behavior relationships in children with learning disabilities: a research program. *American Psychologist,* 1975, *30,* 911-920.

Rourke, B. P. Issues in the neuropsychological assessment of children with learning disabilities. *Canadian Psychological Review,* 1976, *17,* 89-102.

Rourke, B. P., Young, G. C., & Flewelling, R. W. The relationships between WISC verbal-performance discrepancies and selected verbal, auditory-perceptual, visual-perceptual, and problem-solving abilities in children with learning disabilities. *Journal of Clinical Psychology,* 1971, *27,* 475-479.

Rugel, R. P. WISC subtest scores of disabled readers: A review with respect to Bannatyne's recategorization. *Journal of Learning Disabilities*, 1974, *7*, 48–55.

Satz, P. Laterality tests: An inferential problem. *Cortex*, 1977, *13*, 208–212.

Satz, P., & Morris, R. Learning disability subtypes: A review. In F. J. Pirozzolo & M. C. Wittrock (Eds.), *Neuropsychological and cognitive processes in reading.* New York: Academic Press, 1981.

Seashore, C. E., Lewis, D., & Saetveit, D. L. *Seashore measures of musical talent.* New York: Psychological Corporation, 1960.

Segalowitz, S. J., & Gruber, F. A. (Eds.). *Language development and neurological theory.* New York: Academic Press, 1977.

Selz, M., & Reitan, R. M. Neuropsychological test performance of normal, learning-disabled, and brain-damaged older children. *Journal of Nervous and Mental Disease,* 1979, *167*, 298–302. (a)

Selz, M., & Reitan, R. M. Rules for neuropsychological diagnosis: Classification of brain function in older children. *Journal of Consulting and Clinical Psychology,* 1979, *47*, 258–264. (b)

Smith, A. Intellectual functions in patients with lateralized frontal tumors. *Journal of Neurology, Neurosurgery, and Psychiatry,* 1966, *29*, 52–59.

Smith, A. Neuropsychological testing in neurological disorders. In W. J. Friedlander (Ed.), *Advances in neurology.* New York: Raven Press, 1975.

Smith, M. D., Coleman, J. M., Dokecki, P. R., & Davis, E. E. Recategorized WISC-R scores of learning disabled children. *Journal of Learning Disabilities,* 1977, *10*, 444–449.

Spreen, O., & Benton, A. L. Comparative studies of some psychological tests for cerebral damage. *Journal of Nervous and Mental Disease,* 1965, *140*, 323–333.

Spreen, O., & Gaddes, W. H. Developmental norms for 15 neuropsychological tests age 6 to 15. *Cortex*, 1969, *5*, 171–191.

Stuss, D. T., & Trites, R. L. Classification of neurological status using multiple discriminant function analysis of neuropsychological test scores. *Journal of Consulting and Clinical Psychology,* 1977, *45*, 145.

Swiercinsky, D. P. Prediction of specific brain damage location and process by the neuropsychological factor approach. *Journal of Clinical Psychology,* 1976, *32*, 651–654.

Swiercinsky, D. P. Factorial pattern description and comparison of functional abilities in neuropsychological assessment. *Perceptual and Motor Skills,* 1979, *48*, 231–241.

Trupin, E. W., & Townes, B. D. Neuropsychological evaluation as an adjunct to behavioral interventions with children. *Professional Psychology,* 1976, *7*, 153–160.

Tsushima, W. T., & Towne, W. S. Neuropsychological abilities of young children with questionable brain disorders. *Journal of Consulting and Clinical Psychology,* 1977, *45*, 757–762.

Wener, B. D., & Templer, D. I. Relationship between WISC verbal-performance discrepancies and motor and psychomotor abilities of children with learning disabilities. *Perceptual and Motor Skills*, 1976, *42*, 125–126.

Witelson, S. F. Early hemisphere specialization and interhemisphere plasticity: An empirical and theoretical review. In S. J. Segalowitz & F. A. Gruber (Eds.), *Language development and neurological theory*. New York: Academic Press, 1977.

Wittrock, M. C. Education and the cognitive processes of the brain. In J. S. Chall & A. F. Mirsky (Eds.), *Education and the brain, 77th yearbook of the National Society for the Study of Education, part II*. Chicago: University of Chicago Press, 1978.

Zurif, E. G., & Carson, G. Dyslexia in relation to cerebral dominance and temporal analysis. *Neuropsychologia*, 1970, *8*, 351–361.

Charles J. Golden

8
The Luria-Nebraska Children's Battery: Theory and Formulation

The Luria-Nebraska Neuropsychological Battery for adults has been available since 1979. In that short period, the battery has gained an unusual amount of acceptance. It has become increasingly clear that the popularity of the battery is at least partially due to its reliance on, and relationship to Luria's neuropsychological theories, which are increasingly important to neuropsychology.

With the spread of Luria's ideas and theories to other areas of psychology, the need for a children's test battery based on Luria's theories has become evident. Modern texts on learning disabilities and other learning disorders have increasingly included chapters on Luria's basic theory (or some simplification of this theory) as a means for understanding childhood brain disorders. While Luria's theories are applicable to standard American tests (e.g., WISC-R), they are much more useful when applied to a test battery specifically designed for them.

To understand the design and rationale of the Luria-Nebraska Children's Battery, it is first necessary to understand Luria's basic theories and their implications for performing psychological evaluations.

BASIC CONCEPTS IN LURIA'S THEORIES

There are several basic concepts in Luria's theories that must be understood in order to use his work in a clinical setting (Luria, 1966, 1973). Of these, the concept of functional systems is the most important. Luria defines a functional system as the interacting areas of the brain that must be coordinated in order to produce a given behavior.

This concept should be compared to other basic theories of brain functions, e.g., localization theory and equipotential theory. Localization theory suggests that all behaviors result from a single part of the brain. In this system, a particular area of the brain can be identified as a "walking" area and all disorders of walking can be blamed on injury to this area. In contrast, equipotential theorists suggests that for all human behaviors, all areas of the brain participate on an equal basis; no one area specifies a particular behavior.

Luria's theory differs from both of these. No single area of the brain is considered responsible for any particular overt behavior. However, neither are all the areas of the brain considered to contribute equally to all behaviors. In the functional system theory, a limited number of brain areas are involved with each behavior, each in a specific and predictable manner within the functional system. It is this idea that differentiates this theory from the equipotential theories.

A functional system may be thought of as a chain with each link of the chain representing a particular area of the brain. Each link is necessary for the chain to be complete, yet each plays its own specific role in the overall chain. If any part of a functional system is broken, the behavior represented by the chain is injured.

Another important concept is the notion of pluripotentiality. This concept suggests that any specific area of the brain can participate in numerous functional systems. Thus, if one area of the brain is injured many behaviors are disrupted, depending on the number of functional systems in which the given area plays a part. The role of the brain area is similar in each system; for example, one area may be involved in a variety of tasks requiring visual and tactile integration. This concept appears similar to standard localization concepts in which specific skills are assigned to one area of the brain. However, according to this concept and in opposition to localization theories, the various areas of the brain cannot operate in isolation: actual behavior can only result from cooperation of numerous areas of the brain.

The final concept of importance is the lack of uniqueness of functional systems. Multiple functional systems may be responsible for any given behavior. Thus, while one system may be injured, the behavior can be continued because of the availability of an alternate functional system. Indeed, the number of functional systems available may be an index of intelligence and frontal lobe functioning. In general, the more functional systems there are, the more the individual can minimize the effects of brain injury. This fact accounts for the severity of the effects of brain injury in some children: a lack of alternate functional systems arises from being too young to have the opportunity (or neurological circuits) to have developed more complex functional systems. As a result, the effects of a given brain injury may be more devastating in a child than in an adult.

From these basic concepts, several important conclusions can be reached. First, there is no one-to-one correspondence between any specific behavior and any specific area of the brain. If a child cannot read for neurological reasons, the functional system necessary for reading (a tremendously complex system) is impaired in *at least* one place and *possibly more.* Conversely, the absence of a deficit does not indicate that any particular area of the brain is intact, only that some functional system for that behavior is intact. Since there can be multiple functional systems using different areas of the brain, the lack of a deficit does not necessarily yield a great deal of information.

With this information, one can analyze the nature of psychological tests for brain damage. In general, Luria's theory would predict that the more areas of the brain required to perform on a given test, the more likely that a brain injury will disrupt part of the functional system necessary to successfully complete that task. The ultimate test—with a 100 percent hit rate (100 percent accuracy in identifying brain-injured clients)—would be one that involved every area of the brain, or nearly every area. Indeed, it is this ideal test that the American neuropsychological literature has aimed for, with numerous publications by researchers attempting to out-perform the hit rate of the previous researcher.

While this ideal test, or something close to it, is theoretically possible, one must question why it is needed. To know that a person fails the test is similar to knowing that there is a break in a telephone system between Los Angeles and New York. What good is such gross information in identifying the precise spot in the 3000 miles of telephone line that is dysfunctional? Much more precise evaluation is necessary before useful information can be extracted.

It should be noted that, by comparing the results of a battery of complex and simple tests, brain dysfunction can be localized and lateralized. The simpler motor and sensory tests add more to such analysis than do the complex, summary tests. Such results can be accomplished, especially by increasing the number of tests (which, in mathematical terms, provides the ability to solve for a larger number of unknowns). However, while possible, this is the hard way of doing things.

Luria adopted the opposite strategy. Instead of using complex tests with high hit rates, Luria focused on simple tests that attempt (ideally) to focus on one specific, brain-based behavior. Since complex tests simply represent longer chains of simple behaviors, they are not necessary for testing the effectiveness of any given area of the brain. If the disorder does not show up in a simple system using the skill, then the skill is not impaired. This also has the advantage of minimizing errors by normal controls; as many tests gain higher hit rates with the neurologically impaired, they become more likely to falsely identify normals as brain injured. The tests in Luria's Battery—with a few exceptions—are uniformly easy and (on the Children's Battery) can be performed by a normal child of 8 years without difficulty.

Luria recognized that the results of one test item are not sufficient to diagnose an injury in a given part of the brain. Thus, he pursued what he thought was the deficit by giving other test items that measured alternate skills based on the same area of the brain, and looked for the pattern of errors predicted by pluripotentiality. Once a pattern had been established that was associated with a given injury, other areas of injury would be investigated until the full pattern of the insult was outlined.

An alternate way of testing a particular level in a chain is to substitute different links at a given point in the chain. For example, if the chain sequence $a\ b\ c\ d\ e\ f$ has been tested and shown to be intact, but $a\ b\ c\ d\ e\ g$ is not intact, we can infer that the problem may be due to presence of link g. An examination of other items containing link g can confirm or contradict this assumption. Substitutions may be used to similar effect in other parts of the chain. The simpler the basic chain, and the less time it takes, the more efficient the testing of a wide range of alternate links.

In practice, Luria applied these procedures qualitatively. He would give an initial test item and decide on the basis of the result what would be done next. The use of further items would be decided in the same manner—on the basis of the patient's response and on Luria's clinical judgement and intuition as to what was wrong. The result would determine future procedures. This process would continue until Luria was satisfied that an accurate diagnosis had been achieved. This could take as little as 10 minutes, or last hours, days, or even weeks.

It is obvious that a standardized test cannot follow the identical methodology Luria employed. First of all, Luria did not use standardized testing procedures or standardized scoring procedures. He gave test items in the way he thought best in the situation. Scoring (usually a rating of normal, borderline, or abnormal) was based on Luria's clinical analysis of the patient's performance. Further, since Luria used no specific set of tests, what would or would not be given to a patient could not be predicted.

These procedures have several drawbacks. First, there is no way to analyze the effectiveness of Luria's test procedures, except to note that Luria said they worked. As a consequence, replication (a significant aspect of any standardized system) is essentially impossible. In addition, learning the system was difficult unless one simply followed Luria around for several years (or more).

Thus, the standardized system must use a more systematic approach to testing than Luria used himself. This system was developed by including items that test all possibilities in breaking down the major functional systems into their specific links. Using this system, a person administering the battery does more testing than Luria, who would choose to skip items when he felt them unnecessary. Another change was in the multiple use of single items. While Luria might have used the same item to evaluate multiple dimensions of behavior, each item in the standardized system focuses on only one aspect (e.g., motor skills) of behavior, although this might be done in multiple ways (evaluate motor skills for quality and speed, for example).

Because of the need to limit the length of the entire battery, some compromise was made. An initial battery, comprising all of the Luria items (Christensen, 1975), took over 6 hours to administer — clearly too long for the purpose of the battery. Thus, a wide variety of items were eliminated or modified. Items that were short were given priority over longer items. Redundant items were eliminated, as were items difficult to standardize or score reliably. Items that did not differentiate brain-damaged from normal individuals, or that only measured rarely occurring deficits, were eliminated as well.

The remaining items theoretically allow the interpreter to examine each area of the brain (by looking at the pattern of performance on items using that area) and the specific skill areas (e.g., motor skills). Skill areas may be further analyzed in terms of either basic deficits or identification of those input, output, or integrative situations where the deficit occurs. Through these methods, the status of specific functional systems and their various links can be determined. This allows the examiner to both localize the site of a lesion or dysfunction and to determine which alternative functional systems using the intact areas of the brain may be employed.

To fully understand how each functional system (represented by a single item) is formed and changed to produce the test items, it is necessary to both understand how a functional system is formed in adults and the effects of developmental processes on such systems.

THE THREE UNITS OF THE BRAIN

As noted earlier, all functional systems must consist of interactions of at least several areas of the brain. More specifically, all functional systems must involve the three basic units of the brain. These units are the (1) arousal unit, (2) the sensory input unit, and (3) the output planning unit.

The Arousal Unit

The arousal unit consists of those parts of the brain identified as the reticular activating system (RAS). This system is a collection of diffuse intertwined structures that act to raise or lower cortical arousal. The structure itself extends from the pons and medulla through the thalamus to the cortex. The system is necessary for survival and behavior since without arousal the cortex is unable to respond to incoming stimuli. Disorders of the reticular system, in the extreme, can vary from narcolepsy (chronic, pathological sleep) to insomnia.

In addition to its role in arousal, the reticular system is also responsible for filtering sensory input, especially from those senses that are always "on" (tactile/kinesthetic and auditory). This prevents the cortex from being flooded with constant, irrelevant stimuli, which can interfere with cognitive processing. Thus, this system plays an important role in attention, concentration, and other similar processes.

Reticular system defects in the child can result in a wide variety of disorders, ranging from schizophrenia to hyperactivity. Hyperactive syndromes may result from two mechanisms. In the first, the child is "underaroused:" the reticular system is not producing sufficient cortical arousal or is not letting through enough stimuli to maintain cortical arousal. This induces a state of "sensory deprivation," a situation that, when prolonged, is highly aversive to most living organisms. In response, the child will attempt to generate additional input and arousal in the only manner open to him or her: motor movements, including vocalizations. Theoretically, it is this type of child who responds to drugs like Ritalin (Ciba). The drug raises arousal levels, thereby allowing the child to reduce activity.

It should be noted that the failure of Ritalin or other similar drugs, when prescribed correctly, does not rule out this mechanism for hyperactivity. While the hyperactive behavior may begin as a result of reticular dysfunction, it may be maintained by secondary gains, and essentially become independent of its physiological origins. Such emotional and learning factors complicate the diagnosis of all of the problems discussed here. Indeed, avoiding these secondary problems is an important aspect of treating the brain-injured child.

The opposite of the underaroused child also exists: the overaroused child. In these cases, the reticular system may fail to screen stimuli, flooding the cortex with excess information. The child becomes stimulus bound, unable to focus on any one thing. Unlike the underaroused child, Ritalin given to the overaroused child will cause the child's hyperactive behavior to increase dramatically. This child is unable to sit still for any length of time, although some improvement may occur if the child is put in a quiet, low stimulus environment (unless, again, secondary gains interfere with the child responding to such environmental manipulations). Unlike the first type of child, who sometimes improves in a high-activity environment, the overaroused child will deteriorate in such situations.

In a few cases, reticular system dysfunction can be cyclical, going from one extreme to another. In these cases, few solutions seem effective for very long because of the child's changing physiological condition.

The Sensory Input Unit

This unit is responsible for most early learning skills, as well as for many of the abilities measured by intelligence tests. As a result, this unit plays a critical role in neuropsychology.

The second unit can be subdivided into three types of areas: primary, secondary, and tertiary. Of all of the areas of the cortex, the primary are the most "hard wired." By this it is meant that the functions of the primary areas and the connections within the area are largely predetermined by genetics. The primary areas act as sensory reception areas; input is received on a general "point-to-point" basis from the appropriate sensory organs. It is here that initial integration of the material occurs. In the sensory input unit, there are three primary areas, each devoted to a specific sense. The auditory primary area is in the temporal lobe; the visual primary area is in the occipital lobe; and the tactile/kinesthetic primary area is in the parietal lobe. There is little difference between the primary areas of the two hemispheres. One can be eliminated early in life with only minor effects. Destruction of both primary areas results in such conditions as cortical blindness or cortical deafness.

There is a secondary area corresponding to each of the primary areas of the sensory input unit. The secondary area analyzes and integrates the information received at the primary areas. Thus, for example, the acoustic secondary area (in the temporal lobe) is responsible for analyzing sounds, organizing them into phonemes, pitch, tone, rhythm, and so on.

The secondary areas of the sensory input unit process information sequentially. This allows the brain to be aware of stimulus changes (e.g., to detect movement) and to link events temporally. This is quite important, for example, in the case of speech, in which phonemes must be sequentially linked to form words and sentences. Injuries to the secondary area will generally first affect the sequential nature of the analysis. For example, a person with a partial injury to the auditory secondary area may be able to understand two phonemes in a row, but not three. An individual with injuries to the secondary visual area may only be able to examine one object at a time, or one word (or letter) at a time. Injuries to the secondary parietal area will not impair sensation but may inhibit two-point discrimination, detection of direction of movement, or recognition of shapes or letters traced on the skin.

At the secondary level, there is more specialization in the role of the hemispheres. The left hemisphere (in most individuals) predominates in analysis of verbal material, while the right hemisphere predominates in the analysis of nonverbal material, including music. However, both play a role in recognizing phonemes and letters, while the left hemisphere also plays a role in rhythmic analysis and visual-spatial perception. In understanding hemispheric differentiation, one must carefully analyze the skills required of the functional system. For example, reading, in its early stages, requires the recognition of unfamiliar shapes (called letters), a task that is predominantly done in the right hemisphere. Only after the letter is learned does it become a verbal symbol primarily detected by the left hemisphere. Similarly, writing, in its initial stage, is a right-hemisphere dominated, visual-motor construction task. Later, switching from printed to cursive writing involves right-hemisphere coordination, as does reading or learning unfamiliar alphabets. Some languages—based on pitch discrimination or picture representation rather than letters—remain right-hemisphere dominated processes.

The tertiary level of the sensory input unit, located primarily in and around the patietal lobe, is responsible for cross-modality integration. It is at this level that auditory, visual, and tactile information can be fused and analyzed simultaneously. This simultaneous integration across senses complements the sequential analysis of the secondary units. However, these areas are also capable of sequential analysis of material that is initially integrated.

The tertiary parietal area plays a primary role in many of the tasks commonly subsumed under "intelligence." Auditory-visual integration is necessary for reading, while auditory-tactile integration is necessary for writing. Arithmetic, as well as body location in space and visual-spatial skills, depends upon visual-tactile integration. Grammatical skills, syntax, abstractions, logical analysis, understanding of prepositions, spatial rotation, angle determination, and stereognosis are just a few of the skills mediated by the tertiary area of the sensory input unit.

There is increasing hemispheric differentiation of tasks at the tertiary level of the second unit. The left hemisphere is largely responsible for reading, writing, and understanding arithmetic symbols and processes. Grammar, syntax, and other language-related skills are generally of the left hemisphere. The left tertiary area also is involved in the reproduction of complex figures, especially in the reproduction of details (rather than major outlines). The right hemisphere is responsible for the visual-spatial relationship of parts, the spatial nature of arithmetic (such as "borrowing" or "carrying over"), verbal-spatial skills, facial recognition, recognition of emotional (nonverbal) facial and postural reactions, and analysis of unusual or unknown pictures (as well as handwriting).

Injuries to the tertiary area, depending on location and severity, can lead to loss of or impairment of any of the above skills, usually through the loss of the ability to integrate effectively across two or three sensory modalities.

This can lead to profoundly obvious symptoms – dysnomia, dyslexia, dysgraphia, or any of the many dyspraxias – or very subtle symptoms (e.g., inability to recognize emotional states, or inability to understand complex grammatical structures.)

The Output/Planning Unit

The tertiary area of the output/planning unit represents the highest level of development of the mammalian brain. Before looking at the tertiary area, however, the functioning of the primary and secondary areas should be examined.

The primary area of the output/planning unit is the motor output area of the brain. Commands are sent from this area (through the motor tracts of the brain) to the specific muscles needed to perform any given behavior (including speech functions). The secondary area of the output/planning unit is responsible for organizing the sequence of motor acts. Whereas the primary areas send individual commands, the secondary area must organize and sequence the temporal pattern of movement.

These two areas do not function by themselves. In order for motor movements to take place, there must be adequate information available on muscle and joint status (kinesthetic and proprioceptive feedback). To allow this, there are heavy connections between the motor and tactile primary areas, as well as between the motor and tactile secondary areas. In addition, 20 percent of the cells in the primary motor area are tactile cells and 20 percent of the cells in the primary tactile area are motor cells. Thus, the primary and secondary areas interact strongly on a behavioral level. They also tend to develop in tandem (i.e., the primary areas and secondary areas develop about the same time, in the absence of injury).

Injuries to the motor area can produce severe dysfunctions such as hemiplegia (paralysis of one side of the body). However, injuries of a limited nature that occur early in life may cause temporary dysfunction that essentially disappears through adoption of the function by the other hemisphere (this frequently occurs with injuries to the nondominant, usually right, hemisphere) or by reorganization within the injured hemisphere. Injuries later in life generally are manifested by clumsiness or by less control (or strength) of one side of the body. Injuries may also be expressed as speech disorders, including stuttering, lack of fluency, impairment in tongue or lip movements, and similar kinds of problems.

The functions of the tertiary area of the output/planning unit, most commonly called the prefrontal lobes, are in many ways dramatically different from the functions of the primary and secondary areas. The major tasks of the tertiary area are planning (decision-making), evaluation, temporal continuity, impulse and emotional control (delay of gratification), focusing of attention, and flexibility (creativity).

The planning function is unquestionably central to human behavior. The prefrontal lobes receive information from the tertiary area of the sensory unit. They then analyze this information and plan behavioral reactions. This function allows a person to respond rationally to environmental changes and demands according to sensory input and past experiences. This function is especially important for long-range planning, as opposed to the short-term reactions that dominate the behavior of most animals as well as of children. This ability is closely-related to the skill of delaying gratification (without external reward or restraint) and impulse control (again without external restraint or reward), which are two more important functions of the prefrontal lobes.

As the prefrontal lobes develop, they assume dominance over the arousal unit of the brain (reticular system). The prefrontal tertiary areas thereafter regulate attentional focus and can directly and consciously modulate level of arousal. Thus, at around puberty, many symptoms of reticular system dysfunction may disappear as the tertiary areas achieve behavioral dominance. This is the reason why many cases of hyperactivity with a physiological basis disappear at or around puberty. (However, it should be remembered that if the frontal lobes themselves are dysfunctional, new symptoms may appear at this age or old symptoms may worsen.)

Another major function of the frontal lobes is evaluating behavior. The frontal lobes must evaluate whether a person's behavior is consistent with long-term goals and plans, much as the secondary (pre-motor) area monitors behavior to insure that short-term goals are accomplished (e.g., walking across a room or communicating specific information). Evaluative skills, when intact in the injured person, can cause depression. The injured individual can clearly recognize that he or she is unable to formulate or put long-term plans into action.

Injuries to the frontal lobes can cause a wide variety of disorders, although these disorders are generally more difficult to discriminate from psychiatric and behavioral problems than are disorders of the sensory input unit.

Injuries to the tertiary area of the frontal lobe prior to adolescence are essentially impossible to detect. Children may show "symptoms" associated with frontal lobe dysfunction—irritability, hyperemotionality, impulsiveness, rages, etc.—but these symptoms are usually the result of injury to the arousal unit; i.e., the reticular system in the neonatal period or the limbic system thereafter. Such symptoms may or may not improve when frontal lobe development occurs, depending on whether the frontal lobes themselves are intact. This cannot be determined behaviorally except indirectly (i.e., if other nearby areas are injured, the prefrontal lobes may also be injured). As a result, in the absence of definite neuropathological information (e.g., the frontal lobes were destroyed), it cannot be predicted with certainty whether a child will, when reaching adolescence, begin to show signs of frontal lobe dysfunction.

Since many of the skills mediated by the tertiary frontal lobe area can be subsumed under the word *maturity,* it is difficult to be sure if the observed behavior is a result of a frontal lobe deficit or immaturity due to environmental training. Thus, the patient may be in late adolescence or young adulthood before the behavioral pattern of such a deficit is clearly discriminable from childishness, juvenile delinquency, or psychiatric disorders common to the adolescent period.

Early injury to the prefrontal areas can theoretically lead to adult-onset schizophrenia, with the first serious episode occurring somewhere between the ages of 17 and 26, and usually secondary to some stressful event. Such schizophrenics will generally prove to be, as adults, process schizophrenics who respond poorly to treatment. It is not unusual to find adult-onset schizophrenics with a history of early brain injury or a history of early drinking or drug abuse (e.g., glue sniffing) that could damage the brain.

DEVELOPMENTAL SEQUENCING

In adult neuropsychology, all the units of the brain are theoretically fully functioning before the onset of a given disorder. Thus, all the neuropsychologist has to do is identify deficits in order to identify brain injury (assuming a normal environment). However, child neuropsychology presents a unique problem: the child is developing and changing, so that not all skills exist at any given age. Thus, it is of no concern to anyone that a 6-month-old child does not speak. Such an infant is not expected to talk. The major problem this causes in neuropsychological evaluation is the need to be able to identify, for a given child, what skills *should* exist. This is, of course, further complicated by the fact that children develop neurologically at different rates, making any such list of expected skills debatable. At any given age, a lack of some skills might be considered sure signs of brain damage, a lack of others might be considered normal, while a lack of still others may be seen as indicating dysfunction, *perhaps.* To complicate matters even further, neurological growth must interact with an appropriate environment: if one is raised by monks who never speak, one will never learn to speak.

Given this situation, it is essential for anyone practicing child neuropsychology to be aware of the developmental sequences likely to be reflected in testing. In general, there are two major types of theories to describe neurodevelopmental processes. The first type assumes that the child's brain is the equal of an adult's brain. It is capable of all skills and skill levels; however, it must develop sequentially each year with quantitative gains being made as the child grows older. Thus, a 3-year-old child can fingertap 12 times, a 4-year-old 16 times, and so on, until adult speeds are reached. Similarly, the young child is viewed as having all essential problem-solving skills: only the complexity of the problems the child can solve changes with age.

Other theories assume that there are distinct neurodevelopmental periods in which qualitative rather than quantitative changes in skills occur. Thus, a child is not able to use certain problem strategies intelligently until a certain stage of growth is reached. This type of theory is very similar to the developmental theories advocated by Piaget and others.

It is this latter theory on which the Luria-Nebraska Children's Battery is based. It is assumed that certain skills are more developmentally advanced than others and that the child cannot learn them until the neurological stage is reached. Thus, if frontal lobe skills do not develop until age 12, it is senseless to include a test of frontal lobe abilities in a battery designed for the 8-year-old. While the child may respond, the answer's correctness or incorrectness will not measure frontal lobe activity because that area is essentially useless to the child at that age.

Before describing the theoretical developmental system assumed in interpreting and designing the Luria-Nebraska Children's Battery, it is necessary to describe what is meant by neurological development. In the present context, neurological development is the end product of several factors: mylenization, dendritic growth, growth of cell bodies, establishment of pathways among neurons, and other related physical and biochemical events. All of these processes are necessary for complete neurological development and none alone is sufficient. Thus, there is at present no one-to-one relationship between periods of physical growth in the brain (such as mylenization) and psychological maturation: any such relationship remains poorly understood. As a result, the times for various developmental periods given here are based on behavioral rather than physiological observations. As such, they are subject to change as our understanding increases and should not be considered rigid or essential to the basic theory.

In addition to the necessary physiological substrate, there is also an environmental requirement before behavior emerges. Thus, at any level above the basic sensory and motor skills, physiological maturation serves only as a base for the skills resident in each area. Without appropriate experience, the abilities will not emerge. Thus, while the secondary visual area can differentiate red from blue, one will not perceive these colors as different unless one is taught to perceive them. This is true of all the skills that are mediated by secondary or tertiary levels of the brain. In the following discussion, for the sake of simplicity, normal environmental experience will be assumed.

Five Stages of Development

Overall, there are five major stages of development: (1) development of the arousal unit; (2) development of the primary motor and sensory areas; (3) development of motor and sensory secondary areas; (4) development of the sensory input unit tertiary areas (parietal lobe); and (5) development of output/planning unit tertiary areas (prefrontal lobes).

STAGE 1

The most basic part of the brain is the reticular system and related structures. This system is generally operative by birth and is certainly fully operative by 12 months after conception. The neuropsychologist, in working with infants, should be clearly aware that the development of this unit depends upon time since conception, not since birth. A premature infant born 6 months after conception cannot be expected to show behavior that is seen in a full-term baby. Before development of the reticular system, the premature child would be expected to show disorders of arousal and attention as compared to the full-term baby, although such deficits need not be permanent if the problem is only developmental and not related to brain dysfunction.

The reticular activating system (RAS) is particularly sensitive to damage during the time it is being formed. More severe disorders often lead to death or severe retardation. However, disorders of attention and/or filtering appear to be much more likely with injuries that occur prior to 12 months after conception. Indeed, Rutter (1980) has found that childhood head injuries that occur after this period produce no unusual attention deficits. As a result, true physiological hyperactivity (as discussed earlier) probably is due only to these early injuries.

After this initial period, injuries to the RAS appear to result more often in disorders of consciousness (coma, stupor, etc.) than in disorders of attention. Injuries to the nearby limbic system may cause emotional disorders that simulate hyperactivity to some degree. These disturbances are qualitatively different from true attention disorders and are more stress and anxiety related.

STAGE 2

Stage 2 of neurological development proceeds concurrently with stage 1 development. Stage 2 involves the four primary areas of the brain. Generally, these areas are fully operational within 12 months after conception, similar to the timing in the arousal unit.

During the early part of life, cortical response to the outside world is dominated by these primary areas. Built into these areas are basic motor behaviors—for example, crying and grasping,—and basic sensory behaviors—depth discrimination, recognition of high-pitched voices, etc. All of these behaviors are genetically "built in," and all appear to have (or have had) some definitive survival function. In general, however, these behaviors last only as long as the primary areas dominate cortical functioning. As secondary areas take over, these behaviors drop out or become quiescent. For example, a baby may be able to make a differential response to certain sounds, but, if not taught the differential response on a secondary level, the child may be unable to make the discrimination at age 3.

Depending upon the age and extent of injury, children respond differently to damage to the primary areas of the cortex. If the injury occurs early—before birth or shortly thereafter—the complete destruction of the primary area in one hemisphere can be compensated for by the primary area in the opposite hemisphere. This, of course, only applies to unilateral injuries. For example, a child might be born partially paralyzed on one side of the body due to primary level injuries. But at age 5, there may be no residual problems: i.e., the child may have apparently normal motor and sensory function. If the injury occurs early enough in fetal development, no deficit may be seen, even at birth. One child seen by this author was born without a right hemisphere, yet showed no motor, tactile, visual, or auditory deficits. Caution should be exercised in applying these results, however. Injuries might have to be of a certain size or severity for this takeover to occur. Also, many motor deficits and sensory deficits arise from injuries to places other than the four primary areas.

Injuries after this early postnatal period are more serious, but many can be compensated for by the brain. Thus, loss of a primary auditory area on one side of the brain will result in a higher threshold of hearing, i.e., auditory acuity will be diminished, but otherwise not interfere with day-to-day life. Loss of the primary visual area will cause the loss of half of the eye fields, which can be compensated for partially by eye movement. Motor loss can cause hemiplegia, but with proper therapy and exercise some control can be regained. Bilateral injuries are much more serious. These can cause deafness, blindness, or paralysis. Partial injuries produce some fraction of the above results, depending upon the seriousness of the injuries.

STAGE 3

This stage begins concommittent with the first two stages but extends through about age 5. Secondary level discriminations begin to develop as soon as the adequate attentional focus of stage 1 and the capacity to relay information from the primary areas to secondary levels via dendritic connections is developed. Such behavior as fear of strangers marks the emergence of important secondary visual discriminations, while such behavior as differential responses to an individual woman's voice as opposed to other women's voices marks auditory development. Eye-hand coordination, crawling, early walking, and so on mark secondary motor milestones.

The secondary areas are highly related to the concept of dominance. It is at this level of the brain that the first important differentiation of the brain into verbal and nonverbal hemispheres is seen. However, the brain is not committed to the left hemisphere as verbal—as it is in 93 percent of the population (Milner, 1975)—until the development of the secondary areas is markedly advanced. This occurs at about age 2, or more precisely, when the child develops consistent verbal skills. Injuries to the left hemisphere prior to this time will result in much less deficit than injuries after this time. In general, left-hemisphere injuries prior to 2 years will result in the transfer of dominance for verbal skills to the right hemisphere; the earlier this occurs, the better and more complete the transfer. After age 2, some transfer may occur, but this is usually minimal (e.g., Hebb, 1942; Smith, 1975). The results of injuries incurred after 2 years of age begin to resemble the results of adult injuries more and more (Golden, 1978). Thus, there appears to be a critical period in which these unilateral injuries are minimized; thereafter, they are much more serious (Dikman, Matthews, & Harley, 1975). Such plasticity mechanisms do not apply when the injury is diffuse.

This plasticity of the brain also does not occur with small injuries—it occurs only when there is significant injury to the secondary areas (DeRenzi & Piercy, 1969). As a consequence, there is the paradox that a small injury at birth may produce more deficit than larger injuries. This, theoretically, is a primary cause of learning disabilities limited to a single modality (Golden & Anderson, 1979).

During the first 5 years of life, the secondary areas are the primary sites of learning in the human cortex. (This age limit, like others in this chapter, is only approximate: there are extensive individual differences both up and down at this age.) During this period, the child's primary and most important learning occurs within single modalities rather than between them. Cross-modality learning, at this stage, is not integrative learning but rather rote memory. The child learning to read at this level must memorize each letter or word-sound combination. The visual symbol for a word lacks meaning for the young child except through its association with the spoken word. Thus, the child must say the word to understand it, or repeat the phonemes in an attempt to integrate the sounds and recognize the word. It is not until stage 4 that the child is capable of true, integrative cross-modality learning.

STAGE 4

Stage 4 is primarily concerned with the tertiary area of the sensory input unit, located mainly in the parietal lobe. The tertiary parietal area is responsible for efficient performance in most major educational skills. Injuries to this area of the brain can have disastrous effects on learning. Major injuries can result in mental retardation (as can more basic injuries, of course), while smaller injuries can cause specific learning disabilities that interfere with the integration of two or more sensory modalities (Luria, 1966). Which sensory modalities will be effected depends upon the location of the injury (Luria, 1966).

The tertiary parietal area is not psychologically active until a child is 5-8 years old. As a result, the effect of earlier injuries to the tertiary area may not be seen until ages 8-12. Thus, if a child has an injury limited to this area at age 2, one might conclude when the child is 3 that he or she is normal and unharmed, only to discover that at age 10 the child has serious learning impairments. This consideration is extremely important in legal cases or situations in which one is asked to predict future behavior. It is essentially impossible to do better than quote actuarial data in predicting whether a 4-year-old will have tertiary level problems (except, of course, in cases where brain damage in other areas is already obvious.) In those cases where the entire injury is limited to tertiary areas, real prediction is impossible.

An important problem in evaluating the development that occurs during stage 4 is the concept of developmental lag. This will be discussed in the next section.

STAGE 5

During this stage, the prefrontal areas of the brain that serve as the tertiary level of the output/planning unit develop. In general, stage 5 does not begin until adolescence. As a result, tests measuring the skills at this level are not appropriate in a test for 8-12-year-olds and have not been included in the Luria-Nebraska Children's Battery. Frontal lobe injuries incurred earlier in life, such as those occuring during infancy, will now be seen at this stage. Children with a disorder of the frontal area can be symptomless until ages 12-15, or even older. In many people development in stage 5 may not be complete until age 24.

General Considerations

In general, the time a child enters any given stage is independent of the time he or she will enter later stages. Also, the quality of performance in any one stage does not predict the quality of performance in the next or subsequent stages. (As a consequence, IQs across stages or predictions across stages—except in extreme cases—tend to be of little use. This is especially true in borderline individuals.) A child may be slow in stage 4 and blossom in stage 5—or do the opposite.

Clearly, when evaluating a child, it is necessary to estimate what stage the child is in as well as what stage the child should be in. This determines how the child's behavior should be viewed, and is useful in helping to discriminate deficits due to emotional factors versus those due to neurological disorders. In cases where clear impairment in a current stage is due to injury, such an analysis is useful for prognosis. Alternatively, the analysis can also serve as a reminder of prognostic limitations. Many "miracles" occur when physicians or psychologists make predictions about a child's prognosis without being aware of the brain's potential or developmental structures. In the same way, many seriously injured children have been declared "normal" because physicians and psychologists have been unaware of the development of psychological processes.

DEVELOPMENTAL LAGS

Another important concept in examining the child neuropsychologically is the concept of developmental lag. As described above, development is sequential in most individuals. As the individual progresses from one stage to another there are *qualitative* as well as *quantitave* changes in the neurological base of abilities. Thus, while a form of later skills can be seen in an earlier stage (e.g., reading during the secondary stage), the behavior is *not* identical in quality or method to the behavior in the appropriate (tertiary) stage. The child who does not steal a cookie because he or she will be punished is not showing the same behavior as the adult who leaves the cookie alone because it belongs to someone else.

As a result, the concept of developmental lag is an important one. If two children are the same age but one is more advanced neuropsychologically, the advanced child will have many advantages in both school and personal situations.

One problem with the concept of developmental lag is the need to establish at what ages a true lag exists. We are, at present, limited to largely behavioral data in determining the ages at which a child should enter a given stage. It is evident from watching children who turn out to be normal that the ranges are rather large, especially for the transition from stage 3 to 4, which may occur, it appears, in children as young as 2 or 3 or as old as 10 to 12. Under such ranges, few children would be classified as delayed—indeed, using the 2-standard-deviation statistical method, only 2 percent or so of children would be classified as "lagging." These would largely be children who did not enter the stage 4 level until age 9 or later.

Unfortunately, a more stringent criterion is typically used—the ability to perform most basic educational skills in the first grade. Using this definition, some schools classify 10-40 percent of their children as developmentally abnormal. The absurdity of this definition arises from the assumption that if the brain does not develop by an arbitrarily set date—a date set more for parental and societal convenience with no reference to brain development—there is something wrong with that brain. Most such lags can be eliminated by resetting the age to 8, rather than 6, for stage 4 skills. The problem lies not in our children, but in our expectations. ("Hyperactivity" can also be traced to these same expectations in a number of cases.) Thus, while the concept of developmental lag has a role in neuropsychology, the present use of the term is highly questionable from this theoretical point of view.

DEVELOPMENT OF THE CHILDREN'S BATTERY

Two viewpoints may be followed in developing a children's version of any test, as we have seen. The first view sees children as essentially less-sophisticated, less-skilled adults. Thus, one uses the same basic tests but makes them easier—such an approach is clearly taken in the Wechsler Intelligence Scale for Children-Revised, for example, or in the Halstead-Reitan Children's Batteries.

The second approach views children as developing through succeeding stages, each of which is qualitatively different in nature than the others. At each stage, assuming an appropriate environment, the child is able to do certain tasks, though they are not done in the same manner during the different stages. Thus, while a simpler version of an adult test can be devised for children, the test will not measure the same thing in children as in adults. A good example of this is the Halstead Category Test. The Reitan-Indiana Battery has a children's "version" of this test. However, while the adult test measures certain frontal lobe skills, the children's test does not (except when given to an adult!). The test measures something completely different at the child's level—such as ability to memorize a complex pattern of results, or luck—rather than frontal lobe skills, as such. The use of these tests can easily lead to misinterpretation.

In the alternative methodology, the child's version is made by eliminating those items that measure skills of a higher developmental level. Thus, the adult Luria test becomes a child's test for ages 8-12 (during which time a child should be in the tertiary parietal but not tertiary frontal stage) by eliminating items intended for measuring prefrontal skills. The remaining items are then analyzed for age appropriateness of the instructions and material (e.g., an 8-year-old would not be expected to be familiar with the word "industrious" or aware of different types of alcoholic beverages).

It was essentially this approach that was used in developing the children's version of the Luria-Nebraska Battery. A small group of above-average youngsters were given the adult test to identify inappropriate items and places where procedural changes might be necessary. Two revisions of this were tested on small groups. Finally, a third version was tested on 60 children. From the results of this work, the final (fourth) version was created. In order to establish initial norms, 120 normal children were chosen to be tested (24 at each age level from 8 to 12 years). At the time of writing (1981), the children have been tested and the subsequent results are clearly in line with theoretical expectations — basic test items (secondary level or less) generally show little age effect. Tertiary parietal test items show improvement with age as more children enter this level and become more proficient with the tasks demanded at the level.

DESCRIPTION OF THE SCALES

The final version of the Luria-Nebraska Children's Battery consists of 11 subtests covering the following areas.

Motor skills. This section measures basic motor speed, coordination, imitation, and construction skills. More complex items, involving frontal lobe control of behavior, have been eliminated from the adult battery for the development of the children's battery.

Rhythm. This section evaluates the child's ability to hear and repeat simple tonal discriminations, to sing a song from an example and from memory, to count and to repeat rhythmic patterns. Except for more complex discrimination items, this scale is intact from the adult version.

Tactile. This scale measures finger and arm localization, two-point discrimination, strength discrimination, movement detection, shape discrimination, and stereognostic skills in the right and left hands and arms.

Visual. This section measures simple visual recognition from actual objects as well as pictures, as well as visual recognition of unusual or shaded figures, recognition of multiple objects, comparisons of rotated figures, and visual memory. Complex spatial relationship and three-dimensional block design have been removed from this section.

Receptive speech. This section evaluates the child's ability to decipher phonemes, follow simple commands, and to follow visual-verbal instructions. Somewhat shorter than the adult version, the receptive speech scale on the children's battery differs from the adult battery only in the elimination of the most complex items.

Expressive language. This scale evaluates the ability to read and repeat words correctly (eliminating words that younger children might not recognize), to repeat sentences, to use automatized speech, to name objects from visual and oral descriptions, and to speak in response to several stimuli. Items requiring reorganization of mixed-up sentences, which have heavy right frontal loadings, were eliminated.

Writing. This scale measures the ability to analyze letter sequences, to spell, to copy, and to write from dictation.

Reading. This section measures sound synthesis, letter recognition, nonsense syllable reading, word reading, sentence reading, and paragraph reading.

Arithmetic. Number recognition, number writing, number comparison, and simple mathematical processes are evaluated on this scale.

Memory. This scale evaluates verbal and nonverbal memory with and without interference.

Intelligence. The items on this scale cover content similar to the Picture Arrangement, Picture Completion, Vocabulary, Comprehension, Arithmetic, and Similarity scales of the WISC-R appropriate for this age range. In addition, the ability of the child to make simple generalizations and basic deductions is also measured.

SCORING OF THE BATTERY

Normative data (currently being published) are used to establish a 3-point scale for each item. A score of 0 represents performance equal to or less than one standard deviation below the mean. A score of 1 represents performance between one and two standard deviations worse than the mean. A score of 2 represents performance more than 2 standard deviations below the mean. Items in which the worst possible answer was within two standard deviations of the normal mean were discarded as ineffective. Norms were established at each age group, although for over half the items norms are identical for most or all age groups used for the present test (8-12-year-olds).

After item scores are determined, total scores for each scale are determined by adding up the results for each item on the *0, 1, 2,* scale. These scores are then transformed into *t* scores, using the mean of the normative group as 50 and then assigning the standard deviation as 10. Tables to do this are enclosed with the test booklet (Golden, 1980).

ITEM EXAMPLES

The following pages present sample items from the Luria-Nebraska Children's Battery along with the scoring procedures for raw scores. This information is available in the test form and test manual that accompany the test. Italic material shows what is said to the patient.

Motor Skills. *Using your right hand, touch your fingers in turn with your thumb as quickly as you can while you count them.* With palms facing up, demonstrate and then have the subject practice before timing. Record the number of correctly completed four-finger sequences that the subject completes in 10 seconds. Do not count sequences in which the subject fails to touch all fingers or to maintain sequence with fingers. Sequences in which the fingertips are not in direct contact with the tip of the thumb are not counted as correct. Instances in which contact is made below the last joint of the fingers are not counted as correct.

Without lifting your pencil from the paper, I want you to draw the best square you can. Score for quality and time until completion. Scoring (time): 0, 1-3 seconds; *1,* 4-5 seconds; *2,* 6 and above. Scoring (quality): Score *0* for responses that are not in violation of any of the 1- or 2-point criteria. Score *1* if one or two violations occur, including lack of closure by 2-6 mm; overlapping by 2-6 mm; a mild tremor in at least half the figure which does not distort the figure; any of the 1-point criteria. Score *2* if any of the following occur: three or more 1-point criteria; lack of closure greater than 6 mm; tracing overlap greater than 6 mm; overall distortion of the figure (e.g., an extra side); greater than 15 seconds to complete; lifting the pencil; and additional 2-point criteria.

Rhythm Skills. *Please make a series of . . .* (if subject fails to make a series, say, *I want you to make a series* or *do the rhythms more than once*) Examiner asks the subject to perform each of the following series: *two taps*; *three taps*; *two taps*; *two strong and three weak taps*; *three weak and two strong taps*; and *a series of two and three taps*. Items are given individually. Score an error when the tap groupings are not clearly discernable or taps fail to clearly reflect intensity differences.

Tactile Skills. Subject is blindfolded. *Am I touching you with the point or the head of a pin?* Touch the back of the appropriate hand with the head (H) or point (P) as indicated. Hold touch for each hand for 1 second, alternating between hands. Sequence: Right hand: P, H, P, P, H. Left hand: H, P, P, H, H. Score errors for each hand individually.

Visual Skills. *What do you call this object?* Examiner presents objects, one at a time, beginning with pencil, then eraser, rubber band, and quarter. Score number of errors. Scoring: *0*, 0 errors; *1*, 1 error; *2*, 2-4 errors.

Receptive Skills. *I will say some sounds. What I want you to do is first repeat exactly the sound you hear. For example, if you hear "ta" say "ta."* Circle the letters on the score sheet when a repetition error is made.

What do the following words mean: cat? bat? pat? Accept as correct any definition that indicates that the subject has differentiated between the initial consonants. For example, an adequate response to cat would be "it goes meow." However, "it is an animal" is not sufficient since that would be true for cat or bat. Request more information when the answer in unclear or incomplete. Score an error if, after questioning, the answer is still insufficient or if the initial answer is wrong.

Now I will show you a grey card and a black card. If it is night now, point to the grey card and if it is day now, point to the black card. Or If it is day now, point to the black card and if it is night now, point to the grey card. Score errors. Both must be correct in order to get credit for the item. Scoring: *0*, correct; *2*, any errors.

Expressive Skills. *Repeat after me: a* (as in later); *i* (as in light); *m* (as in milk); *b* (as in baby); *sh* (as in shine). Perfect performance is required for credit on any item. Expressive difficulties such as stuttering, slurring, undue hesitation, mispronounciation, or dysfluency should be scored as errors. Spontaneous corrections are not accepted as correct.

What do you call this object with which you fix your hair each morning? Comb, hairbrush, or brush. *What do you call the object that shows you what time it is?* Watch, clock, or any time piece. *What do you call the object that protects you from the rain?* Umbrella or raincoat. Accept only the first answer. Allow 10 seconds to answer each question.

Writing Skills. *Copy these in your own handwriting.* Show the child the following: pa, an, pro, pre, sti. Allow 30 seconds. Score responses as errors if misspellings occur, the transcripton is illegible, or the item was not completed within the time limit. *Write the letter I say: f, t, h, l.*

Reading Skills. *Tell me what you see here.* Present card with k, s, w, r, t, Score the number of letters misidentified.

Read these sentences. "The man went out for a walk." "There are flowers in the garden." Score an error if any of the words are mispronounced, slurred, or omitted, or if any words are added.

Arithmetic Skills. *Write the following numbers: 27, 34, 158, 396, 9845.* Allow 10 seconds for each item. Score any number incorrectly written as an error.

Tell me which number is larger: 17 or 68? 23 or 56? 189 or 201?

How much is 3 plus 4? 6 plus 7? Subject may write the items down Allow a maximum of 10 seconds, including writing.

Memory Skills. *I am going to show you a card and I want you to look at it carefully. When I remove the card, I want you to draw as much as you can remember.* Show card for 7 seconds. Score as errors figures not reproduced or figures sufficiently distorted so as not to be recognizable. Serial order on the picture is not required.

I want you to remember some words I am going to say: house, tree, cat. Repeat those words. Now look at this picture. What do you see? Have subject describe the picture for 15 seconds. Score errors.

Intelligence. *What is meant by the expressions: "iron hand," "green thumb"?* Iron hand scoring: *0*, the response defined the expression as an adjective connoting a condition of absolute government or ruling policy, e.g., tyrannical, authoritarian, despotic. "A person who rules with an iron hand is tyrannical" or "A strict (stern, rigid) policy of rule,", etc. *1*, the response defined the expression as a person with tyrannical characteristics or the response uses less than absolute adjectivial connotations, e.g., "a tyrannical ruler," "a person who governs despotically," "a person who is strict like a principal." *2*, Any other response such as "a tough man" or "a heartless ruler," "an arm of steel," or "it means having no compassion for others." Green thumb scoring: *0*, response implies an exceptional ability at gardening, e.g., "good at growing plants," "lucky at growing flowers." *1*, response does not imply an exceptional ability at gardening, e.g., "can grow plants." "able to grow flowers." *2*, Any other response, e.g., a gardener, farmer, or plant grower. Overall scoring for this item is based on summing the points given to each phrase.

Peter had two apples and John had six apples. How many did they have together? Begin timing after finishing the question. Item is scored for both time and accuracy.

RESEARCH OF THE LURIA-NEBRASKA
CHILDREN'S BATTERY

Research on the battery just began in 1980. Early data (based on N = 50) has indicated that the battery is effective in predicting both IQ and WRAT reading levels, with multiple correlations across the 11 Luria scales of .70-.85 ($p < .05$). An initial group of children with brain injury documented (N = 50) to areas other than the tertiary frontal area show significantly poorer performance than matched controls on the scales. (Patients with injury *only* to tertiary frontal areas must be examined separately since the theory does not expect to be able to identify such children in this age range.) Clearly though, this research is only preliminary at present.

Future research will extend the coverage of the battery to larger populations as well as to such groups as children with specific learning disabilities.

DISCUSSION

Although the qualitative/theoretical formulation of the battery is fairly well established (although much of this is expected to be highly controversial), the quantitative support for the battery is only in its infancy. While the original results have been promising, much more extensive research is necessary to show that the battery has the practical ability to live up to the expectations set up by the theory. The author strongly feels that this will be done; and the Luria-Nebraska Battery, as well as other instruments based on this neuropsychological theory, will significantly alter the practice of child assessment during the next two decades.

CASE STUDY

Commentary—L. L.

L. L. was an 8-year-old female caucasian who was hit by a car 12 months before the examination. She was unconscious for only a short period of time, and she appeared to recover physically without deficit. However, several months after the accident, a behavioral change was noted in the child. She became introverted, sensitive to criticism, unable to interact with others, easily frustrated, prone to temper tantrums, and anxious. She was referred for evaluation to see if the symptoms could be blamed on brain dysfunction secondary to her trauma. Her neurological examination was normal, as was her CT scan and EEG.

BEHAVIORAL OBSERVATIONS

L. L. was an extremely cooperative girl whose behavior in general belied the description given us by her parents, as described above. She showed some slowness in motor skills, but not enough to be alarming by itself. Her visual functioning was excellent, while verbal functioning in general was superior. Her one area of difficulty was in auditory functioning. When asked to repeat or write simple phonemes, she had inordinate trouble, although her reading and writing scores were in general well above grade level.

It became clear after an analysis of her results, that she was able to do quite well on things learned before her accident (when she had been at the top of her class) but had subsequently lost the ability to do phonetic discrimination, especially for letters closely related to one another. Thus, while she could continue to do well based upon previously learned material, she was having a difficult time with new material, which required extensive studying and effort for her to keep up with her former expectations. It was then increased effort and strain, combined with the fear that she was stupid and would not be able to keep up, that had led to the personality change that had occurred rather than it being a direct result of the accident itself.

VALUE OF TESTING

The importance of the Luria-Nebraska Battery in this case cannot be underestimated: on traditional tests, such as the WISC-R, WRAT, PIAT, and Bender, this child had performed at superior levels, making her seem normal and inviting speculation that she had an "organic personality change" or that she needed "psychiatric therapy." Deficits like those seen in L. L. are missed by these tests, especially when the deficits are subtle. It is in these subtle injuries that the diagnostic ability of the Luria-Nebraska can be the most useful, as in many other cases the presence of brain damage is obvious. In cases where brain damage is clear, the Luria-Nebraska can be helpful in detailing the nature of the deficits.

In the present case, identification of the deficit allowed the child, parents, and teachers to better understand what was happening. The teachers changed training to a visual approach, avoiding the auditory except for special training to improve L. L.'s skills in this area. This eliminated a major source of frustration. Also, the parents now knew to reduce the pressure for success on the child. The combination led to a lessening of symptoms and a slow return to normal.

REFERENCES

Christensen, A. L. *Luria's neuropsychological investigation.* New York: Spectrum, 1975.

DeRenzi, E., & Piercy, M. The fourteenth international symposium of neuropsychology. *Neuropsychologia,* 1969, *7,* 583–585.

Dikman, S., Matthews, C. G., & Harley, J. P. The effect of early versus late onset of major motor epilepsy upon cognitive intellectual performance. *Epilepsia*, 1975, *16*, 73–77.

Golden, C. J. *Diagnosis and rehabilitation in clinical neuropsychology*. Springfield, Il.: Charles C Thomas, 1978.

Golden, C. J. *Luria-Nebraska Neuropsychological Battery for Children*. Unpublished experimental test form, 1980. (Available from Charles J. Golden, Ph.D. University of Nebraska Medical Center, 42nd and Dewey Avenues, Omaha, Nebraska 68105).

Golden, C. J., & Anderson, S. *Learning disabilities and brain dysfunction*. Springfield, Il.: Charles C Thomas, 1979.

Hebb, D. O. The effect of early and late brain damage upon test scores and the nature of abnormal adult intelligence. *Proceedings of the American Philosophical Society*, 1942, *85*, 275–319.

Luria, A. R. *Higher cortical functions in man*. New York: Basic Books, 1966.

Luria, A. R. *The working brain*. New York: Basic Books, 1973.

Milner, B. Psychological aspects of focal epilepsy and its neurosurgical management. *Advances in Neurology*, 1975, *8*, 299–329.

Rutter, M. *Childhood disorders due to brain injury*. Speech given to the Conference on the Hyperactive Child, Omaha, Nebraska, April 1980.

Smith, A. Neuropsychological testing in neurological disorders. *Advances in Neurology*, 1975, *7*, 49–115.

P. G. Aaron

9
Diagnosis and Remediation of Learning Disabilities in Children — A Neuropsychological Key Approach

A rational approach to the treatment of any disorder, whether physical or psychological, should begin with proper diagnosis. This principle is equally applicable to learning disabilities. Reliable and accurate diagnosis should, therefore, constitute the first step in dealing with any form of learning disorder. With this rationale in mind, a Neuropsychological Key approach was proposed in the diagnosis and remediation of learning disabilities. It follows a deductive method in reaching conclusions about the etiology, nature, and treatment of such disorders (Aaron, 1979). Such an approach has been found to be useful in the areas of biology, medicine, and even in psychology (Russell, Neuringer, & Goldstein, 1970).

The Neuropsychological Key (hereafter referred to as the Key) is intended not to be an aid in classifying or labeling a child, but rather a means of determining the cause of learning disability the child might have and devising appropriate remedial measures. Further, the Key is not considered to be in its final format; rather it represents a logic which, when applied, can provide much needed order and schema in the field of learning disability while also providing a scientific basis for the diagnosis and treatment of learning disorders. The different diagnostic tests and remedial methods incorporated in the key are, therefore, presented as modules that can be replaced by other tests and methods if proved inadequate. The first part of the chapter presents the Key as it was originally proposed; then, the validity of the model as well as the refinements that have to be introduced are discussed; and, finally, the Key is presented in its final form.

The entire Key is based on a neuropsychological model that recognizes two forms of information-processing strategies of the brain—analytic and holistic—as well as the two aspects of linguistic competence—receptive and expressive. Since its publication, the validity and utility of the model have been assessed by the testing of many learning-disabled students from both elementary-school and college levels. Results of these investigations indicate that the Key needs to be modified in several important ways.

The entire Key is intended for use by school psychologists and learning-disability specialists. Consequently, the tests utilized in the model are, for the most part, easily accessible and could be administered without much prior experience. Furthermore, they are not very time consuming.

DESCRIPTION OF THE KEY

Rationale

The rationale for the Key rests on four premises that are derived from existing clinical and experimental neuropsychological data. The first premise is that not all learning-disabled (LD) children manifest the same pattern of deficits and that, consequently, they constitute a heterogenous group. Often, each child shows a unique pattern in which one area of performance is more affected than others. For example, Rutter (1970), who studied 86 dyslexic children with reference to language abnormalities, motor incoordination, constructional difficulties, and right–left confusion, found that none of these children showed all of these characteristics; more than one fourth of the children had only one. Koppitz (1971), in her longitudinal study, observed that some youngsters had difficulty in visual-motor perception only, while others had problems in the area of auditory recall or auditory perception but not in the visual-motor area. The 54 dyslexic children studied by Symmes and Rapoport (1972) had no emotional, motor, or language difficulties. Denckla's (1973) study showed that 42 subjects had reading-spelling difficulty alone and were free from attentional or motor deficiencies. Furthermore, Denckla and Rudel (1976) differentiate dyslexia from other forms of learning disabilities because of the unique information-processing deficit found in reading-disabled children. It also appears that hyperactive children generally do not show any language deficiency, and their reading performance is adequate (Douglas, 1974). Even specific areas of learning disabilities such as dyslexia ✍ em not to represent a homogeneous defect but are made up of clinical subtypes. Recently, Pirozzolo (1979) has provided convincing evidence for the existence of two groups: audiolinguistic and visuospatial dyslexics. In fact, the term "specific learning disabilities" reflects the heterogeneous nature of LD children. Therefore, in clinical practice it becomes necessary to diagnose accurately the deficits of the LD child and to focus remedial methods on those specific deficits.

The second premise is based on the belief that learning disability is the result of an imbalance in the subject's information-processing abilities and not the outcome of a generalized cognitive deficit. LD children tend to over-utilize certain cognitive strategies to the exclusion of others, resulting in serious imbalances. For example, some children possess better than average or superior visual memory and relatively poor auditory memory, whereas other children show exactly the opposite profile. The former tend to utilize the visual modality more than the auditory modality; the latter do exactly the opposite.

The reported instances of learning disability in men of eminence such as Leonardo da Vinci and Albert Einstein may have been due to such imbalances. Unfortunately, many experimental investigators look for cognitive deficits and have failed to explore the associated strengths of LD children. One research study that investigated such an imbalance (Aaron, 1978a) found that one subgroup of dyslexic children was poor in holistic simultaneous information-processing ability but above average in analytic-sequential information-processing ability, whereas another subgroup of dyslexic children showed the opposite pattern of performance. A control group of normal readers did not show such an imbalance. When dealing with LD children, it becomes necessary, therefore, to look not only for deficits, but also for assets, which often tend to be used as crutches and are consequently overutilized.

The third premise supporting the usefulness of the Neuropsychological Key is that learning disability, in children, is due to some form of anomalous neurological development, the consequences of which can be ameliorated through appropriate remedial treatment. In contrast, learning deficits resulting from organic brain damage have a different prognosis. Delayed maturation as a contributing factor to learning disability in general, and reading disability in particular, has been advanced by many neurologists and psychologists (Critchley, 1966; De Hirsch, Jansky, & Langford, 1966; Eustis, 1947; Geschwind, 1964; Kinsbourne, 1973; Money, 1966; Satz & Friel, 1974). "Maturational lag" implies that with proper training, learning deficits can eventually be overcome or at least ameliorated. Impressive success for retarded readers, as they grow older, has been reported by Robinson and Smith (1962) and Rawson (1968). Contradictory results, however, have been reported by Silver and Hagin (1964) and by Trites and Fiedorowicz (1976).

It should be noted that reading-disabled children studied by Trites and Fiedorowicz gained 1.3 grades in reading after 2½ years, whereas a comparable brain-damaged group progressed only .7 grade during that span of time. A recent study (Rourke, 1976) addressed directly to this issue found that some children initially classified as retarded readers, if not all, made substantial gains in reading. Yet such a prognosis could not be extended to children who had sustained organic brain lesions. There is evidence to conclude that children who manifest organic symptoms associated with a history of neurological involvement constitute a distinct clinical category (Doehring, 1976; Gallagher, 1966).

The general notion that the child's brain is plastic and, therefore, can recover almost all lost functions lacks firm support (Kaste, 1972; McFie, 1961; Moskowitz, 1964). It is also known that early damage to the subcortical region, such as the basal ganglia, frequently results in mental retardation (Tobin, 1969). Basing his argument on animal studies, Isaacson (1975) concludes that it is quite possible that early brain damage can be more disastrous than later brain damage. Studies by Teuber and Rudel (1962), B. T. Woods and Teuber (1973), and Isaacson (1975) indicate a clear possibility that certain forms of early brain damage in children may have disproportionately serious consequences for later development.

After examining some of the research findings in this area, Rudel (1978) concludes that the consequences of brain damage can be classified into three categories: (1) those that appear early and disappear, (2) those that are present at all ages, and (3) those that are apparent only after a delay. Further, she cites evidence that brain damage at any age seems to lead to a slowing of reaction time, slowness on tests of language, impaired visual storage, and repetitive movements, and that these deficits are demonstrable in children with a variety of developmental anomalies including dyslexia. It seems, then, that after early brain damage, reaching an acceptable level of mental functions is the exception rather than the rule. Even though language may be an exception, such a linguistic precedence does not seem to include reading and writing and is limited to the spoken form (Smith, 1974). Translated into clinical terms, this means designing an individualized remedial approach utilizing the brain-damaged child's strengths rather than attempting to rectify his or her deficient processes. Helping brain-damaged individuals find alternative ways to achieve the required ends is a recommended method in clinical practice (Isaacson & Noneman, 1972). In contrast, the LD child without a history of brain damage is more likely to benefit from training methods that attempt to remediate his or her deficiency.

The fourth premise supporting the Key is based on the findings that remedial methods such as perceptual and motor training, visual discrimination, and auditory sequential training (which allegedly train the presumptive psychological processes underlying reading and language functions) are unable to show consistently positive results (Koppitz, 1971).

A review of 81 such studies by Myers and Hammill (1976) showed that an overwhelming majority of those that employed perceptual motor or similar methods proved to be ineffective. Calling these methods "diagnostic-prescriptive teaching," Arter and Jenkins (1979) reviewed research that utilized remedial methods such as auditory discrimination, visual discrimination, and training about spatial relationships, auditory-visual integration, and psycholinguistic abilities such as the ones included in the Illinois Test of Psycholinguistic Ability (ITPA). They concluded that there exists little evidence to support the idea that underlying psychological abilities can be taught and that children do not appear to profit from such approaches. They go on to say that unsupported expert opinion and teacher training programs resulting from these approaches appear to have a deleterious effect on teacher behavior and a similar effect on children's learning as well.

In contrast to these process-oriented methods, task-oriented remedial methods such as the phonetic approach to teaching reading and an emphasis on language development have been found to be more successful (Lee, Koenigsknecht, & Mulhern, 1975). Also, in utilizing such a direct approach in remediating reading or language deficits, the perennial problem of transfer of specific skills from the training situation to actual learning can be avoided.

The general principles that govern all remedial programs are equally applicable in these training programs. On the basis of available empirical data, Guthrie (1978) concluded that such principles would include providing instruction in all deficient areas, providing intensive interaction between the instructor and the students (by keeping the pupil-teacher ratio low), and maximizing the amount of instructional time.

A schematic representation of the Key is shown in Fig. 9-1. The different steps where decisions are made with the Key are numbered consecutively, 1 through 5. The rationales for decisions made at each step are given below.

Procedure

(1) IDENTIFYING THE LD CHILD

Attempts to identify the LD child have resulted in numerous definitions, elaborate formulas, and much controversy. The complex formula developed a few years ago by the Department of Health, Education and Welfare (Education of Handicapped Children, 1976) has recently been scrapped and replaced by a criterion wherein subjective decisions of personnel who serve the child play a more important role (APA Monitor, 1978). In light of these controversies, it was decided in the present context to take into account the discrepancy between the child's potential and actual achievement while at the same time keeping the procedure uncomplicated. The Key, therefore, utilizes a simple rule based on the IQ score obtained from WISC-R. Any child whose

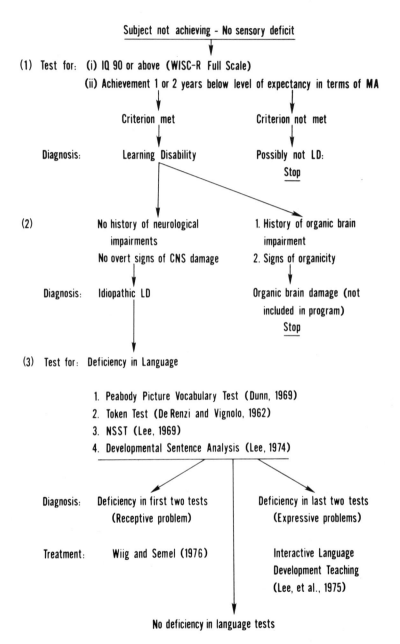

Subject not achieving - No sensory deficit

(1) Test for: (i) IQ 90 or above (WISC-R Full Scale)
(ii) Achievement 1 or 2 years below level of expectancy in terms of MA

Criterion met   Criterion not met

Diagnosis: Learning Disability   Possibly not LD:
                                         Stop

(2)   No history of neurological   1. History of organic brain
              impairments   impairment
              No overt signs of CNS damage   2. Signs of organicity

Diagnosis: Idiopathic LD   Organic brain damage (not
                                              included in program)
                                              Stop

(3) Test for: Deficiency in Language

1. Peabody Picture Vocabulary Test (Dunn, 1969)
2. Token Test (De Renzi and Vignolo, 1962)
3. NSST (Lee, 1969)
4. Developmental Sentence Analysis (Lee, 1974)

Diagnosis: Deficiency in first two tests   Deficiency in last two tests
              (Receptive problem)   (Expressive problems)

Treatment: Wiig and Semel (1976)   Interactive Language
                                              Development Teaching
                                              (Lee, et al., 1975)

No deficiency in language tests

Figure 9-1. A schematic representation of the Neuropsychological Key
(Adapted from "A Neuropsychological Key Approach to Diagnosis and
Remediation of Learning Disabilities" by P. G. Aaron. *Journal of Clinical*

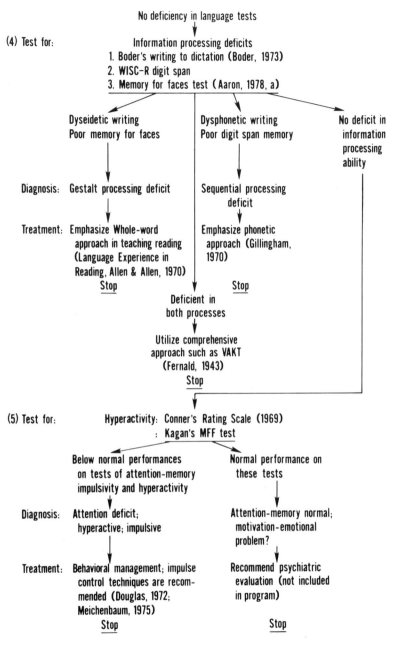

No deficiency in language tests

(4) Test for: Information processing deficits
1. Boder's writing to dictation (Boder, 1973)
2. WISC–R digit span
3. Memory for faces test (Aaron, 1978, a)

Dyseidetic writing	Dysphonetic writing	No deficit in
Poor memory for faces	Poor digit span memory	information processing ability

Diagnosis: Gestalt processing deficit   Sequential processing deficit

Treatment: Emphasize Whole-word approach in teaching reading (Language Experience in Reading, Allen & Allen, 1970)   Emphasize phonetic approach (Gillingham, 1970)

Stop   Stop

Deficient in both processes

Utilize comprehensive approach such as VAKT (Fernald, 1943)

Stop

(5) Test for: Hyperactivity: Conner's Rating Scale (1969)
                : Kagan's MFF test

Below normal performances on tests of attention-memory impulsivity and hyperactivity   Normal performance on these tests

Diagnosis: Attention deficit; hyperactive; impulsive   Attention-memory normal; motivation-emotional problem?

Treatment: Behavioral management; impulse control techniques are recommended (Douglas, 1972; Meichenbaum, 1975)   Recommend psychiatric evaluation (not included in program)

Stop   Stop

Psychology, 1979, *35,* 328–329. Copyright 1979 by P. G. Aaron. With permission.)

IQ score is 90 or above and is achieving 1 or 2 years below his or her mental age (MA) is considered learning-disabled. A child with poor achievement associated with an intellectual ability below 90 IQ points is usually considered to have multiple involvement accompanied by mild retardation (D. Johnson & Myklebust, 1967) and is not considered to be learning disabled.

(2) DISTINGUISHING THE LD CHILD FROM THE BRAIN-DAMAGED CHILD

The Key does not make any provision for treatment of learning deficits that result from organic brain damage. Treatment of brain-damaged children should be built around a strategy that circumvents deficits and utilizes the child's existing strengths. Such an approach is markedly different from the one recommended for LD children. Diagnosis of organic brain damage is based on the developmental history of the child rather than results obtained from psychological tests of brain damage. The complex nature of such tests, the excessive amount of time required for administration, and the absence of clearly established test validity (Yates, 1954) render these tests impractical.

Aspects of developmental history that would suggest brain damage are prenatal infection, perinatal anoxia, premature birth,* below-average APGAR score, prolonged neonatal jaundice, childhood infection of the central nervous system (such as meningitis and encephalitis), traumatic brain injuries, and hard neurological signs such as cerebral palsy and hemiplegia. The significance of the early history, particularly that of the perinatal period and its sequelae, is well-documented (Pasamanick & Knobloch, 1966). None of the above-listed developmental events by itself is sufficient to unequivocally establish a condition of organic brain damage. When such an event is coupled with persistent learning failure, however, it could be concluded with reasonable certainty that such learning difficulty is a sequela to brain damage.

(3) INVESTIGATING LANGUAGE DEFECTS IN THE LD CHILD

At this level, language defect as a possible etiological factor in learning disability is considered. Some children with learning disability are found to have either overt speech problems or some form of language difficulty (Trantham & Pederson, 1976). The association between learning disability

---

*Prematurity is often causally connected with psychological problems. By itself, prematurity may not cause any organic brain damage. The physiological events that antedate birth and cause premature birth, however, may result in impairments. Consequently, prematurity in conjunction with learning disability may be suspected of indicating prenatal physiologic, organic problems.

and language deficits has been recognized (Cruickshank, Bentzen, Ratzeburg, & Tannhauser, 1961; Myklebust, 1954; Strauss & Kephart, 1955). Empirical support for such a view has been provided by Wiig and Semel (1973), Wiig and Harris (1974), and Wiig and Roach (1975).

Vellutino (1979) believes that in a majority of cases, reading disability is caused by basic inadequacies in one or more aspects of linguistic functioning; most research studies show this to be the case and three of the five types of featural information contained in a printed work (graphic, orthographic, semantic, syntactic, and phonological) correspond with the major components of language. Of the three linguistic components—phonetic, semantic, and syntactic—the latter two contribute significantly to learning in the classroom.

Recent studies (R. F. Cromer, 1978; Menyuk, 1978) investigating the language defects of developmentally dysphasic children show that these children are deficient in the production of grammatical categories, resulting in poor syntactical and semantic abilities. Language-retarded children were found to be particularly deficient in the usage of plural markers, possessive markers, articles, conjunctions, and verb-tense markers. Further, existence of subclasses of language deficiencies in children has also been supported by both empirical data and clinical observations.

Aram and Nation (1975) administered tests to measure comprehension and different aspects of expression to 47 children with developmental language disorders. Factor analysis revealed six patterns of language performance. On the basis of these findings, the authors concluded that children can be differentiated on the basis of their ability to express and comprehend syntactic, semantic, and phonologic features and that these abilities can be differentially disrupted.

The present Key does not attempt to assess the phonological aspects of spoken language since simple tools of assessment of phonology are not available and research literature in this area is sparse. Thus, the focus is on the semantic and syntactic aspects of language. The possibility that a LD child could be deficient in semantic or syntactic aspects of language and that these deficiencies could either be limited to the expressive aspect or may involve both expressive and receptive domains was also taken into account in the construction of the Key.

Tests. The Peabody Picture Vocabulary Test (Dunn, 1969) is utilized in assessing the receptive semantic ability of the child. The Token Test (DeRenzi & Vignolo, 1962; Hahn & Weiss, 1973) and the Token Test for Children (DiSimoni, 1978) are recommended for assessing receptive syntactic ability. Assessment of Children's Language Comprehension (Foster, Giddan, & Stark, 1973) is yet another test of receptive language ability. The Northwestern Syntax Screening Test (NSST) (Lee, 1969) evaluates both the receptive and the expressive aspects of the syntactic structure of the language and has been found successful in differentiating LD from normal children (Semel and Wiig, 1975). The Developmental Sentence Analysis (Lee, 1974) provides a more refined measure of the child's syntactic expressive ability and is reportedly successful in identifying LD children (Vogel, 1974).

Treatment. Since language comprehension precedes production, the child who is found to be deficient in receptive aspects of language has to receive intensive training designed to improve his or her comprehension. Wiig and Semel (1976) have described suitable techniques for improving such linguistic-processing ability. For an LD child whose problem lies mainly in the area of language production, interactive language development teaching (Lee et al, 1975) holds much promise. This method of teaching aims at improving the child's ability to spontaneously produce mature forms of grammatical structure and sentences. Significant improvement in the syntactical ability of language-disabled children has been reported (Lee et al, 1975). Several other language-training programs are also available (Bricker, 1972; Leonard, 1974; MacDonald & Blott, 1974). In general, the choice of language therapy should be governed by the following two observations made by Stark (1980): (1) highly programmed syntax teaching kits are usually sterile, and (2) having the child experience meaningful encounters with the environment is very important for language development.

(4) INVESTIGATING READING DEFICITS IN THE LD CHILD

If the child's language competency is within normal limits, a reading deficit should be considered as a possible source of learning disability. Efficient reading involves at least two operations — decoding and comprehension (Bateman, 1969). The decoding process, also referred to as word naming or identification (Wiener & Cromer, 1967), involves the association of a visual stimulus with its linguistic equivalent. Comprehension, on the other hand, is primarily a linguistic operation, and any language deficiency serious enough to impair comprehension would have been detected at step 3 in the Key. The decision-making process will, therefore, focus on the decoding of reading.

Decoding in reading has continued to be a topic of controversy. While it is true that the fluent or skilled reader may utilize semantic and syntactical cues in addition to orthography, and gain access to the semantic store directly without letter-by-letter decoding, the beginning reader, in order to gain access to the lexical store, most likely depends a great deal on decoding. Furthermore, decoding, in the present context, does not necessarily refer to converting the visual symbol into its oral counterpart but refers to the interpretation of the written word into its linguistic equivalent. Whether such interpretation is accomplished via oral language or not is unimportant. Regardless of the route the reader takes—visual to oral to meaning, or visual to meaning, or a mixture of the two—visual perception of the word is the essential first step in the process of reading.

If reading is merely a psycholinguistic guessing game, as some authorities claim, reading-disabled children should have little or no difficulty reading words in isolation. This clearly is not the case. A large number of dyslexic children are also impaired in their ability to read individual words. It should also be pointed out that some authorities do consider reading to involve a direct transition from letters and letter patterns to a corresponding level of oral language representation (Gough, 1972; Brown, 1980).

According to the neuropsychological theory on which the Key is based, specific reading disability in the absence of a linguistic deficit is due to a weakness in the information-processing abilities involved in the decoding aspect of reading. Analytic-sequential and holistic-simultaneous information-processing operations are two fundamental strategies of the human being (Bever, 1975). Others have referred to similar abilities as *successive* and *simultaneous* processes (Das, 1973; Das, Kirby, & Jarman, 1979). Evidence that these two operations are involved in the decoding aspects of reading comes from studies of normal subjects as well as of those neurologically impaired. Tachistoscopic studies of normal subjects have shown that word identification is a multistage process with analysis of the gross visual feature of the word carried out from information reaching the parafoveal region, with a more detailed analysis of the foveal input. Such a feature analysis seems to be carried out primarily by the right cerebral hemisphere with the phonetic analysis of more detailed foveal information carried out by the left hemisphere (Geffen, Bradshaw, & Nettleton, 1972; Pirozzolo & Rayner, 1977). Observations of brain-damaged patients by Conrad (1948), Kinsbourne and Warrington (1962a, b), Albert, Yamador, Gardner, and Howes (1973), and Hécaen and Kremin (1976) revealed that some patients could name individual letters but could not read whole words, while others could name the word but no individual letters. This suggests that these two processes are independent and separable. Further support of this view comes from observations that in a majority of human beings the left hemisphere mediates analytic-sequential information whereas the right hemisphere specializes in handling information that is in the form of simultaneous gestalts (Gazzaniga, 1970; Kimura, 1967; Sperry, 1962, 1967). It is possible, therefore, that any anomalous maturational trend of the central nervous system could cause an imbalance between these processes wherein the individual becomes overdependent on one of the two strategies. Such an anomalous pattern of development where one process is overutilized at the expense of the other has been reported (Bakker, Smink, & Reitsma, 1973; Rudel, 1974; Symmes & Rapoport, 1972; Witelson, 1976; Yeni-Komshian, Isenberg, & Goldberg, 1975). Idiosyncratic patterns of response found in some poor readers (W. Cromer & Wiener, 1966) may be another example of such an imbalance. Since efficient decoding involves a proper blend of both these operations—sequential processing of a selected sample of series of letters in a word and the holistic-simultaneous processing of the salient feature of the word itself (F. Smith and Holmes, 1971)—it is logical to expect deficiency in either one of the two information-processing strategies to adversely affect reading ability and to produce different patterns of symptoms.

Tests. Three tests are employed to identify the deficient information-processing strategy. Boder's (1971, 1973) analysis of children's writing to dictation is a simple means of identification. On the basis of their unconventional written spelling errors reflecting sequential analytic difficulties, children are divided into two major categories: dysphonetic and dyseidetic. When asked to write "stop," the dysphonetic child may write "sotp" or "spto;" for "book," he or she may write "koob." The dyseidetic child, on the other hand, tends to spell by the ear and writes "bloo" for "blue" and "gal" for "girl," thus revealing poor visual gestalt for the word.

The Memory for Faces Test (Aaron, 1978b) consists of 41 transparent slides of faces of college students. Each slide is exposed for a period of 8 seconds, and after all the 41 faces are shown, the subject is asked to identify each face he had seen before from an array of four faces. The total number of faces correctly identified provides an index of holistic-simultaneous information-processing ability. A facial identification test in book form has been standardized for use with adults by Benton and Van Allen (1973).

Facial perception requires a great deal of nonverbal ability since language cannot be used successfully to encode and recall human faces. Even though a limited amount of language may be involved in facial perception (Benton, 1980), a Memory for Faces Test is the best tool we have for assessing nonverbal memory. In addition, since the human face is best remembered as a single gestalt, it is considered a valid test of holistic-simultaneous ability.

The Digit Span subtest of WISC provides a relatively good measure of sequential-processing ability (Das et al, 1979).

Treatment. Decisions regarding the nature of the deficit as well as the kinds of remedial teaching methods to be used are based on the child's performance on Boder's Writing Task, the Memory for Faces Test, and the WISC Digit Span. In accord with the general principles stated earlier, remediation aims at strengthening the deficient process. Evidence exists to indicate that children with different forms of symptoms respond differently to the two basic forms of teaching reading—phonetic and whole word approaches (Aaron, Grantham, & Campbell, 1978). LD children found to be deficient in the analytic-sequential processes, should benefit from the phonetic approach (e.g., Gillingham, 1970), while those who are weak in the holistic-simultaneous processes should profit from methods that emphasize the whole word or look-say approach (e.g., Allen & Allen, 1970). Brown (1980), who subscribes to a model that recognizes decoding, has recommended the teaching of letter-sound correspondences as an exact left-to-right sequential processing. If the child's performance indicates deficiency of both processes, a comprehensive approach that utilizes several modalities and processes simultaneously is recommended (e.g., visual-auditory, kinesthetic, tactile, Fernald, 1943).

(5) INVESTIGATING ATTENTION DEFICITS
IN THE LD CHILD

The absence of language deficiency, along with normal or above-normal performance on tests of analytic and holistic processes, suggests the possibility of attention deficit as an etiological factor. Such a deficit may manifest symptomatically in the form of extremely short attention span, distractibility, and impulsivity (Ross, 1976; Sykes, Douglas, Weiss, & Minde, 1971). Collectively, these symptoms constitute the hyperactive syndrome.

Tests. Hyperactivity is most difficult to assess and in spite of the concerted efforts of experts for many years, no single satisfactory test for this syndrome exists. Consequently, a combination of the Conners Behavior Rating Scale (Conners, 1969) and the Matching Familiar Figures Test of Kagan (O. G. Johnson & Bommerito, 1971) is utilized. Individually, these tests have been shown capable of differentiating between hyperactive and normal children and can detect the difference between behaviors of hyperactive children before and after drug administration. Standardized normative data for Conner's rating scale are provided by Sprague, Christensen, and Werry (1974) for children in grades K through 6. The Matching Familiar Figures Test has been found to be a valid measure of impulsivity (Sandoval, 1977), and normative data for children are provided by Salkind (undated). A rough index of the cut-off point that separates normal from impulsive children could be derived from two other studies (Ault, 1973; Campbell & Douglas, 1972). The two measures that are used as indices of hyperactivity in the Matching Familiar Figures Test are reaction time and number of errors committed.

If the findings of these tests of hyperactivity turn out to be negative, the possibility of motivational and emotional disturbances as etiological factors should be seriously considered. Under such circumstances, a thorough psychiatric evaluation of the child becomes necessary.

Treatment. Stimulant medication is frequently used in extreme cases of hyperactivity and has been reported to be an effective form of treatment (Safer & Allen, 1976). Behavior therapy is considered the most successful psychological form of treatment. Behavior therapy could range from modification of behavior through the judicious utilization of reinforcers to a combination of reinforcement and cognitive processes such as self-instruction and modeling (Douglas, 1972; Meichenbaum, 1975; Meichenbaum & Goodman, 1971). Recently, Mash and Dalby (1979) reviewed the effectiveness of behavioral intervention strategies in the treatment of hyperactive children. This survey included procedures such as reinforcement applications, cognitive behavior modification, progressive relaxation-biofeedback training, and family therapy. The authors concluded that more empirical information is needed before the effectiveness of specific behavioral interventions can be evaluated; however, it is unlikely that major questions such as "Is behavior therapy more effective than drug therapy?" can be satisfactorily answered.

EVALUATION OF THE KEY

The validity and utility of the Neuropsychological Key's diagnostic aspect were tested by administering the tests in the Key to 28 children who were reading at least 1 year below their grade level. These children came from grades 3-7. There were 19 boys and 9 girls in the group. Administration of the Henmon-Nelson or Wechsler's Intelligence Tests revealed that their IQs ranged from 81 to 121, with 13 children scoring below 90. The reading performance of the subjects was assessed with the aid of the Durrell Analysis of Reading Difficulty (Durrell, 1955). In addition to the tests recommended in the Key, the following tests and tasks were also administered: (1) audio taping of the child reading a passage from Durrell's test; (2) audio taping of the child's description of two pictures from the Stanford-Binet Intelligence Test; (3) Goldman-Fristoe-Woodcock Test of Memory for Sequence (Goldman, Fristoe, & Woodcock, 1974); (4) Revised Minnesota Form Board Test (Likert & Quasha, 1970); (5) Color Recall and Color Identification Task; and (6) Small Parts Dexterity Test (Crawford & Crawford, 1956). Interpretation of the test results and analysis of data indicated that many of the premises on which the Key was based were valid even though some revisions and modifications in the administration of the Key were necessary. There were five major findings that led to the modified Key.

Problems in the Original Key

• Accurate diagnosis could not be based on the findings of a single test alone. This is because no test is "pure" or capable of accurately assessing a single psychological ability or disability. This makes interpretation of test results a very risky affair. For example, poor performance on the Peabody Picture Vocabulary Test may indicate a deficit in the semantic aspect of language or poor memory for pictures. In order to rule out the latter possibility, the Memory for Faces Test, as well as the language test, also must be administered. Another example is the WISC Digit Span subtest, which is generally considered a test of sequential ability. Poor performance on this test may be due to the subject's poor memory for sequences or due to a short attention span. To be certain that the subject's poor performance is attributable to a deficit in sequencing, and to eliminate the possibility of impaired attention, a test of attention also must be administered. In the Key, therefore, the diagnostic decision at each node must be based on the subject's performance on more than one related test.

• Reading disability and language disability did not emerge as clearly isolable defects. All the subjects who had language deficits were also retarded in reading. The converse, however, was not true. There were three children in the group who had reading deficits but normal language ability. Reading defects in these children were due to poor visual gestalt memory ability. The revised Key has been modified in order to accommodate this finding.

• Contrary to expectation, children with poor visual memory fell into a single group, rather than two subgroups, with an apparent holistic or gestalt processing deficit. No subject studied showed evidence of having a visual sequence-processing deficit. Consequently, the classification of children with poor visual memory into two subgroups has been abandoned.

• The classification of language-disabled children into the "expressive" and "receptive" subgroups as suggested in the Key could not be carried out successfully. This is primarily because many of the children who did poorly on the (NSST) receptive test did perform normally on the expressive part of the same test. This is clearly a logical incongruity since reception precedes expression and since a child who has poor receptive ability cannot have normal expressive ability. This unexpected outcome could be due to the possibility that items in the expressive part of the NSST can be answered by relying on rote memory (the subject has to repeat the same sentence the examiner had said earlier). Data obtained in the present study, however, revealed that a more reliable basis for classification of language deficits exists in the form of the syntactic–semantic dichotomy. It is, of course, not always easy to categorize children's language errors as semantic or syntactic since these two linguistic features tend to overlap at times. Nevertheless, it was found that when the results of children's oral language analysis, their reading error analysis, and language tests were all taken together, a reliable classification was possible. In general, children who make errors that affect the grammar of a sentence, speak in short sentences, and misread more functional words than content words are considered to have poor syntactical ability; children who show poor comprehension, misread more content words than functional words, and commit errors that affect meaning rather than grammar are considered to be deficient in the semantic aspect of language.

Another difficulty encountered in assessing children's language ability involved the eliciting of spontaneous and complete utterances that could be used for linguistic analysis. Many children have a tendency to answer in incomplete sentences, others were reticent; still others refused to talk except in the form of an occasional "yes" or "no." This obstacle was overcome to a certain extent by asking the child to describe the story in a picture or the story he or she had just read. Frequently, this procedure yielded copious linguistic output that was sufficient for analysis.

• Some tests in the Key did not yield unequivocal supporting information regarding the placement of LD children in the various diagnostic categories. Examples of such tests are the WISC Digit Span, Color Recall, and Color Identification Tasks, and Boder's Spelling Error Analysis. These tests, however, could provide some useful information when used as adjuncts to other tests in the battery. On the other hand, some tasks that were not part of the original Key were found to yield very valuable information. These are analysis of reading errors, estimation of listening comprehension (Durrell), and sight vocabulary. These tasks are, therefore, incorporated in the revised battery while others are dropped.

The following observations obtained from administering the Key to the group of 28 children tend to support some of the premises that constitute the basis of the Key.

Observations Supporting the Usefulness of the Key

• Children with an IQ of 90 or below tend to have a uniformly depressed test performance profile. On the contrary, LD children with normal intelligence invariably show profiles suggestive of cognitive imbalance; their performance is average or superior in certain areas and below average in certain other areas. Of the 28 children who were administered the tests in the Key, 13 had an IQ of 90 or below. The performance profile of 12 of these children was flat; the only child who showed above-average performance in certain areas of the Key had an IQ of 86 on the Henmon-Nelson Intelligence Test; his IQ as determined by the Peabody Picture Vocabulary Test was, however,

103. Data pertaining to the performance of children belonging to the different diagnostic categories are shown in Table 9-1.

• As mentioned earlier, a vast majority of LD children with IQs of 90 or above did show an uneven neuropsychological profile. The view proposed earlier – that learning disability is the result of an imbalance in information-processing strategies – is, therefore, confirmed by the data. On the basis of these data, four different subgroups of LD children could be identified; representative cases of these subgroups are shown in Table 9-1. The four subgroups and their characteristics are (1) Visual-gestalt-deficient group. Subjects in this group performed poorly in oral reading, and on tests of sight vocabulary and memory for faces, but did well in listening comprehension and language tests; they had good memory for digits. Their reading errors were limited to misreading of content words with no signs of agrammatism; (2) Semantic-language-deficient group. Children in this category showed a profile almost opposite of that of the visual-gestalt deficient group. Their listening comprehension scores were lower than those of their oral reading; their NSST expressive scores were very low, but they had good sight vocabulary and excellent memory for faces. Analysis of reading showed that subjects decoded slowly, almost in a letter-by-letter fashion, with few or no signs of agrammatism. They were, however, extremely poor in oral description of stories or pictures and missed the main theme very often; (3) Syntactic-language-deficient group. These children had good listening comprehension but poor reading comprehension; their performances on language tests, including the Token Test, were well below average. Equally poor were scores on Sequential Memory and Digit Span tests. Their visual memory was within normal limits and both their reading and oral utterances showed signs of agrammatism arising primarily from omission or substitution of prepositions, conjunctions, and inflectional word endings; and (4) Attention-deficient, impulsive group. There was only one boy who could be considered to belong to this category. His reaction time on the Matching Familiar Figures Test was very short and his errors numerous. His digit span was good but his memory for faces was poor. However, he also showed signs of agrammatism when reading.

• No attempt was made to collect perinatal and postnatal health history from the subjects in the study. Such information, however, was obtained from another group of older subjects (college students) to whom the tests in the Key were administered. Two "unusual cases" that illustrate the utility of the Key as an instrument in differential diagnosis will be described.

A male freshman drop-out suspected of having sustained brain damage during childhood was referred to our laboratory by his mother. His neuropsychological profile was, however, uniformly superior. A lengthy counseling session revealed that his poor academic performance was due to emotional

Table 9-1

Performance of Children Belonging to the Different Diagnostic Categories – Representative Cases

	K. B.: Borderline Intelligence	A. L.: Deficit in Visual Information Processing	T. B.: Deficit in Semantic Aspects of Language	H. S.: Deficit in Syntactic Aspects of Language	D. D.: Impulsive
CA[a]	9 years, 8 months	10 years, 6 months	10 years, 2 months	9 years, 11 months	9 years, 8 months
Grade	4	4	4	4	4
IQ	85^b	100	97	102	104
Durrell (Grade) Oral Reading[d]	3.0^b	3.0^b	3.5^b	1.4^b	3.5^b
Listening Comprehension	2.0^b	6.0^c	3.0^b	5.0^c	4.0
NSST[a]					
Receptive[e]	10.0%^{b}	25.0%^{b}	50.0%	50.0%	50.0%
Expressive	10.0%^{b}	99.0%^{c}	25.0%	10.0%^{b}	99.0%^{c}
Token Test	1.0%^{b}	50.0%	50.0%	60.0%	55.0%
Sequential Memory Test	30.0%^{b}	84.0%^{c}	70.0%^{c}	09.0%^{b}	60.0%
Digit Span	75.0%^{c}	75.0%^{c}	37.0%^{b}	37.0%^{b}	50.0%
Manual Dexterity Test	12R; 9L^b	16R; 13L^c	16R; 12L^c	—	12R; 9L^b

Memory for Faces Test	16.0%[b]	10.0%[b]	84.0%[c]	69.0%	8.0%
Sight Vocabulary	40.0%	5.0%[b]	90.0%[c]	60.0%	85.0%[c]
MFF[a]					
Total errors	83.0%	92.0%[b]	91.0%[b]	62.0%	67.0%
Response time	44.0%	40.0%	25.0%	28.0%	18.0%[b]
Reading					
Comprehension	Poor	Good	Poor	Poor	Good
Oral expression	Short sentences; uses only "and."	Uses embeddings; uses "might be."	Short sentences; uses only "and."	Short incomplete sentences; agrammatism in expression.	Uses "wh" questions; tells complete story.
Error analysis	Errors of meaning; neologisms.	Misreads content words; no agrammatism; self-corrects.	Steady decoding; few oral errors; no agrammatism.	Omits functional words; no self-correction; agrammatism.	Omits some words; self-corrects; decoding problems.

[a]CA, chronological age; NSST, Northwestern Syntax Screening Test; MFF, Matching Familiar Figures Test.
[b]Very poor performance.
[c]Very good performance.
[d]Durrell's Reading Test was administered during the end of the academic year. Reading at grade level 3.5, therefore, reflects approximately 1.5 years of retardation.
[e]All percentile ranks are approximations.

problems involving his girlfriend and that the suspected organic problems could be attributed to his occasional bouts with migraine headaches – which ran in his family. His reading level, as assessed by the Stanford Diagnostic Reading Test, was at the graduate level. It was concluded, therefore, that his academic problems were not due to any specific learning disability.

The second subject was a sophomore who had found reading a very laborious and difficult task but, nevertheless, was able to maintain an acceptable grade point average by dint of sheer hard work. Her neuropsychological profile did not fit any expected pattern. She scored high on WISC Comprehension, NSST, and the Token Test, but her reading comprehension was poor. Nevertheless, she showed signs of agrammatism while reading. Her digit span and memory for faces were poor, but her rate of reading and vocabulary were at the graduate level. She encountered a great deal of difficulty with tests of spatial ability and also showed some parietal signs such as finger agnosia. Her past health history revealed that while pregnant, her mother had had measles, and immediately after birth, the subject had to be treated for Rh incompatibility. The erratic neuropsychological profile and her prenatal and perinatal history, along with her reading difficulty, naturally led to the conclusion of organic impairment.

THE REVISED NEUROPSYCHOLOGICAL KEY

Neuropsychological data obtained from LD children show that the different types of learning disabilities bear close resemblance to the different forms of acquired disabilities described in clinical literature. It appears logical, therefore, to place the theory of diagnosis and treatment of developmental disabilities securely within a neuropsychological model derived from clinical neurology. Such a model is briefly described below.

The human brain is an information-processing organ, and the two major information-processing strategies of the brain are sequential-analytic and holistic-simultaneous. Disruption of one or the other of these two strategies results in specific cognitive deficits.

Developmental dysphasia resembles aphasia resulting from loss of language. Since there are at least two major types of aphasias (Broca's and Wernicke's), one can expect to see at least two groups of language-retarded children. Language defects of children that resemble Broca's aphasia are likely to be in the form of agrammatism, poor syntactical ability, and telegraphic expressions. These children are further likely to be deficient in sequential information-processing as well as motor tasks that involve sequential movements. Many of the "clumsy children" who are considered learning disabled may very well belong to this category. Comprehension of spoken language remains essentially intact in these children. On the other hand, language deficits that resemble Wernicke's aphasia are semantic in nature and may show few or no signs of agrammatism; defects of comprehension and meaningful expression, however, dominate the picture. Both forms of language disorders affect reading, but in different ways.

The clinical literature describes two major kinds of alexias – alexia without agraphia and alexia with agraphia. The existence of a third kind of alexia associated with Broca's aphasia has been reported recently (Benson, 1977). The similarity between alexias and developmental dyslexias has also been recently documented (Aaron, 1980). It is reasonable, therefore, to expect three kinds of reading disabilities: (1) those arising from defective visual-gestalt processing ability, (2) those associated with semantic-linguistic deficits, and (3) those associated with agrammatism and syntactic-linguistic defects.

On the basis of the research findings, the Key has been revised and elaborated within the framework of the neuropsychological model described above.

Instruments

The revised Key incorporates the following tests: (1) intelligence test, preferably WISC-R; (2) Durrell Analysis of Reading Difficulty (oral reading, silent reading, listening comprehension, and spelling subtests); (3) taping of subject's oral reading from Durrell for the analysis of reading errors; and taping of oral description of two pictures; (4) sight vocabulary, using a graded word list from Classroom Reading Inventory (Silvaroli, 1976) or Analytical Reading Inventory (M. L. Woods & Moe, 1977); (5) Northwestern Syntax Screening Test; (6) Token Test for Children (DiSimoni, 1978); (7) Memory for Faces Test (Aaron, 1978b); (8) Digit Span from WISC; (9) Sequential Memory Test (Goldman et al, 1974); (10) Manual-Dexterity Test (Crawford & Crawford, 1956); and (11) Matching Familiar Figures Test (Salkind, undated).

Procedure

All of the 11 tests and subtests are to be administered to the subject, and the data collected and recorded.

Step 1. If the subject's IQ is 90 or below and, in addition, the subject shows uniformly depressed performance on all the tests in the Key, he or she is not to be considered learning disabled. Instead, the subject has a generalized learning disability and should receive remedial help in all aspects of learning.

Step 2. If the subject's performance shows imbalances in the form of an uneven neuropsychological profile, he or she is considered a learning-disabled child. Under such circumstances, the psychologist must decide whether the child's learning disability is language related or visual-gestalt-process related.

If the subject performs poorly on the Memory for Faces Test and on sight vocabulary tests but shows average or above-average performance on language tests, Digit Span, Sequential Memory Test, and the Matching Familiar Figures Test, the etiology of learning disability is considered to be due to a visual-gestalt deficiency. Corroborating data are obtained from the analysis of reading errors and oral language.

Reading error analysis with visual-gestalt-deficient LD subjects should reveal that the errors are limited mainly to the misreading of content words. Meaning is often not affected and if reading results in incongruous state-ments, the subject often goes back and self-corrects. Decoding is often accomplished in a letter-by-letter manner. Nonsense words or neologisms do not occur in the process of reading. Listening comprehension (Durrell) is far superior to oral reading. The following is a sample reading of a visual-gestalt-deficient subject:

Subject: L . . a . . t . . e in the summer a man s . . t . . u . . d started
   Text: Late in the summer a man started
Subject: to build a house. He had some men digging the cell
   Text: to build a house. He had some men dig the cellar
Subject: for him. Then he put   the floor and the sides.
   Text: for him. Then he built the floor and the cellar.

Expressive language reveals mature language usage, the presence of a variety of conjunctions, a rich vocabulary, and good comprehension of the theme of the story. A sample of oral-expressive language is "This man, he was building a house with a cellar for him. He, he wanted to finish it before winter winter came. When he couldn't finish it, he told the boys that they might be able to use it." Logically, remediation of a visual-gestalt-deficient child should include efforts to improve sight vocabulary.

Step 3. If the subject has average or above-average visual memory but low language scores, then learning disability may be due to language defi-cits. The next logical step is to decide whether the subject has a semantic-comprehension deficit or a syntactic-grammar deficit.

Step 4. If the subject has a lower score in listening comprehension (Durrell) as compared to his or her oral reading, and also has performed poorly on the language test such as the NSST but shows average or above-average performance on sight vocabulary, Memory for Faces, Digit Span,

Sequential Memory Test, and the Matching Familiar Figure Test, he or she is considered to have a semantic-comprehension deficit.

Reading error analysis should reveal the following. The subject usually reads at a steady rate and may decode well with few or no errors at all. When errors occur, misreading of content words is more frequently seen than misreading of functional words. Reading errors may alter the meaning of the sentence, and the subject is often insensitive to such errors and makes no attempt to self-correct. Misreading of words frequently results in nonsense words and neologisms. The following is a sample reading of a semantic-comprehension-deficit subject:

Subject: In 1807, Robert Fulton took the first long trip in
   Text: In 1807, Robert Fulton took the first long trip in
Subject: a steamboat. He went one hour and fifty minutes.
   Text: a steamboat. He went one hundred and fifty miles.
Subject: According gathered on both bridge of the river.
   Text: Crowds gathered on both banks of the river.
Subject: They (fishermen) were afraind that it its noise
   Text: They were afraid that its noise
Subject: and splarting would drive away all the fish.
   Text: and splashing would drive away all the fish.

Expressive language usually reveals that no theme emerges from the story. Children with a comprehensive deficit usually are not verbally fluent and may limit their expressions to one or two sentences. Their spelling errors are typically phonetic. This is in general accordance with the clinical observation that patients with posterior lesions (Wernicke's and anomic aphasics) produce phonetically acceptable spelling and that patients with anterior lesions (Broca's aphasia) produce phonetically unacceptable ones (Frith, 1980). A sample of oral-expressive language is "Robert Fulton was in a steamboat for an hour and fifty minutes and the fishermen were unhappy because he was trying to scare the fish away."

Step 5. If the subject's performance is poor on Durrell's oral and silent reading subtests as compared to listening comprehension, as well as NSST, Token Test, Sequential Memory Test, Digit Span, and Manual Dexterity Test, but average or above-average in Memory for Faces, sight vocabulary, and the Matching Familiar Figures Test, a diagnosis of syntactic-grammar deficit could be arrived at.

Reading error analysis invariably reveals the following. The subject usually omits or substitutes functional words such as conjunctions and articles as well as inflexive word endings. These errors usually result in grammatically incorrect sentences that the subject seldom corrects. Misreading is limited primarily to functional words, and content words are usually read

correctly. Meaning of the sentence is usually well-preserved. A sample reading
of a syntactic-grammar-deficient subject follows:

Subject: In 1807, Robert Fulton took the first long trip
  Text: In 1807, Robert Fulton took the first long trip
Subject: in a steamboat. This was fast   that and a
  Text: in a steamboat. This was faster than a
Subject: steamboat had ever gone before. They (fishermen)
  Text: steamboat had ever gone before. They
Subject: were afraid it   noise and splash would drive
  Text: were afraid its noise and splashing would drive
Subject: all away all the fish.
  Text: away all the fish

Expressive language usually reveals that the subject's comprehension is
adequate. However, the story is often expressed in short and choppy sentences, which are frequently linked to each other only by the conjunction
"and." The expressive language also may reveal the subject's insensitivity to
grammatical rules. Spelling errors are of the mixed type even though nonphonetic spelling may be a predominant feature. A sample of oral-expressive
language is "In 1807, Robert Fulton-he-he-went five miles an hour in a boat-
and-all people gathered on the banks . . . see the new steamboat and the fish-
erman said 'go away' because they didn't like it, because there is a . . . . . .
and said 'go away.'"

Remedial measures for these two types of language-retarded children naturally would include intensive language therapy. The semantic-comprehension-
deficient child may require more personal experiences and opportunities
to express him- or herself, whereas the agrammatic, syntax-deficient child
may need training in formulating grammatically acceptable utterances.

Step 6. If the subject's performance is poor on the Matching Familiar
Figures Test, along with short reaction time and low scores on Digit Span
and the Sequential Memory Test, but is average or above-average in language
and visual memory, hyperactivity may be suspected. In the present study,
only one subject could be considered to qualify for this diagnostic category.
Since his protocols were not very revealing, no detailed description of reading
or language errors representative of this group can be provided.

DISCUSSION

Very few children described in the present study fell neatly into one
subgroup or another, even though assigning them to one diagnostic category
or another did not pose a major problem. In a majority of cases, the neuro-

psychological profile left little doubt as to which category the child belonged. Whether the subjects diagnosed as belonging to the different learning disability categories respond differently to different forms of treatment will be the ultimate test of the validity of the neuropsychological model on which the Key is based.

REFERENCES

Aaron, P. G. Dyslexia, an imbalance in cerebral information processing strategies. *Perceptual and Motor Skills,* 1978, *47,* 699-706. (a)

Aaron, P. G. A test for facial memory. Unpublished manuscript, 1978. (b)

Aaron, P. G. A Neuropsychological Key approach to diagnosis and remediation of learning disabilities. *Journal of Clinical Psychology,* 1979, *35,* 326-335.

Aaron, P. G. Developmental dyslexia and acquired alexia: Two sides of the same coin? *Brain and Language,* 1980, *11,* 1-11.

Aaron, P. G., Grantham, S. L., & Campbell, N. Differential treatment of dyslexia of diverse etiologies. Unpublished manuscript, 1978.

Albert, M. L., Yamador, A., Gardner, H., & Howes, D. Comprehension in alexia. *Brain,* 1973, *96,* 317-328.

Allen, R., & Allen, C. *Language experiences in reading.* Chicago: Encylopedia Britanica, 1970.

Aram, D., & Nation, J. E. Pattern of language behavior in children with developmental language disorders. *Journal of Speech and Hearing Research,* 1975, *18,* 229-241.

Arter, J. A., & Jenkins, J. R. Differential diagnosis-prescription teaching: A critical appraisal. *Review of Educational Research,* 1979, *49,* 517-555.

Ault, R. L. Problem solving strategies of reflective, impulsive, fast accurate, and slow accurate children. *Child Development,* 1973, *44,* 259-266.

Bakker, D. J., Smink, T., & Reitsma, P. Ear dominance and reading ability. *Cortex,* 1973, *9,* 201-212.

Bateman, B. Reading: A controversial view — Research and rationale. In L. Tarnopol (Ed.), *Learning disabilities.* Springfield, Il.: Charles C Thomas, 1969.

Benson, D. F. The third alexia. *Archives of Neurology (Chicago),* 1977, *34,* 327-331.

Benton, A. L. The neuropsychology of facial recognition. *American Psychologist,* 1980, *35,* 176-186.

Benton, A. L., & Van Allen, M. W. *Test of facial recognition manual.* Iowa City, Iowa: Neurosurgery Center Publication No. 287, University of Iowa, 1973.

Bever, T. G. Cerebral asymmetries in humans are due to differentiation of two incompatible process: Holistic and analytic. *Annals of the New York Academy of Sciences,* 1975, *263,* 215-262.

Boder, E. Developmental dyslexia: Prevailing diagnostic concepts and a new diagnostic approach. In H. R. Myklebust (Ed.), *Progress in learning disabilities.* New York: Grune & Stratton, 1971.

Boder, E. Developmental dyslexia: Diagnostic approach based on three atypical reading-spelling patterns. *Developmental Medicine and Child Neurology,* 1973, *15,* 663–687.

Bricker, W. A. A systematic approach to language training. In R. L. Schiefelbusch (Ed.), *Language of the mentally retarded.* Baltimore: University Park Press, 1972.

Brown, E. R. Theories of reading and language development: An interpretative review. In R. W. Rieber (Ed.), *Language development and aphasia in children.* New York: Academic Press, 1980.

Campbell, S. B., & Douglas, V. I. Cognitive styles and responses to threat of frustration. *Canadian Journal of Behavioral Sciences,* 1972, *4,* 30–42.

Conners, C. K. A teacher rating scale for use in drug studies with children. *American Journal of Psychiatry,* 1969, *126,* 152–156.

Conrad, K. Beitrag zum Problem der parietalen Alexie. *Psychologie,* 1948, *181,* 398–420.

Crawford, J. E., & Crawford, D. M. *Small parts dexterity test.* New York: Psychological Corporation, 1956.

Critchley, M. Is developmental dyslexia the expression of minor cerebral damage? *Clinical Proceedings,* 1966, *22,* 213–219.

Cromer, R. F. The basis of childhood dysphasia, a linguistic approach. In M. A. Wyke (Ed.), *Developmental dysphasia.* New York: Academic Press, 1978.

Cromer, W., & Wiener, M. Idiosyncratic response patterns among good and poor readers. *Journal of Consulting Psychology,* 1966, *30,* 1–10.

Cruickshank, W., Bentzen, F., Ratzeburg, F., & Tannhauser, M. *Teaching method for brain injured and hyperactive children.* Syracuse, N.Y.: Syracuse University Press, 1961.

Das, J. P. Structure of cognitive abilities: Evidence for simultaneous and successive processing. *Journal of Educational Psychology,* 1973, *65,* 103–108.

Das, J. P., Kirby, J. R., & Jarman, R. F. *Simultaneous and successive cognitive processes.* New York: Academic Press, 1979.

De Hirsch, K., Jansky, J. J., & Langford, W. *Predicting reading failure.* New York: Harper & Row, 1966.

Denckla, M. B. Research needs in learning disabilities: A neurologist's point of view. *Journal of Learning Disabilities,* 1973, *7,* 441–450.

Denckla, M. B., & Rudell, R. G. Rapid automatized naming: Dyslexia differentiated from other learning disabilities. *Neuropsychologia,* 1976, *14,* 471–479.

DeRenzi, E., & Vignolo, L. A. The token test: A sensitive test to detect receptive disturbances in aphasics. *Brain,* 1962, *85,* 665–678.

DiSimoni, F. *The token test for children.* Boston: Teaching Resources, 1978.

Doehring, G. D. Evaluation of two models of reading disability. In R. M.

Knights & D. J. Bakker (Eds.), *The neuropsychology of learning disorders.* Baltimore: University Park Press, 1976.

Douglas, V. I. Stop, look, listen: The problem of sustained attention and impulse control in hyperactive and normal children. *Canadian Journal of Behavioral Science,* 1972, *4,* 259-282.

Douglas, V. I. Difference between normal and hyperactive children. In C. K. Conners (Ed.), *Clinical use of stimulant drugs in children.* New York: American Elsevier Publishing, 1974.

Dunn, L. M. *Peabody Picture Vocabulary Test.* Nashville: American Guidance Service, 1969.

Durrell, D. D. *Durrell analysis of reading difficulty.* New York: Harcourt, Brace, Jovanovich, 1955.

Education of handicapped children. *Federal Register,* 1976, *41,* (230), 52404.

Eustis, S. R. The primary etiology of the specific language difficulties. *Journal of Pediatrics,* 1947, *31,* 448-455.

Fernald, G. *Remedial techniques in basic school subjects.* New York: McGraw Hill, 1943.

Foster, C. R., Giddan, J., & Stark, J. *Assessment of children's language comprehension.* Palo Alto, Ca.: Consulting Psychologist Press, 1973.

Frith, U. Unexpected spelling problems. In U. Frith (Ed.), *Cognitive processes in spelling.* New York: Academic Press, 1980.

Gallagher, J. J. Children with developmental imbalances: A psychoeducational definition. In W. M. Cruickshank (Ed.), *The teacher of brain injured children.* Syracuse, N.Y.: Syracuse University Press, 1966.

Gazzaniga, M. S. *The bisected brain.* New York: Appleton-Century-Crofts, 1970.

Geffen, G., Bradshaw, J. L., & Nettleton, N. C. Hemispheric asymmetry: Verbal and spatial encoding of visual stimuli. *Journal of Experimental Psychology,* 1972, *95,* 25-31.

Geschwind, N. The development of the brain and evolution of language. In C. J. Stuart (Ed.), *Monograph series on language and linguistics.* Washington, D.C.: Georgetown University Press, 1964.

Gillingham, A. *Remedial training for children with specific disability in reading, spelling, and penmanship* (7th ed.). Cambridge, Mass.: Educators Publishing Service, 1970.

Goldman, R., Fristoe, M., & Woodcock, R. W. *Auditory memory tests.* Circle Pines, Minn.: American Guidance Service, 1974.

Gough, P. B. One second reading. In J. F. Kavanagh & I. G. Mattingly (Eds.), *Language by ear and by eye.* Cambridge, Mass.: MIT Press, 1972.

Guthrie, J. T. Principles of instruction: A critique of Johnson's remedial approaches to dyslexia. In A. L. Benton & D. Pearl (Eds.), *Dyslexia: An appraisal of current knowledge.* New York: Oxford University Press, 1978.

Hahn, W. J., & Weiss, M. *New scoring criteria for use of the token test in identifying language disabilities in children of low socioeconomic status.* Paper presented at the Annual Convention of the American Speech and Hearing Association, Detroit, 1973.

Hécaen, H., & Kremin, H. Neurolinguistic research on reading disorders resulting from left hemisphere lesions: Aphasic and "pure" alexia. In H. Whitaker & H. A. Whitaker (Eds.), *Studies in neurolinguistics.* New York: Academic Press, 1976.

Isaacson, R. L. The myth of recovery from early brain damage. In N. R. Ellis (Ed.), *Aberrant development in infancy-human and animal studies.* Hillsdale, N. J.: Lawrence Erlbaum, 1975.

Isaacson, R. L., & Nonemann, A. J. Early brain damage and later development. In P. Satz & J. T. Ross (Eds.), *The disabled learner: early detection and intervention.* Rotterdam: Rotterdam University Press, 1972.

Johnson, D., & Myklebust, H. *Learning disabilities: Educational principles and practices.* New York: Grune & Stratton, 1967.

Johnson, O. G., & Bommarito, J. W. *Tests and measurement in child development: A handbook.* San Francisco: Jossey Bass, 1971.

Kaste, C. M. A ten-year follow-up of children diagnosed in a child guidance clinic as having cerebral dysfunction. *Dissertation Abstracts International,* 1972, *33,* 1797–1798.

Kimura, D. Functional asymmetry of the brain in dichotic listening. *Cortex,* 1967, *3,* 163–178.

Kinsbourne, M. Minimal brain dysfunction as a neurodevelopmental lag. *Annals of the New York Academy of Science,* 1973, *205,* 268–273.

Kinsbourne, M., & Warrington, E. A variety of reading disability associated with right hemisphere lesions. *Journal of Neurology, Neurosurgery and Psychiatry,* 1962, *25,* 330–334.(a)

Kinsbourne, M., & Warrington, E. A disorder of simultaneous form perception. *Brain,* 1962, *85,* 461–486.(b)

Koppitz, E: *Children with learning disabilities – A five-year follow-up study.* New York: Grune & Stratton, 1971.

Learning disabilities regulations. *APA Monitor,* February 1978, *9* (2).

Lee, L. *Northwestern syntax screening test.* Evanston, Il.: Northwestern University Press, 1969.

Lee, L: *Developmental sentence analysis.* Evanston, Il.: Northwestern University Press, 1974.

Lee, L., Koenigsknecht, R. A., & Mulhern, S. T. *Interactive language development teaching.* Evanston, Il.: Northwestern University Press, 1975.

Leonard, L. B. A preliminary view of generalization in language training. *Journal of Speech and Hearing Disorders,* 1974, *4,* 429–436.

Likert, R., & Quasha, W. H. *Revised Minnesota Paper Form Board Test.* New York: The Psychological Corporation, 1970.

MacDonald, J. D., & Blott, J. P. Environmental language intervention: The rationale for a diagnostic and training strategy through rules, context, and generalization. *Journal of Speech and Hearing Disorders,* 1974, *39,* 244–256.

Mash, E. J., & Dalby, T. J. Behavioral intervention for hyperactivity. In R. W. Trites (Ed.) *Hyperactivity in children.* Baltimore: University Park Press, 1979.

McFie, J. The effect of hemispherectomy on intellectual functioning in cases of infantile hemiplegia. *Journal of Neurology, Neurosurgery, and Psychiatry,* 1961, *24,* 240-249.

Meichenbaum, D. Self-instructional methods. In F. Kanfer & A. Goldstein (Eds.), *Helping people change.* New York: Pergamon Press, 1975.

Meichenbaum, D. H., & Goodman, J. Training impulsive children to talk to themselves: A means of developing self-control. *Journal of Abnormal Psychology,* 1971, *77,* 115-126.

Menyuk, P: Linguistic problems in children with developmental dysphasia. In M. A. Wyke (Ed.), *Developmental dysphasia.* New York: Academic Press, 1978.

Money, J. On learning and not learning to read. In J. Money (Ed.), *The disabled reader.* Baltimore: Johns Hopkins Press, 1966.

Moskowitz, S. *The program for brain injured children in the NYC public schools – An appraisal* (pamphlet). New York: NYC Board of Education, New York Bureau of Educational Research, 1964.

Myers, P., & Hammill, D. *Methods for learning disorders.* New York, John Wiley, 1976.

Myklebust, H. R. *Auditory disorders in children.* New York: Grune & Stratton, 1954.

Pasamanick, B., & Knobloch, H. Retrospective studies on the epidemiology of reproductive casualty – old and new. *Merrill Palmer Quarterly of Behavior and Development,* 1966, *12,* 7-26.

Pirozzolo, F. J. *The neuropsychology of developmental reading disorders.* New York: Praeger, 1979.

Pirozzolo, F. J., & Rayner, K. Hemispheric specialization in reading and word recognition. *Brain and Language,* 1977, *4,* 248-261.

Rawson, M. B. *Developmental language disability.* Baltimore: Johns Hopkins University, 1968.

Robinson, H. M., & Smith, H. K. Reading clinic – Ten years after. *The Elementary School Journal,* 1962, *63,* 22-27.

Ross, A. *Psychological aspects of learning disabilities and reading disorders.* New York: McGraw-Hill, 1976.

Rourke, B. P. Reading retardation in children: Developmental lag or deficit? In R. M. Knights & D. J. Bakker (Eds.), *The neuropsychology of learning disorders.* Baltimore: University Park Press, 1976.

Rudel, R. G. The neurological assessment of learning disabilities. In S. G. Brainard (Ed.), *Learning disabilities: Issues and recommendations for research.* Washington, D.C.: U.S. Department of Health, Education and Welfare, 1974.

Rudel, R. G. Neuroplasticity: Implications for development and education. In J. S. Chall & A. F. Mirsky (Eds.), *Education and the brain.* Chicago: University of Chicago Press, 1978.

Russell, E. W., Neuringer, C., & Goldstein, G. *Assessment of brain damage – A neuropsychological approach.* New York: Wiley Interscience, 1970.

Rutter, M. *The concept of dyslexia.* Paper presented at the Sixth International Study Group on Child Neurology and Cerebral Palsy.

Safer, D., & Allen, R. *Hyperactive children – Diagnosis and management.* Baltimore: University Park Press, 1976.

Salkind, N. J. *The development of norms for the Matching Familiar Figures Test.* Unpublished manuscript, University of Kansas, Undated.

Sandoval, J. The measurement of hyperactive syndrome in children. *Review of Educational Research,* 1977, *47,* 293-318.

Satz, P., & Friel, J. Some predictive antecedents of specific reading disabilities: A preliminary two-year follow-up. *Journal of Learning Disabilities,* 1974, *7,* 48-55.

Semel, E. M., & Wiig, E. H. Comprehension of syntactic structures and critical verbal elements by children with learning disabilities. *Journal of Learning Disabilities,* 1975, *8,* 53-58.

Silvaroli, N. J. *Classroom reading inventory* (3rd ed.). Dubuque, Iowa: William Brown, 1976.

Silver, A. A., & Hagin, R. A. Specific reading disability: Follow-up Studies. *American Journal of Orthopsychiatry,* 1964, *35,* 95-102.

Smith, F., & Holmes, L. D. The independence of letter, word and meaning identification in reading. *Reading Research Quarterly,* 1971, *6,* 394-415.

Sperry, R. W. Some general aspects of interhemispheric integrations. In V. B. Mountcastle (Ed.), *Interhemispheric relations and cerebral dominance.* Baltimore: John Hopkins Press, 1962.

Sperry, R. W. Split-brain approach to learning problems. In G. C. Quarton, T. Melnechnuck, & F. O. Schmitt (Eds.), *The neurosciences.* New York: The Rockefeller University Press, 1967.

Sprague, R. L., Christensen, D. E., & Werry, J. S. Experimental psychology and stimulant drugs. In C. I. Conners (Ed.), *Clinical use of stimulant drugs in children.* Amsterdam: Excerpta Medica, 1974.

Stark, J. Aphasia in children. In R. W. Rieber (Ed.), *Language development and aphasia in children.* New York: Academic Press, 1980.

Strauss, A. A., & Kephart, N. C. *Psychopathology and the education of the brain-injured child.* New York: Grune & Stratton, 1955.

Sykes, D. H., Douglas, V., Weiss, G., & Minde, K. Attention in hyperactive children and the effects of methylphenidate. *Journal of Child Psychology and Psychiatry,* 1971, *12,* 129-139.

Symmes, S. J., & Rapoport, L. J. Unexpected reading failure. *American Journal of Orthopsychiatry,* 1972, *42,* 1, 82-91.

Teuber, H. L., & Rudel, R. G. Behavior after cerebral lesions in children and adults. *Developmental Medicine and Child Neurology,* 1962, *4,* 3-20.

Tobin, A. Mental retardation due to germinal matrix infarction. *Science,* 1969, *164,* 156-158.

Trantham, C. R., & Pederson, J. K. *Normal language development – The key to diagnosis for language disturbed children.* Baltimore: Williams & Wilkins, 1976.

Trites, R. L., & Fiedorowicz, C. Follow-up study of children with specific reading disability. In R. M. Knights & D. J. Bakker (Eds.), *The neuropsychology of learning disorders.* Baltimore: University Park Press, 1976.

Vellutino, F. R. *Dyslexia: Theory and research.* Cambridge, Mass.: MIT Press, 1979.

Vogel, S. A. Syntactic abilities in normal and dyslexic children. *Journal of Learning Disabilities,* 1974, *7,* 47–53.

Wiener, M., & Cromer, W. Reading and reading difficulty—A conceptual analysis. *Harvard Educational Review,* 1967, *37,* 620–643.

Wiig, E. H., & Harris, S. P. Perception and interpretation of nonverbally expressed emotions by adolescents with learning disabilities. *Perceptual and Motor Skills,* 1974, *38,* 239–245.

Wiig, E. H., & Roach, M. A. Immediate recall of semantically and syntactically varied sentences by learning-disabled adolescents. *Perceptual and Motor Skills,* 1975, *40,* 119–125.

Wiig, E. H., & Semel, E. M. Comprehension of linguistic concepts requiring logical operations by learning-disabled children. *Journal of Speech and Hearing Research,* 1973, *16,* 627–636.

Wiig, E. H., & Semel, E. M. *Language disabilities in children and adolescents.* Columbus, Oh.: Charles Merrill, 1976.

Witelson, S. Abnormal right hemisphere specialization in developmental dyslexia. In M. R. Knights & D. J. Bakker (Eds.), *The neuropsychology of learning disorders.* Baltimore: University Park Press, 1976.

Woods, B. T., & Teuber, H. L. Early onset of complementary specialization of cerebral hemispheres in man. *Transactions of the American Neurological Association,* 1973, *98,* 113–117.

Woods, M. L., & Moe, A. J. *Analytical reading inventory.* Columbus, Oh.: Charles Merrill, 1977.

Yates, A. The validity of some psychological tests of brain damage. *Psychological Bulletin,* 1954, *51,* 359–377.

Yeni-Komshian, H. G., Isenberg, D., & Goldberg, H. Cerebral dominance and reading disability: Left visual field deficit in poor readers. *Neuropsychologia,* 1975, *13,* 83–93.

Robert M. Knights
Clare Stoddart

10

Profile Approaches to Neuropsychological Diagnosis in Children

Problems in differential diagnosis have plagued psychologists since the introduction of the first standardized tests. The history of the measurement of
intelligence and the assessment of personality variables is replete with examples of the difficulty of defining reliable subcategories of individuals who
share some common characteristics. Many methods have been used in attempts
to summarize and describe the similarity among individuals on certain types
of measurable behaviors. Much of the literature on individual assessment is
devoted to finding the commonality of those characteristics that have been
measured. A variety of multivariate statistical techniques have been developed, including factor analysis, cluster analysis, regression analysis, and linear
discriminant function analysis. These techniques are often used to determine
the unique features of groups of individuals with common symptoms or
etiologies. In the area of child neuropsychology, these methods have sometimes been used to derive a profile characteristic of a particular group of
children.

A *neuropsychological profile* is a set of scores that provide a pattern that
uniquely describes the performance of an individual or a particular group on

The authors appreciate the assistance of Jan Norwood in the preparation of this
paper.

335

a variety of neuropsychological tests. This technique allows examination not only of the level of performance but also of the pattern of abilities and deficits. The importance of not relying solely on level of performance in neuropsychological diagnosis has continuously been stressed by Reitan (1967). In clinical and research work on minimal brain dysfunction and learning disorders, the differences in characteristics leading to a particular diagnosis are frequently subtle, confusing, and difficult to quantify. Given these difficulties in diagnosis, the profile approach has been advocated because it has greater sensitivity than other methods.

An additional advantage associated 'with the use of profiles is that it provides a visual representation of the pattern of scores. Some neuropsychologists find this a definite advantage, since it allows a more configural interpretation of the test scores.

A number of the difficulties common to all neuropsychological research have been discussed in detail by Parsons and Prigatano (1978). However, there appear to be further difficulties inherent in the use of children's neuropsychological profiles that should also be considered. For example, one of the basic assumptions underlying the derivation of neuropsychological test profiles is that a similar etiology or a similar educational deficit, such as a visual or perceptual deficit, will result in a similar pattern of abilities and deficits consistent across age. That is, the child who is classified as a dyslexic at age 6 will have characteristics similar to those of a child who is classified dyslexic at age 9. The profile approach is based on the assumption that these disorders have a common set of characteristics as measured by neuropsychological tests. On the other hand, the plasticity of the young brain makes the determination of consistent brain-behavior relationships difficult.

A study of the literature on the neuropsychological assessment of children reveals that there have been consistent attempts to define specific subgroups of children classified as minimally brain damaged, hyperactive, or learning disabled. Although there appears to be general agreement that there are subcategories of each of the above groups (which are suggested clinically by selective responsiveness to specific therapies), attempts to define consistent unique patterns of abilities and deficits have, so far, remained tentative.

In reviewing the use of a neuropsychological test battery for the development of profiles, only a limited number of studies may be considered relevant. It should be noted that this chapter does not refer to profiles specific to individual tests, such as the WISC-R, or to neuropsychological studies of adults. Table 10-1 summarizes three methods for using profiles or patterns of test scores and notes the rather specific methodological problems involved in each type of profile analysis.

Table 10-1
Profile Approaches and Pattern Analysis

	Group to Subgroup	Individual into a Group	Individual to Individual
Statistical method	Statistical analysis of group data to form subgroup profiles	Statistical classification of a child to category on basis of test pattern	Statistical matching of individual test profile to others with similar disorders
Studies	Conners, 1973; Doehring, 1974; Doehring et al, 1979; Mattis et al, 1975; Petrauskas and Rourke, 1979	Fletcher et al, 1979; Selz and Reitan, 1979	Knights, 1973; Knights and Watson, 1968
Clinical method	Clinical formation of subgroups and examination of test score profiles	Clinical sorting of child to category on basis of test pattern	Clinical practice, individual case interpretation
Studies	Finlayson and Reitan, 1976; Reitan and Boll, 1973; Rourke and Finlayson, 1978	Doehring, 1974; Reitan and Boll, 1973	
Specific methodological problem	Crossvalidation difficulties in small sample studies that may not be replicated in other research studies	Base rates in the clinic population and selection of cases meeting criteria for research studies	Number of cases for matching in the data bank, or relevant clinical experience

GROUP TO SUBGROUP

Statistical Analysis

A recent excellent example of the first method of profile production in which subgroups are formed from a larger group on a post hoc basis is Petrauskas and Rourke's (1979) study. This study analyzed the neuropsychological test battery results of retarded readers in order to identify subtypes. The study involved 160 children, 133 of whom were retarded readers. The 44 test variables were categorized into 6 abilities: tactile, sequencing, motor, visual-spatial, auditory-verbal, and abstract-conceptual. Statistical analysis consisted of a Q factor analysis of a Pearson product moment correlational analysis. This method permitted the drawing of profiles of five subtypes of retarded readers with scores on each of the variables in the six categories. Visual inspection indicated differences in the pattern of results and statistical analysis suggested that at least three of the subtypes are quite reliable. For example, the first subtype profile showed above-average visual, spatial, and motor skills and very poor expressive language; the second subtype was somewhat below average in most skills but much below average on tactile and visual memory. The third subtype profile differed primarily in poor abstract-conceptual performance.

Petrauskas and Rourke related these characteristic subtypes to the work of other investigators who have indicated similar subclassifications of retarded readers. This provides that a degree of semblance exists among the subtypes of retarded readers within a variety of different approaches.

As indicated in Table 10-1, one continual problem in this type of study is that of crossvalidation. Petrauskas and Rourke addressed this problem by splitting their group into two subsamples and performing different statistical analyses, on each half and then on the total sample. The three profiles for the three reliable retarded subtypes were surprisingly consistent.

Doehring and co-workers conducted two separate studies in which subgroups of retarded readers were formed. The first study (Doehring, 1968), consisted of a comprehensive statistical analysis of the test scores of 78 boys who were given a complete neuropsychological test battery. Doehring compared the performance of 39 10–14-year-old boys who were 2 years below expected reading level with the performance of 39 control youngsters. The pattern of differences between the groups was analyzed with factor analysis, multiple stepwise regression, and discriminant function analysis. The factor analysis used a Principal Components solution and found the major differences to be on reading-spelling ability and visual-perceptual speed. The multiple stepwise regression showed that the best differentiation between the nonreaders and the readers was on two spoken language abilities, while the discriminant analysis demonstrated excellent separation on the basis of the two language measures plus age. In general, the various methods of analysis showed poor readers to be associated with a pattern of poor reading and spelling, as expected, and to have problems in spoken language and difficulty in visual-perceptual speed and a variety of nonlanguage tasks.

The study is comprehensive in the use of a variety of statistical procedures, but other than the two factors revealed in the factor analysis, the study is primarily directed toward separating the two groups rather than comparing patterns or profiles associated with each group.

In the second study, by Doehring, Hoshko, and Bryans (1979), a statistical analysis of test scores was again used to form specific reading subgroups. Doehring et al describe a series of studies in which subgroups of poor readers were formed by the Q technique of factor analysis and by cluster analysis to provide crossvalidation data on three retarded-reader subtypes. Both of these statistical methods classify children in terms of indices that reflect the degree of test profile similarity.

The first sample in this series of studies consisted of 34 children who were registered in a summer reading program for poor readers. They were given 31 tests of reading-related skills, including seven tests of visual matching, seven tests of oral and written material, nine tests of oral reading, and eight tests of visual scanning. Factor analysis of the test scores by the Q technique was used to define three specific subtypes of reading disability. The first group was poor at general oral reading, the second group slow in matching letters, and the third group poor in matching syllables.

On the basis of this sample of problem readers, Doehring et al provided several crossvalidation studies using both the Q factor technique and cluster analysis to illustrate that these subgroups continue to exist in a variety of samples of children. One of the interesting findings was that a group of normal readers did not load on the original factors in a manner similar to that of the poor readers. This was interpreted to indicate that reading difficulties in retarded readers do not represent exaggerated forms of normal readers' problems. The six types of cluster analysis included four methods of squared Euclidian distance and two methods of shape difference. Doehring et al found very close agreement between the original Q technique classifications and the cluster analysis solution using McQuitty's method. Doehring et al also provided a third crossvalidation study of 26 children with a variety of learning problems and found consistent and similar results.

This study differs from that of Petrauskas and Rourke (1979) and the earlier study by Doehring (1968) in that the tests used were measures of reading skills rather than measures of neuropsychological functioning. It is, therefore, difficult to make direct comparisons. Another drawback to the Doehring et al study is that no visual representation of the subgroup profiles was provided. The positive aspect is the crossvalidation studies, which stand up with a variety of methods and again suggest that the subgroups are reliable and exist in poor reading populations.

In a neuropsychological study of dyslexia, Mattis, French, and Rapin (1975) examined the pattern of test battery results in 113 children classified into three groups: brain damaged with no reading problems, brain damaged with dyslexia, and dyslexia with no brain damage (developmental dyslexia). They found no significant differences between the two dyslexic groups and suggested that three identifiable syndromes may be seen in both groups of dyslexics: the first characterized by a general language disorder, the second by motor-speech difficulty, and the third by a visuospatial perceptual impairment. Unfortunately, the authors did not present a visual representation of the test data, although the differences in patterns of performance could have provided an interesting visual comparison between each subtype.

The results of this study provide some support for the Doehring (1968) factor analysis study, since two of the three subgroups seem to correspond with the factors of general language ability and visual-perceptual disorder.

The above-mentioned studies all examined subgroups of children with reading difficulties. In contrast, Conners (1973) formed subgroups of children with minimal brain dysfunction (MBD) on the basis of neuropsychological test profiles. His sample of 267 children had been referred for evaluation of behavior and learning disorders. He first performed factor analyses on their test results from the neuropsychological test battery and identified five factors: general IQ, achievement, rote learning, attentiveness, and impulse control. He then conducted a cluster analysis in order to identify separate patterns of scores. He found six rather distinct subgroups, which differed on five factors. Conners speculated on the validity of the real differences among the different profile groups and conducted some interesting comparisons that suggested the subgroups were reliable. For example, the six groups were compared on motor tests, parent and teacher ratings, drug response, and cortical evoked response, and showed significant differences that are psychologically sensible. Unfortunately, crossvalidation was not provided for these different profile patterns.

A consistent problem in the crossvalidation of studies using multivariate statistical methods is the large amount of shrinkage that occurs when replication studies are conducted. This issue is directly addressed by Fletcher, Rice, and Ray (1978) in an article on linear discriminant function analysis in neuropsychological research. They discussed the relationship between the number of subjects, the number of variables, and the artificial inflation of classification rates. They further discuss the care that must be taken in the interpretation of multivariate analysis of small samples when a large number of dependent variables are involved. This is particularly applicable to those studies that have used all the scores in the neuropsychological test battery as dependent variables. Furthermore, many test scores do not provide "pure" measures of one particular function, and deficits in different functional systems may result in the same poor performance on individual tests of the battery. This makes interpretation of multivariate analysis particularly difficult.

Both Petrauskas and Rourke (1979) and Conners (1973) formed the subgroup profiles post hoc on the basis of statistical analysis. The other way to form profiles is to derive subgroups, a priori, on the basis of clinical, educational, or behavioral information and then analyze the neuropsychological test scores to determine whether pattern differences exist between the subgroups.

Clinical Formation of Subgroups

Reitan and Boll (1973) separated children into four groups: those with minimal brain dysfunction who had academic difficulties, those with MBD who had behavioral difficulties, those with neurological evidence of brain damage, and those with no evidence of brain damage. The scores on intelligence tests, achievement tests, and the Reitan-Indiana Neuropsychological Test Battery for Children were converted into mean t scores for each group. The pattern of mean t scores for the four groups appears impressive in the figure presented but the ordinate only represents one standard deviation on each side of the mean, and statistical analyses generally failed to show significant differences between the control and MBD groups.

Another study that formed subgroups, a priori, is Finlayson and Reitan's (1976). They used scores on tactile-perceptual tasks for normal younger (6-8) and older (12-14) children as the basis of classification. These two groups were compared on the Category Test of abstract reasoning, three WISC IQ scores, and reading ability. Finlayson and Reitan found that the group with poor tactile skills performed less well, especially in the older age group. This study demonstrated the differences in the pattern of skills that exist between sensorimotor performance and higher-order cognitive abilities in normal children.

A third study in which learning-disabled children were classified into subgroups is that of Rourke and Finlayson (1978). They studied three subgroups of children with learning disabilities on the basis of academic achievement scores in reading, spelling, and arithmetic, and examined the pattern of scores on 14 tests classified as either verbal and auditory-perceptual or visual-spatial and visual-perceptual. Examination of the t score figure illustrating the profile results clearly shows the groups to be different either in level of performance or in pattern. Again, however, the entire figure shows only two standard deviations and the score differences are visually magnified. The statistical comparisons are less impressive because only one subgroup has a unique pattern. Rourke et al stated in the conclusion that the pattern of results was far more important than the level of performance.

Other studies that might be considered relevant in that they compare neuropsychological test scores in brain-damaged and non-brain-damaged children (for example, Reitan, 1974; Tsushima & Towne, 1977) have not been included in this section as they do not examine the pattern or profile of results.

INDIVIDUAL INTO A GROUP

As suggested in Table 10-1, the individual-into-a-group category includes those studies that look at the profile of neuropsychological test results in order to place the child in a particular category, such as brain damaged or learning disabled. These studies either use a statistical method for analyzing the pattern or a clinical method in which the investigator categorizes individuals on the basis of a blind interpretation of the test scores pattern.

Statistical Classification

In an attempt to improve on clinical methods of inference, Selz and Reitan (1979) classified children into either control, learning-disabled, or brain-damaged groups using a system of rules. These taxonomic rules included not only level of performance and patterns of performance among various tests, but also right–left differences and pathognomonic signs. On the basis of cut-off scores for each of the variables, each child was given added points if he or she was out of the normal range. The cut-off score was determined by the authors in order to produce the fewest number of misclassifications. Using this technique, they recorded an overall correct classification rate of 73 percent. However, when the classification rate was broken down into groups, it can be seen that this apparently satisfactory overall rate can be attributed to the high correct classification rate, 82 percent, for the control and brain-damaged groups; in the case of the learning-disabled group the correct classification rate dropped to 56 percent.

It is apparent that, in this study, although several methods of inference were used for capitalizing on the pattern differences in results, in the final analysis it was the level-of-performance score that was utilized because of the additive effects in the methods of calculation of normal or abnormal categories. That is, although a pattern approach was used in analyzing the individual neuropsychological data, the overall method of categorization was based on a total score or level-of-performance procedure. The study might have been even more informative if the four methods were not used in an additive manner, but rather used so that more emphasis was placed on the configural pattern of scores to determine the child's classification. For example, children with only right-left differences of a certain magnitude could have been classified as brain damaged, whereas level of performance could have been used primarily to differentiate the control group from the other two groups. Similarly, errors on the Aphasia Screening Test could have been weighted most heavily in categorizing the child as learning-disabled. An approach such as this would have relied more heavily on the four inference methods originally described by Reitan (1967) than on the procedure used in the 1979 study.

Despite an early article by Meehl and Rosen (1955), which illustrated the importance of the prior probability, or base-rate frequency of outcomes, and a more recent article by Gordon (1977), which demonstrated the problems of ignoring base rates in neuropsychology, this issue is still not dealt with in research that classifies patients into groups. Much of the research literature reports studies with experimental and control groups of equal size, as is the case with the Selz and Reitan study, with the result that there may be an inflated estimate of actual utility of the procedure in situations where the prior probabilities are unbalanced. Although the actual incidence of children in each category undoubtedly varies from clinic to clinic, it presumably does not correspond to these optimal conditions, and the effect of extreme base-rate asymmetry should be considered.

The construction of groups based on neurological criteria used in neuropsychological experimental research may also be open to question in terms of applicability to problems of clinical diagnosis. A recent study by Anthony, Heaton, and Lehman (1980) is an example of the difficulties involved. In this study, only 150 patients of 1500 met all criteria for classification in the "experimental" or brain-lesioned group. Attempts to determine the validity of testing procedures using such highly selected groups may not be indicative of actual clinical utility. It appears that in clinical neuropsychological laboratories the vast majority of patients seen cannot be neatly classified into well-defined groups, such as brain damaged or non-brain damaged, but instead fall into the category in which the possibility of brain damage is equivocal (Snow, 1981).

A second classification study was Fletcher, Smidt, and Satz's (1979) in which children were classified on the basis of predictions of who would or would not have reading difficulties 3 years after initial assessment. This study was one of a series by Paul Satz and co-workers conducted as the Florida Longitudinal Project (Satz, Taylor, Friel, & Fletcher, 1978). Statistical classification in this study was based on the use of discriminant function analyses, and Fletcher et al (1979) provide an excellent discussion of some of the problems related to the statistical assumptions and methodological concerns involved when this method of analysis is used. In this study, they first administered 14 neuropsychological tests to 497 kindergarten children and subsequently selected 5 tests with the greatest predictive value. At the end of the 3-year follow-up, information on reading achievement was obtained on 417 children. The discriminant function was used to predict four levels of reading ability: severely disabled, mildly disabled, average, and superior. An excellent feature of the Fletcher et al study is that it takes into account base-rate information and incorporates this into the calculations. In the first prediction, where the prior probability of falling into one of the four groups was 25 percent, the overall hit rate was 77 percent. When using the actuarial base rates of .15, .20, .50, and .15 for the severe, mild, average, and superior reading groups, the overall hit rate increased to 79 percent. The authors discuss the difficulty of predicting the two middle groups and also demonstrate that small numbers left at the extreme may lead to artificially high hit rates. An additional aspect of this study is the discussion of the effect of a dichotomous variable, finger localization, in the discriminant function analysis. Fletcher et al describe several discriminant function analyses after breaking the four groups in different ways in order to show the effects on the overall hit rate.

In summary, this is a very thorough study that looks at the pattern of test results in kindergarten children in order to predict reading disability 3 years later and takes into account methodological difficulties that are too often ignored in neuropsychological research. The study, unfortunately, does not provide visual profiles of results, although they probably exist in the authors' data. It would be interesting to see whether differences not only in the level of performance of the four groups but also in the pattern of results on the five most predictive tests could be presented visually in a meaningful way.

Clinical Classification

The first study to demonstrate classification of individuals into categories on the basis of clinical sorting was that of Reitan and Boll (1973). The first part of this study is discussed above in the review of group-to-subgroup studies. As is noted, statistical comparisons between groups generally failed to show significant differences between the control and each of the two MBD groups. In the second part of the same study, a clinical approach was employed in which blind ratings of each child's protocol were made that indicated whether the test results implied a deficit in each of 17 areas. Highly significant results were obtained as a result of this analysis among the four groups in terms of the mean number of psychological deficits judged to be present in each group. The brain-damaged group showed the most deficits, followed by the group with MBD and academic difficulties, whereas the group with MBD and behavior problems showed the second lowest deficits next to the control group, which had the best performance. This clinical approach, therefore, was more successful in separating the four groups than were comparisons based on statistical analyses.

Reitan and Boll did a second clinical categorization of the children, who were sorted into three groups as having normal, mildly impaired, or abnormal brain functions. In this clinical classification, the authors were relatively successful in classifying normal and abnormal subjects, but were less successful with the mildly impaired category. The apparent difference in findings between these statistical and clinical approaches is attributed by the authors to the limitations of the statistical model in which valuable information regarding intraindividual differences is lost in statistical comparisons based on measures of averages or central tendencies. This difficulty has been noted before in neuropsychological research with adults (Reitan, 1964).

Doehring's (1968) study of retarded readers also presented a clinical sorting by two judges of normal and poor readers into four classifications on the basis of a set of rules describing patterns of neuropsychological test results. These descriptions could be considered an early version of the rules used by Selz and Reitan (1979). In Doehring's (1968) classification, the categories were normal, MBD, or definite cerebral dysfunction. Doehring also provided an estimate of probable location and extent of the presumed lesion. The judges had good agreement on classification but there were no outside criteria with which to evaluate the actual hit rate. One judge also clinically classified the children into retarded or normal reader groups on the basis of the neuropsychological test patterns. This was quite successful, and he correctly identified 84 percent of the retarded or possible retarded readers and 82 percent of the normals. This high hit rate is considered good because only the Halstead tests were used and no measure of reading skills was involved.

INDIVIDUAL TO INDIVIDUAL

Statistical Comparisons

The third method of classifying children according to neuropsychological test profiles was discussed by Knights and Watson (1968), and Knights (1973). In this procedure, a computer was used to compare the child's scores on 17 tests and 106 subtest variables with normative data derived from the performance of control children of the same age (Knights & Norwood, 1980).

The computer program translated the raw scores into t score form and plotted a profile in mean and standard deviation units. This procedure was adopted in order to account for differences in level of performance across age, while allowing for consistency in the pattern of abilities and deficits, on an individual rather than a group basis. The profile approach allows intra-individual differences to be taken into account in a way that is not possible in statistical comparisons among group means.

To statistically compare the profiles of individual children, a second computer program was written that compared the criterion child with every other previously tested child whose data was stored in the computer data file. The comparison statistic was Cohen's r_c (1969), which is a coefficient of profile similarity derived from Cattell's r_p (Cattell, 1949). This coefficient is invariant over profile reflection and takes into account both the level of performance and the pattern of high and low scores. Examples of this profile and the matching profile procedures are presented in Knights (1973).

CASE EXAMPLES

To illustrate the utility of the matching-profile program, several cases from Knights's neuropsychology laboratory are presented that demonstrate the potential positive aspects of the method. It should be noted these cases illustrate the successful contribution of the matching procedure in discovering etiology or in considering possible diagnostic classifications.

The first case provides not only some indication of the reliability of the procedure, but also demonstrates that the pattern of test results is consistent over a 3-year period. The patient, R. L., was given the full neuropsychological test battery (Knights & Norwood, 1979) in 1977, 1978, and 1980. In 1977, the 7-year-old patient was referred to the laboratory because of his learning difficulties. The neuropsychological tests revealed that he had particular difficulties in tactile perception, visual-motor, and spatial skills. The matching-profile program selects the ten best matches from the entire data bank, that is, ten cases with the highest correlation with the criterion subject. In the case of R. L., the 1980 profile correlated most highly with his previous assessment in 1977 (r_c = .68), followed by the profile of a child with learning difficulties (r_c = .67), followed by R. L.'s second testing in 1978 (r_c = .66). Over a 3-year period, therefore, R. L. had maintained a very similar pattern of test results in spite of an overall improvement in the level of performance. Another feature of this matching technique was illustrated when R. L.'s 1977 results were rerun with the subsequent cases in the file. R. L. then matched with both his future results. That is, the profile in 1977 is predictive of his 1980 profile and indicates, unfortunately, in his case, a long-standing and permanent pattern of deficits.

A second case, G. G., illustrates how the matching profile can assist in ruling out a pathological etiology. G. G. was a 15-year-old rural boy referred by his father because of writing difficulty, continuous poor school performance, and concern over his problems in relating to peers. The medical history indicated some difficulties at the time of birth and a mild head injury. G. G.'s test results were relatively normal with the exception of poor fine motor coordination and low academic achievement. The matching-profile program found that eight of the ten best matches were with children with relatively normal test results, and the remaining two were children with behavior problems. An interview with the father revealed that G. G. had been raised on an isolated farm with limited opportunity to socialize and that he preferred working on mechanical tasks around the farm. Academically, G. G.'s main difficulties stemmed from a very poor writing style, which was unacceptable at his school. It was recommended that G. G. be allowed to print his work, which he could do very neatly, and the father was given reassurance that the boy did not suffer from any serious learning disability.

The next case illustrates the particular advantage of the profile approach in diagnosing a child with a serious behavior problem. C. G., an 11-year-old girl, was referred from the psychiatry inpatient ward and had a history of long-standing emotional and behavior problems, including hysterical seizures. The referral to the neuropsychological laboratory was made to ascertain whether there was any indication of brain dysfunction that might account for the seizures. On clinical examination of the test profile, both the level and the pattern of performance appeared to be within the normal range. The computerized matching-profile program, however, selected nine children who had either closed head injuries or seizures. Both these disorders have similar patterns of mild scattered deficits in a variety of functions. This finding, therefore, suggests that brain dysfunction may well have contributed to this girl's serious emotional difficulties and seizures.

A final illustration of the use of the profile approach and its potential contribution to managing the child with learning disorders is the case of C. L. This 7-year-old boy could be considered a classic example of the distractible, impulsive, hyperactive child with an attention disorder. He could watch cartoons for hours, interrupted adults' conversation frequently, and was unresponsive to reward and punishment. Treatment included an unsuccessful attempt at diet manipulation and a relatively good response to methylphenidate. The interesting aspect of C. L.'s matching profiles, aside from selecting a variety of children with attention deficits, was that two of the ten matches also responded well to drugs. Although this may not seem to be a high selection ratio, the number of drug responders in the data bank is as yet very limited.

Clinical Interpretation

In clinical practice, the neuropsychologist typically uses his or her experience with previous similar cases in order to interpret a child's test results. This method often results in accurate inferences regarding the child's functioning in a variety of abilities. However, such a method necessarily relies on the skill and experience of the individual clinician. In addition, a consistent problem in this method is how to convey to others the weighting of the cues used in analysis, interpretation, and diagnosis.

DISCUSSION

A review of Table 10-1 suggests several general comments regarding the efficacy of the three types of profile approaches. In the first category, the formation of subgroups from group data, the profile approach has been relatively successful in delineating several subtypes of reading disabilities, MBD, and learning disorders. The studies presented have provided some interesting methods of crossvalidation and future research should add to the reliability of these subcategories.

It should be noted that so far there are no studies that provide subgroups of children labeled hyperactive on the basis of neuropsychological test results. There are two possible explanations for this apparent omission. First, the concept of hyperactivity may not represent a coherent unique entity, due to the variety of proposed etiologies and the selective effectiveness of different treatment programs. Second, the central issue in hyperactivity is frequently considered to be an attentional deficit, and neuropsychological test batteries usually do not provide a detailed assessment of this deficit. A variety of behavioral assessments and ratings would provide more relevant information in defining the characteristics of the hyperactive child.

In the second category, where the studies classified children into groups either statistically or clinically, a fairly high rate of accuracy was achieved. The importance of taking into account base-rate information has been discussed. An additional consideration in evaluating the validity of these studies is the use of highly selected cases for classification, when in fact the majority of cases referred to the neuropsychologist are equivocal with respect to the presence or absence of mild brain dysfunction. The persistent difficulty in neuropsychological research remains that of establishing criteria. Although neurodiagnostic evidence frequently provides objective criteria for either normality or brain damage, the evidence is commonly not as clear-cut for the MBD and the learning-disabled child.

In the future, a more fruitful use of the neuropsychological battery in research with children may be to provide descriptions of the patterns of abilities and deficits in a variety of other nonneurological medical disorders, such as asthma (Dunleavy & Baade, 1980), rather than to classify children into predetermined diagnostic categories.

In the third category of profile approaches, individual to individual, the computerized profile matching, like all profile approaches described in Table 10-1, is based on the assumption that specific etiologies result in a similar pattern of performance on the neuropsychological battery and that this pattern is relatively consistent across age. The cases presented tend to support these assumptions. The advantages of the individual-to-individual approach using computer techniques lie in the ability of the computer to accurately and reliably compare test scores using a large number of variables and a large sample population.

In conclusion, profile approaches are an attempt to describe the unique characteristics that can be attributed to subgroups of children. Progress in the understanding of brain–behavior relationships in children with learning and behavior disorders will depend on better and more accurate descriptions of these subtypes. The various profile approaches described are moving toward this more precise characterization of various disorders. For example, there has been a definite advance from the misunderstanding of the child with difficulties in school to some appreciation of more specific impairments such as hyperactivity, reading disabilities, and MBD. Profile approaches continue to further differentiate the nature of difficulties experienced by such children.

REFERENCES

Anthony, W., Heaton, R., & Lehman, R. Actuarial neuropsychological test interpretation. *Journal of Consulting and Clinical Psychology,* 1980, *48,* 317–326.

Cattell, R. B. r_p and other coefficients of pattern similarity. *Psychometrika,* 1949, *14,* 279–298.

Cohen, J. r_c: A profile similarity coefficient invariant over variable reflection. *Psychological Bulletin,* 1969, *71,* 281.

Conners, C. K. Psychological assessment of children with minimal brain dysfunction. *Annals of the New York Academy of Sciences,* 1973, *205,* 283–302.

Doehring, D. G. *Patterns of impairment in specific reading ability.* Bloomington, Indiana University Press, 1968.

Doehring, D. G., Hoshko, I. M., & Bryans, B. N. Statistical classification of children with reading problems. *Journal of Clinical Neuropsychology*, 1979, *1*, 5–16.

Dunleavy, R. A., & Baade, L. E. Neuropsychological correlates of severe asthma in children 9–14 years old. *Journal of Consulting and Clinical Psychology*, 1980, *48*, 564–577.

Finlayson, M. A., & Reitan, R. M. Tactile-perceptual functioning in relation to intellectual, cognitive and reading skills in younger and older normal children. *Developmental Medicine and Child Neurology*, 1976, *18*, 442–446.

Fletcher, J. M., Rice, W. J., & Ray, R. R. Linear discriminant function analysis in neuropsychological research. Some uses and abuses. *Cortex*, 1978, *14*, 564–577.

Fletcher, J. M., Smidt, R. K., & Satz, P. Discriminant function strategies for the kindergarten prediction of reading achievement. *Journal of Clinical Neuropsychology*, 1979, *1*, 151–166.

Gordon, N. G. Base rates and the decision making model in clinical neuropsychology. *Cortex*, 1977, *13*, 13–10.

Knights, R. M. Problems of criteria in diagnosis: A profile similarity approach. *Annuals of the New York Academy of Sciences*, 1973, *205*, 124–132.

Knights, R. M., & Norwood, Jan A. *A neuropsychological test battery for children: Examiner's manual.* Published by RMK Psychological Consultants, Inc., 41 Grove Avenue, Ottawa, Canada, K1S 3A5, 1979.

Knights, R. M., & Norwood, Jan A. *Revised smoothed normative data on the neuropsychological test battery for children.* Ottawa: Carleton University, 1980.

Knights, R. M., & Watson, P. The use of computerized test profiles in neuropsychological assessment. *Journal of Learning Disorders*, 1968, *12*, 696–709.

Mattis, S., French, J. H., & Rapin, I. Dyslexia in children and young adults: Three independent neuropsychological syndromes. *Developmental Medicine and Child Neurology*, 1975, *17*, 150–163.

Meehl, P. E., & Rosen, A. Antecedent probabilities and the efficiency of psychometric signs, patterns, or cutting scores. *Psychological Bulletin*, 1955, *52*, 144–216.

Parsons, O. A., & Prigatano, G. P. Methodological considerations in clinical neuropsychological research. *Journal of Consulting and Clinical Psychology*, 1978, *46*, 608–619.

Petrauskas, R. J., & Rourke, B. P. Identification of subtypes of retarded readers: A neuropsychological, multivariate approach. *Journal of Clinical Neuropsychology*, 1979, *1*, 17–38.

Reitan, R. M. Psychological deficits resulting from cerebral lesions in man. In J. M. Warren & K. A. Akert (Eds.), *The frontal granular cortex and behaviour.* New York: McGraw-Hill, 1964.

Reitan, R. M. Psychological assessment of deficits resulting from cerebral lesions in subjects with normal and sub-normal intelligence. In J. L. Khanna (Ed.), *Brain damage and mental retardation: A psychological evaluation.* Springfield, Il.: Charles C Thomas, 1967.

Reitan, R. M. Psychological effects of cerebral lesions in children of early school age. In R. M. Reitan and L. A. Davison (Eds.), *Clinical neuropsychology: Current status and applications.* New York: John Wiley & Sons, 1974.

Reitan, R. M., & Boll, T. J. Neuropsychological correlates of minimal brain dysfunction. *Annals of the New York Academy of Sciences,* 1973, *205,* 65–89.

Rourke, B. P., & Finlayson, M. A. J. Neuropsychological significance of variations in patterns of academic performance: Verbal and visual-spatial abilities. *Journal of Abnormal Child Psychology,* 1978, *6,* 121–133.

Satz, P., Taylor, H. G., Friel, J., & Fletcher J. M. Some developmental and predictive precursors of reading disabilities: A six year follow-up. In A. L. Benton & D. Pearl (Eds.), *Dyslexia: An appraisal of current knowledge.* New York: Oxford University Press, 1978.

Selz, M., & Reitan, R. M. Rules for neuropsychological diagnosis: Classification of brain funtion in older children. *Journal of Consulting and Clinical Psychology,* 1979, *47,* 258–264.

Snow, G. W. A comparison of frequency of abnormal results in neuropsychological vs. neurodiagnostic procedures. *Journal of Clinical Psychology,* 1981, *37,* 22–28.

Tsushima, W. T., & Towne, W. S. Neuropsychological abilities of young children with questionable brain disorders. *Journal of Consulting and Clinical Psychology,* 1977, *45,* 757–762.

SECTION IV

Neuropsychology
in the Schools

Lawrence C. Hartlage
Cecil R. Reynolds

11

Neuropsychological Assessment and the Individualization of Instruction

The foremost prerequisite to the ability to cogently translate the results of a comprehensive neuropsychological assessment of a child experiencing learning or other behavior difficulties is thorough comprehension of neuropsychological, psychometric, and related theories of the human intellect and of the interaction of its components. These various theories have been well articulated elsewhere in this volume (e.g., see Chapters 3, 4, and 8) and in the general psychological literature (e.g., Cattell, 1963; Guilford, 1967; Halstead, 1947; Jensen, 1979; Luria, 1966, 1970). It is imperative that psychologists understand each of these theories if they are to function as psychologists and not stimulus-bound technicians. Without the foundation of theory, even as imperfect as our theories are at present, the psychologist is limited to working with only the empirical experience generated from trial-and-error methods or the reading case examples. Thus, when encountering a child with a fresh set of problems and nuances of behavior and psychometric data, there is little basis for developing any sort of therapeutic or remedial effort. The same is true for other areas of psychology. A psychologist could certainly not function as a behavior therapist without extensive comprehension of operant and classical conditioning theories.

Many see the field of clinical neuropsychology as a set of tests and techniques for relating observed, quantifiable behavior to the integrity of an individual's functional neurological organization and structure. Moreover, many believe that to become a clinical neuropsychologist, it is only necessary to master the technical skills involved in administering and scoring tests such as the Halstead-Reitan Neuropsychological Test Battery (HRNTB) and the Luria-Nebraska Neuropsychological Battery. This is a gross oversimplification of clinical neuropsychology that borders on the fallacious. Much more than a set of techniques, clinical neuropsychology offers a paradigm for viewing and interpreting individual test data. Without a strong paradigm, clinical neuropsychology could not have progressed to the applicability it has reached today. As with other areas and subspecialities of psychology, several competing paradigms exist in clinical neuropsychology, any one of which may be more appropriate for a given case than another.

Several testing methods and paradigms have been developed over the past decades, each offering salvation for the child with learning problems. Some of the more unsuccessful approaches include the ITPA Model (Kirk & Kirk, 1971) and the Doman and Delacato method previously discussed in this volume (see Chapter 3). In contrast to these methods, the neuropsychological model, especially the strength model described here, has been shown to be quite effective in designing rehabilitation programs for adults (e.g., Golden, 1978; Reitan & Davison, 1974) and shows great promise for applications to children. Gaddes has reviewed much of the primary evidence favoring neuropsychological techniques (see Chapter 2). The requirements for such assessment need to be considered in detail.

REQUIREMENTS FOR ASSESSMENT
AND THE RATIONALE FOR THE
NEUROPSYCHOLOGICAL ASSESSMENT

Quantifiable, Replicable, and Valid

The assessment of a child's constellation of intellectual and academic strengths and weaknesses for remedial or rehabilitative purposes, such as constructing an individual educational program (IEP), is maximally useful only when certain requirements are met. The first requirement is that all, or at least a majority, of a child's educationally relevant cognitive abilities and methods of higher-order information-processing skills be assessed in a quantifiable, replicable, and valid manner. Many of the comprehensive assessment batteries designed by school psychologists or school psychological service departments meet this requirement when the psychologist interpreting the test results is well grounded in theories of individual differences and information processing.

Translation into an Educational Plan

A second requirement is that the findings from such an assessment be translated into a meaningful, relevant, and valid educational plan. To be meaningful, the translation of test findings to recommendations must be based on a theoretically sound rationale, ideally one that is in agreement with (or at least not contradictory to) current knowledge of educational, psychological, neurological, genetic, and related behavioral sciences. Again, this requires that the individual responsible for making such translations have considerable knowledge of the core areas of psychology. To be relevant, there must be a logical, as well as theoretical, relationship between the test findings and the practices that are feasible for the teacher or school system. Validity most commonly refers to the demonstrated ability that the recommendations for educational practices based on test findings have a better than chance probability of success. There are other types of validity that are also relevant here, especially in light of the dearth of research evaluating neuropsychological models of remediation and habilitation for school-age learning-disabled children. The most important of these is construct validity.

CONSTRUCT VALIDITY

Construct validity is a complex concept that, in this instance, refers to whether test findings are correctly translated into educational recommendations and whether the neuropsychological theory guiding the translations is itself valid. Currently, the most comprehensive neuropsychological model of human information processing and brain–behavior relationships is the Luria model, as described by Reynolds in this volume (Chapter 3). Yet even this theory will not be adequate for all children evaluated. The numerous individual differences found among children indicate that of the many proposed neuropsychological models of brain–behavior relationships (e.g., Knights & Bakker, 1976; Pirozzolo, 1980; Pribram, 1971; Tarnopol & Tarnopol, 1977; Wittrock, 1980), all will be the "best" model for describing some particular youngster who has learning problems. It is up to the psychologist to uncover the theoretical model of "best fit" for each child evaluated and to develop a programmatic educational plan on the basis of this particular model. The psychologist must thus play detective in neuropsychological models of test interpretation much as Kaufman (1979) has described for more traditional models of test interpretation.

THE DEFICIT MODEL

The meaningfulness of many translations of test findings into educational recommendations has been increasingly challenged in recent years (Hammill & Larsen, 1974; Ysseldyke, 1973; Yssledyke & Mirkin, in press). The greatest challenges have been directed (appropriately, we believe) towards the deficit model of remediation, whereby deficit or weakness areas are identified for subsequent intervention. Special emphasis in training is then focused on the child's area of greatest weakness (e.g., Ayres, 1974; Bannatyne; 1980; Ferinden & Jacobsen, 1969; Ferinden, Jacobsen & Kovalinsky, 1970; Getman,

1974; Kephart, 1963; Kirk & Kirk, 1971; Vallett, 1967). A major limitation of the deficit model has been suggested by findings in neurological, genetic, and related studies demonstrating neurological (L. C. Hartlage, 1975, 1979; L. C. Hartlage & P. L. Hartlage, 1978; L. C. Hartlage, Stovall, & P. L. Hartlage, 1980) and/or genetic bases (L. C. Hartlage, 1970; P. L. Hartlage & L. C. Hartlage, 1973a, b) for many common academic or intellectual disabilities. To focus attention on such deficits has been likened to using flash cards with blind readers to remedy their weak word-recognition skills (P. L. Hartlage & L. C. Hartlage, 1973b). Viewed from a neuropsychological model, the deficit approach is theoretically doomed to failure since it "teaches to dead tissue." In other words, under the deficit approach remedial attention is focused on developing dysfunctional areas of the brain. Not only does current knowledge in neurology predict failure for such efforts (Kolb & Whishaw, 1980), but also, evaluations of these efforts have found them to be ineffective in remedying learning problems (e.g., Glass & Robbins, 1967; Levine, Brooks, & Shonkoff, 1980; Myers & Hammill, 1976). Whether one accepts the anatomical basis of the argument against the deficit approach is irrelevant, however. Many researchers do not accept localizationist approaches to the diagnosis and descriptive etiology of learning problems. The paramount consideration is that these approaches do not seem to be effective.

Several other arguments against the deficit model can be used as long as alternative approaches exist. The strongest argument is the stress and anxiety created in the child by focusing on the child's poorest abilities—the areas in which failure has most frequently occurred. Such an inherently unpleasant focus for a remedial program surely cannot be in the child's best interest. Rather, to be meaningful and to increase the probability of success, a remedial approach to a child's learning problems need to be based on abilities that are sufficiently *intact* in the child, so as to promote successful accomplishment of the steps in the educational program; this way the interface between the strengths (rather than the weaknesses) determined from the assessment and the intervention strategy is a cornerstone of meaningfulness for the entire diagnostic-intervention process. In the language of Luria, it is necessary to locate an intact complex functional system capable of taking over and moderating the learning processes that are necessary for acquiring the academic skills in question.

INTERPRETING TEST SCORES

Reliable and accurate determination of a child's cognitive strengths and weaknesses requires considerable psychometric sophistication in addition to knowledge of theory. The psychometric methodology necessary to examine a single individual's scores and determine whether fluctuations in performance represent real differences in abilities and processing functions or are simply due to the random fluctuation inherent in all tests with less than perfect reliability has been described in a variety of sources (e.g., Field, 1960; Kaufman, 1979; Kaufman & Kaufman, 1977; Payne & Jones, 1957; Reynolds, 1979a, b; Reynolds & Gutkin, 1979, 1980; Sattler, in press). It is necessary to be conversant with ipsative (as contrasted with normative) test score interpretation in which general ability level is considered in determining specific areas of strength and weakness.

The relevance and practicality of educational recommendations based on test data pose special problems for school psychologists who serve many schools. These psychologists may not be aware of specific classroom management problems, available community resources, the presence or absence of special support services within a school, and the availability of supplementary teaching materials. In such situations, relevance is best attained by using the broad guidelines for teaching methods that utilize a child's intact processing modalities, capitalizing on his or her cognitive strengths and limiting the debilitating nature of the child's weaknesses, e.g., traditional orthographic, whole-word, look-say approaches to the teaching of reading likely have a higher probability of success with Johnny than will heavily linguistic approaches to reading, such as phonics-dependent or special alphabet methods that would call more upon his deficient left-hemisphere processing skills. The choice of a specific set of stimulus materials is then left to the learning-disabilities or other resource teacher, who is an expert in curriculum materials, whereas the psychologist conducting the evaluation is the expert in learning and information processing.

The validity of such test interpretations is important not only to the child's learning, but also to maintaining good rapport with teachers and other support staff. Predictive validity is essential to future good working relationships, and a certain amount of "face validity" may even be necessary to persuade teachers to follow through on recommendations. Unfortunately, there has been little empirical research on either relevance or validity of the neuropsychological assessment of children as it relates to intervention or intervention outcomes, but there is evidence that interest in such research is growing (e.g., Gutkin, 1980).

Future school psychological assessment batteries will probably be viewed more critically with respect to these issues than have existing batteries. The significance and utility of neuropsychological assessment data have been aptly demonstrated with adult patients (Golden, 1978; Heilman & Valenstein, 1979; Luria, 1969; Reitan & Davison, 1974), which is encouraging. Gaddes has also provided an excellent review of neuropsychological knowledge in the assessment and remediation of children's learning problems (see Chapter 2). The validity of educational recommendations drawn from neuropsychological assessment has undoubtedly been insufficiently researched thus far. Available results are promising, though, and neuropsychology has a major advantage over many other proposed systems in that it offers a sound theoretical foundation from which to develop activities.

Efficiency

A third requirement for assessment is that the procedures used should be reasonably efficient in terms of time and effort needed to administer and interpret them. The assessment should sample the relevant abilities without unnecessarily redundant or overlapping evaluation. Many school psychological assessment batteries do not meet this requirement since, frequently, the aggregation of tests in most batteries is designed to comply with some sort of general mandate that the battery include "measures of intelligence, achievement, adaptive behavior, perceptual-motor skill, and language" or other areas specified by a state or local education agency. As a result, many batteries require several hours or more to administer, and they yield a somewhat haphazard accumulation of data. These data require considerable ingenuity on the part of the psychologist to pull together any sort of comprehensive picture of how the child receives, associates, processes, or retrieves specific information via various modalities. In effect, when confronted by an unusual problem, many such batteries may yield a diagnostic picture as accurate as the conclusions reached by the three fabled blind men who combined their findings about elephants. Neuropsychological assessment procedures, as with other approaches to testing, should be designed to test the specific referral problem and to provide the information needed to devise an appropriate program for the individual in question.

Neuropsychological Assessment and
The Three Requirements

Neuropsychological differentiation meets the requirements for translation into a maximally effective individualized program of instruction. The assessment of abilities in quantifiable, replicable, and valid ways based on a sound concept of cerebral organization and functioning is, of course, the basis of neuropsychological assessment. This holds equally true for a battery based on the Halstead-Reitan (Reitan & Davison, 1974) approach, the Luria-Golden System (Golden, Hemmeke & Purisch, 1978), or other combinations (e.g., L. C. Hartlage & P. L. Hartlage, 1977). The validity of these procedures has been reported in a number of studies (L. C. Hartlage & P. L. Hartlage, in press; Hevern, 1980; Luria & Majovski, 1977; Matarazzo, Matarazzo, Wiens, Gallo, & Klonoff, 1976; Matarazzo, Wiens, Matarazzo, & Goldstein, 1974;

Moses & Golden, 1980). The soundness of translating neuropsychological assessment results into educational recommendations has been consistently demonstrated (L. C. Hartlage, 1979a; Hartlage & Haak, 1980; L. C. Hartlage & P. L. Hartlage, 1977), as has the educational relevance of these results (L. C. Hartlage, 1975a, in press; L. C. Hartlage & P. L. Hartlage, 1978), though certainly more research is needed.

The potential efficiency of a neuropsychological assessment battery derives from it being based on considerations of how the brain processes information, so that careful selection of tests to survey relevant functional brain areas can result in little or no redundancy. Furthermore, because it systematically surveys all relevant functional brain areas, the neuropsychological assessment does not leave the interpreter wishing that additional tests had been given.

THE NEUROPSYCHOLOGICAL TEST
BATTERY AND FORMULATING THE IEP

Characteristics to Test

Hemispheric efficiency. As Reitan (1966) pointed out, one of the unique, valuable aspects of a neuropsychological approach to assessment is the ability to compare the functional efficiency of one area of an individual's brain with another area, independently of such factors as general intelligence or level of education (though the latter two factors must surely be considered in designing an individual educational program). Of course, ipsative interpretation is (or should be) at the root of any interpretive approach for developing individualized programs. As has been recently observed (L. C. Hartlage, 1979a), an additional special advantage of this approach is its relative freedom from cultural influences, since it is highly unlikely that cultural phenomena affect one side or part of the body differently than the other.

An important first step in developing a battery to provide information for an IEP is to sample the relative functional efficiency of the two sides of the brain. While an initial estimate can be made by comparing the verbal and performance portions of one of the Wechsler Scales (Reitan, 1955), there are genetic (Karlsson, 1978; Nance, Allen, & Parisi, 1978), sex (Arnold, 1980; Dawson, Farrow, & Dawson, 1980; McKeever & Hoff, 1980), and cultural (Berg & Berg, 1971; Hartlage & Lucas, 1976) influences that can sufficiently affect this level of inference to make it dangerous to base any implications on this measure alone. A very powerful refinement of this initial estimate can be made by adding measures of comparative efficiency of motor and sensory functions of the two sides of the body. Specifically, such motor measures as rate of rapid finger oscillation and sensory measures such as fingertip number (or symbol) writing add considerable information to the verbal–performance comparison, and are culture-fair measures of neurological functional level.* Further, the motor measures given information about the efficiency of the frontal portions of the (contralateral) cerebral hemispheres, while the sensory measures provide information about the more posterior (contralateral parietal) areas.

Acuteness/chronicity. The element of acuteness/chronicity is usually not a major consideration in school psychological assessment, since problems that are referred are much more likely to be chronic problems than, for example, rapidly infiltrating tumors or vascular insults. However, a useful estimate of chronicity can often be made by comparing data from current functional levels (e.g., Wechsler standard scores) with data from measures that are typically more resistant to decline (e.g., achievement test standard scores, such as those obtained from the Wide Range Achievement Test), perhaps in conjunction with demographically derived estimates of a child's expected normal functional level (Reynolds & Gutkin, 1980).

Receptive language. Because of their common use in school psychology settings, and their usefulness for developing individual educational programs, separate measures of receptive language (e.g., Peabody Picture Vocabulary Test; PPVT) can be profitably incorporated into a neuropsychological battery since they provide information complementary to other language measures. Thus, in a child with a comparatively high PPVT score compared to his or her extrapolated Wechsler Vocabulary subtest standard score, there would be reason to consider possible expressive (i.e., frontal) language problems. Further evaluation of this possibility can then be made by comparing the rates of finger tapping, to determine whether indeed the right-hand tapping rate is comparatively slower than would be expected. On a more neuropsychologically refined basis, a comparison of spoken language facility with written language facility will permit inferences about whether the area of presumed dysfunction involves more inferior or superior areas of the language

---

*Normative data with children for these measures are available from a number of sources, including Boll and Reitan (1972), Finlayson and Reitan, (1976), Hughes (1976), Knights and Moule (1968), and Spreen and Gaddes (1969), though most traditional neurological and neuropsychological measures do not, as yet, have the careful, comprehensive normative data that have come to be associated with tests such as the Wechsler Scales. Some of the implications of these normative problems have been discussed elsewhere (Reynolds, in press).

cortex. Translation of these findings into an IEP is fairly straightforward, since if the child can express him- or herself more fluently in verbal than written language, measuring his or her knowledge by verbal questioning would be more likely to result in an accurate estimate than would written responses.

Constructional praxis. Measures of constructional praxis, as provided by such tests as the Beery Developmental Test of Visual-Motor Integration (VMI) and the Bender Visual-Motor Gestalt Test, add useful information to the more cognitively dependent Wechsler Block Design subtest and the more motor-dependent tapping rate. If a child is able to perform adequately on the fairly straightforward copying requirements of the Beery VMI yet has difficulty on Block Design, this may suggest relatively intact sensory and motor functions, with the deficit more related to cognitive weakness. This suggestion would be easy to verify by comparing left-hand performance on sensory (number writing) and motor (tapping) measures with right-hand performance. Or, if poor Beery and Block Design performances are noted in a child with good left-hand tapping but depressed number writing, the problem may be due to more posteriorly located deficits, compatible with spatial-perceptual rather than perceptual-motor problems. Translation of these findings into an IEP could profitably de-emphasize visual-spatial input, such as from flashcards or pictorial representation, and concentrate more on intact input modalities such as language-mediated instructional approaches. Alternatively, of course, a child with depressed performance on Beery VMI, Block Design, and left-hand tapping, but intact left-hand number writing recognition, may have problems with translating spatial material into an expressive form. In such children, performance on Picture Completion, with its relatively motor-free demands, would normally be fairly intact and would be higher than the more motor-dependent Wechsler subtests such as Object Assembly. One implication for the IEP of this constellation of performances could involve de-emphasis of such activities as art production; for example, art appreciation could be substituted for drawing requirements.

Maximizing the Child's Strengths

A very real consideration in the use of neuropsychological assessment as the basis for formulating an IEP is that the data from a good neuropsychological battery can be used to maximize the child's strengths toward the accomplishment of a given educational goal. This can be a positive and powerful strategy for helping prevent the frustration that can result from random attempts at enhancing a child's performance in weak academic skill areas, which can require the child to perform certain tasks that are beyond his or her cortical functional abilities. An example of how the focus of instructional strategies may be manipulated to capitalize on children's cerebrally mediated information-processing strengths to facilitate an instructional goal may help illustrate this point.

All the first-grade students in one school ($N = 1132$) were screened with a group battery that permitted classification on the basis of relative information-processing efficiency involving visual screening, auditory sequencing, and auditory and visual space (L. C. Hartlage & Lucas, 1973a, b). Subsequent matching was done with a specific reading instructional approach based on each child's profile. Those children who scored highest on visual sequencing were taught reading with a special alphabet approach (ITA), which is heavily dependent on such skills. Children who scored highest on auditory sequencing were taught reading with a system that emphasized phonics. Children who scored highest on auditory and visual space were taught reading by a traditional orthographic, whole-word, look-say approach. Due to logistic considerations such as having only one reading teacher in a school where children with all three types of profiles were enrolled, slightly more than half ($N = 684$) of the children were (operationally) randomly assigned to a reading approach; these children served as controls.

Mean Metropolitan Readiness Test scores were essentially identical for both experimental (106.7) and control (107.1) groups. At the end of first grade, all children were tested with the Reading scale of the Wide Range Achievement Test. Mean reading score for control group children was 106.0, compared with 129.0 for the children matched with the teaching method that the screening test profile suggested would be most compatible with their information-processing strengths. It was interesting to note that the teacher rankings of children's reading skills and the children's Wide Range Achievement Test score were significantly correlated ($p < .001$), suggesting that the differences in test scores did not represent an artifact related to testing method (L. C. Hartlage, 1975b).

The tests used to screen these children are not specifically neuropsychological tests, but rather are tests that were interpreted within a neuropsychological paradigm. This paradigm accurately relates cognitive performances on specific tests to the complex functional systems of the cortex mediating such performances; programs are then designed to utilize each child's most effective processing method. The simple screening procedures described above undoubtedly prevented much early reading failure among the experimental groups. Such interpretations of test results as made above and in the following case studies require considerable knowledge of neuropsychological, psychometric, and neurological theory as well as the basic foundations of neuroanatomy and physiology.

CASE STUDIES

Commentary — James

REFERRAL PROBLEM

James, a 9 1/2-year-old, white, right-handed boy whose Metropolitan Readiness Test scores were average, had experienced some difficulty since entering school, but never to a sufficient degree to warrant retention. At the end of the third grade, his teacher reluctantly passed him, but requested a psychoeducational evaluation for possible learning disabilities. When we saw him, he had just started fourth grade, and was one of the first children to be evaluated at the beginning of the school year.

All of his previous teachers had expressed concerns about James to his parents, who were described as cooperative and supportive. Both parents were high school graduates, and the father, a plant foreman, had taken several college courses. There was no family history of learning problems, epilepsy, or mental illness.

DEVELOPMENTAL HISTORY

James had a normal birth, with no significant illnesses or injuries. He walked at 14 months; spoke several words at 18 months; put together 2–3 words at 21 months; used plurals correctly at 30 months; learned to ride a tricycle by his fourth birthday, and mastered a bicycle by his sixth birthday. His mother had always considered him bright, alert, and inquisitive. His pediatrician felt he was normal.

CLASSROOM BEHAVIOR

There was no unanimity among his four teachers concerning his classroom behavior. James's first-grade teacher thought he was immature because of his impulsiveness and messy work. His second-grade teacher thought he was bright enough, but that he was a marginal student due to his carelessness, especially on his workbooks and written assignments. His third-grade teacher thought he might be learning disabled, since he seemed to be successful at reading but had some difficulty with writing and special problems on perceptual-motor tasks. His fourth-grade teacher was not aware of any serious problems.

BEHAVIORAL OBSERVATIONS

James was neatly dressed but his hair was unkempt, and he had recently acquired some spots on his shirt. Although he was quite friendly and outgoing and seemed to be at ease, he gave the impression of being impatient and wishing the session would soon be over. His responses tended to be verbose, with frequent tangential comments. He could, however, refocus when his

Results of Neuropsychological Examination

Patient James Age 9⁵ Sex M Education in 4 Handedness R

Wechsler Intelligence Scale for Children–Revised

Information	10	Picture Completion	10
Similarities	12	Picture Arrangement	9
Arithmetic	10	Block Design	8
Vocabulary	9	Object Assembly	8
Comprehension	12	Coding	7
(Digit Span	NA)	(Mazes	NA)

VIQ 103   PIQ 88   Full Scale IQ 96

Wide Range Achievement Test
Grade level   R 4.1   S 3.7   A 3.2
Standard score   R 95   S 91   A 87

Beery Developmental Test of Visual-Motor Integration
Age level   8–7
Standard score   89

Peabody Picture Vocabulary Test
Mental age   10–8
Standard score   106

Finger Tapping Test
R 39   L 33

Finger-tip Number Writing Test
R 17/20   L 15/20

attention was directed. Although his activity level was higher than average for his age, he was not hyperactive. There was no evidence of pressured speech, but phrase length was slightly above average for his age. Syntax, grammar, comprehension, articulation, and other aspects of his speech and language were essentially normal. He related easily, and came across as being slightly overconfident. He tended to ignore his mistakes, and to gloss over items with which he had difficulty.

The results of James's neuropsychological examination are shown above.

SYNTHESIS OF DATA

James's developmental history suggests that language development was chronically superior to nonlanguage development, in that the language milestones tend to be approximately average, with nonlanguage milestones generally several months to a year below expected norms. From these early developmental history data, it would be reasonable to expect a subsequent language ability; as reflected in average verbal IQ, or PPVT, with nonlanguage functions approximately a standard deviation below average. This nonlanguage development, if continuing at the same rate suggested by early development milestones, might show up as performance IQ or constructional praxis (Beery VMI) standard scores in the mid-80s range. These expectations can be helpful as a first step in assessing the chronicity (versus acuteness) of the difference between language and nonlanguage ability, by providing a tentative baseline for rate of development.

Classroom behavioral data, although apparently contradictory or at least inconclusive, actually are compatible with a chronic dysgenesis of the right hemisphere. James's carelessness, messy written work, impulsiveness, and perceptual-motor problems are fairly common behaviors in normal classroom students with marginal chronic deficiencies of right cerebral hemisphere development (L. C. Hartlage, 1980). Although not by itself diagnostic, poor monitoring of their own behavior is a very common behavioral trait reported in children with less efficient right-hemisphere functioning, independent of level of global mental ability. Thus, teacher comments such as "He can do better when he tries" may be a behavioral cue to cerebral functional asymmetry favoring the left hemisphere. The consistencies of teacher reports concerning this aspect of his behavior further lend slight but consistent support to the chronicity of the hypothesized cerebral functional asymmetry.

The psychometric profiles, which reveal 15-point WISC-R superiority of verbal over performance IQ and 17-point superiority of receptive language (PPVT) over constructional praxis (VMI) scores, support consistent superiority of left-hemisphere functioning. The pattern of slightly higher Wide Range Achievement Test (WRAT) skills on word recognition than on calculation of visually presented arithmetic problems is further compatible with chronically more efficient function of the left cerebral hemisphere (although the small magnitudes of James's differences among the diverse abilities measured by the WRAT are not by themselves necessarily indicative of functional cerebral asymmetry, especially since these scores may be confounded to some extent by teaching method).

The superiority of right-hand function on both motor (Finger Tapping) and sensory (Finger-tip Number Writing) tasks, at levels beyond what might be attributable to hand preference, strongly supports a cerebral organization discrepancy, since it is highly unlikely that cultural enrichment or deprivation would affect only one side of the body. James's distinct right-hand superiority is a very important finding, since the direction of the discrepancy between hands on motor and sensory functions is consistent with the discrepancies on psychometric, developmental, behavioral, and academic skill measures. The relatively small degree of subtest scatter within WISC-R verbal and performance subtests, and the good agreement between performance IQ and VMI scores, further indicates functional asymmetry of long duration.

The score configurations, in addition to supporting hypotheses of chronic functional superiority of the left hemisphere, suggest that, while both anterior and posterior portions of the right hemisphere are depressed when compared with the left hemisphere, there may be slightly less impairment on posterior portions of the right hemisphere than on anterior portions. Specifically, the purely receptive functions (i.e. posterior functions of the right hemisphere, reflected in such measures as Picture Completion and Finger-tip Number Writing) show slightly less comparative weakness than those left hemisphere functions with an executory component (e.g., tapping, Block Design, Object Assembly, Coding), which indicates slightly less perceptual than motor (anterior) impairment.

EDUCATIONAL IMPLICATIONS

Although the sight-word approach is a favored method of instruction for many individuals (Knight, 1980), for James (and other children with less efficient right- than left-hemisphere function) such an approach presents information in the way he is least able to process it. Thus, although he probably can and eventually would develop improved academic skills in subjects presented by flashcards, blackboard illustration, pictures, and related educational media, he would acquire such information in a much more efficient—and less painful—way if it were presented to him in a manner more oriented to his comparatively stronger left hemisphere. Specific recommendations for James thus included:

• Using linguistic-phonetic approaches to word attack skills. This strategy utilizes the analytic-sequential skills of the left hemisphere, and de-emphasizes visuospatial cues, which for James are less effective.

• Teaching "rules," such as "i before e, except after c," for reading and spelling. This technique presents spatial configuration material in the logic of language, i.e. a left-hemisphere approach.

• Encouraging him to read assignments twice: once quickly for overview, then more carefully for context. This procedure encourages James to use his intact logical organizational skills to develop information in what is for him a meaningful, sequential system. Such studying techniques as the OK4R (Overview, Key Words, Read, Recite, Recall, Review) may be especially appealing to James and students like him.

• Having teachers handle his behavioral transgressions with emphasis on verbal understanding of causes and consequences, for instance, having him write a 300-word paper on "Why I should not talk in class" will put the matter in his own perspective. Contingency contracting, i.e., spelling out the rules for him, along with sanctions, puts behavioral expectancies in a context meaningful to him. The use of verbal mediation is especially effective when used with children like James with superior left hemispheres.

These approaches avoid spatial, gestaltic, and emotive strategies (which would depend on James's weaker information-processing systems) and accentuate his more adaptive and efficient systems. At the same time, essentially the same academic and behavioral goals have been maintained; the process, not the procedure, has been altered.

FOLLOW-UP

At the end of fourth grade, James was promoted without reservation. The teacher's report indicated that she did not consider him to have any important learning or behavioral problems, although her ratings of his classroom behaviors on a 49-item classroom behavior inventory were not strikingly different from those of his third-grade teacher, who had considered him in need of referral. While at first glance this represents a contradiction between teachers, the inconsistency is actually a function of our educational system. Most academic programs generally emphasize right cerebral hemisphere-mediated abilities in early school grades, as demonstrated by the acquisition of early letter recognition and printing skills. As a child moves into fourth grade and beyond, much less reliance is placed on simple visuo-spatial matching, copying, and reproducing than on listening comprehension, automatic (deep structure) decoding of printed language, and synthesis of material. Thus, educational requirements gradually shift from a heavy reliance on right- to progressive dependence on left-hemisphere functioning, so that a youngster like James will often appear to "outgrow" any problems in early school grades resultant from weak right-hemisphere development. Actually the learning styles most compatible with the task have shifted.

Repeat examination by the school psychologist 8 months later revealed, as might be expected, no change on WISC-R, PPVT, or constructional praxis (Bender-Gestalt instead of VMI) scores. There was a slight improvement on WRAT standard scores: up 5 on scaled score points on Arithmetic, 6 on Spelling, and 8 on Reading. These are all in the range of possible standard error and cannot be considered indicative of any important change. During a brief visit with James's mother at the end of fourth grade, she reported some improvement in his attitude toward school, which she attributed to his growing up.

SUMMARY

James's case is not a dramatic illustration of how school psychological examination produced an instant miracle. Rather, it was chosen to demonstrate how the application of neuropsychological principles to the interpretation of developmental, behavioral, and test data of an essentially average child can provide a systematic framework for understanding patterns of learning strengths and weaknesses and for making fairly direct translations of these findings into intervention strategies uniquely relevant to the given child's cerebral organization. In light of the fact that approximately 76 percent of children and adults have significant cerebral asymmetry (Chi, Dooling, & Gilles, 1977; Geschwind & Levitsky, 1968), neuropsychological interpretation of data can provide a useful approach for developing optimal educational and behavioral intervention strategies for children with a wide range of school problems.

Commentary—Martin

REFERRAL PROBLEM

Martin, a 12-year-old, white, right-handed boy, was hit by a bat on the left frontal area of the head while playing baseball, and was unconscious for nearly 2 days. The injury occurred 4 months prior to the time of referral,

Results of Neuropsychological Examination

Patient Martin Age 12 Sex M Education in 7 Handedness R

Wechsler Intelligence Scale for Children–Revised

Information	10	Picture Completion	10
Similarities	13	Picture Arrangement	15
Arithmetic	8	Block Design	12
Vocabulary	9	Object Assembly	12
Comprehension	11	Coding	10
(Digit Span	7)	(Mazes	NA)

VIQ 101   PIQ 112   Full Scale IQ 106

Wide Range Achievement Test
Grade level R 11.1 S 8.9 A 9.9
Standard score R 127 S 112 A 119

Bender Visual-Motor Gestalt Test
Standard score 102 did not recognize errors

Peabody Picture Vocabulary Test
Standard score 134

Finger Tapping Test
R 36.2 L 36.0

Finger-tip Number Writing Test
R 20/20 L 16/20

Benton Visual Retention Test
Correct 7 (average)
Errors 6 (low average)
errors mainly distortions or omissions of left peripheral figures

which was initiated by his teacher. Martin had just begun seventh grade, and was in no apparent difficulty, but his teacher wondered whether his head injury might have some effect on his school performance.

He had always been a very good student, and 11 months before his injury had been tested for placement in the school's enrichment program. Previous teachers had described him as an eager student with good self-assurance and no discipline problems. Both parents had graduate degrees, the father in law and the mother in library science. Martin was an only child.

DEVELOPMENTAL HISTORY

Birth and early developmental history were described as unremarkable. Mother recalled that he was walking before his first birthday, and occasionally spoke in complete sentences around his second birthday, but admitted she was preoccupied with her graduate work during his early years and didn't remember them very clearly.

BEHAVIORAL OBSERVATIONS

Martin was outgoing and task oriented, and seemed comfortable in the examiner's company, although he wanted a good deal of assurance that he was doing well. His general demeanor suggested a bright, insightful understanding of most verbal test items, although his actual responses were not particularly impressive.

The results of Martin's neuropsychological examination are shown on p. 370.

SYNTHESIS OF DATA

The sketchy developmental milestones recalled by Martin's mother, if accurate, suggest accelerated language development, and his evaluation for placement in the school's enrichment program is compatible with above-average academic performance. His behavior during testing, although by no means diagnostic, did not sound like that reported by previous teachers, because although he had been described as self-assured, he required a good deal of assurance. This could be of some significance, since severe damage to the left cerebral hemisphere can result in what neurologists have described as the "catastrophic reaction," manifested by such traits as loss of self-assurance, feelings of impotence, and need for considerable assurance and support.

His psychometric profile, while superficially puzzling, came into fairly sharp focus when the nature of his injury was considered. The comparatively depressed Vocabulary scaled score, when contrasted with the much higher PPVT score, reflected the effect of anterior left damage on expressive language, while the more posteriorly mediated receptive language on the PPVT was unimpaired and compatible with his WRAT reading level. The simultaneous verbal sequencing in the Arithmetic scale and the auditory sequencing involved in Digit Span further reflected the sorts of problems compatible with damage to left frontal areas.

Since in many closed-head injuries the brain often suffers damage at an area opposite the site of injury (caused by the brain's bouncing against the contralateral skull area), those functions subserved by the right posterior parietal area had to be checked. One of the most direct measures of the functions of this cortical area is Finger-tip Number Writing, and the 20 percent deficiency in recognizing numbers written on left-hand fingertips when compared to the right hand lends strong support to damage to this area. This is further reflected in Martin's poor performance (when compared with his performance IQ) on the Benton Visual Retention Test, and slightly depressed performance on the Bender-Gestalt. The damage to the right hemisphere seems to be confined mainly to posterior areas, since the left-hand tapping rate is within expected rates and there is no global depression of performance IQ. The impairment of the left frontal (motor) area, determined by comparing depressed right-hand tapping rate (normally at least 5 percent greater than left in right-handed individuals) with left-hand rate and by depressed spelling compared to word recognition, provides fairly consistent evidence of primary residual impairment involving the left frontal (site of injury) area and the contre coup right posterior parietal area.

EDUCATIONAL IMPLICATIONS

Although Martin's IQ level was still within the average range, there was considerable evidence that it was currently reduced from prior levels. Perhaps of much more immediate consequence, there will be a recovery period during which he may function at levels below his measured IQ, and quite possibly with some variability from week to week. During this period restraint should be used with respect to involving him in demanding educational activities geared toward helping him "catch up." Instead the focus should be on helping him maintain residual skills during the convalescent period. For purposes of long-term educational planning, at least 1 year and even 2 years following Martin's injury needs to elapse before his possible long-term status can be assessed with formal IQ testing. This is important not only for making realistic plans for Martin's education based on his altered neurological status, but also for those instances where school psychologists may be asked to testify in personal injury cases, since frequently the neuropsychological picture does not stabilize in the immediate post-traumatic period. Specific recommendations for Martin thus included:

• Making maximal utilization of the intact middle and posterior portions of the left cerebral hemisphere. Examples of the residual strengths involved include excellent word recognition (left posterior parietal) and abstracting ability (left temporal). Martin can profit from reading for comprehension and information acquisition.

• Not focusing too much attention on expressive language, either spoken or written. The anterior portions of his left hemisphere still demonstrate signs of residual deficit, and calling attention to these deficit areas by requiring him to make major spoken class presentations or prepare extensive written reports should be avoided. He will probably perform better on multiple choice, matching, or true-false examinations than on essay or short answer questions. If he is to be tested to determine what he knows, rather than what he can express, the former types of questions will provide more fair and accurate indications.

• Not being surprised if he shows signs of mental fatigue after comparatively short periods of concentration. Try to break up periods of intense study, memorization, etc. with less mentally demanding periods. This condition will gradually improve over a few months, but in the months following the injury it can be a potential problem if it is not taken into account.

• Not being concerned about variability in his written productions. Because of the combination of mild spatial perceptual deficits from his right parietal injury, and expressive language problems, from his left frontal injury, he may write familiar words and phrases, or draw familiar objects from memory, with more facility than when attempting to compose new prose or copy from a visual stimulus.

Table 11-1
Martin's WISC-R Scores 11 Months Prior to Head Injury

Information	13	Picture Completion	12
Similarities	14	Picture Arrangement	15
Arithmetic	12	Block Design	13
Vocabulary	14	Object Assembly	12
Comprehension	12	Coding	12

VIQ 119 PIQ 120 Full Scale IQ 121

• Keeping in mind that, although his handicap is hidden, and he can still perform at average or above levels on standardized tests, he is suffering from a significant injury, and will be at risk for frustration, disappointment, and depression over not being able to perform intellectually with as much facility as in the past.

FOLLOW-UP

Results of Martin's Wechsler testing 11 months before his injury were obtained, and are listed in Table 11-1.

Although his earlier full scale IQ did not qualify him for the school's enrichment program (which required a full scale IQ of 125 or greater), it documents the extent of his loss following the head injury. His Wide Range Achievement Test scores are compatible with his previous rather than current levels of function, and there is room for some cautious optimism that he may regain some degree of the level of ability reflected in his prior scores. Recommendations were made for follow-up evaluations at least 1 year after this evaluation, since maximum recovery cannot be expected to occur much before then. The examination at that time should provide a fairly stable profile of what to expect in subsequent years, and thus could be used as the basis for possible educational and career planning.

DISCUSSION

The preceding cases illustrate how neuropsychological assessment can provide relevant information for writing IEPs for both chronically and acutely neurologically disordered children. By carefully determining the integrity of cortical areas underlying either general or specific abilities, the neuropsychological examination can provide information uniquely relevant for developing an IEP based on a given child's configuration of strengths and weaknesses, and can do so in such a way as to maximize the likelihood that the child will profit from the proposed educational plan.

REFERENCES

Arnold, A. P. Sexual differences in the brain. *American Scientist,* 1980, *68,* 165-173.

Ayres, A. J. *Sensory integration and learning disorders.* Los Angeles: Western Psychological Services, 1974.

Bannatyne, A. *Neuropsychological remediation of learning disorders.* Paper presented at the NATO/ASI International Conference on Neuropsychology and Cognition, August, Georgia, September, 1980.

Berg, N. L., & Berg, S. D. Comparison of verbal intelligence of young children from low and middle socioeconomic status. *Psychological Reports,* 1971, *28,* 559-562.

Boll, F. J., & Reitan, R. M. Motor and tactile-perceptual deficits in brain damaged children. *Perceptual and Motor Skills,* 1972, *34,* 343-350.

Cattell, R. B. Theory of fluid and crystallized intelligence: A crucial experiment. *Journal of Educational Psychology,* 1963, *54,* 7-22.

Chi, J., Dooling, E., & Gilles, F. Gyral development of the human brain. *Annals of Neurology,* 1977, 1, 88-93.

Dawson, G. D., Farrow, B. J., & Dawson, W. E. *Sex differences and haptic cerebral asymmetry.* Paper presented at the annual meeting of the Midwestern Psychological Association, St. Louis, 1980.

Ferinden, W. E., & Jacobsen, S. *Educational interpretation of the Wechsler Intelligence Scale for Children (WISC).* Linden, N.J.: Remediation Associates, 1969.

Ferinden, W. E., Jacobsen, S., and Kovalinsky, T. *Educational interpretation of Stanford Binet Intelligence Scale Form LM and the Illinois Test of Psycholinguistic Abilities.* Linden, N. J.: Remediation Associates, 1970.

Field, J. G. Two types of tables for use with Wechsler's Intelligence Scales. *Journal of Clinical Psychology,* 1960, *16,* 3-7.

Finlayson, M. A. J., & Reitan, R. M. Handedness in relation to measures of motor and tactile perceptual functions in normal children. *Perceptual and Motor Skills,* 1976, *43,* 475-481.

Getman, G. N. *How to develop your child's intelligence* (8th ed.). Wayne, Pa.: Research Publications, 1974.

Geschwind, N., & Levitsky, W. Human brain asymmetries in temporal speech region. *Science,* 1968, *161,* 186-187.

Glass, G. F., & Robbins, M. P. A critique of experiments on the role of neurological organization in reading performance. *Reading Research Quarterly,* 1967, *3,* 5-52.

Golden, C. J. *Diagnosis and rehabilitation in clinical neuropsychology.* Springfield, Ill.: Charles C Thomas, 1978.

Golden, C. J., Hammeke, T. A., & Purisch, A. D. Diagnostic validity of a standardized neuropsychological battery derived from Luria's Neuropsychological Tests. *Journal of Consulting and Clinical Psychology,* 1978, *46,* 1258-1265.

Guilford, J. P. *The nature of human intelligence.* New York: McGraw-Hill, 1967.

Gutkin, T. B. Teacher perceptions of consultation services provided by school psychologists. *Professional Psychology,* 1980, *11,* 637–642.

Halstead, W. C. *Brain and intelligence.* Chicago: University of Chicago Press, 1947.

Hammill, D. D., & Larsen, S. C. The effectiveness of psycholinguistic training. *Exceptional Children,* 1974, *41,* 5–14.

Hartlage, L. C. Sex-linked inheritance of spatial ability. *Perceptual and Motor Skills,* 1970, *31,* 610.

Hartlage, L. C. Neuropsychological approaches to predicting outcome of remedial educational strategies for learning disabled children. *Pediatric Psychology,* 1975, *3,* 23. (a)

Hartlage, L. C. *Preventing initial reading failure by prescreening for learning style.* Paper presented at the annual meeting of the Association for Children with Learning Disabilities, New York, 1975. (b)

Hartlage, L. C. *Relationships of neurologic status to exceptional education outcomes.* Paper presented at the annual meeting of the Council for Exceptional Children, 1975. (c)

Hartlage, L. C. *Applying behavioral technology in school settings.* Paper presented at the annual meeting of the National Association of School Psychologists, San Diego, March, 1978.

Hartlage, L. C. *Clinical neuropsychology in the 70's.* Presidential address to the National Academy of Neuropsychology, 1979. (a)

Hartlage, L. C. Management of common clinical problems: Learning disabilities. *School Related Health Care,* 1979, (Ross Laboratories Monograph #9), 29–33. (b)

Hartlage, L. C. *Developmental aspects of brain-behavior relationships.* Invited paper presented at North Atlantic Treaty Organization (NATO) Advanced Study Institute on Neuropsychology and Cognition, Augusta, Ga., 1980.

Hartlage, L. C. Neuropsychological assessment techniques. In C. R. Reynolds & T. B. Gutkin (Eds.), *The handbook of school psychology.* New York: John Wiley, in press.

Hartlage, L. C., & Haak, R. *Reitan-Indiana Battery correlates of academic and developmental variables in learning disabled children.* Paper presented at the annual meeting of the International Neuropsychological Society, San Francisco, 1980.

Hartlage, L. C., & Hartlage, P. L. The application of neuropsychological principles in the diagnosis of learning disabilities. In L. Tarnopol (Ed.), *Brain function and learning disabilities.* Baltimore: University Park Press, 1977.

Hartlage, L. C., & Hartlage, P. L. Clinical consultation to pediatric neurology and developmental pediatrics. *Journal of Clinical Child Psychology,* 1978, *7,* 52–53.

Hartlage, L. C., & Lucas, D. G. Group screening for reading disability in first grade children. *Journal of Learning Disabilities,* 1973, *6,* 48–52. (a)

Hartlage, L. C., & Lucas, D. G. *Pre-reading expectancy screening scales.* Jacksonville, Il.: Psychologists and Educators, 1973. (b)

Hartlage, L. C., & Lucas, D. G. *Mental development evaluation of the pediatric patient.* Springfield, Il.: Charles C Thomas, 1973. (c)

Hartlage, L. C., & Lucas, T. L. Differential correlates of Bender-Gestalt and Beery Visual Motor Integration Test for black and white children. *Perceptual and Motor Skills,* 1976, *43,* 1039-1042.

Hartlage, L. C. Stovall, K. W., & Hartlage, P. L. Age related neuropsychological sequelae of Reye's Syndrome. *Clinical Neuropsychology,* 1980, *2,* 83-85.

Hartlage, P. L., & Hartlage, L. C. Comparison of hyperplexic and dyslexic children. *Neurology,* 1973, *23,* 436-437. (a)

Hartlage, P. L., & Hartlage, L. C. *Dematoglyphic markers in dyslexia.* Paper presented at the annual meeting of the Child Neurology Society, Nashville, 1973. (b)

Heilman, K. M., & Valenstein, E. *Clinical neuropsychology.* New York: Oxford University Press, 1979.

Hevern, V. W. Recent validity studies of the Halstead-Reitan approach to clinical neuropsychological assessment: A critical review. *Clinical Neuropsychology,* 1980, *2,* 49-61.

Hughes, H. E. Norms developed at the University of Chicago for the neuropsychological evaluation of children. *Journal of Pediatric Psychology,* 1976, *1* (3), 11-15.

Jensen, A. R. The nature of intelligence and its relation to learning. *Journal of Research and Development in Education,* 1979, *12,* 79-95.

Karlsson, J. L. *Inheritance of creative intelligence.* Chicago: Nelson-Hall Paperback, 1978.

Kaufman, A. S. *Intelligent testing with the WISC-R.* New York: Wiley Interscience, 1979.

Kaufman, A. S., & Kaufman, N. L. *Clinical evaluation of young children with the McCarthy Scales.* New York: Grune & Stratton, 1977.

Kephart, N. C. *The brain injured child in the classroom.* Chicago: National Society for Crippled Children and Adults, 1963.

Kirk, S., & Kirk, W. *Psycholinguistic learning disabilities: Diagnosis and remediation.* Urbana: University of Illinois Press, 1971.

Knight, J. The nonreading adult student—A question of method. *Orton Society Newsletter,* 1980, 4, 1-4.

Knights, R. M., & Bakker, D. J. (Eds.). *The neuropsychology of learning disorders: Theoretical approaches.* Baltimore: University Park Press, 1976.

Knights, R. M., & Moule, A. D. Normative data on the Motor Steadiness Battery for children. *Perceptual and Motor Skills,* 1968, *26,* 643-650.

Kolb, B., & Whishaw, I. Q. *Fundamentals of human neuropsychology.* San Francisco: W. H. Witt-Freeman, 1980.

Levine, M. D., Brooks, R. & Shonkoff, J. P. *A pediatric approach to learning disorders.* New York: John Wiley & Sons, 1980.

Luria, A. R. *Higher cortical functions in man.* New York: Basic Books, 1966.

Luria, A. R. *Cerebral organization of conscious acts: A frontal lobe function.* Invited address to the XIX International Congress of Psychology, London, 1969.

Luria, A. R. The functional organization of the brain. *Scientific American.* 1970, *222,* 66–78.

Luria, A. R., & Majovski, L. V. Basic approaches used in American and Soviet clinical neuropsychology. *American Psychologist,* 1977, *32,* 959–968.

Matarazzo, J. D., Matarazzo, R. G., Wiens, A. N., Gallo, A. E., & Klonoff, H. Retest reliability of the Halstead Impairment Index in a normal, a schizophrenic, and two samples of organic patients. *Journal of Clinical Psychology,* 1976, *32,* 338–349.

Matarazzo, J. D., Wiens, A. N., Matarazzo, R. G., & Goldstein, S. G. Psychometric and clinical test retest reliability of the Halstead Impairment of healthy, young, normal men. *Journal of Nervous and Mental Diseases,* 1974, *158,* 37–49.

McKeever, W. F., & Hoff, A. L. Spatial ability: Familial sinistrality effects in left-handers. *Midwestern Psychological Reports,* 1980, *28,* 559–562.

Moses, J. A., & Golden, C. J. *The Luria-Nebraska neuropsychological battery: Updated review.* Paper presented at the conference on Neuropsychology and Cognition, North Atlantic Treaty Organization Advanced Study Institute, Augusta, Georgia, 1980.

Myers, P. I., & Hammill, D. D. *Methods for learning disorders* (2nd ed.). New York: John Wiley & Sons, 1976.

Nance, W. E., Allen, G., & Parisi, P. (Eds.). *Twin research.* New York: Alan R. Liss, 1978.

Payne, R. W., & Jones, H. F. Statistics for the investigation of individual cases. *Journal of Clinical Psychology,* 1957, *13,* 115–121.

Pirozzolo, F. J. *The neuropsychology of developmental reading disorders.* New York: Praeger Publishers, 1980.

Pribam, K. H. *Languages of the brain.* Englewood Cliffs, N.J.: Prentice-Hall, 1971.

Reitan, R. M. Certain differential effects of right and left cerebral lesions in human adults. *Journal of Comparative and Physiological Psychology,* 955, *48,* 474–478.

Reitan, R. M. A research program on the psychological effects of brain lesions in human beings. In N. E. Ellis (Ed.), *International review of research in mental retardation.* New York: Academic Press, 1966.

Reitan, R. M., & Davison, L. A. (Eds.). *Clinical neuropsychology: Current status and applications.* New York: Winston, 1974.

Reynolds, C. R. Factor structure of the Peabody Individual Achievement Test at five grade levels between grades one and twelve. *Journal of School Psychology,* 1979, *17,* 270–274. (a)

Reynolds, C. R. Methodological and statistical problems in discerning profile reliability: Comment on Roffe and Bryant. *Psychology in the Schools,* 1979, *16,* 505–507. (b)

Reynolds, C. R. The importance of norms and other traditional psychometric concepts to assessment in clinical neuropsychology. In R. N. Malatesha & L. C. Hartlage (Eds.), *Proceedings of the NATO/ASI International Conference on Neuropsychology and Cognition.* Anphen Aan Den Rijin, Holland: Sijithoff and Noordoff, in press.

Reynolds, C. R., & Gutkin, T. B. Predicting the premorbid intellectual status of children using demographic data. *Clinical Neuropsychology,* 1979, *1,* 868-870.

Reynolds, C. R., & Gutkin, T. B. Statistics related to profile interpretation of the Peabody Individual Achievement Test. *Psychology in the Schools,* 1980, *17,* 163-167.

Sattler, J. M. *Assessment of children's intelligence and special abilities.* Boston: Allyn & Bacon, in press.

Spreen, O., & Gaddes, W. H. Developmental norms for fifteen neuropsychological tests age 6-15. *Cortex,* 1969, *5,* 170-191.

Tarnopol, L., & Tarnopol, M. Introduction to neuropsychology. In L. Tarnopol & M. Tarnopol (Eds.), *Brain function and reading disabilities.* Baltimore: University Park Press, 1977.

Vallett, R. E. *The remediation of learning disabilities: A handbook of psychoeducational resource programs.* Palo Alto, Ca.: Fearon Publishers, 1967.

Wittrock, M. C. Learning and the brain. In M. C. Wittrock (Ed.), *The brain and psychology.* New York: Academic Press, 1980.

Ysseldyke, J. Diagnostic prescriptive teaching: The search for aptitude-treatment interactions. In L. Mann & D. Sabatino (Eds.), *First review of special education.* New York: Grune & Stratton, 1973.

Ysseldyke, J., & Mirkin, P. K. The use of assessment information to plan instructional interventions: A review of research. In C. R. Reynolds & T. B. Gutkin (Eds.), *The handbook of school psychology.* New York: John Wiley, in press.

George W. Hynd

12

Training the School Psychologist in Neuropsychology: Perspectives, Issues, and Models

Since the 1950s, truly remarkable progress has been made in increasing our understanding of brain–behavior relationships in children with learning disorders. The chapters by Rourke and Gates (Chapter 1) and Gaddes (Chapter 2), as well as other chapters in this volume, clearly articulate the present state of knowledge in the area of clinical child neuropsychology as well as the related problems and issues.

The volume of research that has been generated since 1970 alone represents the efforts of a growing number of researchers in the fields of neurology, psychology, and education who see promise in new theoretical approaches to old problems and in the innovative diagnostic procedures and intervention programs for children with suspected neuropsychological disorders. Directed at both researchers and practitioners within these fields, a number of books have recently been published (e.g., Benton & Pearl, 1978; Cruickshank & Hallahan, 1975; Knights & Bakker, 1976) that attempt to present an overview of this progress in child neuropsychology. Other books, which are directed specifically at the psychologist who must work with these children, either take a neuropsychological perspective (e.g., Kaufman, 1979), include specific chapters about the neuropsychology of learning disorders (Hartlage, 1980; Schroder, 1980), or address issues and procedures related to neuropsychological assessment within chapters covering a broad range of topics (e.g., Oakland & Goldwater, 1979). Finally, one need only review various professional journals or convention proceedings to find articles aimed at informing both special educators (e.g., Fletcher & Satz, 1979; Harris, 1979; Pettit &

Helms, 1979; Vellutino, 1979) and psychologists (e.g., Dean, 1979; Hartlage, 1971; Hynd & Obrzut, 1980, in press; Reynolds & Gutkin, 1979; Reynolds, Shellenberger, Paget, & Hartlage, 1979; Rourke, 1976; Sloves, 1978) of new innovations in diagnosis, theory, and remediation.

With this explosion of knowledge, one can well imagine that the student or practicing psychologist who works with learning-disabled children feels inundated with information and uncertain as to how to pursue training or continuing education in neuropsychology. Certainly, there is a rationale for pursuing graduate education in neuropsychology, especially for the school psychologist. Federal legislation has all but required some basic knowledge of neuropsychology as is illustrated by the following definitions of specific learning disability (SLD),

> a disorder in one or more of the basic psychological processes involved in understanding or in using language, spoken or written, which may manifest itself in an imperfect ability to listen, think, speak, read, write, spell or do mathematical calculations. The term includes such conditions as perceptual handicaps, brain injury, minimal brain dysfunction, dyslexia, and developmental aphasia. (Federal Register, 1976, p. 56977)

While the specifics of this definition may change (and probably will based upon its past history), clearly one must be familiar with the basics of brain–behavior relationships in order to determine whether or not a child is learning disabled. This is indeed important when one considers that approximately 7-10 percent of the entire school population in the United States might qualify as learning disabled. Furthermore, there is every reason to suspect that as public schools become responsible for *all* handicapped children from 3 to 21 years of age, there will be a dramatic increase in the need for psychologists who understand the neuropsychological nature of a wide range of handicapping conditions. The arguments in favor of adopting a neuropsychological perspective in the schools seem even more relevant now than when they were first proposed (Gaddes, 1968, 1969, 1975; Hynd & Obrzut, in press; Rourke, 1975, 1976; Sloves, 1978).

Undoubtedly, there are those who will argue that recent court decisions (see Reschley, 1979 for a review) all but mandate a moratorium on all assessment practices due to bias inherent in the procedures used. While there is much favorable in the behavioral approaches that are typically offered as an appropriate alternative for the assessment of learning-disabled children (Tombari & Davis, 1979), it seems that the era of strict "behaviorism" in the schools is past (Hammill, 1980). This is not to discount the value of behavioral approaches in the public schools, as it is clear that there is much merit to such techniques, especially as they pertain to intervention of overt problem behaviors (Horton, 1979, 1981). However, recent advances in neuropsychology and the case study method advocated and outlined by Aaron (see Chapter 9) and Obrzut (1981) allow for appropriately flexible assessment practices, which could very well incorporate behavioral procedures. Measures of adaptive behavior and multifactored pluralistic assessment procedures (Mercer & Lewis, 1978) are also consistent with a comprehensive neuropsychological perspective. What *is* needed is a comprehensive and integrated viewpoint on children with learning disorders so that the advantages of all approaches and knowledge from a variety of fields can be brought to bear in assisting the child to develop his or her abilities to the fullest extent.

It should be pointed out that the identification of this need is not limited to those few researchers or trainers who could have a vested interest in neuropsychology. Surveys of practitioners seem to indicate that school psychologists overwhelmingly perceive their own lack of training and experience in this area. Furthermore, they express a strong desire for the dissemination of such training through extended workshops and continuing education programs offered by training institutes and colleges or universities (Mowder & DeMartino, 1979; Ramage, 1979). Certainly, this interest is not just another passing fad in the field of psychology, as the history of the interaction between education and the medical perspective is indeed long standing and spans many decades (Bannatyne, 1971; Burt, 1937; Chalfant & Schefflin, 1969; Delacato, 1954; Strauss & Lehtinen, 1947; Strauss & Kephart, 1955).

This chapter addresses this need for a comprehensive point of view and is specifically aimed at the graduate student and the school psychologist. As reflected in the title of the chapter and the emphasis throughout this book, the editors believe that it is the school psychologist who is the logical professional to pursue training in this area and subsequently provide services to the schools. It is not our intent to discount or ignore the consulting clinical neuropsychologists. Rather, the school psychologist is fully trained in both educational and psychological matters and, thus, should be most sensitive to the uniqueness of the educational enterprise while incorporating a neuropsychological perspective in the provision of psychological services.

HUMAN NEUROPSYCHOLOGY

Definitions of Clinical Neuropsychology

Attempts at defining any profession are fraught with pitfalls and typically seem incomplete in light of recent advances in our knowledge. This certainly seems to be the case with school psychology, and issues related to the definition of clinical neuropsychology are equally as complex. It is important, however, to accurately define a profession since associated roles and expectations are generated from such definition.

In 1976, Lezak defined clinical neuropsychology as "an applied science concerned with the behavioral expression of brain dysfunction. It evolved in response to practical problems of assessment and rehabilitation of brain-damaged patients" (p. 3). Hécaen and Albert (1978) prefer the broader term "human neuropsychology" and define the profession as "the study of neural mechanisms underlying human behavior. This discipline is based on a systematic analysis of disturbances of behavior following alterations of normal brain activity by disease, damage or experimental modifications" (p. 1). These writers suggest that neuropsychology is at the "intersection" of the neurosciences and the behavioral sciences and can be divided into two areas of specialization: adult neuropsychology and developmental neuropsychology. Others (e.g., Davison, 1974) would argue that there are three areas of specialization within the profession of neuropsychology: clinical neuropsychology, experimental neuropsychology, and behavioral neurology. The specialists in these three fields are perceived as having unique roles and responsibilities.

The Clinical Neuropsychologist's Roles and Responsibilities

While all professionals in the field of neuropsychology contribute greatly to our conceptual understanding of the brain, the specialty of clinical neuropsychology is most relevant to the present discussion. According to Davison (1974), the clinical neuropsychologist has as his or her roots academic psychology, behavioral neurology, and the psychometric-measurement disciplines. While the clinical neuropsychologist may have much in common with the clinical psychologist, they differ in many critical ways. Most importantly, as Lezak (1976) points out, the clinical psychologist is primarily interested in *effecting* behavioral change whereas the clinical neuropsychologist is interested in *assessing* behavioral change. Furthermore, there are a number of other minor but nonetheless important theoretical differences between the approaches used in diagnosing "organicity." The point is that the clinical neuropsychologist has a set of professional responsibilities distinct from the field of clinical psychology.

In discussing the clinical neuropsychologist's roles, Lezak (1976) suggests that three different functions exist: differential diagnosis, assisting in patient care, and conducting research. Under patient care, Meier (1981) would most likely include the design of rehabilitation strategies, consultation with families and other health care providers, and providing some services relative to "consumer" or patient education.

THE ROLE OF ASSESSMENT

Despite the delineation of a number of professional roles, it seems clear that the primary emphasis in clinical neuropsychology (and indeed school psychology) is assessment. What of the tests and evaluation procedures used by the clinical neuropsychologist? Estimates of the number of neuropsychological evaluation instruments vary from less than 100 (Golden, 1978) to over 200 (Lezak, 1976). While the Wechsler Adult Intelligence Scale (WAIS), the Bender Visual-Motor Gestalt Test, and the Halstead-Reitan Neuropsychological Test Battery seem to be the tests most commonly administered (Craig, 1979), the diversity of assessment instruments and the variability in evaluation practices is truly remarkable. Craig (1979) makes the point that the era of using one test to diagnose organicity is over. However, while there is much validity to neuropsychological batteries, they are somewhat limited in their ability to reliably detect impaired psychological processes or to determine the site of impairment and the degree of chronicity. They are reasonably accurate in determining presence or lack of brain impairment (Hevern, 1980; Spreen & Benton, 1965; Wedding & Gudeman, 1980).

Although such batteries as the Halstead-Reitan Neuropsychological Test Battery do seem to be as diagnostically accurate as pneumoencephalograms and arteriograms and even superior to the EEG and skull x-ray (Filskov & Goldstein, 1974; Russell, Neuringer, & Goldstein, 1970), the recent advent of computerized axial tomography (CAT scan—sometimes referred to as the EMI procedure after the corporation that developed the prototype) has remarkably altered the role of assessment in clinical neuropsychology (Wedding & Gudeman, 1980). While there are some drawbacks to using this procedure (e.g., expense), the available data suggest that the diagnostic accuracy of axial tomographic procedures often approximates 100 percent (Dublin, French, & Rennick, 1977; Huckman, Fox & Ramsey, 1977; Wedding & Gudeman, 1980). Although some might feel that this diagnostic procedure will make neuropsychological batteries "obsolete" (Wedding & Gudeman, 1980), a more moderate approach is that the neuropsychological test battery and axial tomographic techniques can complement each other (Bigler, 1980). This appears to be especially true in formulating rehabilitation plans in which the assessment of cognitive skills and deficits is most important. In fact, there is an increasing emphasis on the roles of the clinical neuropsychologist in rehabilitation planning and in the remediation of learning disorders (Bradley, Battin, & Sutter, 1979; Brinkman, 1979; Diller, 1976; Golden, 1976,

1978; Lipowski, 1978). Furthermore, neuropsychological evaluations are obviously needed to provide a data base for research, especially research on innovations in neurosurgical procedures that directly alter cognitive abilities (e.g., Rosenstock, Garner, Jaques, & Majovski, 1979). Consequently, while the future of the clinical neuropsychologist seems assured, important changes in his or her role could well occur.

Education in Neuropsychology

In any profession, especially one that is growing so rapidly, the curriculum of a training program needs to provide not only a solid foundation but also a broad enough coverage of material that modifications in roles and responsibilities can easily be accommodated. Historically, the training of clinical neuropsychologists seems to complement this view as most have been trained as "generalists" within another area of specialty (clinical or perhaps counseling) and have then developed more refined professional competencies postdoctorally (Meier, 1981).

The issue of training in clinical neuropsychology is an important one especially since it has potential implications for training school psychologists in neuropsychology. As will be seen, in clinical neuropsychology, there are no agreed-upon standards for training but, unlike school psychology, there is complete agreement that the doctorate degree is a minimal requirement for entry into the profession.

At present, the formal training of neuropsychologists is considered generally inadequate (Craig, 1979). While there are at least 18 identifiable graduate training programs that offer specialization in neuropsychology (Golden & Tupperman, 1980), there are no agreed upon competency standards for training. Although some progress appears to be forthcoming through the cooperative efforts of the International Neuropsychological Society (INS), the American Psychological Association (APA), and the American Board of Professional Psychology (ABPP), training remains an unsettled issue. For instance, Craig (1979) found that, of those psychologists offering neuropsychological services in public psychiatric hospitals, 28 percent had not received *any* specialized (unspecified) education in neuropsychology. Of those who had received such training, the majority (52 percent) identified Ralph Reitan's workshops as their primary source. In this survey, only one practitioner identified his graduate training as being in neuropsychology.

MODELS FOR TRAINING

Reflecting his own concern about training, Meier (1981) has identified several models for training in neuropsychology:

- Model I: subspeciality for students in an applied psychology program
- Model II: interdepartmental supporting program in neuropsychology and clinical neurosciences
- Model III: integrated scientist/practitioner curriculum for Ph.D.
- Model IV: coordinated graduate curriculum with speciality credentialed Ph.D. and Psy.D. components

While the latter two models seem the most inviting, logical, and appropriate alternatives for training specialists in human neuropsychology, they really do not relate to the model that will be proposed for the school psychologist. Models I and II are probably the most common vehicles for training neuropsychologists today. In particular, Model II has great potential for providing graduate students in school psychology with appropriate experiences in neuropsychology.

Model II entails the incorporation of training in neuropsychology into a traditional applied psychology program. Appropriate coursework, practicum, and internship experiences are imbedded as a subspecialty within the student's major area of studies. As described, this approach uses the credits earned outside the student's major area of studies. The greatest advantage to such an approach is that little or no extra teaching load is placed on the psychology department faculty as the majority of the elective course work would be taken in other departments. Like Model I, Model II's other advantages are that such an approach least disrupts the current organization structure, is cost efficient, and has a history of being reasonably effective. Disadvantages seem obvious: such training might be viewed as a lower-order priority, and the depth of experience that may be gained is limited. Furthermore, an affiliated neuroscience program would be needed. Despite these potential problems, the benefits of such a model may far outweigh the inadequacies for the profession of school psychology. Prior to incorporating this model into the training of school psychologists, the development of school psychology as a profession needs to be reviewed.

THE PROFESSION OF SCHOOL PSYCHOLOGY

It is indeed ironic that the provision of psychological services to school-age children is considered by many to be a relatively recent development. Like the history of clinical neuropsychology, school psychology is a product of early efforts to develop quantitative measures of behavior.

The numerous social, legal, and professional forces that have contributed to the remarkable growth of school psychology since 1950 are only the most obvious events and seem somewhat diminished in importance when viewed from a historical perspective. The unique historical developments of school psychology as a speciality within the field of applied psychology are important to understanding current dilemmas over training and appropriate professional services. These dilemmas have influenced the proposed educational models for providing school psychologists with a neuropsychological perspective, since to be truly valuable, any proposed roles or responsibilities must be theoretically and practically consistent with existing standards for training and practice.

Early Influences

Some have argued that school psychology is unique among the applied professions. The proposed uniqueness of school psychology lies in the fact that it is, in reality, a product of the times and has survived and thrived in response to the needs of other professionals (Bardon, 1976).

First and foremost, school psychology has traditionally served the needs of special educators. Binet's seminal work in devising a scale to differentiate cognitive abilities among children for educational purposes set the stage for involving psychologists in education. The development of classes for delinquent and retarded boys in Providence, Rhode Island in 1896 proved to be a forerunner and model for the incredibly rapid spread of such classes in the United States. That same year Lightner Witmer founded the first psychological clinic at the University of Pennsylvania. Interestingly, at that early time Witmer recognized the potential of his clinic and recommended, "the training of students for a new profession—that of the psychologist expert, who should find his career in connection with the school system, through the examination and treatment of mentally and morally retarded children, or in connection with the practice of medicine" (cited in Brothmarkle, 1931, p. 346).

The rapid growth of special classes for the mentally retarded at the turn of the century had been nothing short of phenomenal. A 1911 U.S. Office of Education report noted that there were over 200 cities that had included such special classes in their accepted public school curriculum.

The extended use of the 1908 Binet-Simon Scale by H. H. Goddard and his students at the Vineland Training School and the 1916 revision and publication of the Stanford-Binet Scale solidified the role of the psychologist as a clinical psychometrician. In 1919, the State of Missouri was the first state to require psychological testing of all special education children as a prerequisite for placement. While this had been a generally accepted practice following the lead of Goddard, Gessell, and Witmer, it was an important development because for the first time schools were mandated to employ psychologists for the specific purpose of clinically assessing school children (Herron, Green, Guild, Smith, & Kantor, 1970).

Other landmarks that contributed to the rapid growth of school psychology included the certification of school psychologists by the State of New York in 1935, the continued enactment of laws governing the identification and education of retarded children, and subsequent increased employment opportunities for psychologists in schools (Gray, 1963). In addition, the group testing movement, the child guidance movement, and the influences of experimental and cognitive psychology all added new dimensions and responsibilities to the role of the school psychologist. (Tindall, 1964, 1969). Between 1915, when Arnold Gessell was first employed as a (school) psychologist by the State of Connecticut to assist in identifying retarded children in rural areas, and the late 1940s, the profession of applied psychology in the school setting became an accepted reality.

The Thayer Conference

By the 1950s, there were increased employment opportunities for psychologists sensitive to the needs of educators and of children with special learning difficulties. This suggested to many the need for a national conference to define the nature of the school psychologist. Sponsored by Division 16 of the American Psychological Association (APA) and financed by a grant from the Public Health Service, a conference was held at the Thayer Hotel in New York. The steering committee was comprised of a number of nationally known psychologists including Dale Harris of the University of Minnesota, Nicholas Hobbs of George Peabody College, and Samuel Kirk of the University of Illinois. The participants of the conference were to define the role of the school psychologist, agree on training levels, and attempt to resolve various professional issues.

Certainly, some landmark progress was made along these lines but the perceived definition of a school psychologist remained relatively unchanged since that of Witmer's time. The report of the conference proposed that the school psychologist is "a psychologist with training and experience in education. He uses his specialized knowledge of assessment, learning and interpersonal relationships to assist school personnel in enriching the experience and growth of children, and to recognize and deal with exceptional children" (Cutts, 1955, p. 177).

Importantly, some progress was made in defining appropriate professional roles in that the conference members decided that the school psychologist was to serve in an "advisory capacity" to school personnel. Within this conceptualization, he or she might perform a number of functions including (1) measuring intelligence and social and emotional development; (2) differentially diagnosing children with exceptionalities and assisting in the planning of remedial services; (3) assisting in the development of curriculum methods to facilitate and encourage learning; (4) conducting appropriate research, especially as it related to children's learning problems; and (5) performing other services as needed by school personnel (Herron et al, 1970).

Finally, and perhaps most critical to the future of school psychology as a profession, the conference recommended two levels of training as vital to the provision of psychological services in the schools.

Two levels of training are recommended. The position of *school psychologist* involves such broad comprehensive preparation at a high level that these responsibilities can only be met with doctoral training or equivalent. This training should consist of four years of graduate study, one of which should be a year of internship. The position of *psychological examiner* is considered essential. The training for this position should be a two-year graduate program of which one-half year should be an internship. Such training should equip the examiner to perform many psychological services. (cited by Herron et al, 1970, p. 5)

As will be seen in the following sections, the recommendation that two levels of academic preparation were appropriate for providing school psychology services probably did more to shape the current state of affairs in school psychology than any other factor.

Developing a Professional Identify

By 1960, there had been a 300 percent growth in the membership of APA's Division 16 (School Psychology), and only four states did not have school psychologists employed at some level within the public schools (Magary & Meacham, 1963). In fact, by 1960, 22 states and the District of Columbia certified school psychologists (Hodges, 1960). This rapid increase in the number of school psychologists indicated a need for journals germane to the practice of psychology in an educational environment. In 1963, the Ohio State Department of Education sponsored the development of the *Journal of School Psychology,* which was followed by the first issue of *Psychology in the Schools* the next year (Reger, 1965).

Generally, the 1960s might be viewed as a period of growth to the point where a number of practicing school psychologists demanded the establishment of a formal professional organization. A number of factors having to do with the perceived role and appropriate preparation of the school psychologist led to the organization of a separate association, one free from the jurisdiction of the American Psychological Association. The role of the school psychologist had been a matter of disagreement since the term "school psychologist" first appeared in the literature in the early 1920s (Hutt, 1923). The identification with clinical psychology was ever popular (e.g., Cornell, 1942; Symonds, 1942) and many believed that the term "school" simply described the employment setting of the clinical psychologist (Lantz, 1960). Others argued just as cogently that the school psychologist was in reality a mental health specialist (Bardon, 1963), a child growth and developmental specialist (McIntire, 1959), a child guidance specialist, or a pupil personnel specialist (Johnson, Steffire, & Edelfelt, 1961). While arguments over professional roles and appropriate employment settings are certainly not unusual, and similar discussions may be found in the human neuropsychology literature (Davison, 1974; Meier, 1974, 1981), they are important to any profession attempting to establish itself as unique and valuable in its contribution to society.

In many respects, school psychology had reached a watershed in terms of perceived roles and professional identity. The testing movement as well as the child guidance movement had had such a direct affect on school psychology that legitimate specialities were now being discussed openly and often heatedly. Controversies over levels of entry to the profession added fuel to the fire, which still consumes enormous energies.

In response to APA's exclusion of subdoctoral professionals, its perceived "academic" orientation that was seen as irrelevant to the practicing school psychologist, and the APA's conservative "posture" (Farling & Anger, 1979), the National Association of School Psychologists (NASP) was founded on March 15, 1969. Approximately 400 school psychologists from 24 states met at a 2-day planning conference in St. Louis to outline the development of this subdoctoral practitioner-oriented organization. The establishment of this national association firmly entrenched school psychologists in the field as the providers of subdoctoral services to school children and undoubtedly served to reinforce the skeptics who wondered about the true nature of the school psychologist.

Current State of Affairs

The controversy over training continues unabated and needs to be addressed, especially since it relates to the criteria that will be proposed in a later section dealing with training school psychologists in neuropsychology.

The dichotomy in training suggested at the Thayer Conference still remains as a central issue. Both APA and NASP are adamant as to what they perceive as appropriate standards for graduate training in school psychology. Each organization's standards are articulated below.

Professional school psychologists have a doctoral degree from an organized, sequential school psychology program in a regionally accredited university or professional school. The program of study shall be provided in a department of psychology in a university or college, in an appropriate department of school of education or other similar administrative organization or in unit of a professional school. School psychology programs that are accredited by the American Psychological Association are recognized as meeting the definitions of a school psychology program.*

Sixth-year programs shall consist of a minimum of three years of full-time academic study or the equivalent beyond the baccalaureate, including at least 60 graduate semester hours or the equivalent, one year's supervised experience, and shall culminate in institutional documentation. *Rationale:* Sixth-year programs are the entry level of planned systematic study in the discipline. A minimum of three years and 60 semester hours are needed to assure the coverage of necessary theoretical and applied issues, the mastery of technical professional skills, the understanding of alternative professional roles and professional responsibilities, and the acquisition of sufficient professionally supervised experience in order to satisfy minimum requirements for credentialing as a school psychologist.†

Clearly, there is considerable disagreement between these two organizations. Both, in reality, recognize that doctoral and subdoctoral training is both necessary and desired. The central issue is what constitutes an appropriate *entry* level standard for the provider of psychological services. In many respects, the reason for this disparity is related to the composition of state certification and licensure boards. State departments of education typically certify school psychologists at the specialist or 60-semester-hour level (Brown, Sewell, & Lindstrom, 1977). In fact, at the time this chapter was written (1980), only a few states required a doctoral degree for certification. Obviously, the precedent set early in the development of the profession of school psychology is difficult to change. The point to understand, however, is that school psychologists are usually certified by educators. Clinical psychologists or other applied psychologists are generally licensed by psychological examining boards which require the doctorate at a minimum for entry to the examination of credentials. Clearly, the public (as viewed through the

*From *Standards for Providers of School Psychological Services* by the American Psychological Association. Working draft #8, June, 1978. Copyright 1978 by the American Psychological Association. Reprinted by permission.

†From *Standards for Training Programs in School Psychology* by the National Association of School Psychologists. Washington, D.C., February, 1978, pp. 11–12. With permission.

eyes of state departments of education) has fewer expectations about perceived appropriate training for psychologists than do state medical or psychological examining boards. Needless to say, issues related to the existence of a national registry for mental health care providers and association with the medical establishment certainly have influenced existing standards for applied psychologists in the private sector.

Sincere attempts have been made to reconcile these differences, and generally they relate to the recommendations of the 1963 Vail Conference. The Vail Conference report recommended that the doctorate of psychology (Psy.D.) be awarded through professional schools of psychology as the appropriate degree for applied professional psychologists. Bardon (1976) suggests that this model could foster a "multipurposed professional psychologist" who could easily fit into one setting or another. The scope of training would be broad, encompassing many aspects of present school, clinical, and counseling programs. Upon graduation, the psychologist could easily adapt to the demands of most applied settings. The benefits of such a program are obvious. The Psy.D. could be viewed as a compromise between the Ph.D. and specialist degree requirements, would certainly satisfy APA's standards, and would still be oriented toward the practitioner. Furthermore, as Bardon (1976) points out, the broad training might provide a basis for a lessening of intraprofessional rivalry and competition.

Some compromise is necessary. APA has approximately 50,000 members and is growing by several thousand each year (Bardon, 1979). NASP has about 6,000 members (NASP, 1980) and continues to attract new members. While NASP has been accepted by the National Council for Accreditation of Teacher Education (NCATE) as an associate member and has developed appropriate training standards for school psychologists, the reality is that doctoral training is increasing (Ramage, 1979) and the issue of doctoral training in school psychology cannot be ignored or wished away.

All of these developments serve to complicate the lives of those responsible for training school psychologists. Many programs that offer both doctoral and subdoctoral training in school psychology now need to apply to NCATE-NASP for accreditation of their certification subdoctoral program and to APA for approval of doctoral training. These issues and problems are complex and are reviewed in detail elsewhere (e.g., Bardon, 1979; Brown, 1979 a, b; Brown & Lindstrom, 1978; Hyman, 1979). They are important and relevant to any discussion of training in school psychology especially when proposing new specialties. Needless to say, the issues briefly discussed in this section are reflected in the curricula of school psychology programs. Any proposal for changing or modifying existing programs needs to take into account the present structure typically found in training.

EFFECTS OF CERTIFICATION AND ACCREDITATION
STANDARDS ON TRAINING

The tremendous growth in school psychology since the turn of the twentieth century has resulted in the development of numerous professional programs in school psychology throughout the United States and Canada. Many studies have reported the results of surveys of school psychology programs, which now number over 200 (Bardon, Constanza, & Walker, 1971; Bardon & Wenger, 1974; Brown & Lindstrom, 1977; French, Smith, & Cardon, 1968; Goh, 1977; Hynd, Quackenbush, & Obrzut, 1980; Smith, 1964).

The increase in training programs reflects directly the number of students in training. According to Brown (1979a), well over 7000 graduate students are currently enrolled in school psychology programs throughout the United States. This includes approximately 1700 each in master's or doctoral programs and over 4000 students in sixth-year/certification programs. Training school psychologists is indeed a thriving business, and the fact that many school districts are not able to fill available positions suggests a continued need for such programs.

While there seems to be considerable variability in what is perceived as an appropriate training model (Brown, 1979a) as well as the appropriate role of school psychologists (Gilmore, 1974), in reality most school psychology programs are bound by state certification requirements that, more than any other factor, determine the curricula. Surveys of state certification agencies (Brown et al, 1977) indicate that, most typically, advanced course work is required in the broad areas of (1) consultation and intervention; (2) educational foundations; (3) psychological foundations; (4) special education; (5) tests and measurements; and (6) statistics and research methodology. Not surprisingly, Goh (1977) found in surveying graduate training programs that the various categories of certification requirements were well reflected in most school psychology programs.

The vast majority of states still employ course-based certification standards, and a question might be raised as to how these courses relate to doctoral training in school psychology. In analyzing the course requirements of doctoral programs, Goh (1977) found that the only important differences between the preparation of the sixth-year student and the doctoral student were in consultation and quantitative methods. Since the doctoral programs require more graduate hours, they include more electives as well as areas of emphasis beyond those required for state certification as a provider of school psychology services. Goh (1977) makes the point that the sixth-year/certification-level school psychologist still functions in the area of assessment while the doctoral-level school psychologist seems to act as a trained organizational consultant in the school.

The NASP Standards

As previously outlined, NASP and APA differ considerably on what constitutes an appropriate entry level for the provision of psychological services in the schools. The following discussion will focus on the NASP standards, however, since, no matter what level of training he or she has had, the school psychologist must still meet the minimum requirements for state certification. The NASP standards are most relevant in this regard since its association with an education accreditation body (NCATE) coincides with the philosophy of most state departments of education. This should not be interpreted as a preference by the author but merely a realistic reflection of the current state of affairs. Certainly the APA standards are appropriate in designing doctoral programs in school psychology and are especially relevant should the program's focus be to produce psychologists who will practice in the private sector.

The training standards developed by NASP in 1978 require 60 graduate semester hours plus a 1-year internship as the minimum for program accreditation by NCATE-NASP. The standards for the training of the subdoctoral school psychologist require objectives and/or competency standards for the following core content areas:

1. Psychological foundations. Human learning; child and adolescent development (normal and abnormal); human exceptionality and cultural diversity
2. Educational foundations. Organization and operations of the schools; instructional and remedial techniques; special education
3. Psychoeducational methods. *Evaluation:* psychoeducational assessment; research design and statistics; *Intervention:* consultation; behavior modification; counseling; organizational and administration of pupil services
4. Professional school psychology. Professional issues; standards and ethics in school psychology

For a doctorate in school psychology, the NCATE-NASP standards require a minimum of 90 graduate semester hours in these broad curriculum areas. The internship requirement for both levels of preparation is 1000 clock hours of experience of which at least half must be in a public school (National Association of School Psychologists, 1978b).

Observations and Proposals

An analysis of current issues suggests that the following statements regarding curricula in school psychology can be made with some assurance of accuracy.

1. Most state department of education certification divisions are not likely to adopt new standards for certification in the foreseeable future. Consequently, the curricula of most school psychology programs will probably remain essentially unchanged with respect to sixth-year/certification requirements.
2. If change is to take place, it will be at the doctoral level, and present programs that typically are merely an extension of the sixth-year/certification program will need to be considerably modified to best reflect APA standards for doctoral training in school psychology. This is especially important if doctoral-level school psychologists wish to maintain their identity as applied psychologists trained at a similar level of expertise as clinical or counseling psychologists.
3. With an increasing emphasis on the service/practitioner model (Brown, 1979), even at the doctoral level, the proponents (e.g., Bardon, 1976; Hyman, 1979) of practitioner-oriented doctoral programs are gaining support. It might be reasonably proposed that there will be an increase in the offerings of the Psy.D. or Ed.D. in school psychology. Considerable curriculum changes would be needed to accommodate this shift in emphasis.
4. As school psychology attempts to adjust to recent developments (e.g., court decisions and federal legislation), there will be an increasing need for specialization in the training of school psychologists, especially at the doctoral level. Such specialization could be in vocational assessment, preschool services, organizational research and evaluation, consultation, and neuropsychology.
5. As Meier (1981) has suggested relative to the training of neuropsychologists, there will be a place for subdoctoral support professionals. Consequently, it is proposed that advanced course work in these areas be made available to both subdoctoral as well as doctoral students, as each could provide valuable and needed services respective to their levels of academic preparation.

Germane to these statements are the projected roles for school psychologists educated in the area of neuropsychology. These roles need to be addressed in making recommendations regarding required course work to ensure minimum competencies in the provision of services.

PROPOSED NEUROPSYCHOLOGICAL ROLES AND TRAINING FOR THE SCHOOL PSYCHOLOGIST

It is at this juncture that it should be stated firmly that the typical role envisioned for the school psychologist is *not* to diagnose the site of brain impairment through the use of neuropsychological assessment techniques. First, school psychologists do not achieve the level of expertise currently proposed in the training of clinical neuropsychologists (Meier, 1981). Second, the use of computerized procedures to locate functional impairments has altered the significance of neuropsychological assessment. Third, school psychologists are exactly what their title implies — psychologists in the school environment; consequently, their services should be directed toward the remediation of learning deficits by providing direct or indirect services.

What is envisioned is training school psychologists to a sufficient degree of expertise in neuropsychology so that they can bring a *perspective* to the problems and challenges of working in a school setting. This is entirely consistent with the present wide-ranging services provided by the school psychologist.

There is one very important assumption that underlies the following discussion. For any school psychology program offering a subspeciality in neuropsychology, student access to a neuroscience training facility is absolutely necessary. While some appropriate course work can be completed within an academic psychology department, course work and field experiences must be provided in settings not typically used in training school psychologists. Consequently, it is assumed that appropriate facilities are available for training and that cooperative arrangements have been made between the neuroscience programs and the school psychology program. With this consideration in mind, the following roles are elaborated and curriculum additions proposed.

The Sixth-Year/Certification-Level School Psychologist

Due to the limited number of electives and training experiences that can be realistically included in the typically rigid sixth-year/certification-level school psychology program, an obviously restricted role is foreseen for this school psychologist. Consistent with the usual assessment-oriented training program as well as the role suggested at the Thayer Conference and by the APA for subdoctoral psychologists, the following roles and responsibilities are proposed as functions of a neuropsychological technician under the supervision of an appropriately trained doctoral level school psychologist:

1. Administers the neuropsychological test battery to children with suspected neuropsychological disorders
2. Collects behavioral data on children requiring medication so that appropriate conclusions may be reached by medical personnel
3. Assists in the collection of research data
4. Collects ongoing data as to effectiveness of neuropsychologically based intervention programs

The training of specialists at this level must take into account current practices. For instance, Hynd et al (1980) have documented the general lack of training in physiological psychology at the sixth-year/certification level. Yet such preparation is absolutely necessary. Based on such an analysis, the following training experiences are deemed minimally appropriate as they relate to NASP's standards for training (1978a). Where courses are not believed necessary, the content area has been omitted.

1. Psychological foundations: cognitive psychology; physiological psychology; and psychopharmacology
2. Psychoeducational methods: neuropsychological assessment and vocational assessment
3. Practicum and internship experiences. A separate practicum experience in neuropsychological assessment with a consulting neuropsychologist should be required. Some (perhaps 200 hours) of the school psychology internship should be spent in a setting where experiences could be gained with neurologically or neuropsychologically handicapped children. The emphasis should be on those aspects of behavioral and neuropsychological assessment and evaluation of behavior that are relevant to the provision of intervention services.

Doctoral-Level School Psychologist

Consistent with the notion of the doctoral-level school psychologist serving as an organizational consultant (Goh, 1977) and with the training model of the generalist in neuropsychology (Meier, 1981), the doctoral-level school psychologist will need to devote a major portion of his or her program to course work in the neurosciences and behavioral sciences. Projected roles might include the following:

1. Interprets the results of the neuropsychological assessment and develops strategies of intervention
2. Presents recommendations for remediation strategies at case staffings
3. Consults with curriculum specialists in designing curriculum objectives and programs that reflect normal development from a neuropsychological perspective

4. Acts as an organizational liaison with the medical community in the provision of health care services to children enrolled in the public schools
5. Consults with and supervises other psychologists in the school system in the area of neuropsychological services
6. Conducts in-service workshops for educational and lay groups in the area of the neuropsychology of learning and development
7. Conducts basic and applied research as needed

Training school psychologists at the doctoral level to provide such services in the school community could very well extend currently organized doctoral programs by as much as a year to a year and a half. To develop the level of skill proposed here even as a generalist, a 5-year doctoral program is probably minimal. This includes education at the master's level. The additional course work and experiences listed below may be most appropriate for psychologists pursuing a practitioners program (Psy.D. or Ed.D.). Certainly, a school psychologist employed to provide primarily research services would need considerably more course work in the neurosciences as well as quantitative research methodology. However, the need for such an individual seems very limited at present and hence is not fully elaborated.

1. Psychological (and neuroscience) foundations: physiological psychology; advanced physiological psychology; psychopharmacology; functional neuroanatomy; neuropathology; and cognitive psychology
2. Psychoeducational methods: neuropsychological assessment; rehabilitation planning and vocational assessment; and behavior therapy
3. Seminar, practicum, and internship experiences: Similar to the specialist-level school psychologist, a separate practicum experience is believed necessary, and following such an experience, a seminar on the provision of health care services is appropriate. In addition to the 1000 hours of internship (1200 according to APA Standards) in the public school setting, an additional 500 hours should be required in a health care facility where children are served. In this fashion, the school psychologist can develop minimal competencies in working with health care providers and will feel comfortable in the role as a liaison once he or she is employed in a school setting.

The Practicing School Psychologist

The school psychologist who is currently employed and who seeks to acquire knowledge and some expertise as a generalist in neuropsychology should first complete the minimum training requirements noted for the sixth-year-level school psychologist. Once this minimum level of sophistication is gained, two choices seem apparent. First, and least desirable, continuing education could be sought through the many workshops and seminars offered throughout the country. While the need for continuing education certainly exists for school psychologists (Hynd & Schakel, in press), a sequential program of supervised experiences seems more desirable. Thus, the second choice, that of pursuing advanced training in a program offering such specialized training, is recommended. As of 1980, the vast majority of directors of school psychology training programs indicated a desire to see their students receive education in this area (Hynd et al, 1980). Furthermore, several doctoral programs indicated that such specialization was available to their students. Certainly, it seems as though appropriate avenues for training are readily accessible to the interested and motivated school psychologist.

CONCLUSIONS

Bardon (1976) has accused school psychology of being an "intermediate" specialty, in that school psychologists have tended to "put into practice whatever in psychology might be of benefit in the school," and has consequently "tended to adopt whatever is in vogue at the time and quickly press it into service without much quality control" (p. 786). This indeed seems to be an accurate statement insofar as school psychology is concerned.

While the interest in neuropsychology and its relevance to the practice of school psychology never seemed greater, there is certainly a potential danger if this interest leads to an uncritical and inappropriate application in the school environment. Considering legal and professional issues that have recently affected the profession of school psychology, it would seem that caution should be the watchword in the adoption of a neuropsychological perspective in education.

As outlined elsewhere (Hynd & Obrzut, in press), there is no urgent need to develop new programs offering such a specialty. In a moderately large school district of 30,000 pupils, there should be a need only for one doctoral- and one sixth-year/certification-level school psychologist, each trained in neuropsychology. It is necessary that programs that have established relationships with neuroscience programs and health care facilities organize and formalize their efforts in training school psychologists in this subspeciality.

The chapters in this book have outlined and documented an exciting and dynamic area of endeavor. Despite the enormously important developments in conceptualizing the brain and its functional organization in children, the issues and problems in the application of our knowledge are incredibly complex and demand careful study. Certainly, as our ability to successfully apply this knowledge increases, so will the satisfaction we receive in assisting children to reach the fullest extent of their potential.

REFERENCES

American Psychological Association. *Standards for providers of school psychological services.* Working draft #8, June, 1978.

Bannatyne, A. *Language, reading, and learning disabilities: Psychology, neurology, diagnosis and remediation.* Springfield, Il.: Charles C Thomas, 1971.

Bardon, J. I. Mental health education: A framework for psychological services in the schools. *Journal of School Psychology,* 1963, *1,* 20–27.

Bardon, J. I. The state of the art (and science) of school psychology. *American Psychologist,* 1976, *31,* 785–791.

Bardon, J. I. Debate: Will the real school psychologist please stand up? Part I: How best to establish the identity of professional school psychology. *School Psychology Digest,* 1979, *8,* 162–167.

Bardon, J. I., Costanza, L. J., & Walker, N. W. Institutions offering graduate training in school psychology, 1970–71. *Journal of School Psychology,* 1971, *9,* 252–260.

Bardon, J. I., & Wenger, R. P. Institutions offering graduate training in school psychology, 1973–1974. *Journal of School Psychology,* 1974, *1,* 70–83.

Benton, A. L., & Pearl, P. *Dyslexia: An appraisal of current knowledge.* New York: Oxford University Press, 1978.

Bigler, E. D. Neuropsychological assessment and brain scan results: A case study approach. *Clinical Neuropsychology,* 1980, *2,* 13–24.

Bradley, P. E., Battin, R. R., & Sutter, E. G. Effects of individual diagnosis and remediation for the treatment of learning disorders. *Clinical Neuropsychology,* 1979, *1,* 25–32.

Brinkman, S. D. Rehabilitation of the neurologically impaired patient: The contribution of the neuropsychologist. *Clinical Neuropsychology,* 1979, *1,* 39–47.

Brothmarkle, R. A. (Ed.). *Clinical psychology: Studies in honor of Lightner Witmer to commemorate the thirty-fifth anniversary of the founding of the first psychological clinic.* Philadelphia: University of Pennsylvania Press, 1931.

Brown, D. T. Issues in accreditation, certification and licensure. In G. D. Phye & D. J. Reschly (Eds.), *School psychology: Perspectives and issues.* New York: Academic Press, 1979. (a)

Brown, D. T. Debate: Will the real school psychologist please stand up! Part 2: The drive for independence. *School Psychology Digest,* 1979, *8,* 168–173. (b)

Brown, D. T., & Lindstrom, J. D. The training of school psychologists in the United States: An overview. *Psychology in the Schools,* 1978, *15,* 37–45.

Brown, D. T., Sewall, T. J., & Lindstrom, J. P. *The handbook of certification/ licensure requirements for school psychologists* (2nd ed.). Washington, D.C.: National Association of School Psychologists, 1977.

Burt, C. *The backward child.* London: University of London Press, 1937.

Chalfant, J. C., & Scheffelin, M. A. *Central processing dysfunction in children: A review of research.* Bethesda, Md.: U.S. Department of Health, Education and Welfare, 1969.

Cornell, E. L. The psychologist in a school setting. *Journal of Consulting Psychology*, 1942, *6*, 185–195.

Craig, D. L. Neuropsychological assessment in public psychiatric hospitals: The current state of the practice. *Clinical Neuropsychology*, 1979, *1*, 1–7.

Cruickshank, W. M., & Hallahan, D. P. *Perceptual and learning disabilities in children. Vol. I: Psychoeducational practices; Vol. II: Research and theory.* Syracuse: Syracuse University Press, 1975.

Cutts, N. E. *School psychology at mid-century.* Washington, D.C.: American Psychological Association, 1955.

Davison, L. A. Introduction. In R. M. Reitan & L. A. Davison (Eds.), *Clinical neuropsychology: Current status and applications.* New York: John Wiley & Sons, 1974.

Dean, R. S. Cerebral laterality and verbal performance discrepancies in intelligence. *Journal of School Psychology*, 1979, *17*, 145–150.

Delacato, C. H. *The treatment and prevention of reading problems.* Springfield, Il.: Charles C Thomas, 1954.

Diller, L. A mode for cognitive retraining in rehabilitation. *Clinical Neuropsychologist*, 1976, *29*, 13–16.

Dublin, A. B., French, B. N., & Rennick, J. M. Computerized tomography in head trauma. *Radiology*, 1977, *122*, 365–369.

Farling, W. H., & Agner, J. History of the National Association of School Psychologists: The first decade. *School Psychology Digest*, 1979, *8*, 140–152.

Federal Register. *Education of handicapped children and incentive grants program: Assistance to states.* December, 1976.

Filskov, S. B., & Goldstein, S. G. Diagnostic validity of the Halstead-Reitan Neuropsychological Battery. *Journal of Consulting and Clinical Psychology*, 1974, *42*, 382–388.

Fletcher, J. M., & Satz, P. Unitary deficit hypothesis of reading disabilities: Has Vellutino led us astray? *Journal of Learning Disabilities*, 1979, *12*, 155–159.

French, J. L., Smith, D. C., & Cardon, B. W. Institutions offering graduate training and financial assistance in school psychology. *Journal of School Psychology*, 1968, *6*, 261–267.

Gaddes, W. H. A neuropsychological approach to learning disorders. *Journal of Learning Disabilities, 1968, 1*, 523–534.

Gaddes, W. H. Can educational psychology be neurologized? *Canadian Journal of Behavioral Sciences*, 1969, *1*, 38–49.

Gaddes, W. H. Neurological implications for learning. In W. M. Cruickshank & D. P. Hallahan (Eds.), *Perceptual and learning disabilities in children; Part I: Psychoeducational practices.* Syracuse: Syracuse University Press, 1975.

Gilmore, G. F. Models for school psychology: Dimensions, barriers, and implications. *Journal of School Psychology*, 1974, *12*, 95–101.

Goh, D. S. Graduate training in school psychology. *Journal of School Psychology,* 1977, *15,* 207–218.

Golden, C. J. The role of the psychologist in the training of the neurologically impaired. *Professional Psychology,* 1976, *7,* 579–584.

Golden, C. J. *Diagnosis and rehabilitation in clinical neuropsychology.* Springfield, Il.: Charles C Thomas, 1978.

Golden, C. J., & Tupperman, S. K. Graduate training in clinical neuropsychology. *Professional Psychology,* 1980, *11,* 55–63.

Gray, S. W. *The psychologist in the schools.* New York: Holt, Rinehart, & Winston, 1963.

Hammill, D. D. The field of learning disabilities: A futuristic perspective. *Learning Disabilities Quarterly,* 1980, *3,* 2–9.

Harris, A. J. Lateral dominance and reading ability. *Journal of Learning Disabilities,* 1979, *12,* 337–343.

Hartlage, L. C. A look at models for training school psychologists. *Psychology in the Schools,* 1971, *8,* 304–306.

Hartlage, L. C. Neuropsychological assessment techniques for the school psychologist. In C. R. Reynolds & T. B. Gutkin (Eds.), *A handbook for the practice of school psychology.* New York: John Wiley & Sons, 1980.

Hécaen, H., & Albert, M. L. *Human neuropsychology.* New York: John Wiley & Sons, 1978.

Herron, W. G., Green, M., Guild, M., Smith, A., & Kantor, R. E. *Contemporary school psychology.* Scranton: Intext Educational Publishers, 1970.

Hevern, V. W. Recent validity studies of the Halstead-Reitan approach to clinical neuropsychological assessment: A critical review. *Clinical Neuropsychology,* 1980, *2,* 49–61.

Hodges, W. State certification of school psychologists. *American Psychologist,* 1960, *6,* 346–349.

Horton, Jr., A. M. Behavioral neuropsychology: Rationale and research. *Clinical Neuropsychology,* 1979, *1,* 20–24.

Horton, A. M., Jr. Behavioral neuropsychology in the schools. *School Psychology Review,* 1981.

Huckman, M. S., Fox, J. H., & Ramsey, R. G. Computerized tomography in the diagnosis of degenerative diseases of the brain. *Seminars in Roentgenology,* 1977, *12,* 63–75.

Hutt, R. B. W. The school psychologist. *Psychological Clinic,* 1923, *15,* 48–51.

Hyman, I. A. Debate: Will the real school psychologist please stand up? Part 3: A struggle for jurisdictional imperialism. *School Psychology Review,* 1979, *8,* 174–180.

Hynd, G. W., & Obrzut, J. E. *Neuropsychological assessment and consultation in the public schools.* Paper presented at the annual convention of the National Association of School Psychologists, Washington, D.C., April, 1980.

Hynd, G. W., & Obrzut, J. E. School neuropsychology. *Journal of School Psychology,* in press.

Hynd, G. W., Quackenbush, R., & Obrzut, J. E. Training school psychologists in neuropsychological assessment: Current practices and trends. *Journal of School Psychology,* 1980, *18,* 148–153.

Hynd, G. W., & Schakel, J. A. Continuing professional education and school psychology: A review of state requirements. *Psychology in the Schools,* in press.

Johnson, W. F., Steffire, B., & Edelfelt, R. A. *Pupil personnel and guidance services.* New York: McGraw-Hill, 1961.

Kaufman, A. S. *Intelligent testing with the WISC-R.* New York: Wiley-Interscience, 1979.

Knights, R. M., & Bakker, D. J. *The neuropsychology of learning disorders.* Baltimore: University Park Press, 1976.

Lantz, B. The school psychologist in the deprived neighborhood. In M. G. Gottsegen & G. B. Gottsegen (Eds.), *Professional school psychologist.* New York: Grune & Stratton, 1960.

Lezak, M. D. *Neuropsychological assessment.* New York: Oxford University Press, 1976.

Lipowski, Z. J. Organic brain syndromes: A reformulation. *Comprehensive Psychiatry,* 1978, *19,* 309–322.

Magary, J. F., & Meacham, M. L. The growth of school psychology in the last decade. *Journal of School Psychology,* 1963, *1,* 5–13.

McIntire, H. C. *The school psychologist in Ohio.* Columbus, Oh.: Superintendent of Public Instruction, 1959.

Meier, M. J. Some challenges for clinical neuropsychology. In R. M. Reitan & L. A. Davison (Eds.), *Clinical neuropsychology: Current status and application.* New York: John Wiley & Sons, 1974.

Meier, M. J. Education for competency assurance in human neuropsychology: Antecedents, models and directions. In S. B. Filskov & T. S. Boll (Eds.), *Handbook of clinical neuropsychology.* New York: John Wiley & Sons, 1981.

Mercer, J., & Lewis, J. *Technical manual: SOMPA: System of multicultural assessment.* New York: The Psychological Corporation, 1978.

Mowder, B. A., & DeMartino, R. A. Continuing education needs in school psychology. *Professional Psychology,* 1979, *10,* 827–833.

National Association of School Psychologists. *Standards for training programs in school psychology,* Washington, D. C., February, 1978. (a)

National Association of School Psychologists. *Standards for field placement programs in school psychology.* Washington, D. C., February, 1978. (b)

National Association of School Psychologists. *Membership directory.* Washington, D.C., 1980.

Oakland, T., & Goldwater, D. L. Assessment and interventions for mildly retarded and learning disabled children. In G. D. Phye & D. J. Reschly (Eds.), *School psychology: Perspectives and issues.* New York: Academic Press, 1979.

Obrzut, J. E. Neuropsychological assessment in the schools. *School Psychology Review,* in press.

Pettit, J. M., & Helms, S. B. Hemispheric dominance in language disorders. *Journal of Learning Disabilities,* 1979, *12,* 71–76.

Ramage, J. C. National survey of school psychologists: Update. *School Psychology Digest,* 1979, *8,* 153–161.

Reger, R. *School psychology.* Springfield, Il.: Charles C Thomas, 1965.

Reschly, D. J. Nonbiased assessment. In G. P. Phye & D. J. Reschly (Eds.), *School psychology: Perspectives and issues.* New York: Academic Press, 1979.

Reynolds, C. R., & Gutkin, J. B. Predicting premorbid intellectual status of children using demographic data. *Clinical Neuropsychology,* 1979, *1,* 36–38.

Reynolds, C. R., Shellenberger, S., Paget, K., & Hartlage, L. C. *School psychology and primary health care: The many roles we play.* Paper presented at the annual convention of the National Association of School Psychology, San Diego, March, 1979.

Rosenstock, J., Garner, J. T., Jaques, S., & Majovski, L. V. Improvement in cognitive functions by increased blood flow to the brain. *Clinical Neuropsychology,* 1979, *2,* 25–27.

Rourke, B. P. Brain-behavior relationships in children with learning disabilities: A research program. *American Psychologist,* 1975, *30,* 911–920.

Rourke, B. P. Issues in the assessment of children with learning disabilities. *Canadian Psychological Review,* 1976, *17,* 89–102.

Russell, E. W., Neuringer, G., & Goldstein, G. *Assessment of brain damage: A neuropsychological key approach.* New York: Wiley, 1970.

Schroeder, C. An overview of common medical problems encountered in the schools. In C. R. Reynolds & T. B. Gutkin (Eds.), *A handbook for the practice of school psychology.* New York: John Wiley & Sons, 1980.

Sloves, R. *Neuropsychological assessment and individual perscription writing for brain damaged children.* Paper presented at the annual convention of the National Association of School Psychologists, New York, March, 1978.

Smith, D. C. Institutions offering graduate training in school psychology. *Journal of School Psychology,* 1964–1965, *3,* 58–66.

Spreen, O., & Benton, A. L. Comparative studies of some psychological tests for cerebral damage. *Journal of Nervous and Mental Disease,* 1965, *140,* 323–333.

Strauss, A. A., & Kephart, N. *Psychopathology and education of the brain injured child. Vol. II: Progress in theory and clinic.* New York: Grune & Stratton, 1955.

Strauss, A. A., & Lehtinen, L. E. *Psychopathology and education of the brain injured child.* (Vol. I). New York: Grune & Stratton, 1947.

Symonds, P. M. The school psychologist – 1942. *Journal of Consulting Psychology,* 1942, *6,* 173–176.

Tindall, R. H. Trends in the development of psychological services in the schools. *Journal of School Psychology,* 1964, *3,* 1–12.

Tindall, R. H. School psychology: The development of a profession. In G. D.

Phye & D. J. Reschly (Eds.), *School psychology: Perspectives and issues.* New York: Academic Press, 1979.

Tombari, M., & Davis, R. A. Behavioral consultation. In G. D. Phye & D. J. Reschly (Eds.), *School psychology: Perspectives and issues.* New York: Academic Press, 1979.

Vellutino, F. R. The validity of perceptual-deficit explanations of reading disability: A reply to Fletcher and Satz. *Journal of Learning Disabilities,* 1979, *12,* 160–167.

Wedding, D., & Gudeman, H. Implications of computerized axial tomography for clinical neuropsychology. *Professional Psychology,* 1980, *11,* 31–35.

Glossary

Acoustic cortex. The primary acoustic cortex receives all auditory stimuli and is located in the temporal region.

Agenesis. The failure of a particular area of the brain or body to develop.

Agnosia. An inability to comprehend the meaning of perceptual stimuli.

Agraphia. Loss of the ability to express thoughts in writing because of a lesion of the cerebral cortex.

Alexia. Loss of the ability to read.

Angiogram. X-ray studies of the cerebral blood vessel system following injection of radiopaque material into the arterial system.

Angiography. The practice of studying the circulatory system with angiograms.

Angular gyrus. A convolution located in the parietal cortices believed to be involved in crossmodal integration.

Aphasia. An inability, partial or complete, to understand or express language, whether written or spoken, because of injury or disease of the language centers in the brain.

Appreciation is expressed to William H. Gaddes who provided many of the definitions included in this glossary.

Apraxia. A defective ability in the absence of severe sensory or motor loss for carrying out neuromuscular acts normally, even though the subject understands what is expected of him or her.

Astereognosis. An impaired ability to recognize objects by touch alone.

Brain scan. A technique for detecting pathological brain tissue using radioactive material injected into the blood stream. A radiation detector picks up the gamma rays emitted by the damaged tissue and produces a type of x-ray picture of the brain structure.

Broca's area. A convolution in the left frontal lobe usually involved in mediating motor speech.

Callosal. Pertaining to the corpus callosum.

CAT (CT scan). Computerized axial tomography (sometimes known as the EMI procedure) is a new x-ray scanning method that has been developed in the last 10 years. This method is much more accurate than former brain scan methods in detecting lesions in soft tissue because the radiation is confined to a thin "slice" of brain tissue.

Closed head injury. Damage to the brain tissue resulting from a violent blow to the head, where the skull is not fractured, but the brain tissue is bruised or damaged by concussion.

Commissurotomy. The severing of the corpus callosum, which connects the two cerebral hemispheres.

Contralateral. Relating to the opposite side of the body.

Corpus callosum. The wide band of neural fibers interconnecting the two cerebral hemispheres.

Craniotomy. Generally refers to any operation involving the brain.

Dichotic listening. A technique for stimulating simultaneously both ears of a subject with different words, usually with similar initial sounds and lengths. This procedure is used to study auditory perception and cerebral dominance for language.

Encephalitis. Infection or inflammation of the brain tissues.

Epilepsy. A seizure condition resulting from intense and abnormal electrical activity in the brain.

Hemianopia. A half visual field defect; blindness or impaired vision in the left or right visual field.

Hemiparesis. Partial paralysis on one side of the body.

Hemiplegia. Paralysis of one side of the body.

Hyperglycemia. An unusually high level of glucose in the blood.

Ipsilateral. On the same side of the body; an antonym for contralateral.

Lesion. Any tissue that is damaged or abnormal, due to infection, trauma, tumor, etc.

Ontogenetic. Related to the beginning or origin of an organism.

Stereognosis. Tactile perception; the ability to recognize two- and three-dimensional objects by touch alone.

Visual cortex. The primary visual cortex receives all visual stimuli and is located in the occipital lobe.

Wada amytal test. A clinical test of speech dominance first developed by Dr. Juhn Wada in 1949. When sodium amytal is injected into the left carotid artery, it is carried to the left cerebral hemisphere in a matter of seconds where it has an anesthetizing effect on the left hemisphere. In most patients, this produces a temporary aphasia, alexia, and agraphia. When injected into the right carotid artery, it usually interferes with the patient's ability for pictorial interpretation and spatial perception.

Wernicke's area. The cerebral cortical area, usually in the left temporal lobe, which mediates the understanding of language. It is believed to include one-third of the left superior temporal gyrus and part of the middle temporal gyrus.

Index

Abstraction factor, in biological intelligence, 97
Acalculia, 243, 244
Achievement tests, 258–259
Acoustic cortex, 405
Age
  and cerebral lateralization, 145–152, 291
  and effects of brain damage, 306
  and performance patterns in childhood, 9–10
  and predictors of reading achievement, 12–14
  and stages of development, 289–292
  and subtype persistence in learning disabilities, 19–20
Aggressive behavior, and brain dysfunction, 55–56
Agnosia, 405
  auditory, 244
  finger, 244
  visual, 242–243
Agraphia, 243, 405
  alexia with, 72
Alexia, 405
  with agraphia, 72
  without agraphia, 72
Alphabet recitation test, 12, 36, 39
Ambidexterity, and learning disabilities, 126
American Psychological Association, 387, 391
  standards for training of school psychologists, 390
Amytal test, 61, 130, 407

Analytic information processing, compared to holistic processes, 109–111, 240, 313
Angiography, 405
Angular gyrus, 405
Antisocial behavior in children, 56–57
Anxiety, behavioral effects of, 106–107
Aphasia, 243, 405
  Broca's, 177, 325
  developmental, 176–177
  motor, 245
  recovery from, in childhood, 146–147
  semantic, 177
  Wernicke's, 177, 325
Aphasia Screening Test, 199, 206, 257
  scaled scores for, 217
  simplified for children, 208
Apraxia, 406
  constructional, 243
Arithmetic ability
  impairment in, 243, 244
    subtypes of, 17
  tests of, 258
    Luria-Nebraska test for children, 296, 299
Arousal unit in brain, 281–283
Articulation disorders, 168–170
  assessment of, 169
  treatment of, 170
Assessment of Children's Language Comprehension, 311
Assessment, neuropsychological, requirements for, 356–361. *See also* Tests, diagnostic

Delayed feedback, auditory
effects of, 68
in treatment of stuttering, 174
Delinquency in children, 56–57
Developmental lag, 293–294, 305
and learning disabilities, 35–36, 48
and reading retardation, 12–13
Developmental learning problems
aphasia, 176–177
causes of, 48–50
reading disorders, 5, 180–183
in adults, 72
in children, 73
Developmental processes, 287–293
stages in, 289–292
Developmental Sentence Analysis,
312
Developmental Test of Visual-Motor
Integration, 37, 39, 256, 363
Diagnostic procedures, 31–33
Neuropsychological Key approach
to, 303–327
profile approaches to, 335–349
tests used in, 33, 35–38, 258–259.
See also Tests, diagnostic
Dichotic listening. See Listening tests,
dichotic
Digit Span Test, 314, 317, 323
performance profile for, 320
Directional factor, in biological
intelligence, 97–98
Doman and Delacato theory of
cerebral dominance, 92–95
Draw-A-Person Test, 256
Durrell Analysis of Reading
Difficulty, 316, 323
performance profile in, 320
Dynamometer Test (Grip Strength
Test), 206–207, 208, 253
Dysarthria, 175
Dyslalia, 169
Dyslexia, 179–183
backwardness compared to
retardation in, 4–5
and brain function, 71–73

definitional issues in, 3–6, 179
developmental, 5, 72–73, 180–183
biological basis for, 181
cytoarchitectonic studies in,
181–182
definition of, 179
topography of brain in, 182–183
dysphonetic and dyseidetic, 259,
314
remedial methods for, 314–315
subtypes of, 73, 183, 304,
339–340
traumatic
in adults, 71–72
in children, 73

Ear dominance. See Listening tests,
dichotic
Education
and individualization of instruction,
355–373
in neuropsychology, 384–385
models for training in,
384–385
and school psychology. See School
psychology
and training of school psychologists
in neuropsychology, 389–391
Electrophysiological studies, 15–16
of hemispheric asymmetry, 62–63
Endocrine pathology, and learning
deficits, 51–52
Epilepsy, 406
neural dyssynchrony in, 68
Event-related brain potentials,
15–16
Expressive skills. See Language,
expressive
Eyedness
and cerebral lateralization, 91–92,
133–134
and learning disabilities, 127

b
3 c
4 d
5 e
6 f
7 g
8 h
9 i
8 0 j